THE
TEMPLES
OF
KARNAK

THE
TEMPLES
OF
KARNAK

—◆—

R. A. Schwaller de Lubicz

Photographs by Georges and Valentine de Miré

Illustrations by Lucie Lamy

Inner Traditions
Rochester, Vermont

Inner Traditions International
One Park Street
Rochester, Vermont 05767
www.InnerTraditions.com

First published in the USA by Inner Traditions International, Ltd. 1999
Originally published in French under the title *Les Temples de Karnak*
Copyright © 1982, 1999 by Éditions Dervy
Translation copyright © 1999 by Inner Traditions International

Library of Congress Cataloging-in-Publication Data

Schwaller de Lubicz, R.A.
    [Temples de Karnak. English]
    The temples of Karnak : a contribution to the study of Pharaonic thought /
R.A. Schwaller de Lubicz ; photographs by Georges and Valentine de Miré ; diagrams
and drawings by Lucie Lamy ; notes on the plates compiled by Lucie Lamy and translated by Jon Graham.
    p.   cm.
    Includes index.
    ISBN 0-89281-712-7 (alk. paper)
    1. Karnak (Egypt)—Antiquities. 2. Temples—Egypt—Karnak. I. Miré,
Georges de. II. Miré, Valentine de. III. Lamy, Lucie. IV. Title.
DT73.K4S3913   1999
932—dc21   98-31742
                                                   CIP

Printed and bound in Hong Kong

10 9 8 7 6 5 4 3 2 1

Text design and layout by Virginia L. Scott and Peri Champine.
This book was typeset in Adobe Caslon with Centaur MT as the display typeface.

CONTENTS

THE LAND OF THE NILE

It has been said: Egypt is the greatest oasis in the world's greatest desert. It has also been said: The Nile is Egypt; should it ever run dry, all life in that country would cease. But what has not been told is the country's influence on the mentality of men inhabiting this narrow band of fertile land imprisoned by stretches of desert.

It is as much a prison as may be the brief span of human life zoned in eternity. This the Ancients symbolized by inscribing the personal royal name within a loop (the cartouche): a knot on the endless thread of continuity.

There is Upper Egypt of the single river and Lower Egypt of the Delta, which once was watered by several branches of the Nile, now reduced to two offshoots ramified in countless canals. Flat country where one is surprised to see immense sails gliding through the middle of the fields: feluccas navigating upon invisible waters.

There are two peoples, differentiated by their mentality, which is the result of their surrounding medium: the desert, nourished by only one artery, and the fertile Delta, irrigated by numerous rivulets. As a group, the former—in Upper Egypt—is simple, faithful to its traditions, mystically religious. The latter, in Lower Egypt, is unstable, rapacious, turbulent.

Upper Egypt of the single river extends from Cairo to Aswan, which is already the beginning of the black land: Nubia, reaching as far as Wadi Halfa, and then the Sudan, whose capital, Khartoum, is at the confluence of the two Niles—the Blue coming from Abyssinia and the White from Lake Victoria.

The Ancients said: "The Nile has two sources: one is in heaven, the other in earth, and they spring forth at Bigeh" (near Aswan).

Some have claimed the ancient Egyptians were ignorant of the real sources of this extraordinary river; others, more enlightened, know

that old Egypt had commercial relations with the heart of Africa and Abyssinia since remotest times;

that monuments were erected as far as the Sudanese desert, which is watered by the river;

that ever since prehistoric times, annals have existed concerning inundations of the Nile, floods conditioned by seasonal intertropical rains and by solar and lunar-solar cycles that govern their intensity.

But indeed, the true sources of the Nile are in heaven and in earth.

Flowing from the south northward, this magnificent river alone waters an immense arid desert for more than 3000 kilometers.

The Nile is life; it is androgynous, male in its role as a quickener, female in its fecundity; it links the influence of heaven and its celestial bodies to the salt of the earth. Normally calm, it becomes spirited during the months of strongest heat—swelling, inundating the entire land so as to deposit the extremely fertile black silt whence comes one of the most ancient names for Egypt: Kemit, the "Black Land," which prompted the Muslims who later came to study there, to speak of the science of Al-Kemit.

The Nile has carved its valley, forming, to the west, the cliffs of the Libyan Desert plateau; on the east it borders the Arabian mountain chain that separates Egypt from the Red Sea.

While a man bathes his feet in the life-giving river, his gaze loses itself in the infinite void of the desert, where the great mystics have always revealed themselves. There the heavens are richly studded with stars and deep as the divine mystery.

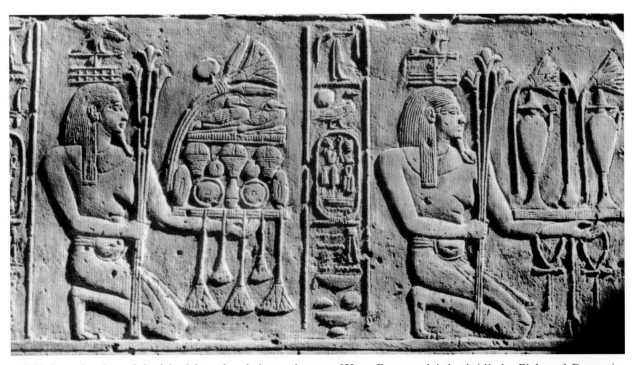

"Niles" wearing the symbols of the eighteenth and nineteenth nomes of Upper Egypt on their heads (Abydos, Eighteenth Dynasty)

Similar magic is known to the sailor, but for him the parturition of Nut—who brings the sun into the world—takes place within a moving medium, while in Egypt "the master of day" emerges from the shadowy earth, from the caverns of the netherworld, the world of the Dwat.

But every night, at the moment the Eye of Ra goes to visit the souls of that Dwat, when dusk has already invaded the earth, Ra once more radiates a crimson glimmer, auspicious harbinger of another life.

And in the morning when the jackal Anubis, he who digests (his mission being to transform all dead things into reanimated matter), slips into his lair, jubilation bursts from everything that lives again.

Then in the evening, when Ra "become old" approaches his descent toward the *amenti* (the west), a religious silence settles even on the birds, the animals do reverence, and men fold their hands. This is peace, a peace no longer known to the world.

CONTEMPORARY EGYPT

Summoned by the muezzin from the heights of the minaret, the fellah says his prayers, and rests limbs wearied from a day of drawing the blessed Nile's water by means of the *shadouf* or the *sakkieh*, to the intoning of psalms thousands of years old. In summer, very often at night, chants and tom-toms resound: we are in Africa.

Under the sun, work in the fields is arduous, but the fellah turns his back on modernizations: electricity or underground water mains would mean working even harder in order to pay for them.

Painting from the tomb of Menna (Eighteenth Dynasty)

Painting from the tomb of Menna (Eighteenth Dynasty)

Furthermore, the water of the Nile is a source of life, *particularly when it is muddy,* because it contains alumina and salts necessary to blood thinned by the sun's fire, whereas the well water is nitrous and magnesian. People from there know very well what suits them, better than do our engineers and chemists.

The habits and customs of ancient Egypt have left many a trace on the practices of the people. To the east of Cairo at the foot of the Mokkatam hills, the city of the dead extends from the Citadel to the beautifully domed Tomb of the Caliphs. Every well-to-do family has its "house of eternity" there, and constructed on every tomb is a miniature dwelling with nothing lacking. These families congregate there on certain holidays in order that the dead may participate in the festivities.

Likewise in Upper Egypt, a diminutive "house of the soul" is built on each tomb, where the unfortunate survivors place nourishment for the departed, who must share the enjoyment of those still waiting to go toward Allah when the "earth *shall have eaten* their mortal body."

And suddenly, be it night or day, a door opens somewhere and a wife or a son shouts to the villagers that there has been a death. Then all the neighbors proclaim aloud the merits and qualities of the deceased, the widow laments the departure of her *gamal* (her "camel"—symbol of patience and power). The wailers then appear—like those depicted in the tomb of Ramose, throwing mud on their hair, beating their faces in "anguish"; ritually, their hands drive out the malefic spirits and with beckoning gestures, summon the soul to reincarnate in "the woman"; all this to the accompaniment of cries and a treading dance that becomes frantic. . . . Afterward, it is in the name of the One and Only Allah that the body is buried in the earth whence it came.

Allah is omnipresent in these places, everything here recalling the reality of an eternal continuance: life on earth is but a transitory passage.

Painting from the tomb of Ramose (Eighteenth Dynasty)

It is due to the survival of these ancient traditions that, for example, the temple of Luxor has never ceased to be respected as a sacred spot. Close to the east wing of the pylon inside the court of Ramesses have been successively interred a Christian woman martyr and the Muslim saint Abu el-Haggag, who still counts numerous descendants in the land.

Represented in the temple of Luxor, on the walls of the "nave," is the annual procession of the golden barques of Amun, Mut, and Khonsu (the triad protecting Thebes), going from Karnak to Luxor and back again. Now, it happens that in the mosque built upon the tomb of Abu el-Haggag, at the height of the capitals, three wooden barques are kept. On the occasion of the annual celebration in honor of the saint, these barques, placed on chariots and filled with gaily dressed children, are carried along the Nile as the crowd chants praises of the holy man to cries of "*Ya Amun! Ya Amun!*" as did the pharaonic people thirty centuries ago.

How can these barques of Abu el-Haggag be explained except as the continuation of a tradition characteristic of the temples of Luxor and Karnak?

Furthermore, he was a wise man, this saint whose words have been thus transcribed by G. Legrain:

I asked myself who is God and I cried out: "It is Allah-the-greatest!" when I heard a voice saying: "It is I who am your own God, for if I tell you 'I am hungry,' you nourish me; when I am tired, you make me sleep; when I wish to move about, you make me walk; when I want to hear, you make me listen; and when I hate a man, I make you kill him. Hence it is to me you are obedient, it is I who am your true and only God and you are my slave."

I remained a long time listening to this voice that rose inside me, and then, in the Book, I searched to find whose this voice was and lo, I found what should answer it: "Resist that one who would command thee in order to understand his weakness and if he tells thee: 'I am hungry,' fast; if he says to thee, 'I wish to sleep,' be vigilant; if he says, 'I want to move about,' stay; if he wants to hear, close thine ears; and if he urges thee to shed blood, then tell him: Thou shalt not kill! Resist thyself, act against the instinct within thee and thou shalt have a crown of glory." (G. Legrain, *Louqsor sans les Pharaons*)

We can thank the cult of the venerable Abu el-Haggag for having preserved the temple of Luxor from demolitions such as were suffered by the great temple of Karnak.

THE LAND OF THE PHARAOHS

All along this artery of life that the Nile represents, a people stirred by a faith based upon conviction, and according to a scrupulous logic, built temples dedicated to the proof that confers such conviction.

This people whose land, according to a Babylonian saying, overflowed with gold, knew how to concentrate its riches exclusively on service to its faith and science, while using sunbaked brick for secular buildings and even for the construction of royal palaces. To the one and only God and his emanations, the *neters,* were devoted the perishable riches given by God as evidence of his power; to men, bodily health, the strength of faith, the certitude of the continuity of being.

Painting from the tomb of Menna (Eighteenth Dynasty)

Altogether, this produced a hardworking and joyous people, for on the whole, ancient Egypt discloses neither melancholy nor wretchedness, except for brief periods of famine, occurring rarely enough to have been recorded on the stelae or papyri. With its knowledge, the Temple was able to prognosticate the alternating cycles of abundance and drought that conform to the eleven times eleven years of solar influence.

Our view of ancient Egypt tends to minimize its achievements, condensing into a narrow scope its more than four thousand years of history. *Yesterday* there was grave famine, *today* the land abounds in riches and power ... but between *yesterday* and *today,* four or five centuries have elapsed. If we would thus reduce our own history from the year 1000 to this day, what incredible turbulence we would perceive: changed mores, faith lost, differences in dress, language, and writing, civilization turned upside down, and a science having nothing left in common with that of yesteryear.

In ancient Egypt, on the other hand, symbols, language, and the hieroglyphic writing remained unvarying for a span of almost four thousand years, the religious foundation remained unalterable, and there is an astounding stability in the essential data. It could be asked if this stability is a sign of perfection or, on the contrary, an absence of evolution. Another question can serve as answer: what evolution is there to be expected once the aim—knowledge—is attained?

The giant builders transmitted knowledge. Cities now vanished sprang up from other centers as beautiful and wealthy, and the elite does not die once its faith is based on the imperishable realities of the spirit.

Wisdom teaches that the perishable must be allowed to perish without regret in order better to distinguish that which is real and which serves as groundwork for a new destiny. In its greatness, ancient Egypt knew how to apply this wisdom consciously.

Our present error is to *endure* what we do not know how to *will through wisdom.*

Hieroglyph of the phonetic character m *(Eighteenth Dynasty)*

THE WRITING

The first contact with the monuments of ancient Egypt always creates the same impression: the confrontation with another world. It is not so much the colossal massiveness that is striking but rather the cohesion of style, which does not speak to the ordinary sentiments of man and leaves no place for sensuality. In architecture, the curve occurs only to indicate an Osirian aspect: death and resurrection (the cyclic principle); elsewhere, all consists of straight lines, the writing is guided between rectilinear borders, the statuary displays severe hieratic bearing. Walls are covered with bas-reliefs where human figurations obey a rigid canon and are charged with attributes obviously having a definite meaning; headdresses and crowns bear no resemblance to what can be seen in the traces of any other civilization.

Ancient Egypt is surreal. It evokes respect, imposing itself by a royal style. Projecting itself toward a beyond, it remains rooted in all that which composes natural and human life. In its traditional figurations, rich in symbols, there is a serene simplicity and also a sureness that conviction alone can inspire.

At all times, people have searched for the causes of the force radiating from the vestiges of this civilization.

This curiosity was of course first applied to the unviolated writings carved into the stone of the monuments. But from Clement of Alexandria to Champollion the Younger, this writing had kept its secrets. It was an important moment in the history of mankind when Champollion rediscovered one of the meanings of these inscriptions—*one* of the meanings, because the other cannot be dissociated from the very spirit of the master builders' thought. It is one self-contained whole, a synthesis that cannot be transcribed in the words of a dictionary.

With the Maya, for example, we find a manner of writing composed of images, but they are intricate and tortured images, while in Egypt we are confronted with objects, animals, and human gestures whose lines are descriptive in the purest sense, avoiding all mental complications.

In the midst of the bas-reliefs—those speaking images—flows the stream of thought, expressed with the same images guided between straight lines as between the banks of a river, and this stream contains no interruption: nothing separates the words, neither hiatus nor conventional signs. A single exception is the royal name encircled by a "cartouche."

Under such conditions, how could this writing be deciphered? In order to separate possible words, it was necessary to know the methods of reading, and in order to know how to read the signs, it was necessary to know the words. The discovery of the Rosetta Stone inscribed with a bilingual text (the Egyptian hieroglyphic and demotic juxtaposed with the Greek) raised great hopes of solving this problem, but its solution had to wait for Champollion, who to his knowledge of Latin and Greek had added Hebrew, Chaldean, Syriac, Ethiopic, Arabic, and Coptic. In spite of this, it was necessary for him to employ a singular intuition—which could almost be called a *reminiscence*—in order to lay down all the foundations of the writing and language.

Champollion left behind a solid basis on which, after the correction of several errors, a corpus could be founded, permitting today a fairly good reading of the profane sense of the glyphs. But it is easy to forget that Champollion is the man of genius who, in ten years, with rudimentary means, and after only eighteen months in Egypt, was able to create the bases from which our philologists have been working for a century and a half.

He never got to know the great number of stelae and papyri that his successors were able to study (and the latter, moreover, achieved excellent work). When Champollion made his voyage to Egypt (1828–30), many of the monuments now excavated were then still partially buried (such as Edfu, Dendera, Esna, and Luxor, where only the tip of the colonnade of Amun was visible), and yet one remains surprised and filled with admiration for the greatness of the work this scholar

Hieroglyphs for "the gift of life," "stability," and "strength"

Hieroglyphs

accomplished in such a brief time, for he died in 1832 at the age of forty-two, exhausted by his unflagging studies.

Perhaps it would be useful here to reproduce certain forgotten passages from the *Introduction à la Grammaire égyptienne* by Champollion the Younger, the cornerstone he bequeathed us, which after his death was piously edited by his elder brother, Champollion-Figeac.

EXCERPTS FROM THE *INTRODUCTION À LA GRAMMAIRE EGYPTIENNE* BY CHAMPOLLION THE YOUNGER

Going back through the ages, archaeological science, after having reached the original source of Roman arts and civilization, concentrated its means and efforts on studying the monuments of ancient Greece. That famous land had been considered, in general and as a result of the basic education of successive European generations, as the primitive cradle of our civilization, the veritable native soil of the arts and sciences.

A conscientious examination of Hellenic monuments and traditions, however, singularly weakens and modifies this opinion. Such a study would have to disengage itself from the popular prejudice that tended to establish the system of spontaneous generation in the arts, sciences, and all social institutions on

Phonetic group un *("to be")*

the soil of ancient Greece, *in spite of factual evidence and positive testimony by the ancient Greeks themselves. This study would also have to prove that here, as perhaps everywhere else, the country was first inhabited by barbaric hordes and later occupied by a succession of foreign populations, whose arrival produced great changes and important modifications in the language as well as in the religion, in the practices of the arts, and in the customs of civic life.*

The truly Hellenic population descended from the north, and then civilization came to it from the south through foreigners who had been expelled from the eastern regions of the ancient world by political circumstances. Such is the epitome of historical documents that the Greeks themselves transmitted and that concern their own primitive times. Thus it is in the Orient we must search for Hellenic origins; and archaeology, imbued with this truth, first of all proclaims the sublime perfection and incomparable superiority of the arts of ancient Greece. . . .

Historians affirm that the first somewhat evolved forms of civilization were introduced among the small Hellenic tribes of Argolis and Attica by men from the shores of Egypt, who had come by sea. From that moment on, according to these historians, Egypt became a school where Greek legislators, reformers of its cult, and particularly Hellenes of Europe and Asia, went for instruction. The latter speeded up the development of Greek society in being the first to propagate, by their example, the study of sciences, history, and philosophy. It is thus by a thorough knowledge of the Egyptian monuments that we can trace the origin of the arts of Greece, as well as the source of a major part of its religious creeds and the exterior forms of its cult. We should particularly note the factual evidence as to the antiquity of the civilization on the

Nile's shores, anterior to even a political existence of the Greeks, and further, the numerous relations of a nascent Greece with a venerable Egypt.

The renown and wealth of Egypt's soil, as well as its political importance from time immemorial, have bound the history of this country to that of all the great peoples of ancient Africa and Asia. But the annals of most of those nations having irrevocably perished, it is the written monuments of Egypt we must interrogate: they will recall for us the names of the small tribes, now forgotten, who in those times were submitted to Egyptian power by the pharaohs' penetration into the interior of Africa, a summoning of barbaric tribes to civilization by contact or by example. . . .

The number of variously dated monuments on Egyptian soil that have escaped both the devastation of centuries and hostile religions is still such that an abundance of direct evidence can be gathered concerning the ever increasing degree of civilization attained by an industrious people who pioneered the lower Nile valley at a remote epoch. For it must be said: Egyptian monuments of the most ancient times show no traces of the infancy of art; to the contrary, they all manifest mature and experienced art. . . . *It is true that Egypt retains no trace of its own origin; it is in that region, however, that we must seek the origins of both Greek art and civilization and, consequently, our modern civilization's point of departure.*

The study of Egyptian monuments and texts will lead us to the source of the first political institutions in Greece, those of Argos and Athens, by presenting in its true light the political and religious state of the ancient empire of the pharaohs while also substantiating the advanced state of Egyptian arts, long before the production of those same arts in Europe. Such a study will undoubtedly demonstrate the Egyptian origin of a very important part of Hellenic myth and religious practices, about which much uncertainty

Nekhebet, the guardian deity of the South

remains, and it has not as yet been possible to reduce them to a regular system, owing to the general failure to distinguish what is proper to the Hellenic population from that which it received from eastern colonies.

One will recognize the obvious origin of the Greek Doric arch in the porticos of Beni Hasan and in the galleries of Karnak, executed by the Egyptians well before the epoch of the siege of Troy. An unprejudiced examination of the historic bas-reliefs of Nubia and Thebes will convince us that Greek art took from Egyptian sculpture its first models, which it servilely imitated while absorbing the wise simplicity of their style; its means thus enriched, the art of Greece adopted a principle that never belonged to Egyptian art: *it bound itself to the reproduction of nature's beautiful forms, thereby moving further and further away from the primitive approach in order to attain a sublimity that can perhaps never be reached by the efforts of our modern artists.*

The Egyptian origin of the sciences and the main philosophical doctrines of Greece shall perhaps become still more evident through the interpretation of Egypt's monuments. The Platonic school is nothing but Egyptianism that has left the sanctuaries of Saïs, and the old Pythagorean sect propagated psychological theories that are developed in the paintings and sacred legends found in the tombs of the kings of Thebes, in the desert valley of Biban el-Moluk.

THE ORIGIN OF PHARAONIC THOUGHT

Today Champollion's reflections concerning the pharaonic origin of Greek civilization are confirmed.

Hieroglyph of the phonetic characters aa

Nineteenth-century Hellenists were still ignorant of—or preferred to ignore—the antiquity of the high pharaonic civilization and, remarking the sudden flowering of an exceptional art and science in Hellas, invented what became known as "the Greek miracle." This opinion was perfectly justified as long as a slow development of Egyptian civilization was presumed to have evolved from a primary level. Such a view is today contradicted by the excavations and by documents pertaining to the first dynasties. Indeed, from the very start, there exists a hieroglyphic writing, perfected techniques, and a science that obliges us either to shift further back in time a primitive state of beginning and experimentation or to admit the existence of a humanity both inspired and prehistoric.

It was the intensely rationalist-materialist epoch of our nineteenth century that presupposed an evolution beginning with a primitive cell and progressing toward the human condition, all occurring in a purely material sequence and within the limited framework of our terrestrial evolution.

It is true that Nature shows us living beings at all intermediary stages between the cell and a culmination in human form, but it is nevertheless also certain that she very carefully hides from us the passage of the living organism from one stage to another. The theory of evolution is a purely logical supposition that is absolutely unconfirmed by life, even when we are shown the evolution of the human fetus passing through all the essential aspects typical of animal stages, from the most rudimentary to the human form.

Hieroglyph: ideogram of the falcon of Horus (Eighteenth Dynasty)

Yet the appearance of new microorganisms is constantly observed by our biologists, who speak of mutations, sudden changes in organisms.

This author places his belief in a humanity whose origins are still rich with animal instincts and that (by mutation?—or by a harmonic coincidence of the ambient cosmos?) has received the faculty of reason. This humanity, very close to nature and in direct contact with it, was able "to know" the forces that bring about the becoming of things; but this "knowing" was not a "knowing by learning." The downfall of this state, brought about by a faith placed in mental learning—a kind of scission between innate knowledge and its reflection through the exterior, in short, a dualization—that downfall was the condemnation to search for the source, "the condemnation to work." Now it happens that work for work's sake has never ennobled anyone: in order to harvest its fruit, which is the liberation of consciousness, perfection must be sought and the moment attained when one knows how to live within oneself the task to be achieved; then the performing of it ceases to be work, regardless of the effort involved.

We behold an example of this in the sculpture of ancient Egypt. He who was first to carve the falcon of Horus "lived" the aspect, bearing, and nobility of this bird in such a way that he did not "work" in order to sculpt it: he projected his consciousness—and not his vision—onto the stone. This example serves for the whole of pharaonic expression. Another story is the evolution of the mental faculties, a knowledge of a learned nature that is the "work" of research implied by the esotericism of the words found in the Mosaic Genesis.

This would explain the fact that at the known origin of the pharaonic empire, there was a complete and perfect civilization, a time when thought was translated by geometry and number through the pyramids and other monuments more directly than by the writings.

Historically there is a forfeiture of man's "divinity" to the profit of mental acquisition, accomplished by the Sethian tool of the imitator, the "ape of the Divine."

THE DISCOVERY OF PHARAONIC WRITING
IN ITS HISTORICAL ASPECTS

Ever since the seventeenth century, the curiosity of scholars had been excited by some Egyptian art objects brought back to Europe, but the rare Greek texts concerning pharaonic writing remained inscrutable. Said Champollion: *It was thought that the Egyptian writing called hieroglyphic did in no way represent* the sound of the words *of the spoken language; that each hieroglyphic character was the* specific sign of a distinct idea; *and finally, that this writing proceeded to the representation of ideas through symbols and emblems only (ideogrammatical form).*

Such principles, which the learned of our day have not yet renounced, opened an extremely vast field for the imagination, or rather, gave it free rein. The Jesuit Kircher launched out into this field and, abandoning all reserve, abused the good faith of his contemporaries by publishing, under the title Oedipus Aegyptiacus, *so-called translations of the hieroglyphic legends carved upon obelisks that had been brought to Rome, translations he himself did not believe, since he very often dared to support them with quotations from authors who simply never existed.*

When the study of Coptic was introduced into Europe, P. E. Jablonski set himself the task of classifying those dispersed passages of Greek and Latin authors that concern the religious system of ancient Egypt. With the aid of Coptic vocabularies, he also attempted the interpretation of the names of divinities. But as Champollion observed, he would have to have been certain that the

Greeks and Latins in no way altered these names when transcribing them, and in order to prove this, it would first of all have been necessary to know the Egyptian spelling of these names, and during the whole of the eighteenth century, no progress was made in the deciphering of the hieroglyphic writing.

The mania for a priori systems, going beyond all limits of the possible, still served to turn away the more exacting minds from a type of study held in total discredit owing to the uncertainty of the methods employed or because of the extravagant deductions resulting from these methods.

Champollion cites Zoëga as being among the only true promoters of Egyptian archaeology. This Danish scholar *was profoundly versed in the classics and had a good command of the Coptic language. . . . He was the first to vaguely suspect the existence of the phonetic component in the system of the sacred writing, but he gave no extension to this notion, reducing it to a few signs that led to the expression of sounds by the same method as our writing game called rebus.*

The *Description de l'Egypte,* published after the conquest by the French army, again created considerable interest in the learned world by revealing vast architectural treasures and an abundance of texts. Then, with the announcement of the discovery of the Rosetta Stone in August 1799 by a brilliant French officer named Bouchard, hope flared of at last penetrating the mysteries of the graphic system.

This bilingual inscription is divided into three sections: the upper part is in hieroglyphic writing, the middle in vulgar or demotic writing, and the lower in Greek.

As early as 1802, Silvestre de Sacy undertook its study. Soon afterward, Åkerblad, a Swedish Orientalist, following the same lines as the French scholar, compared the Greek proper names cited in both the Greek and demotic inscriptions, at the same time deriving from this analysis a short demotic or popular Egyptian alphabet.

This initial success seemed at first to confirm the hopes raised by the Rosetta Stone. Åkerblad, however, so successful in the analysis of the Greek proper names, obtained no results in his attempts to apply the fund of signs, whose value he had just noted in the written expression of the Greek proper names, to the reading of other parts of the demotic inscription.

Failing to assume, on the one hand, that the Egyptians could have written the words of their language with the medial vowels for the main part deleted, as has always been the practice with the Hebrews and the Arabs, and on the other hand having no inkling as to the fact that many of the characters employed in this text could belong to the class of symbolic signs, the Swedish scholar, dispirited by his fruitless efforts, ceased to occupy himself with the Rosetta Stone. The work of de Sacy and Åkerblad had proved, however, that the vulgar writing of the ancient Egyptians expressed foreign proper names by means of truly alphabetic *signs.*

But seeing that the Rosetta Stone was partially destroyed, no one had as yet been concerned with deciphering the purely hieroglyphic part of the inscription. It was Dr. Thomas Young, a noted English scholar, who undertook the methodical examination of the three texts.

This work, the result of sagacious comparison, finally established several assured notions concerning the method peculiar to the different branches of the Egyptian graphic system and their respective connections. It furnished material proof of the ancient assertion regarding the use of figurative and symbolic signs in the hieroglyphic writing. The intimate nature of this writing, however, its relation to the spoken language, its number, the essence and the combinations of its fundamental elements—these points remained indefinite and hypothetical.

It is true that the English scholar believed first in the alphabetic nature of all the signs of the demotic text (1816); then, in 1819, he affirmed that the totality of the signs was purely ideographic in nature. The work of Åkerblad having nevertheless proved the existence of phonetic signs for the

Rosetta Stone (British Museum)

transcription of Greek names, Young concluded *that only for the transcription of foreign proper names did the Egyptians, as did the Chinese, use signs that were actually ideographic but deviated from their ordinary expression in order to make them accidentally represent sounds.*

Champollion's great contribution was to have assumed and then recognized the existence of three types of signs, which shows his ability to find the just mean between extremes of hypothesis. He was therefore the first to comprehend the famous words of Clement of Alexandria, subject of so many earlier commentators:

Those among the Egyptians who receive instruction learn first of all the kind of Egyptian letters called epistolographic; *and second the* hieratic, *which is used by the hierogrammats; and finally the* hieroglyphic *kind.*

(There are two kinds of) hieroglyphic letters: *one is curiological, making a first use of alphabetic letters; the other is symbolic.*

The SYMBOLIC (method is subdivided into several kinds): *one literally represents the objects by imitation; another expresses them by trope (in a figurative manner); a third exclusively uses allegories expressed by certain enigmas. Accordingly, the Egyptians inscribe a circle when they want to write* sun *after this fashion, and they trace a crescent form in order to write* moon. *In the figurative method, changing and deviating the sense of objects by means of analogy, they express them either by modifying their image or by submitting it to different kinds of transformation. Thus they employ anaglyphs when they want to transmit praises to the king in the form of religious myth. Now here is an example of the third kind [hieroglyphic writing], which uses enigmatic allusions: the Egyptians depict by serpents the other celestial bodies because of the obliquity of their course, but the sun is portrayed by a scarab.* (Clement of Alexandria, from Letrone's translation)

Inspired mainly by this famous text, Champollion classified the hieroglyphs into three categories:

A. The mimetic or FIGURATIVE signs:

These characters express precisely the object, the more or less faithful and detailed image of which they represent to the eye.

| Sun | Moon | Star | Man | Horse | Crocodile | Offerings |

B. The tropical or SYMBOLIC signs:

The impossibility of expressing certain ideas—especially abstract ideas—by figurative characters led the Egyptians to invent a new order of signs by means of which these ideas were delineated in the images of physical objects having close or distant, actual or supposed relationships with the objects of the ideas to be graphically represented.

Champollion distinguishes four methods:

1. *By* synecdoche, *in depicting the part for the whole; most of the signs formed according to this method, however, are essentially nothing but pure abbreviations of figurative signs; thus two arms, one holding a shield and the other a pike or a shaft, signified an army, or combat.*

| Combat | Bull | Goose | Ram | To sail | To offer | To lead |

2. *Proceeding by* metonymy, *depicting cause instead of effect, effect instead of cause, or the tool instead of the finished work. Thus the month was expressed by the crescent of the moon with the horns downward, as it shows itself toward the end of the month . . . the day, by the figurative sign of the sun, which is its author and cause . . . the night by the sign of the sky combined with a star.*

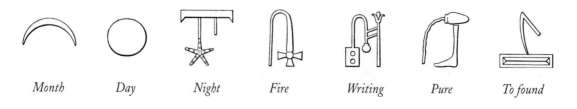

| Month | Day | Night | Fire | Writing | Pure | To found |

3. *In using* metaphors, *depicting an object that had some real or generally supposed similarity with the idea expressed. In this way sublimity was designated by a sparrow hawk because of its very lofty flight . . . the mother by a vulture because such maternal tenderness was attributed to this bird that it was said to nourish its young with its own blood.* (Champollion cites Horapollo for these last interpretations.)

| Sublimity | Mother | Superiority | Royalty | Piety | Judge | Guardian of secrets |

4. *A further and last proceeding was by* enigmas, *employing, in order to express an idea, the image of a physical object related to the object whose idea was to be expressed, but related to it in a very hidden, very remote, sometimes even purely conventional manner. According to this method—which was a most indefinite procedure—justice was signified by an ostrich plume because all the feathers of this bird's wings were said to be equal.* (After Horapollo)

| Truth | Thoth | Years | Bulrush of the South | Papyrus of the North | White crown of the South | Red crown of the North |

C. PHONETIC Signs:

The characters of the third class are the most important, since in the hieroglyphic texts of all times the signs composing this category are much more frequently used than those of the first two. These signs have been qualified as phonetic because they do not actually represent ideas but sounds or pronunciations. (Excerpts from Champollion's *Grammaire égyptienne*)

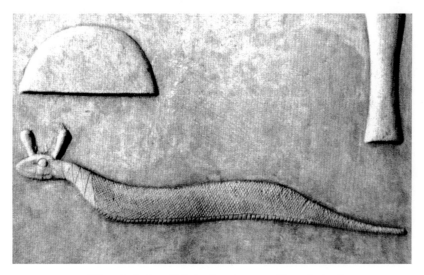

Hieroglyphs in which the characters t *and* f *are depicted*

And so the complete bases of the reading were established. Already in 1822, Champollion's famous letter to Dacier announced the discovery of about fifteen phonetic signs. Ten years later, his *Grammaire* bequeathed a considerable number of words, the main verbal forms, the pronouns, articles, and adjectives and their uses and dispositions in the sentence. It is certainly remarkable that Champollion's thorough knowledge of Coptic, of such precious aid in numerous cases, did not mislead him in others, and that he was able to discern differences where these existed.

Nothing remained to be done but to analyze methodically each point in detail, a meticulous task to which his successors applied themselves. In 1930 the catalog issued by the press of the French Institute of Oriental Archaeology in Cairo contained almost four thousand hieroglyphic signs, and the *Wörterbuch* (the Berlin dictionary) supplied the meaning of about thirty thousand words or variants. The perfecting of the grammar continues year by year, and yet in the 1954 edition of his *Classical Egyptian Dictionary*, G. Lefebvre makes the following observation in his preface:

Hieroglyphs: "Words to be spoken four times"

Vulture belonging to the "two mistresses of the Two Lands" group

Our grammatical structures have by necessity a conventional and provisional character and would no doubt surprise a scribe of the House of Life, could he be called upon to view them. They will be either confirmed by time or modified by our successors; it will perhaps even become possible to "analyze the Egyptian language from within rather than exteriorly," which was Maspero's wish, as Capart recently recalled.

The impressive work of philologists since Champollion has certainly permitted a correct reading of the profane texts; in Champollion's footsteps, research has continued on the phonetic and grammatical aspects of the writing, but the words of Clement of Alexandria have been overlooked: there are at least two possible readings. While one of them is phonetic, the other is symbolic.

The image is neither a rebus nor a cryptogram but, naively, speaks to evoke an intuition. In no case must the latter be translated into words, reduced to a concrete notion such as a useful object or even a mental abstraction, which could distort the reading at first sight. When we designate, for example, by the word *horizon* the apparent line separating earth (or sea) from sky, this visible line is an abstraction, since it is nothing but an appearance: it has no material reality. But in formulating this notion by the word *horizon,* we *see* this line mentally, we are bound to see it if we do not want that word to become devoid of sense. Instead, when the pharaonic mind *represents* the horizon by the image of the sun between two mountains, that representation evokes the moment of the sun's emerging from darkness in the morning and returning to it at night. This is a *function,* a vital state of being. The sign "horizon," in its image, is positive, concrete, and has nothing abstract or conventional about it, but what it evokes is an "intuition" of a function: the function of appearing, of being having emerged from nonbeing. It would again be nothing but a chain of reasoning, hence a concretization of the intuition, were we to say: the sun was merely hidden. . . .

Therefore when Champollion and philologists after him said that the Ancients used certain images in order to signify abstractions, they were not absolutely accurate in terms of truly pharaonic thought: it is rather the evoking of intuitions, which in our way of thinking are mental abstractions. But for the Ancients they were "states of being."

In order to sum up as simply as possible, let us bear in mind that the concrete symbol evokes the abstraction, while in our way of thinking, abstractions necessarily spur the search for the concrete image on which they can lean. This formula must be understood in a vital sense and applies, furthermore, to all the symbols of the hieroglyphs (taken in their hieratic sense).

MYTH

Myth is generally taken to mean an account of the exploits, adventures, or avatars of fabled personnages composing a pantheon. Strictly speaking, however, myth must be seen as the symbol of a theogony. It is symbol inasmuch as it incarnates cosmic functions in human form. Consequently, through images, it evokes the functional principles of the universal law governing the becoming of things, the genesis of that which, from the human point of view, appears to be the effect of an absolute cause variously known as Devas, Theos, or God, and called, in ancient Egypt, *Neter-neteru*, the Principle of principles.

Myth is therefore the anthropomorphization of the elements of a philosophy, and its understanding as such presupposes a knowledge of the natural bases laid down as premises.

Since it is man who judges and thinks the principles of the universe, he concretizes them into human form, which is natural evolution at its highest known state. As a finality of nature, the human being necessarily epitomizes all the phases of this becoming and can thus be regarded as the representative of the universe: *Man, know thyself and thou shalt know the universe and the gods*, it was written at Delphi. This thought has served as the foundation for all revelations concerning the secret of becoming and the return of being to its source.

There are two aspects of this conception of myth: the first gives a *human* nature to cosmic principles by attributing to this symbolization ordinary human feelings and reactions; this lends a historic character to myth. The second, and typically pharaonic, aspect is simply an anthropomorphization of those principles: although represented in human form, human feelings are not attributed to them. It is a kind of synthesis between fable and myth. In order to give life to certain typical

Anubis, Hathor of the amenti, *Horus, Nephthys, Isis, and Osiris (Nineteenth Dynasty)*

qualities that are universal, although they can only be shown in a restricted aspect, the poet chooses among the animals those incarnating these qualities most accurately. Then he makes them speak and behave in the manner of men. In this case we are not concerned with historicity but with pure symbol.

Pharaonic myth combines fable and anthropomorphization into a perfect natural symbol to express a knowledge concerning life's secret. It does not situate in time events that in reality are constant, but it does, on the other hand, situate them in space, that is to say, in situ, taking into account a natural concordance such as orientations, surroundings, and symbioses.

Accordingly, three main centers are found, each revealing the mystery of creation under a different form: Heliopolis, Memphis, and Thebes, and each province, or nome, has its own particular cult with its *local neter,* its myth and legend.

The Osirian myth, which reigned on earth at the beginning of time, signs each site with one of its episodes: it is by the mouth of Tanis that the coffin of Osiris, murdered by his brother Seth, was washed into the sea. It is in Coptos that, through the celestial winds, Isis learned of the death of her spouse, and it was in Byblos that she found the sarcophagus of Osiris, around which a marvelous tree had grown. And it is in the marshes of the Delta that Wadjet, the female divinity of the

North, secretly raised the young child Horus, who was later to engage in interminable combat against Seth in order to reconquer his father's heritage. When Isis brought back the coffin of her husband, Seth dismembered the body of Osiris, flinging the pieces into the Nile, which dispersed them throughout the land. But Isis recovered every part of this *neter's* body; she presented each different part as a relic to the different temples of Egypt, and thus every spot is consecrated by the relic it received or the myth connected with it.

HISTORICAL ACCOUNT OF THE MYTH

When studying pharaonic beliefs, it is tempting to try to unite into a single system all the rites and doctrines dispersed throughout the land. The problem posed by such an "account" of pharaonic "religion" is complex enough to have raised numerous interpretations, each one perfectly defensible from a particular point of view. However, these different theories are in opposition to one another and propose contradictory theses, "from the rudest fetishism to the most subtle symbolism," as the abbé Drioton wrote in 1938.

It is true that there is no hieroglyphic text that presents the religion in the form of a dogma *dictating* a definite set of beliefs. And yet in the temples bordering both banks of the Nile, in tombs, on stelae and papyri, we find innumerable inscriptions relating to all the nuances of cult and myth, to all that can be summarized by the word *religion*. "And yet, in spite of the richness of documentation, which could almost be called excessive, it is impossible to set forth a perfectly coherent synthesis." (E. Drioton and J. Vandier, *L'Egypte*, p. 63)

Indeed, religion such as we conceive it today presupposes the existence of sacred texts expressing in "official and definitive" form a dogma upon which believers bestow their faith. "With the religion of ancient Egypt we have a quite different state of affairs: in order to understand its essence, the terms of the modern conception must be turned upside down. Its basis was not faith but cult and, owing to the circumstances of its development, local cult: the fact of rendering homage to a god of a specific name who was both recognized and proclaimed lord and master of a specific site." (Ibid., p. 64)

This refers to the local cult peculiar to each of the forty-two nomes of the empire of the "Two Crowns." But side by side with this cult, which had as many *neters*—or even triads—as there are

Hieroglyph: "Seth"

Isis (sarcophagus of Ramesses III)

provinces, there is abundant testimony of a sacred history that translates under the form of myth the origins of the world and the mystery of creation. By general agreement the popular cult is therefore distinguished from the teaching of the temples. But this distinction still does not resolve the irritating problem: how could such a collection of creeds be elaborated into a totality that finally constituted a "religion" able to last over four millennia?

Looking back to the origins in prehistory, we note the existence of numerous symbols that will figure as the emblems of nomes throughout the entire historical period; they will be attributed to the local *neter*, as for example the bucranium of Hathor, the crossed arrows of Neith, or the symbol of Min (which some claim to be a thunderbolt and others, a lock).

The first question concerns the choice of these emblems: since we are supposedly dealing with primitive peoples, such a choice could only have been dictated by fear or superstition, which helps explain the case of the crocodile or the serpent but not the symbols for Hathor and Neith, and so many other completely inoffensive objects. It was therefore *supposed* that long before the historical period, the land was peopled by tribes or "clans," each having its particular "gods," their symbols corresponding to a primitive *totemism*. Violently attacked, this interpretation gave way to the theory of *fetishism*, doing no more than replacing one word with another and still bringing no solution to the problem posed by the elaboration of great cosmogonic systems. It was then that scholars turned to the legends to find the historical origins of the religious and political conquest of the country.

According to the Palermo Stone and the Turin Papyrus, there were first of all divine dynasties, then the "Venerable Ones," and finally, the Companions of Horus. A great mystery hovers over the latter, whose reign alone is supposed to have lasted more than thirteen thousand years before the unification of the land by Menes, the first historical king. On the other hand, the monuments show, and tradition affirms, that two important religious centers existed before Menes, the double city of Nekhen-Nekheb for the kingdom of the South (assigned to Seth with the white crown) and the double city of Dep and Pe for the kingdom of the North (assigned to Horus with the red crown). Some scholars have held that perpetual quarrels between Seth and Horus could be found in the myth, and that in the final victory of the latter resided the historic origin of the conquest of the entire territory. But seeing that it has not yet been possible to determine whether the civilizing of Egypt proceeded from the north southward or inversely, the skirmishes between Seth and Horus have had to remain confined to the realm of myth.

And so the historical vision has been extended to the whole of the pantheon, deeming each nome to have originally been a small independant state, conflicts to have broken out between these states, and the triumph of the stronger to have resulted in the supremacy of the victorious *neter*, and, it was logically concluded, this is how Atum, supreme *neter* of Heliopolis, obtained hegemony under the Old Kingdom; a further conclusion was that Menes, a king native to Heliopolis, finally unified Egypt. All told, it was a political conquest in religious guise. But this interpretation still did not explain the origin of the philosophy of the temples nor the coexistence of all the local cults and the four great centers: Heliopolis, Memphis, Hermopolis, and Thebes. And so the notion of *syncretism* was proposed, the fusion of several philosophical systems under the most powerful authority.

Osiris

But however attractive these *totemist, fetishist,* or *syncretist* theories may be, they do not resolve the crux of the problem, which consists precisely in the elaboration of these systems. Furthermore, according to our way of thinking, one of these "systems" should have predominated and gradually smothered the ancient beliefs of the conquered barbarians. No such thing occurred, and the parts coexisted within the whole during the entire pharaonic empire. Such facts, and the quandary one encounters when collecting under the word *religion* creeds and rites of such apparently different nature, lead to the following conclusion:

> Their doctrine spread according to the fame of the temple; it would then emigrate and influence the theology of the more obscure sanctuaries. All told, it was nothing but the collective opinion of those first faithful ones, the priests, seeing that the king was the only lawful pontiff. . . .
>
> [This doctrine] thus left an open field for other opinions to those who frequented the same temple and who practiced the same religion, one as authentically as the other: fetishists or symbolists, anthropomorphists or partisans of the spirituality of divine nature, polytheists, henotheists, or monotheists in varying differences of expression, supporters of the historicity of myth, of its allegoric or naturist interpretation. All these creeds, which can only be expressed in contradictory dogmas, have in fact found their place side by side in Egyptian religion and have left their traces in its writings. This is why it is possible to define Egyptian religion by its cult, which was unified, and impossible to do so by its dogma, which was not only manifold but also diversely interpreted according to religion. (Ibid.)

It would be difficult to present a better summary of the different opinions put forth concerning the apparent multiplicity of pharaonic beliefs. This multiplicity will remain an enigma as long as these creeds are considered to be dogma or even *several* dogmas differently interpreted according to different centers, when it is actually the illustration of a philosophy relating the successive phases of becoming.

Tum

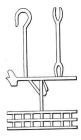

Nome of Heliopolis

Innu (Heliopolis)

THE MYSTERY OF HELIOPOLIS

The Heliopolitan revelation is known mainly through the carved texts lining the long alabaster or limestone walls of the corridors and funerary chambers in the pyramids of the Fifth and Sixth Dynasties: hence their name Pyramid Texts. These inscriptions are worded in archaic style, and this has caused them to be compared with the celebrated Edwin Smith Surgical Papyrus, the original of which is attributed to the time of Djoser (Third Dynasty). But since other medical papyri worded in the same style relate the divine origin of a certain "Treatise of the Heart," found *beneath the feet of Anubis along with other ancient writings* during the reign of one of the first kings of the First Dynasty, there is reason to believe that all these texts go back at least to the time of Menes, at which time the myth, completely formed, appears.

The pyramids affirm the faith in a one and only god, indefinable and eternal, *Neter of neters: He whose name is hidden, He who has no limits,* the incomprehensible.

In Heliopolis, the Innu of the North, the creative act is revealed with the appearance of Tum (or Atum). This word serves to express at once the *affirmation* (of existence) and the *negation* (of the original unity by the very fact of that creation). Accordingly, the word expresses being and non-being; nonbeing becomes the source, and being becomes its negation.

This reversal of notions is typical of pharaonic thought.

Tum will next bring into the world the divine Ogdoad, which, with him, will form the Great Ennead, analysis of this creative act.

It is said of Atum:

> *He who was born in the Nu*
> *when heaven had not yet become,*
> *when earth had not yet become,*
> *when the two supports* [Shu and Tefnut] *had not yet become,*
> *before the* neters *were born,*
> *before death had become,*
> *before there had become the quarrel . . . the voice, anger, and slander . . .*
> *before the Eye of Horus had been put out, before Seth's testes were severed.*
>
> (Pyramid Texts 1040 and 1463–66)

Such is the mystery of creation, the scission of the *oneness,* Nun, whose legend adds, concerning Ra, the universal aspect of Tum:

And Ra said to Nun: O most ancient of gods, Thou in whom I have come into existence.

Nun is the abstract, primordial milieu, symbolized by the waters, the cosmic ocean, as the papyrus of Nesiamsu specifies:

When Atum had emerged from Nun, the primordial waters, before heaven and earth were born, before worm or reptile was created, he could find no place to stand upon. (A. Erman, *La Religion des Egyptiens*)

Then *Tum came into being: Thou hast sprung up as primordial hillock. Thou hast risen like the bird of the stone* [ben-ben] *within the abode of the Phoenix at Heliopolis.*

Thou hast spit forth [ishsh] *Shu, Thou hast hawked up* [tefn] *Tefnut.* (Pyramid Texts 1652)

This mysterious dualization produced Atum, the hillock, for is it not evident that Atum has himself become that primordial knoll? And this polarization *is creation.* Nun and Tum will then

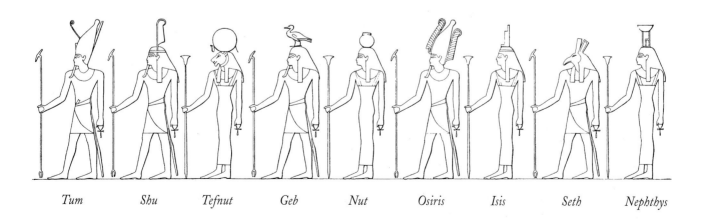

| Tum | Shu | Tefnut | Geb | Nut | Osiris | Isis | Seth | Nephthys |

appear as sky, Nut, and earth, Geb. That which has separated them will also take form, for the legend says that when spitting *(ishsh)*, Atum created Shu, and when expectorating *(tefn)*, he created Tefnut, and together they compose the firmament, which distinguishes and separates heaven and earth. It is the firmament of the Mosaic Genesis. Accordingly, spitting is air and water, the *upward* spouting of the mouth, actually coming from Nun, the primordial ocean, but through Atum.

Shu separating Nut, the sky, from Geb, the earth

Nun, unity or the expression of oneness, *is* but does not *exist* and thus cannot cease to be. Along with the eight principles, four male, four female, who have sprung from the first scission, Atum forms the Great Ennead of Heliopolis:

O Great Ennead of neters in Heliopolis, Tum, Shu, Tefnut, Geb, Nut, Osiris, Isis, Seth, Nephthys, which Tum brings into the world by projection of his heart, as his own birth, in your name of the "Nine Bows" none of you is separated from Tum. (Pyramid Texts 1655)

It would be wrong to consider the ennead as a series of nine principles. It is but a single state that splits up and could symbolically be called "karyokinesis," the function of dualization as it appears in cellular organic life.

With the elements of creation recounted at Heliopolis, all that will constitute the world has been defined: Nut, the sky, supported by Shu and separated from the earth, Geb; then Osiris, the principle of regeneration; Seth, the fallen archangel who opposes the coming forth of the generating fire, Horus. Shu, the air, sustaining life, will make Nephthys, and the invigorating, vitalizing fire in Nut, which animates all life, will make Isis.

This is confirmed by the attribution of the four canopic jars containing embalmed organs: Nephthys protecting the lungs, and Isis, the liver, whose action is well known as the separating and "cooking" of the blood.

Heliopolis gives the entire metaphysics of the cosmic opus, all the bases on which the sensorial world will be grounded to become accessible to human intelligence.

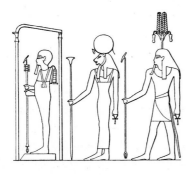

Ptah, Sekhmet, and Nefertum

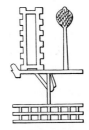

Nome of Memphis

The White Walls (Memphis)

THE MYSTERY OF MEMPHIS

It is at Memphis, the White Walls, in the temple of Ptah, that the metaphysical principles are endowed with bodily form. What is affirmed at Heliopolis is here explained. In Memphis is taught the work of Ptah, that of "giving form" and of animating these forms.

The most ancient known text concerning the Memphite mystery is a copy of an old text said to have been destroyed by worms. This copy, on black granite, was made by the Ethiopian king Shabaka. Sethe, for linguistic reasons, dated the original as stemming from the first dynasties:

It is Ptah, who is called by the great name, Tatenen. . . . He who begot himself, says Atum, he who gave birth to the company of nine neters.

After an account concerning the death of Osiris and the conflict between Horus and Seth, there follows the description of Ptah as creator, he himself being the Ogdoad:

The neters, *which have their shape in Ptah;*
Ptah on the great throne . . .
Ptah-Nun, the father, who [begot] Atum.
Ptah-Nunet, the mother, who bore Atum.
Ptah, the great one—he is the heart and the tongue of the nine neters.
Ptah . . . who gave birth to the neters
Ptah . . . who gave birth to the neters
Ptah . . . Nefertum at the nose of Ra each day.

It is the same fire immanent to the oneness Nun that made Tum appear. This same fire is now Ptah owing to its materialization through Tum.

It arose as heart, it arose as tongue, as a symbol of Atum. . . . Ptah is the very great one. . . .

The heart and tongue have power over all limbs because of the doctrine that it [the heart] is in every body and that it [the tongue] is in every mouth of all neters, *all men, all cattle, all reptiles, all that lives, in that it thinks all that it [the heart] will and commands all that it [the tongue] will.*

His nine neters *are before him as teeth and lips. . . . Atum's nine* neters *have indeed arisen from his seed and his fingers . . . yet the nine* neters *are the teeth and the lips in his [Ptah's] mouth, which told the name of all things, from which Shu and Tefnut proceeded, and which created the nine* neters.

The sight of the eyes, the hearing of the ears, the breathing of the nose, it is communicated to the heart. This it is which lets all knowledge come forth, and it is the tongue that repeats what the heart thinks.

Thus all neters *were born and his [Ptah's] nine* neters *were completed. Every word uttered by Ptah came forth from what the heart had thought and the tongue had commanded. In this way also* kas *were created and* hemsut *determined, which bring forth all nourishment and all food through his word.* (trans., *The God Ptah,* S. Holmberg)

Ptah incarnates himself by being both the fire that will coagulate Nun and the resulting hillock, Tum. As fire he is *active power* and thus, simultaneously, cause and effect.

In the Pyramid Texts, Ptah has already been referred to as "chief artisan" and "creator of forms," and later legends present him modeling the universe and men on a potter's wheel. Ptah is also the "patron" of all artisans and of all human works, and it is therefore said in the text of Shabaka:

He who does that which is loved, and he who does that which is abhorred: Life is given to the peaceful man and death to the wrongdoer. Thus all work is done and all handicraft, the work of the hands and the walking of the legs, and the movement of all [other] limbs according to this command that the heart has thought out and that comes forth through the tongue, which is the being of all things. . . .

Ptah (Turin Museum)

Thus Ptah was content after he had made all things and all neters' *words. He had indeed borne the* neters, *made the towns, founded the provinces, and placed the* neters *at their places of worship. He had determined their offerings and founded their sanctuaries, he had made their bodies as they desired.*

Thus the neters *entered into their bodies of all kinds of wood, all kinds of minerals, all kinds of clay, and all kinds of other things that grow thereon, in which they had taken shape.* (Ibid.)

This text confirms the word *neter* as meaning "specifying functions."

Ptah is "Fire fallen into earth" and he will become the Greek Hephaestos, the divine blacksmith who taught the arts to men. The female principle of Ptah is Sekhmet, the sanguinary lioness who, in a legend connected with the myth of the Solar Eye, almost destroyed all humanity. The child born of the couple Ptah-Sekhmet is Nefer-Tum, "the fulfillment of Tum," who appears as a lotus flower that Ra, according to the Pyramid Texts, wears on his nose each day.

Sekhmet is often called the "Great Enchantress"; she is the protectress of doctors, who were said to be "priests of Sekhmet and magicians." Under the name of Menhit, however, she becomes the preeminent goddess of war. Then, from dreaded lioness, she resumes the peaceful aspect of Hathor upon returning from the South, where she cooled her ardors in the waters of the Abaton (near Philae).

From Hathor, "the house of Hor," will be born the little Ihy who holds the sistrum and the *menat*, which are Hathor's own symbols. In Dendera, Hathor is called "the Golden One." The figure of Ihy, the *neter* of music and harmony, brings to mind the Greek myth of Aphrodite and Ares conceiving Harmonia.

Hathor is venerated throughout Egypt under different names and with different qualities. She is herself the Eye of Ra, the apparent disk, and thus she undergoes the vicissitudes of the solar course. Hathor is also the "mother goddess," and in this capacity she will be identified with Isis. She is the celestial cow as well, the divine nurse whose milk will nourish the kings. Finally, there are the seven Hathors who preside over the destiny of the newborn child.

Thoth   *Nome of the hare*   *City of the Eight, Khemenu (Hermopolis)*

THE MYSTERY OF HERMOPOLIS

The name of Hermopolis, city of Hermes, is but a later Greek appellation of the great religious center of Thoth. The true and sacred name of the capital of Upper Egypt's fifteenth nome was Khemenu, "the city of the Eight," where the eight pristine *neters* appeared. Its civil name, Un, was designated by the nome's emblem, the hare, and signifies "existence."

Thoth, or Djehuty, was likened to the moon, whose birth is recounted in an ancient legend:

While Ra was in the heavens, he said one day: *Have Thoth come unto me, and Thoth was brought to him at once.* The *neter's* Majesty said to Thoth: *Be in the sky in my stead whilst I shine for the blessed in the inferior regions. . . . Thou art in my place, my representative, and thus thou shalt be named: Thoth, the replacement of Ra.* Then all manner of things sprang up as the result of Ra's play upon words. He told Thoth: *I shall make it so that thou wilt embrace* [ionh] *the two skies by thy beauty and thy rays—and thus the moon was born* [ioh]. Further on in the text . . . *I shall make it so that thou wilt send* [hob] *greater ones than thee—and thus the Ibis* [hib], *the bird of Thoth, was born.* (Erman, *Religion des Egyptiens*, p. 91)

Ibis

The baboon of Thoth before the clepsydra (Great hypostyle hall, Karnak)

This is how Ra, the solar light, while beneath the earth, has himself replaced by the moon and its light: Thoth.

Numerous are the legends attributing creative power to the very pronouncing of the name. This efficacity of the word at the source of things sensorial pervades the hymns, prayers, or litanies. These are mainly based on "word games," which lose their meaning in translation. To name is to call into life, and it is said in the legends of Isis and Ra that to know the "secret name" is to know the means of warding off malefic forces. To know the "secret name," then, would be to know the function.

Thoth, Thrice-Greatest (whence Hermes Trismegistos), is the divine scribe who transmitted all science to men, be it astronomy, medicine, or the rituals of the cult. Thoth is the master of *neter-medu,* or divine staffs, the hieroglyphs. He is the inspiration and patron of every scribe or student of the "House of Life." In one of the sanctuaries of each temple are kept the "writings of Thoth," his sacred scrolls, and the priests alone are allowed to consult them.

The animals consecrated to Thoth are the ibis and the baboon. Thoth is the inventor of the calendar, the regulator of time, the dispenser of the years. It is owing to him that the barque of Ra sails the immensity of the diurnal as well as the nocturnal sky, crossing "in peace" each hour protected by the twenty-four *neters* attributed to each division of the daily cycle. Thoth is the Great Judge who "arbitrates" the eternal enemies, Seth and Horus, and he is cited in this capacity as far back as the Pyramid Texts.

In Hermopolis, however, Thoth is never cited in the myth of creation. Here the myth is a resumption of the Ogdoad of Heliopolis, but only abstruse principles appear at the beginning.

Before creation, there existed a serpent named Kem-at-f, "He who has accomplished his time." Although it is said that Kem-at-f died after having given birth to a second serpent, Ir-ta ("creator of the earth"), it is elsewhere affirmed that Amun of the temple of Karnak is himself Kem-at-f. As its name indicates, the second serpent was the true author of the world, and it was this Ir-ta (later merged with the ithyphallic Amun of the temple of Luxor) who created the eight primeval *neters*.

The Eight Primordials form four couples of serpents and frogs whose mysterious names are interpreted as follows:

The first couple, Nun and Nunet, personifies the primeval waters or the space of the world before creation. The second couple, Heh and Hehet symbolizes water "searching for its path" (*heh* means to search). The third couple, Kek and Keket, signifies the darkness that reigned upon the waters before the appearance of the sun. The fourth couple bears several names, the most frequent being Niu, "He who turns away and disappears," and Niat, or Amun, "He whose name is hidden," and Amunet, his female principle. In Hermopolitan cosmogony, the part played by this fourth couple is that attributed to the "spirit of God moving upon the face of the waters" in the biblical account of creation. (From J. Vandier, *La Religion des egyptiens*, p. 63)

And so the Eight Primordials were created, but the world was still darkness and silence. Upon the waves of the primeval waters, these eight were carried to Khemenu, where a hillock of mud had arisen. On this small hill an egg became and of this egg was born a goose, who flew off, cackling. Then day appeared, for this bird was none other than the Great Cackler, the sun itself, author of the first ray of light and of the first noise rending the silence.

When their creative work was accomplished, the Eight Primordials died and were buried at Medinet Habu, across from Thebes. A small temple still stands at their burial place, to which Amun of Luxor went every ten days in order to make offerings to them.

"The idea that a god might die is incompatible with our way of thinking," remarks the great Egyptologist Erman, but he later acknowledges: "The true sense of all the subtleties gathered here escapes our uninitiated minds." (Erman, *Religion des egyptiens*, pp. 121–22)

It is indeed difficult to admit the death of a "god," considering our interpretation of this word. Once again our conceptions must be turned upside down in order to penetrate to the depths of pharaonic thought. For the Ancients, the word *neter* referred to active principles, to the causes of phenomena. This word has been translated as "God"; consequently people speak of pharaonic "gods," and herein lies a source of confusion. To deists, God is the Creator, to whom they attribute a free will similar to man's but situated outside of the world.

This is not the concept pharaonic Egypt attached to the term *neter*, seeing that a clear distinction was made between metaphysical *neters*, cosmic *neters*, and the *neters* responsible for natural facts that concern humanity. These principles are anthropomorphized, but they are not humanized, as are the gods of Olympus, for example.

The "principle," or *neter*, is not a participating agent; it only designates a *mode of action*. The *neters* are the laws of divine harmony; they direct the affinities and concordances, they give rise to forms and signatures, command the phases of becoming and its return to the source; they characterize life. Thus the *neters* are *conscious* principles, but they are without *free will*, without the faculty of deliberate choice.

The philosophy descriptive of the nature of the *neters* is transmitted through legends, which vary with each main center (temple)

because the same "mode of action," or principle, changes its aspect according to the medium upon which it bears; the action of fire, for instance, will be different on fire, on water, on air, or on solid bodies.

Thus, in the Mystery of Heliopolis, Amun is an abstract principle: *He whose name is hidden.* In Hermopolis he becomes the breath that animates air and wind. We have seen before that Kem-at-f, "He who has accomplished his time," is said to have died and also said to be Amun of Karnak himself. This apparent contradiction stems from a misinterpretation of the word *dead:* when activity has produced its fruit, it stops being, as such, since it has fixed itself within the fruit.

THE MYSTERY OF THEBES

The Theban revelation is intimately linked to Hermopolitan cosmogony; in Khemenu, however, the generative "milieu" is described, while at Thebes, the capital of the Wast nome (the key of the Nile), the fruit of this genesis is defined—through Amun, Mut, and Khonsu.

One of the hymns in the Ritual of the Daily Divine Worship defines the nature of the Theban Amun:

Salutations to thee, Amun-Ra, divine form born the first time, Master of Eternity, One and Only One who gives birth to neters, *who gives birth to men, through thee all things come about.*

Master of Life, Thou comest forth as one only, alone in Nun, before thy father Geb [earth] and thy mother Nut [sky].

Thou art as Horus who illuminates the Two Lands with his two eyes.

It is not the solar disk that shows itself to the inhabitants of the sky, but thine head that reaches heaven in thy divine form, exalting thy two plumes and coming forth from the waters. . . .

He [Pharaoh] knows thy perfect names and all that thou didst while [still] the One and Only in Nun, in thine own name of Creator whose heart is tireless.

All the neters *rejoice and worship their Lord, this One and Only One who hides himself [Amun] from his own creations, who ruled this earth upon emerging from the Waters, who veiled the Fire of the Void, who elevated it in his name of "Breath of Life."* (Berlin Papyrus, chapter 40)

Thus Amun is described as he who hides, who contains (like the veil behind which is hidden) the fire of the original void and so becomes the breath of life.

In the Theban triad—Amun, Mut, and Khonsu—the female aspect of Amun is Mut. This can be illustrated in the following manner: the moon, as reflector, is the female aspect of the sun. In this way does a nameless activity become perceptible (physically known) through the obstacle that is of its own nature.

In life, this femininity conceives, incubates, makes live, and makes die at the same time, as the hen brooding her egg puts it into a state of "putrefaction" (death for rebirth) in order to hatch the chick. This illustrates the character of Mut, whose name can be written either with a vulture in which case it signifies "mother," or with an owl (letter *M*), in which case it signifies "death": Mut unites what these two words have in common. The activity of Mut as incubating principle implies the regenerative death symbolized by Sekhmet (who is still known through legend as a slayer of children). She represents the generative "Fire" of Ptah acting "in earth" or "in what is body."

These mythical transcriptions must be understood as "functions"; being of universal nature, their description is bound to be complex.

The set of temples forming Karnak is called the *seats of Apet,* and this word in itself is cabalistic. The female hippopotamus, which symbolizes the gestating matrix, is called Apet. Now

Amun, Mut, and Khonsu

Nome of Thebes

Wast (Thebes)

Apet, or *Ipet*, derives from the root *ip*, "to count" or "to enumerate." It follows that gestation, being a multiplication, is identified with the fact of numbering. In accordance with the *function* taught in that group of temples, the name Karnak therefore means: the site of the *three seats* or phases *of gestation*.

To each phase, Karnak consecrates sanctuaries that are so many chapters of a vast philosophy, each part being linked to the preceding and following parts as the leaf of a plant is to both stalk and flower.

Thus when speaking of Mut generating Khonsu, this principle is not to be separated from Apet, which is simultaneously both the matrix (the matrical vessel containing the egg, or else the animal matrix) and the principle of fixation of what shall live: Osiris in rebirth (death is always synonymous with fixation or, inversely, fixation is synonymous with death).

Khonsu, crowned with the solar disk cupped by the lunar crescent, bears all the scepters with the exception of the *wadj*, symbol of opening, of blossoming. Khonsu is most often represented mummified but may also assume the form of a hawk-headed man, standing or walking; sometimes he is merged with Thoth, master of time.

In a papyrus of the Ramesside era (Leyden Papyrus), the bond of the three mysteries within the Theban Amun is thus defined:

Three gods are all the gods: Amun, Ra, Ptah, who have no equal. He whose nature [literally, whose name] is mysterious, that is Amun; Ra is the head; Ptah is the body. Their cities on earth, forever established, are Thebes, Heliopolis, and Memphis, [lasting] forevermore. When there is a message from heaven, it is heard in Heliopolis; in Memphis it is repeated to Ptah; a letter is made of it written in the signs of Thoth, for the city of Amun [Thebes] with all that pertains to it. The answer and decision are given in Thebes, and that which comes forth is addressed to the divine Ennead, all that comes forth from his mouth, Amun's. The gods are established for him, according to his commands. The message, it is for: to kill or to make live. Life and death depend upon it, for all beings, except for him, Amun, and for Ra [and for Ptah], oneness-trinity. (A. Moret, *Mystères égyptiens* [Paris: Armand Colin, 1913], pp. 127–28)

MYTH AND LEGENDS OF RA

Homage to thee, Ra, who is perfect each day, who rises in the morning without respite and who is Khepri overburdened with labor. . . . The purest gold cannot be compared with thy splendor. Carver who hast carved thyself, thou hast cast thine own body, O sculptor who never hast been sculpted. . . . Thou who travels the eternity above . . . thou makest thy way equally beneath the earth. . . . During a single small day, thou devourest a space of millions of hundreds of thousands of leagues. Each day is merely an instant for thee, and after having journeyed it, thou reclinest. Likewise thou achievest the hours of the night. Thou performest this task without pause in thine efforts. . . .

Homage to thee, Disk [Aten] of the Day, who hast created human beings and made them to live. . . .

He who hastens, he who speeds, he who accomplishes his rotations, Khepri of illustrious birth, elevating his perfection in the belly of celestial Nut, illuminating the Two Lands with his disk [Aten], the primordial one of the Two Lands who has created himself and who saw himself while creating himself. (A. Varille, *Hymne au Soleil des architects d'Amenophis III, Souti et Hor*)

In the royal tombs of the New Kingdom, Ra is represented in the solar barque sailing upon the celestial stream and traveling the regions of day and of night. The sky is depicted by the body of Nut herself, who swallows the sun each evening and brings it back into the world every morning in the shape of a scarab, Kheper. The sun is said to be Khepri when rising, Ra at his culmination of noon, and Atum in the evening, although some texts reverse the roles of Atum and Khepri.

The scarab is chosen to symbolize the dawning sun because it is the only animal known to make the motions of "rolling" a sphere it itself has perfectly molded, and this gesture is comparable to the solar sphere's apparent movement from east to west. Furthermore, the scarab buries this ball in which it has laid its eggs, concealing it *under the earth*. Well known are the characteristic metamorphoses of this egg from worm to nymph before the scarab appears ready to live in the open, the last transformation requiring humidity.

In the hieroglyphic writing, under the name of Kheper, the scarab is used to express *becoming* and *transformations*. Under the name of Khepri, he corresponds to the dawning sun, the daily reminder of Ra's coming forth from darkness and the primeval waters.

Solar scarab, tomb of Ramesses IX

One of the innumerable legends concerning the myth of Ra tells of Isis, *whose mouth is the breath of life, whose sentence drives out evil, and whose very word revives him who no longer breathes.* When Isis desired to know the secret name of Ra, the sole name unknown to her, she artfully fashioned a serpent out of earth and Ra's own saliva, and placed it in the path of that *neter:*

Then the venerable serpent bit him, the living fire born from his own self.

Tormented by pain and fever, Ra then summoned unto him all the *neters* born from his flank. And Isis said to Ra:

Tell me thy name, divine father—for the one upon whose name an incantation is pronounced remains alive!

—I am he who made the waters and the earth, tied the mountains, and created what is above.

I am he who made the waters and created the celestial tides. . . .

I am the one who made the sky and the mysteries of the two horizons wherein I placed the souls of the neters.

I am he who opens his eyes, thus light becomes.

He who closes his eyes, thus darkness becomes;

Upon whose command spread the waters of the Nile, but whose name is unknown to the neters.

I am he who made the hours, and so the days were born.

I am the one who opened the festivities of the year, who created the river. . . . I am he who creates living fire. . . .

I am Khepri in the morning, Ra at his noon, Atum at night.

But the venom was not driven out, the great *neter* was not healed, so Isis said to Ra:

Thy name is not amongst those thou hast told me!

Sacred scarab rolling its ball

And Ra, no longer able to resist the torment, said to Isis: *Hark what I shall say, my daughter, so that my name may pass from my breast to thine. And thou must hide it, but thou mayest tell it to thy son, Horus, as a powerful charm against all poison.* (A. Erman and H. Ranke, *La Civilisation égyptienne*, p. 337)

Another legend tells that Ra once reigned over *neters* and men simultaneously. In the course of time, he grew old, *his bones were of silver, his arms and legs of gold, his hair verily of lapis lazuli.* Men then plotted against him but His Majesty took heed and called upon his Eye, and Shu, Tefnut, Geb, Nut, and all the Primordials, saying to Nun:

O eldest of neters, *in whom I have come into being, and you, primeval gods, lo! The men who have come into existence within my eye have fomented a plot against me. Tell me what there is to be done against that.*

Then the Majesty of Nun said: "My son Ra . . . so great is the fear inspired by thee, it is sufficient that thine eye be turned toward those who have conceived evil against thee. . . . Send thine eye . . . to kill them for thee, when it descends in the form of Hathor."

And so this goddess returned, after having killed the men in the desert. And Ra said: *Thou must be mighty* [sekhem] *amongst them . . .* and it is since that day that Hathor took the name of Sekhmet, the lion-headed. But Ra was dismayed by the bloodshed that so delighted the heart of his messenger:

And Ra said: "Summon unto me swift messengers who can run like the body's own shadow. And these messengers were brought in. And the Majesty of this neter *said to them: "Make ye haste toward Elephantine and bring me back a quantity of red ochre* [didi]." Then Ra ordered that this red ochre be ground at Heliopolis by "the One who wears the buckle" while the servants were grinding barley to make beer, *and this ochre was added to the dough and it resembled human blood. And seven thousand jugs of beer were prepared.* On the dawn of the day when the goddess was supposed to kill the men, this beer was poured upon the ground.

Now when the goddess arrived and found the fields all flooded . . . she looked down at her reflection and *her face was beautiful; she drank and this was pleasing to her heart. So intoxicated did she become, she no longer recognized the men.*

THE SACRED ANIMALS

There is one rite that puzzled the Greek travelers, as it still does the modern commentators: the cult of the sacred animals, among which the bull and the ram are the most prominent.

The bull Hap, better known under his Greek form of Apis, is the oldest evidence of what is called the "divinization of an animal." Some documents dating from the First Dynasty tell us that in that epoch and from the oldest time, a solemn ceremony linked to the royal festival was celebrated in honor of the bull Hap. Moreover, royal onomastics give proof of the importance then ascribed to the bull Hap, whose name forms part of the name of Athotis's mother: Khenethap, and also that of the mother of Djoser: Nimaāthap.

Representations show the sacred bull wearing the solar disk and the uraeus between his horns. He is black and blazed with a white triangle, a white crescent spotting his flank and an eagle on his neck. Hap originally appears as a fecundating and generating power. At the time of his enthronement, Hap was visiting the sanctuary of Hapi, on the isle of Rhoda near Cairo. The first crescent of the new moon appeared at the very moment he was embarking for Memphis, where, on the day of the full moon, his festivities were to be celebrated.

Funerary papyrus of Queen Maātkare (Twenty-first Dynasty)

Little is known concerning the relationship between the bull Hap and Ptah of Memphis. By his titles, we know that he was: *living Apis, herald of Ptah, He who makes truth rise up to the* neter *beautiful of face* (surname of Ptah); he was also called *son of Ptah.*

Heliopolis (Innu of the North) also had its sacred bull—Mnevis, who was black, and was supposed to display ears of corn along his entire body and tail. He was the herald of Ra-Atum, and his symbol, a bull's head surmounting a pillar, became intimately connected with the symbol of the city of Heliopolis: the pillar Innu.

Since ancient times, Armant, or Innu of the South, honored the bull Buchis and then, toward the Eleventh Dynasty, worshiped a hawk-headed *neter* of astral origin, under the name of Mentu-Ra. Armant had four temples situated in the vicinity of Thebes: Armant, Tod, Medamud, and Karnak in which the four bulls consecrated to Mentu were venerated. These four Mentu were assimilated to the four masculine members of the Ogdoad, and so great was their importance that the name Mentuhotep was adopted by the kings of that period between the years 2160 and 2000 B.C.

Then, suddenly, Mentu—the supreme *neter* of such names as Antef and Mentuhotep—lost the supremacy he had exerted and gave place to Amun-Ra and his sacred ram.

There is no doubt as to the astral origin of Mentu, who belongs to the solar cycle (Vandier, *Religion égyptienne,* pp. 161, 236) and is also cited by the Pyramid Texts as being *among the stars.* (Pyramid Texts 1081–1378) It is thus of interest to examine celestial phenomena for the reason behind the disappearance of the Mentu cult and its bull in favour of Amun and his ram. Let us listen to one of our astronomers:

> At the beginning of our era, the equinox reached the first degrees of [the constellation of] Aries, the Ram; 2,150 years earlier, it coincided with the first stars of the constellation Taurus, the

Bull, which had been the equinoctial sign since the year 4300 before our era. It was probably during this epoch that the first stargazers composed the zodiacal constellations, for in all ancient religious myths, the Bull is associated with the Sun's fecundating work upon the seasons and the products of the earth, while no trace is found of an analogous association of [the constellation of] Gemini, the Twins. This was already legend eighteen centuries ago, as Virgil salutes the celestial Bull who opens the yearly cycle with his golden horns:

> *Candidus auratis aperit quum cornibus annum*
> *Taurus, et averso cedans canis occidit astro.*

For the Egyptians, the Chinese, and even the early Greeks, the stars of Taurus, particularly the Pleiades, were the stars of the equinox. The annals of astronomy have preserved a Chinese observation of the η star in the Pleiades as marking the spring equinox of the year 2357 before our era. . . .

The Ancients conjectured that the political state of the globe was periodic as well, and that the Great Year, as they called it, would return to earth the same peoples, the same occurrences, the same history, just as the succession of centuries brings back to the sky the same aspects of the celestial bodies. As it was accepted that human destinies were dependent upon planetary influences, it was natural to believe that the same configurations of these celestial bodies had to reproduce the same events. (Flammarion, *Astronomie populaire*, p. 55)

It is known what events took place in pharaonic Egypt during the passage of Taurus to Aries (2260 B.C.): a celebrated narrative by the sage Ipuwer recounts the grave revolution at the end of

Isis and the bull Apis

The Narmer Palette: lower portion

the Old Kingdom, thought to have taken place around 2720 (Borchardt), 2400 (Moret), or 2242 (Drioton). By speaking of what had been destroyed, these "Admonitions" are invaluable for indicating that which had existed. Here are some excerpts:

Forsooth, the wealthy are in mourning. The poor man is full of joy. Every town says: let us suppress the powerful among us.

Forsooth, the land turns around as does a potter's wheel. The robber is a possessor of riches. [The rich man] is [become] a plunderer.

Forsooth, the splendid judgment hall, its writings are taken away. Laid bare is the secret place that was [such formerly].

Forsooth, public offices are opened and [their] census lists are taken away. Serfs become lords of serfs.

Forsooth . . . [officials] are slain, and their writings are taken away. . . .

Behold, things are done that have never happened since long times past: the king has been taken away by poor men.

Behold, no offices are in their [right] place, like a frightened herd without a herdsman.

Forsooth, princes are hungry and in distress. Servants are served. . . .

Behold, the poor of the land have become rich, and [the possessor of] property has become one who has nothing.

Forsooth, the hot-headed man says: If I knew where God is, then would I make offerings unto him.

But this revolution is joyless:

Forsooth, mirth has perished, and is [no longer] expressed. It is groaning that is heard throughout the land, mingled with lamentations.

. . . The land is given over to its weariness like the cutting of flax. . . . Would that there might be an end of men, no conception, no birth! O that the earth would cease from noise, and tumult be no more! (A. H. Gardiner, *The Admonitions of an Egyptian Sage* [Leipzig, 1909])

Great sacred vase of Amun (painting from tomb of Pinehas, Nineteenth Dynasty)

Amenhotep, son of Hapu; statue from Karnak (Cairo Museum)

The end of the "Admonitions of an Egyptian Sage" is lost, but it can be inferred by the ending of the "Sentences of Neferrehu," priest of Heliopolis, who formulated the following prophecy:

A king shall come from the South, who is called Ameni. . . . He shall take the white crown and wear the red crown, and the two lords [Horus and Seth], who love him, shall delight in him. Rejoice, O ye men who live in his time! Under his reign, the son of a man of quality shall recover consideration for his name forevermore. Those who would do evil and who contemplate hostility, [they] restrain their tongues for fear of him. . . . Law shall recover its place and injustice shall be driven out. Happiness to him who will see these things and who shall serve this king. (Papyrus 1116 B, St. Petersburg, in Moret, *Le Nil,* p. 268)

Now this Ameni, whose name means the Amunian, or He of Amun, will be Amenemhet, Amun at the head (or "in front"), first king of the Twelfth Dynasty (approximately 2000 B.C.), at the outset of the epoch in which the sun stands in the constellation of Aries, beginning the domination of Amun. This king, inaugurating the new order of that era, is in fact the first to have the name of Amun enter into the designation of the royal name.

It is the time when the predominance of Taurus the celestial Bull wanes, to be replaced by Aries, the Ram of the Amunian epoch. This transition is all the more important in that it inaugurates the time of coincidence between the *astrological sign of Aries* in the spring and the *Ram constellation* of the fixed stars. It is the beginning of the brilliant phase of Egypt's historic epoch, which terminated with the end of [the sign of] Aries, the Ram, and the entry of the vernal equinoctial point into Pisces, the Fishes, about sixty years before Christ.

THE ROYALTY

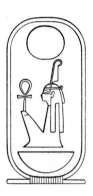

The nobleman, the prince, the administrator of the sovereign's domains in the land of the Bedouins, the truly-known by the king, his beloved one, the companion Sinuhe says:

"I was a follower who accompanied his master. . . .

"In the year XXX, the third month of inundation, the Seventh, the neter *entered his horizon, the king of Upper and Lower Egypt Sehetepibre [Amenemhet I]; he was taken away to heaven and thus found himself united with the solar disk, and the body of the* neter *was absorbed in He who created him. The court was plunged in silence, all hearts in sadness; the great double door remained closed; the courtesans were [sitting on their heels], their heads on their knees, and the people were lamenting."*

And so the story of Sinuhe begins by relating the death of Amenemhet I, son of Ra, and his return toward his father. The heir to the throne, the future Sesostris I, was in Libya at that time. When the messengers told him of the events that had taken place at court, *the falcon took flight with his followers without informing his army.* The future king is here incorporated into Horus, the falcon, for every prince destined to royalty *is* Horus.

Sinuhe, who was among the other royal children following the prince "in that army," heard the words of one of them. What could this be all about? Sinuhe only says: *My heart became troubled, my arms were undone from my body, a trembling settled upon all my limbs. I bounded away to search for a hiding place. I headed toward the South:* [yet] *it was not my intention to go to that court, for I thought there would be conflicts and I did not believe I would be able to [continue] to live after that.*

According to these words, there was doubtless some plot being fostered against the legitimate heir, and in the silence shrouding the actual facts, we have an example of the respect commanded by all members of the royal lineage. This moral decorum can be found not only in the stories but

Stela of the "Serpent King," First Dynasty (Louvre Museum)

also, for instance, in the famous trial that took place under Ramesses III involving a plot in the harem: all those involved were given borrowed names chosen according to the role each had played in that affair, which prevents modern historians from identifying any of the traitors.

Sinuhe walked on and on; he crossed the Nile and went over the border; thirst assailed him in the eastern deserts; he reached Byblos only to start wandering again until a prince of the upper Retenu received him in kindness and asked him the reason for his flight. Sinuhe replied, "disguising the truth," however, and he held his tongue concerning the words he had heard.

The prince inquired: *How then will that country manage without him, the benevolent* neter *who is widely feared among the foreign nations, as is Sekhmet in a year of pestilence?* And Sinuhe answered:

Verily, his son has entered the palace and taken his father's heritage. Surely he is a neter *who has no equal, before whom no other [like him] has existed. He is a master of wisdom, of perfect aims, of excellent commands, on whose order one comes and goes. It is he who tamed the foreign regions while his father stayed within his palace, and he reported to his father when the decisions [of the latter] had been carried out.*

And Sinuhe was profuse in praise of the new king; he glorified his courage, his robust heart, his daring, and his ability in racing and with arms. *He is the well-beloved, full of charms, who has conquered by love. His city loves him more than itself; it rejoices in him more than in its own* neter. *Men and women acclaim him, now that he is king. He conquered [while still being] in the egg, and his face was [turned] toward [royalty] since he was born. He is the one who makes those born with him to multiply, he is the one and only one, the gift of God.*

Sinuhe lived in the country of Retenu, but when he felt old age descending and listlessness stealing over him, his eyes heavy and his arms sapped of strength, his legs refusing to carry him, for his heart was weary, he cried out: *O God! . . . who has predestined this flight, be merciful, lead me back to the court. Perhaps thou wilt grant me to see again the place where my heart has never ceased to be. May the king of Egypt be merciful to me so that I may live by his favor!* Then Sinuhe expresses his desire to be buried in the same earth that saw him born.

This call was transmitted to the king of Egypt and His Majesty immediately responded with great kindness, sending, along with many gifts, the following message:

Horus who lives again by the birth [of the king]. The Two Goddesses: he who lives again by the birth [of the king]. The king of Upper and Lower Egypt, Kheperkare. The son of Ra: Amenemhet, may he live eternally forever!

Royal order for the follower, Sinuhe. Yea, this order of the king is brought to thee to tell thee this: Thou hast wandered the foreign lands, from Qedem to Retenu: one land gave thee to [another], under the impulse of thine own heart [alone]. What hadst thou done, then, in order [to fear] something would be done to thee? Thou didst not blaspheme in such a way that thy words could have been blamed. Thou spokest no harm against the Council of Notables so that it was necessary to oppose thy remarks. This determination possessed thine heart, but in mine own heart it was not. . . .

Return to Egypt, that thou might again see the court wherein thou didst grow up, so that thou mayest again kiss the ground at the great double door and join again with friends. It is [now] too late to lead a wayfaring life. Think of sickness, and return.

It is difficult to imagine Sinuhe's joy in thanking the king for his forgiveness toward him, the deserter, who accuses himself of being a servant led astray by his own heart toward barbaric lands. He evokes all the *neters,* the Great Ennead, and ardently beseeches them to grant unlimited life to his beloved king. Sinuhe blesses the clearsightedness of the king:

Master of knowledge who knows [his] subjects, in the secret of his palace, he realized that this humble servant feared to say these things, and it is indeed a weighty matter to discuss them. Then Sinuhe describes his return to Egypt, his arrival before His Majesty, who was seated on a golden throne.

He admits that fear still remained in his breast and tells how he lost consciousness. . . . Her Majesty, the royal wife, and the royal children then presented their *menat* necklaces and their sistra (attributes of Hathor) to the king, saying: *May thy hands [reach out] toward something beautiful, o king of [eternal] duration, toward the adornment of the Lady of Heaven [Hathor]! May the Golden Goddess give life to thy nostrils and may thee be joined by the Lady of the Stars [surnames of Hathor]!*

May the crown of the South travel downstream and may the crown of the North travel upstream, so as to unite and to assemble, upon the injunction of Thy Majesty! May the uraeus be placed upon thy forehead! And as thou hast kept [thine] subjects sheltered from misfortune, so may Ra, master of the Two Lands, be favorable to thee! . . . Give breath to him who suffocates [Sinuhe, who is gripped by anguish] and grant us our beautiful reward [in the person of] this sheikh, son of Mehyt, [this] barbarian born in Egypt. . . . No more anguish for him who has seen thy face; the eye which has beheld thy face shall be afraid no longer.

We must confine ourselves to citing but a few brief passages of this story. Its translator comments:

> Thus the stories offer us a faithful picture of society, its hierarchy, its different classes, as well as its moral ideas and religious creeds; and this picture, full of life, richly colored and carefully detailed, allows us to enter more deeply into the Egyptian soul. As such they are of interest not only to the history of literature but perhaps even more so to the history of civilization. (G. Lefebvre, *Romans et contes égyptiens de l'epoque pharaonique*, 25 [1949], pp. 5–25)

These texts show the deep-rooted belief that the king is of divine essence, that he himself is Horus, Master of the Two Crowns, Golden Horus, Master of the Two Lands, Son of Ra (the five names of his title). Sinuhe never divulged the reasons for his flight, nor did he utter a single word that could lend credence to dissension at the court of Egypt. He ceaselessly exalts his sovereign's wisdom, his authority over foreign lands. All these tales reveal an unfailing sense of loyalty, and we notice in them a continual associating of the principles, or *neters,* hence of theology, with the actions and behavior of the king as well as of his subjects.

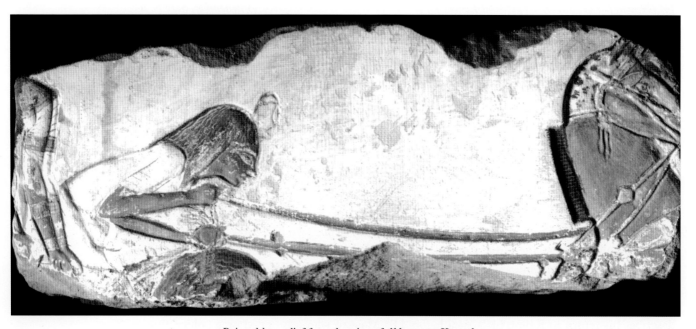

Painted bas-relief from the reign of Akhenaten, Karnak

THE ROYAL NAMES

As early as the first dynasties, kings were designated as Horus bearer of the royal theme. This name is inscribed in a rectangle surmounted by a falcon and placed above the facade of palaces reminiscent of those structures of the Old Kingdom that were characterized by redans. The Horus name is frequently borne by the royal *ka*, whose meaning is symbolized by the image of two uplifted arms.

The second name is that of the two principles Vulture-Cobra, "the Two Goddesses," protectresses of the two kingdoms: Nekhebet of the southern kingdom and Wadjet of the kingdom to the north.

The third is the Golden Horus name, that is to say, the royal fulfillment. In the temple of Karnak, these first three names are put in relation respectively with Amun, Mut, and Khonsu on one of the architraves of the temple of Khonsu.

The fourth and fifth names are King of the South and North (the bulrush and the bee) and Son of Ra, inscribed within two cartouches or within an oblong loop *(ren)*. Prior to the Third Dynasty, these two names were not enclosed by the cartouche but simply followed by a round loop *(chen)* on the endless thread of continuity.

As early as the First Dynasty, the king Den displays, after his Horus name, the uraeus serpent belonging to the second name, the symbol for gold for the third, and the *chen*. Another seal of King Den shows, following the Horus name, the bulrush and the bee of the fourth name, proving that the principles of protocol were established from the very beginnings of the dynastic empire.

With regard to the *bestowal of the name,* here are several excerpts from the Westcar Papyrus concerning the birth of the first three kings of the Fifth Dynasty, born of Redjedet—the wife of Ra-user, priest of Ra—*who was great with three children by Ra, lord of Sakhebu:*

. . . On one of these days, it happened that Redjedet felt the pains [of childbirth], and the delivery was very difficult. Then the Majesty of Ra, lord of Sakhebu, said to Isis, Nephthys, Meskhenet, and Khnum: "Go ye and deliver Redjedet of the three children who are in her womb and who are to exert this beneficient office throughout the entire land. They shall construct your temples, they shall supply your altars with provisions, they shall make prosper your libation tables, they shall increase your offerings." Having transformed themselves into musician-dancers, these neters *went on their way; Khnum, bearing [their] belongings, accompanied them. They arrived at the house of Ra-user and found him holding himself [immobile], his clothes all disheveled. They presented him with their* menat *necklaces and sistra, and he said to them: "Behold, my ladies, it is the mistress of the house who is in labor and her delivery is difficult." Then they said: "Permit us to see her for we know how to accomplish the birth." "Go," he answered, and they went in to Redjedet, closing the chamber upon themselves and upon her. Isis then placed herself in front of Redjedet, Nephthys behind her, and Heket hastened the birth. And Isis said: "Be not too powerful [user] in her breast, in this thy name of User-(ka)-f." This child then glided into her hands; he was one cubit [long] and solid of bone. His limbs were encrusted with gold and he wore a headdress of real lapis lazuli. They bathed him, after having cut the navel string and after placing him upon a brick enclosure. Then Meskhenet went up to him, saying: "A king who will exercise royalty throughout this entire land," while Khnum gave health to his body. [Once again] Isis stood before Redjedet, Nephthys behind her, and Heket hastened the birth. And Isis said: "Do not linger [sah] in her breast, in this thy name of Sah-Ra." This child then glided into her hands: he was one cubit [long] and solid of bone. His limbs were encrusted with gold, and he wore a headdress of real lapis lazuli . . . and soon. (Still one more time) Isis placed herself in front of Redjedet, Nephthys behind her, and Heket hastened the birth. And Isis said: "Be not shadowy [keku] in her breast, in this thy name of Keku."* (Lefebvre, *Romans et contes égyptiens,* pp. 86–87)

The "Two Goddesses" name of Amenhotep I

In this story, each name and word is clearly symbolic, with the musician-dancers referring to harmony.

Thus Userkaf, Sahure, and Neferirkare Kakai were born.

The divine birth of the king is shown for Hatshepsut in the famous bas-reliefs of the temple of Deir el-Bahri and for Amenhotep III in about fifteen scenes represented in the temple of Luxor.

In Deir el-Bahri, Amun informs the Heliopolitan Ennead of the birth of the future pharaoh. He then goes to the queen, while Thoth, with papyrus in hand, recites her official names: Ahmose (birth of the moon), the mother of Hatshepsut. The scene of the theogamy now follows: Amun and the queen are seated upon a sky upheld by Neith (the goddess of weaving) and Selkit (the scorpion divinity presiding over births). The text framing this tableau tells of the union:

Here is what is said by Amun-Ra, king of neters, *master of Karnak, he who presides at Thebes, when he had taken the form of that male, the king of Upper and Lower Egypt, Tuthmosis I. He encountered the queen as she was reclining in the splendor of her palace. She awakened at the fragrance of the* neter *and marveled as His Majesty walked directly toward her . . . placed his heart upon her, and showed himself to her in his form of* neter. *And immediately after his appearing, she exalted at the sight of his beauties; the love of the* neter *suffused her limbs, and the odor of the* neter *as well as his breath were rich with [perfumes] from Punt.*

And this is what the royal wife, the royal mother, Ahmose, said in the presence of the majesty of this august neter, *Amun, master of Karnak, master of Thebes: "Twice great are thy souls! It is a [noble] thing to see thy [face] when thou joinest thyself with all favors to my majesty! Thy dew impregnates all my limbs!"*

Taking literally the words that the royal mother pronounces at that moment, Amun forms the birth name of the child and says:

She who joins Amun, the first of nobles, *indeed that will be the name of this girl who shall open thy womb, since it is the sequence of words that have come from thy mouth. She will conduct a bountiful royalty in this entire land, for my soul is hers, my heart is hers, my will is hers, my crown is hers, verily, that she may govern the Two Lands, so that she may guide all the living doubles.*

The name of Hatshepsut is actually "She who joins herself with Amun, the first (literally, she who is in front) of the nobles." (A. Moret, *Du Caractère religieux de la royauté pharaonique*)

Afterward, on his potter's wheel, Khnum models the child and its *ka*. Heket, the frog divinity, is present and she breathes life into the lungs of two small images of the future being. These images are drawn to adult proportions. Thoth, the divine messenger, presents himself to the queen, who is then led by Khnum and Heket to the place of the lying-in, over which Isis and Nephthys will preside. In Luxor, the *ka*, borne by the divinities, awaits the birth of the royal child.

Hieroglyph: "Son of Ra"

Golden Horus name of Tuthmosis II, Karnak

This child will then be nursed by Hathor, the celestial cow, and its fourteen *ka*s are presented by the same number of divinities, for it is said that in imitation of his father Ra, every pharaoh possesses fourteen *ka*s. In Ptolemaic texts, these "all bear the name of a faculty or one of the senses" (hearing, sight, understanding, strength, and so on) and are "like the emanations of the divinity, through which the divinity lives and which it transmits to man." (Mariette)

The nursing of the king by a divinity is often encountered, and we find an illustration in the temple of Abydos:

This is what Isis says to her son Ramesses II: *"I have taken thee into my two arms so that I might embrace thee like a child [who shall govern] the Two Lands; thou hast emerged from my womb as a benevolent king who rises crowned; it is Khnum who has modeled thee with his own hands, with Ptah who has cast thy limbs. The venerable Hathor of Dendera is thy nurse; Hathor of Diospolis Parva gives thee suck; the mistress of Qes Hathor of Aphroditopolis is the one who nurses thy beauties—together they protect Thy Majesty as master of all the lands."* (Moret, *Caractère religieux,* p. 64)

On the south wall of the "theogamy" chamber in the temple of Luxor, Tum of Heliopolis and Mentu of Thebes purify the prince with water. He is then led toward Amun, who gives him his great names, which Thoth, master of divine words, and Seshat, record in the annals.

THE CORONATION

Well known in the New Kingdom, the consecration rites consist of five series of ceremonies, which can be summarized as follows:

The purification through Thoth and Horus by means of two vases of gold and of silver, each spilling a stream of *ankh* over the prince, sometimes alternating with the symbols *was* and *djed*: life, power, and stability. This scene is repeated during the Ritual of the Daily Divine Worship, which can be performed only by the crowned and purified king himself. When this purification precedes the enthronement, Amun presents the prince to the cycle of *neters* of the South and the North. These *neters* confirm the divine origin of the future king and they reply to Amun: *Surely it is thy son, thine emanation. . . . When still in the body of the one who gave him birth, he already owned the plains and the mountains, all that the heavens cover and all that the sea encircles. Thou hast made for him all that, for thou hast thought the periods of [his reign].* (Ibid., p. 77)

Whereupon the heir to the throne is presented by the reigning king to his people: *His Majesty had come unto him the royal nobles, the dignitaries, the friends . . . the chiefs of the* rektiu *. . . so that they might see their new sovereign rise in the capacity of king* [allusion to the rising sun].

The bee of the North and bulrush of the South (Eighteenth Dynasty)

Then comes the proclamation of protocol, that is, of the *great names,* which are confirmed at the moment of handing over the two crowns. The establishment of the *great names* is thus recounted by Tuthmosis III in his "Text of the Youth," carved on the south exterior wall of Hatshepsut's sanctuary:

Since my majesty was a stripling, while I was a youth in his temple, before occurred my installation to be prophet . . . I was in the capacity of the "Pillar of his Mother," like the youth Horus in Khemmis. [Here, Tuthmosis III compares himself to the young Horus, son of Isis; his mother's name was, in fact, Isis.] I was standing in the northern hypostyle [the hypostyle hall of the temple of Ipet-sut, where on that day great festivities were taking place].

[The neter, *or the procession] made the circuit of the hypostyle on both sides of it. . . . On recognizing me, lo, he halted. . . . (I threw myself on) the pavement, I prostrated myself in his presence. He set me before his majesty; I was stationed at the "Station of the King" . . . , then they revealed before the people the secrets in the hearts of the* [neters]. . . .

(He opened for me) the doors of heaven, he opened the portals of the horizon of Re. I flew to heaven as a divine hawk. . . . I saw the glorious forms of the horizon [neter] *upon his mysterious ways in heaven. . . .*

Re himself established me; I was dignified with the diadems that were upon his head. . . . I was seated with the counsels of the [neters], *like Horus. . . .*

His own titulary was affixed for me. . . .

He fixed my Horus upon the standard; he made me mighty as a mighty bull. He caused that I should shine in the midst of Thebes (in this my name, Horus: "Mighty Bull, Shining in Thebes"). . . .

(He made my kingship enduring, like Re in heaven in) this my (name), Favorite of the Two Goddesses, "Enduring in Kingship, like Re in Heaven. . . ."

He formed me as a Horus-hawk of gold, he gave to me his might and his strength[,] and I was splendid with these his diadems, in this my name, (Golden Horus: "Mighty in Strength, Splendid in Diadems." . . .

King of Upper and Lower Egypt, Lord of the Two Lands: "Menkheperre" . . .

I am his son who came forth from him, a likeness fashioned like the presider over Hesret [Thoth]; he beautified all my forms, in this my name, Son of Re: "Thutmose, Beautful of Form." (Translation from Breasted, *Ancient Records,* vol. 2, §§ 138–47)

The charter of the royal names to be set upon the monuments and on every sealed document is thus established. They are the names under which the new king will celebrate the coronation ceremonies, the festivities of the new year, and myriad panegyrics.

The king must next receive the crowns from the hands of *those who preside at the seats of the* neters, a ceremony consisting of four essential scenes: the bestowal by Seth of Ombos and Horus of Behedet of the two crowns, the white and the red; the union of the Two Lands beneath the king's feet; the "circuit of the wall," and finally, the "royal ascent" toward the supreme *neter* who holds the king in embrace.

The coronation of Ramesses II is represented on the south wall of the great hypostyle hall of Karnak. The king is flanked by the two female divinities Nekhebet of the South and Wadjet of the North. Thoth replaces the figure of Seth.

The imposition of the crowns means the cessation of the king's personality. It is replaced by the principles these crowns represent, directly inspiring the one who is now king by divine right, the intermediary between Heaven and men.

While the Two Lands are being tied together, Horus of Behedet assures the king that the peoples of Nubia and Ethiopia will draw toward him and that he will be as prosperous as Tum in Heliopolis. On his part, Thoth, master of the Eight, unites for the king the bulrush of the South and the papyrus of the North, as well as the countries of the plains and mountains. Meanwhile,

Seti I receiving the panegyrics, north wall of the great hypostyle hall, Karnak

Seshat, mistress of the house of books, "draws up the decree of investiture such as it came forth from the mouth of Ra [Abydos]."

There is little information concerning the ceremony of "walking around the wall," although it is mentioned on the Palermo Stone as being among the royal activities of the First Dynasty. In the pyramid of Unas, it is mentioned in the following terms: *Thou hast seated thyself on the throne, thou holdest the scepters in thy hand, thou walkest around the abodes of Horus, thou walkest around the abodes of Seth.* (Moret)

After the "royal ascent toward the sanctuary," the enthronement is confirmed by the *neter* who holds the pharaoh between his arms or imposes his hands upon the crowns. But the ritual is not yet complete: Thoth and Seshat must inscribe the royal name upon the fruits of the persea tree in the presence of Amun-Ra-Tum.

Finally, there exists a very curious rite that is represented in the temple of Edfu in connection with the crowning of Horus. This ritual, which involved the releasing of four birds, is also figured at Medinet Habu as taking place during the great panegyrics of Min, which coincided with the coronation festivities of Ramesses III. These winged creatures were merged with the four sons of Horus and flew off toward the four cardinal points, announcing (?) the imposition of the double crown to the mysterious *neter* of the horizon.

Great rejoicing follows the coronation ceremonies: *The sky celebrates, the earth exults, the cycle of the* neters *of Egypt has joy in its heart, and as for the men, they are jubilant, they intoxicate themselves [with cheers] unto the sky; great and humble, they take their pleasure therein: the whole earth rings with happiness.*

The undertakings incumbent on the reigning king now begin: *And as soon as the king had taken possession of this land, he reorganized it such as it was in the times of Ra. He restored the* neters' *temples from the marshes of the Adehu [in the Delta] as far as Nubia; he remade all the divine statues more numerous than they had been before, in addition to the embellishments he brought to them. . . . What the king found in ruin from before, he put back into place; he caused one hundred life-size statues to be made out of valuable stone . . . this is what was said after the consecration of Horemheb.* (Translation by Moret)

In wandering through Karnak, we shall see, as the pharaonic formula put it, that "there is no bragging in these words." Next to the well-being of their people, the kings' principal concern was the upkeep and renovation of the temples.

Lid of the Painted Box from the treasure of Tutankhamun (Cairo Museum)

THE MILITARY EXPEDITIONS

From the beginning of its history, Egypt maintained relations with foreign lands, but there is no strictly historical document elucidating to what extent these contacts were commercial or bellicose. The outside walls of the temples of Karnak show us numerous representations of warlike epics, but they are disappointing to the historian: "The long lists of defeated Nubians that decorate the pylons of the temples, the representations of the king slaughtering a black prisoner, these images belong more to the realm of convention and traditional iconography than to the field of history." (Drioton and Vandier, *Egypte,* p. 377)

Of his seventeen campaigns in foreign lands, Tuthmosis III relates in detail the victory of Megiddo alone, inscribed in the very sanctuary of the temple of Ipet-sut, not exactly the place to record a warlike adventure. Seti I is the first to represent his exploits and enumerate the fortified wells of the desert road, but nowhere is his army to be seen. By himself alone, Ramesses II over-throws thousands of enemy chariots through the favor of Amun, who directs his arrows. The celebrated "Poem of Pentaur" "is unfortunately devoid of all historic value," writes Drioton, and he adds, referring to the peace treaty signed between Ramesses II and the prince of the Kheta: "Nowhere is there mention of the essential, that is to say, of the respective borders between the two countries." (Ibid., pp. 408–11)

Indeed under each king the so-called historical accounts keep retracing the same rebellions of the Asians, the same uprisings of the Libyans, the same punishments inflicted on the southern countries. All the kings claim the great domain of their predecessors, which spread out from the Horns of the Earth in the South as far as the Steps of Naharin to the North. All claim to have extended their borders to the sky. It would be vain to argue the authenticity of the conquest or recapture of these "territories" by such and such a king. Along with Breasted, one must recognize the primarily *religious* character of these figurations, all of which converge toward the entrance of the temple and invariably end up with the gift to the Theban triad of all the tribute of the foreign lands.

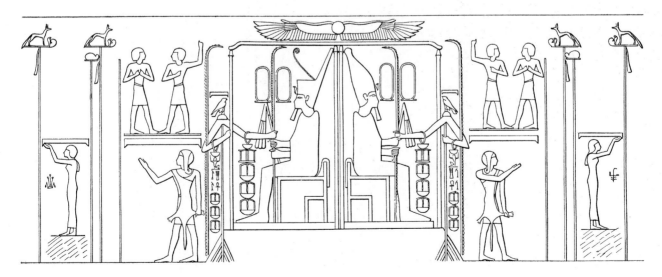

Double pavilion of the sed *festival*

THE *SED* FESTIVAL

"No Egyptian document has left us a coherent account of that ceremony about which scholars are far from being unanimous. One point seems well established, however: the *sed* festival involves a renewal of the consecration rites." (Vandier, *La Religion égyptienne*, p. 200) According to a passage from the decree of Rosetta, it was first thought to have been a thirty-year jubilee, but it is now proved that numerous kings celebrated their *sed* festival before their thirtieth year of regency.

The meaning of the very name of the *sed festival* is highly contested: the word *sed* signifies "tail," hence Spiegelberg's translation "festival of the tail." This scholar deems that on the occasion of this festival, the king solemnly girded his loins with the tail of an animal. Moret, however, underlines the fact that precisely during the *sed* festival, the king *never* dons the artificial tail but a special short garment, and basing himself on philological analogies, Moret translates *heb-sed* as "festival of the royal tunic of one pelt."

In numerous temples there exist more or less complete representations of this enigmatic ceremony. One of the essential scenes—showing the king wearing first a red crown, then a white crown, while seated in the double pavilion of the *sed* festival—is already seen on the seals, palettes, or votive maces dating from the First Dynasty.

Representations of King Narmer and King Den (First Dynasty) associate the image of the *sed* festival pavilion to the ritual race (the "great stride"), which accompanies the gift of the ground during the ritual of a temple's foundation. Furthermore, in front of Narmer there is a formless silhouette placed upon a kind of seat, which evokes a usage of the funerary cult explained in the tomb of Rekhmire as follows: *To make to come to the city of the pelt [Abydos]. Here is the* tikenu *lying under it [the pelt] in the land of transformation* [takheper]. A. Moret comments: "The *tikenu* is in the site of Becoming, of transformations, of life renewed." (*Mystères égyptiens*, p. 50)

Hieroglyph: "Hathor, House of Horus"

Hieroglyph: "Tum of Heliopolis"

In Abydos, Seshat-Sefekht says to Seti I: *Again thou beginnest thy renewal, thou achievest to flower again like the infant moon, thou becomest younger, season by season, like Nun in the beginning of her time, thou art reborn by renewing thy* sed *festivals.*

According to the group of representations in such temples as Abydos, Thebes, Luxor, and Soleb, the king is carried on a throne resting upon a cup *(heb)* toward the hall of panegyrics, while the "pelt," placed on a sled, is also taken to that spot. During this time an oryx (Sethian animal) is slaughtered. Then the king, white-crowned, emerges from his palace, executes the ritual race, and sits down in the southern pavilion. This scene is precisely repeated for the northern pavilion. All the *neters* of the South and the North are witnesses. A bas-relief of Pepi I associates the ritual slaughter of a prisoner with his first *sed*-festival celebration.

The *sed* festival of Osiris is represented on a sarcophagus in the Berlin Museum: the imposing of the two crowns by Iunmutef, the coming forth of Osiris bearing the two scepters *hek* and *nekhakha*, the race with the bull Hap, the setting up of the two obelisks, the presentation of the four calves—black, white, red, and pied—and finally, the ritual race in front of the double pavilion, once with the seal and the *nekhakha* scepter, once with the *akh* bird and the oar.

In the tomb of Kheruef at Thebes, the *sed*-festival ceremony is celebrated in honor of Amenhotep III and accompanied by the erection of the *djed* pillar of Osiris.

Moret relates the characteristically Osirion *sed*-festival with a Vedic ritual: "It pertains to causing the rebirth to another existence of the sacrificing celebrant and his divinization by having him die to the earth and be reborn in heaven." (*Mystères égyptiens*, p. 85) This rebirth can indeed happen only after the death of the preceding form. Thus are explained the sacrifice of the Sethian animal, the passage in the pelt, the representation of the king dressed in a tight shirt as if bound, or in the form of Osiris, the renewal of the royal name—particularly marked in the case of Tuthmosis III, who bears four series of protocolar names—and the handing over of the two crowns in the double pavilion of the South and North.

After his victorious campaigns, Tuthmosis III erected his *sed*-festival temple *(akh-menu)* in Karnak, and its architecture is very strange. In one of the chambers adjacent to the sanctuary, he caused plants and animals to be carved as *emerging from the divine earth in order to be placed in the presence of Amun, in his great temple of Akhmenu [resplendent] forever and ever.*

What is the reason for these plants and for the abnormal growths shown in the lotus? At first considered whimsical representations, similar forms observed in the Paris Museum of Natural History now prove that they existed.

As studied in the light of classical rationalization, the important problem of the *sed* festival remains unsolved.

THE TEMPLES OF KARNAK

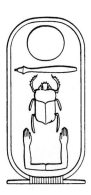

The site of Karnak comprises an aggregate of monuments grouped around the great temple of Amun. A wall of sunbaked brick encloses what would now seem an immense field of ruins, were it not for two very beautiful obelisks and the colossal Amunian colonnade of the hypostyle hall, still rising above the debris.

Two temples were built against that enclosure: to the north, a temple consecrated to Mentu, and to the east, the temple of Akhenaten dedicated to the cult of the solar disk (the physical sun) Aten, a monument that is today completely destroyed. To the south, a road led to the temple of Mut, symbol of maternal femininity.

The surrounding wall of sunbaked brick was approximately 12 meters wide and 16 meters high. It contained four monumental gates: the gate of Nectanebo to the east, that of the first pylon to the west, and the gates of Euergetes and the tenth pylon to the south. In addition there were four entrances of lesser dimensions.

THE DEVASTATION

An attempt to account for the ravaged state of these monuments led to the study of the causes of successive destructions and their dates. The conflagrations by the Persians are known, particularly those brought about by the mad Cambyses, but it is also known that some of the edifices were built *after* the Persian devastations. And although reference is made to a considerable earthquake as having occurred at the beginning of the Christian era, travelers of the seventeenth and eighteenth centuries mention monuments that no longer exist today.

Aerial photograph of the temples of Karnak (1947)

It happened in the last century that the Mamours (the local authorities) systematically destroyed the monuments of Karnak and Luxor to recover the sandstone and saltpeter. To speed and simplify this work, they had no scruples about using explosives to crumble the obelisks, statues, columns, and pylons.

These are the results of the Mamours' operations from 1836 until the winter of 1840:

Beginning with the great pylon of the hypostyle hall, workmen had already begun rapid demolition when the Europeans intervened and the pylon was saved by their courageous efforts. The Mamours then directed their destructive fury toward [other constructions].

At the same time, a protest was addressed to the Ministry of Public Education in Cairo in the hope of saving the ancient monuments, but Mouktar, the director, turned a deaf ear.

The havoc continued, and when the gigantic propylons flanking the entrance to the avenue of the sphinxes were reached, explosives were employed with great success.

The pylon numbered 32 was entirely destroyed. The pylon situated between numbers 36 and 37 was approximately three-quarters demolished.

The pylon marked number 36 was partially wrecked, about half of each wing.

The remainder of the temple marked M was destroyed. Moreover, they removed all of the material strewn in the vicinity of Luxor and Karnak and in differing degrees mutilated other pylons and portions of the great temple itself. (After G. Gliddon, cited by Legrain)

In 1843 the demolitions still continued, and Selim Pasha, governor of Upper Egypt, was exploiting the ruins of Thebes once more; here nine temples and pylons had already disappeared to satisfy the needs of the government. . . .

It was only in 1858 that the viceroy, Said Pasha, attached Mariette to his services and instituted the Service of Antiquities, which was destined to prevent further occurrences of such acts of vandalism. (G. Legrain, *Les Temples de Karnak* [Brussels: Vromant, 1929], pp. 83–84)

The second pylon of the temple of Amun in Karnak, tomb of Pinehas (Nineteenth Dynasty)

A comparison of the photograph showing the actual state of the ninth pylon (pl. 399) and the etching from *Description de l'Egypte* (below) serves to prove that the western wing of this pylon was then still almost intact, missing only seven courses of stone, while by now almost everything has disappeared. Furthermore, this etching verifies that the colossus standing before the gate of this pylon was then intact, while now only the granite base remains.

But whatever the present state of these ruins may be, they still present sufficient evidence of an extraordinary work, and are a source of study that is far from exhausted.

THE FOUNDATION OF THE TEMPLES

The ritual of laying the foundation goes back to the remotest antiquity. Numerous texts affirm that the plans of the temples were conceived according to *divine books.* These were said to have been transmitted in *ancient writings,* either by miracle or by a sage such as Imhotep, son of Ptah (Third Dynasty) or Amenhotep, son of Hapu (Eighteenth Dynasty), who, in the Late Period, were represented on certain Ptolemaic bas-reliefs as "divinized" (see figs. 72 and 104, and pls. 309 and 314).

During the *neters'* reign, *a book of founding of temples for the* neters *of the first Ennead* had been drawn up by Imhotep, "chief celebrant" of the cult of his father Ptah. This book had been taken to the heavens when the *neters* retired from earth, but Imhotep *had let it drop from the sky to the north of Memphis.* It was according to the prescriptions in this book that the general plan of the Ptolemaic temples at Edfu was determined. A similar divine origin was ascribed to the plan of the temple of Dendera; the buildings were reconstructed under the Ptolemies following *a general plan written on a goatskin in ancient writing at the time of the followers of Horus [hence predynastic]. . . . It was found*

View of the ninth pylon in 1799 (Description de l'Egypte)

inside a brick wall of the royal house in the times of King Merire Pepi I (Sixth Dynasty); another text attributes the find *to the time of King Cheops* (Fourth Dynasty). According to a Twelfth Dynasty manuscript on leather, King Senusret I (Sesostris I) did not proceed otherwise in founding or renovating the foundations of the temple of Ra in Heliopolis: there, also, an officiant was provided with the *divine book* in order to draw up the plan of the edifice. We can likewise acknowledge divine origin for the plans of all the Egyptian temples: the king constructed the house of his fathers strictly according to the "projects" they themselves had established while they lived and reigned in the valley of the Nile. (Moret, *Caractère religieux*, p. 131)

At the base of her obelisks in Karnak, Hatshepsut caused the account of their execution to be carved: *I have done this from a loving heart for my father Amun, I have entered upon his project of the first occurrence, I was wise by his excellent spirit, I did not forget anything of that which he exacted. My majesty (fem.) knoweth that he is divine. I did (it) under his command, he it was who led me; I conceived not any works without his doing, he it was who gave the directions. . . . I erred not from that which he commanded, my heart was wise [in Esye, the* neter *of wisdom] before my father, I entered upon the affairs of his heart.* (Breasted, *Ancient Records*, vol. 2, § 316)

These texts indicate that it was not a matter of arbitrary construction according to the whims of a monarch or "the state of his finances" but that the erection of any building whatsoever obeyed theological dictates.

In Karnak, the sanctuary of the Middle Kingdom stood as the now-destroyed heart of the future edifice. Around it the entire temple of Amun was developed according to a complex plan undoubtedly foreseen from the beginning.

In the Eighteenth Dynasty, the temple of Ipet-sut consisted of successive enclosures, to which Tuthmosis III added chapels to the north and east as well as his *sed*-festival temple. This king commissioned a granite stela relating the enlargements he undertook on the temple of Karnak. The text begins: *. . . the king himself commanded to put in writing according to the statement of the oracle, to execute monuments before those who are on earth. . . . I built it for him according to [his] desire. . . . I fulfilled that which was prescribed.* (Ibid., §§ 606–7)

On this same stela, Tuthmosis III states that he gave orders to prepare for the ceremony of *stretching the cord.* It was to take place on the day of the new moon, corresponding to the day of the tenth feast of Amun, in the year 24 of his reign, the last day of the second month of the second season. This inscription confirms the importance of *the choice of day,* the importance, hence, of a precise date of the year for establishing the foundations of the temple. The *stretching of the cord* is the first ceremony of the ritual and consists in defining the orientation of the structure in relation to true north. This is accomplished by means of the "circumpolar stars," an operation described at every epoch, and of which two examples follow:

In the temple of Abydos, Sefekht-Seshat and King Seti I each hold a stake, which they are driving into the ground by means of a mallet: *I have founded it with Sokaris [says Seshat]; I have stretched the cord at the location of its walls; while my mouth recited the great incantations. Thoth was there with his books. . . . In order to establish the enclosure of its walls, Ptah-Tatenen measured the ground, and Tum was there. . . . The mallet in my hand was of gold, I struck with it upon the post and thou [the king], thou wert with me in the form of Hunu [the* neter *of geometry], thy two arms held the mattock; thus the four angles were established as solidly as the four pillars of heaven.*

In the temple of Edfu, the king speaks in this manner: *I have taken the stake and the mallet by the handle, I have grasped the cord with Sefekht; my gaze has followed the course of the stars. My eye was turned toward the Great Bear, I have measured the time and counted [the hour] by the clepsydra, and then have I established the four angles of thy temple.* (Moret, *Caractère religieux*)

These are explicit texts, and it is surprising that some scholars still contest the importance of the orientation, measurements, and geodetic positions of the temples. And yet the investigations and affirmations of such specialists as the architect-Egyptologist Borchardt, the scholar Antoniadi of the Meudon Observatory, the eminent astronomer J.-B. Biot, and the great Laplace, cannot be questioned.

Borchardt is amazed by the extraordinary precision in the execution of the Pyramids, and Antoniadi summarizes earlier studies concerning these structures:

> The partially astronomic character of the pyramids is established by the following facts:
> 1. They rise almost exactly and intentionally on the thirtieth parallel of the northern latitude.
> 2. They are marvelously oriented on the cardinal points, as was pointed out by the Frenchman de Chazelles in 1694.
> 3. The inclined corridors, before their closure, were colossal instruments for measuring when stars crossed the meridian, by far the largest ever built. (Antoniadi, *Astronomie égyptienne,* p. 119)

This astronomer adds, concerning the *orientation* of the Cheops pyramid, whose meridian line, according to Borchardt, does not deviate more than four minutes from the true north-south line:

> This astonishing fact made it possible for Proctor to remark that the orientation of the monument "is much closer to exactitude than the best observation made by Tycho" with the celebrated quadrant of Uranibourg. . . . The base is remarkably horizontal. . . . The precision of the four base angles is nothing short of incredible . . . and Jomard's intuitive discovery of the unexpected fact that the perimeter of the base of Cheops's monument is equal to a half minute of the terrestrial degree seems to indicate that the Egyptians had measured the earth with the greatest success. (Ibid., pp. 119, 142)

In *Description de l'Egypte,* E. Jomard drew up a *table of itinerary measurements in Egypt,* comparing the distances that different classical authors have reported in ancient measurements with the same distances measured on our maps. He noted the existence of several units of measurements:

> *the small stadium of 100 meters* (Herodotus, Diodorus, Strabo);
> *the large stadium of 100 fathoms,* namely, one-tenth of a minute of an arc of the terrestrial meridian (Diodorus, Strabo);
> *the stadium of 300 pharaonic cubits* (Eratosthenes, Hipparchus).

Aristotle wrote (in *De coelo,* 2.16): *The mathematicians who have attempted to calculate the size of the Earth's circumference say that it could reach up to forty myriad stadia* (400,000 stadia). Now, Aristotle is speaking of a stadium of 100 meters, and furthermore, no Greek astronomer is known prior to Aristotle from whom he could have derived this dimension of the earth's circumference. Eratosthenes, to whom history attributes the first attempt to measure an arc of the terrestrial meridian, lived more than a century after the great philosopher; his work has often been commented upon by geodesists and astronomers, and all arrive at the same conclusion: the dimensions were given by Eratosthenes in stadia of 300 *pharaonic cubits,* and the result is surprisingly accurate despite the grave errors committed in his calculations and observations. The fact that Eratosthenes was librarian at Alexandria permitted Laplace to conclude: *Eratosthenes' two errors would have more or less compensated each other, leading one to believe that this astronomer merely reproduced a measure of the earth that had been carefully executed in ancient times and whose origin has gotten lost. (Exposition du Système du Monde)*

Photograph taken before 1945. Scaffoldings of unbaked brick in which the first pylon of the temple of Amun was buried.

We must limit ourselves to these few examples and simply formulate the question posed by all scholars who have been preoccupied with the origin of the first terrestrial measurements: if the Greeks were not their authors, to whom do we owe them? For the clarification of such questions, it is important, each time a pharaonic edifice permits it, to verify the measures inscribed therein and to disclose their nature.

Jomard, Gratien the Elder, Herschel, and Borchardt have studied the astronomical conclusions to be drawn from the orientation and global position of the Cheops pyramid. J.-B. Biot has done likewise with regard to the temple of Dendera, *reconstructed upon an older temple,* and its circular zodiac. Biot noticed that the straight ascension of Sirius brings this star into the axis of the papyrus stem, which is surmounted by a falcon and situated on the principal axis of this monument: *all these special circumstances will later be seen as linked to the original relationships between the orientation of the building, its latitude, and the absolute position of Sirius in the sky.* This scholar further observes that Sirius is recalled by the star sculpted between the horns of the cow, its symbol, precisely in alignment with the β star of Cancer, which indicated *the part of the ecliptic then situating the summer solstice with which Sirius rose simultaneously.*

A mass of literary documents indicates that ancient astronomers frequently made use of simultaneous risings in order to call attention to particular points on the ecliptic. . . . The singular precision with which we here find the emblem of Sirius located close to the solstice *on Dendera's monument seems to indicate that the astronomers who traced this celestial tableau knew how to make uncommonly able use of that procedure.*

Biot then remarks that the longitudinal axis of the temple of Dendera is oriented approximately 18 degrees to the east. It follows that *the true solstitial point was thus directed toward true north and furthermore, that the rising of Sirius was exactly or almost exactly in a horizontal direction, which was that of the south and north walls of the temple. It was therefore feasible to locate Sirius in its rising simply by aligning oneself to the horizontal direction of the transverse walls.*

Subsequently noting that the temple of Esna (which contains a rectangular zodiac), is oriented in such a manner as to form a complementary angle to the angle of Dendera, Biot concluded:

> If, then, we were certain that the two temples really existed at the remote age that the circular zodiac represents; if, further, we could suppose that the Egyptian priests were sufficiently instructed to profit of the advantages offered them by the orientations of these buildings, it would be conceivable that even in relatively few years they could have been able to recognize that the points of the rising and setting of the different stars changed places on the horizon and after a certain time no longer corresponded to the same terrestrial alignment. They would then have been able to observe the general and progressive displacement of the celestial sphere in relation to the meridian line; in other words, the most apparent effect of *the precession of the equinoxes.* (J.-B. Biot, *Recherches sur plusieurs points de l'Astronomie égyptienne*)

A thorough study of the calendars of Egyptian festivals by the chronologist E. Meyer confirms Biot's hypothesis that the priests were acquainted with the phenomenon of the precession, a discovery already attributed to them by Proclus Diadochus.

Great hypostyle hall, north section (photograph by Maxime du Camp)

Similar inquiries should be undertaken for every temple, and it is regrettable that no complete plan of Karnak has ever been drawn up with precision. The Anglo-Egyptian cadastral survey made at the beginning of the century, although very exact in its overall orientations, is on too small a scale to permit precise measurements, and without minute measurements, architectural readings are impossible. What the above citations show in their partial analysis should serve as guide for all the religious edifices of pharaonic Egypt, as the same fundamental principles must always be found in the architecture. In the main, these directives are: the orientations, of prime importance; the trigonometry and measurements, with their geodetic meaning; the axes of construction as well as the way the bas-reliefs are laid out on the walls; the "transparencies" and "transpositions," which complete the meaning of the texts or scenes on each side of the same wall.

In his work entitled *Une Chapelle de Sésostris I à Karnak* (1956), P. Lacau keenly notes the walking direction of the figures and the *incised* inscriptions on the exterior of this small building and those *in relief* that are found inside. He also stresses the importance of the particular placing of certain inscriptions. This scholar insists on the sacred character of ancient measurements, which were placed under the protection of the *neter,* and he ascertains that in the lower level of this *sed*-festival chapel there is, in addition to the ritual list of *names,* a *veritable cadastre* of the entire territory. Further, valuable indications are given concerning the size of Egypt and the levels of floods of the Nile by means of inscriptions on votive cubits. Lacau points to the existence of several fragments of the granite naos of Tuthmosis III, which bear analogous information. It is indeed remarkable that these proofs of geodetic knowledge are echoed on the surrounding wall of the sanctuaries.

It is important to know these details while walking through Karnak because, from the entrance on, noteworthy facts are encountered: the leveling of the base of the first pylon does not deviate from the horizontal for even one centimeter along its entire length. The length, counted *between the tracings on the ground* corresponds to 60 fathoms, that is, to the thousandth part of a degree of the arc of the terrestrial meridian. (See commentary to pl. 9 for the detail of these measurements.)

THE SYMBOLISM OF THE ORIENTATIONS

The course of the starry sky and its luminaries imposes upon natural life its becoming and maintenance. The plant and animal kingdoms are distinctly ordered into categories; some are under tribute to the day, others to the night and, still more specifically, to morning and evening, while all are submissive to the seasons.

The terrestrial globe is first characterized by its own evolution related to solar evolution, and next by energetic effects, magnetic and electric consequences of its own revolution.

Thus the magnetic north pole attracts the electronic effects of solar emission and, mechanically, it resorbs, it *absorbs* the terrestrial continents.

The magnetic south pole *concretizes,* that is, it materializes energy and puts forth the lands as would an immense vortex hollowing itself in the north and rejecting to the south. North is the pole from which the diurnal rotation is observed as going from right to left.

These are realities to which the monumental works of pharaonic Egypt conform.

We already know that the crowns—the white and the red—refer to the two lines of genesis, one lunar, one solar; they are the emblems of the Two Lands, southern and northern, of the empire of the world, namely, of *per-aā,* the pharaoh (or the "great house," as it is translated). More precisely, *per* means "that which encloses," consequently, that which renders the abstract manifest, as the life-bearing seed.

The sun and the celestial bodies appear in the east, whence the identification, through the white crown, of the east with the south, which *gives;* they disappear in the west, whence identification, by the red crown, of the west with the north, which *absorbs.* The same hieroglyph designates "north" and "to fill."

The king's mystic name, the crowns, the attributes—each detail takes on significance by situating these figurations in relation to the orientation. There are four "orients" and two "poles," hence six orientations to be taken into account. Man, for the northern hemisphere, is always situated on the north pole, facing the equator. Therefore his left side is east, and indeed the same hieroglyphic symbol designates east and the left; the right side is west, the *amenti,* where the Eye of Ra, the sun, will set, and again it is one hieroglyph that designates right and the west. Man is considered as looking at the day, and he belongs to the sun. But placing herself opposite and in front of him is woman, who therefore faces the night: the orientations of man and woman are reversed.

The night with its luminary is the kingdom of Osiris wearing the white crown, and the four phases of the moon are disclosed in the symbolism by the position of the hands and scepters of this *neter.* The last quarter, for example, is the time of the passion of Osiris, which ends with his death at the conjunction of the new moon. (The Gospels also associate the time of Christ's death with an eclipse.)

The Osirian principle is that of eternal renewal of nature, for daily as well as for monthly and yearly life, but equally for the universal "continual (or *constant*) creation," for unceasingly, the world ends and begins simultaneously. It is the femininity of nature, the woman-symbol, that restores corporeal being; she perpetuates. The Osirian *function* is therefore feminine but contains, as does woman, rudimentary male organs and seminal possibilities. Osiris is accordingly represented as king but swathed (as a mummy).

It must not be forgotten that Osiris is a *functional* principle, while the king is a definite fact. Thus the deceased is called an Osiris, which means he has entered into the phase of his transformation. When it is said that Isis conceives Horus from the member of the dead Osiris, it is meant that she conceives him from the function of "blackness," of seminal decomposition necessary for a new generation. Horus is the son of a ray of light and not of a mortal seed.

And so whenever a reversal of orientation of the crowns is shown—the white to the north and the red to the south—this must be understood to refer to life's nocturnal face.

Darkness (the night) is symbolic of the enemies of Ra (the light) and constitutes the Dwat—the site of transformations—which, in living nature, is represented by the world of insects whose metamorphoses—egg, nymph, chrysalis—symbolically correspond to the phases of the generation preparing the morning's birth.

The Dwat is therefore the reverse of the world; it is the netherworld, where the soul undergoes judgment, be it to go higher, be it to grope in the eclipse of all light. It is in this world of the Dwat that Ra wanders during his nightly course, being swallowed every evening by Nut, to be brought back into the world in the morning. The course from west to east is in a natural way symbolic of the soul desiring reincarnation. It is also the nocturnal course toward the nascent light.

On the contrary, the progression from east to west is notably a *conscious* ascending toward the culmination of noon. Day knows renewal in the morning, noontime maturity of visible life, and decline toward evening *(amenti),* where "Ra is an old man."

All these phases of life are noted on the royal figurations by the proportions of the head in relation to the height of the body and by the golden mean, with the umbilicus being the point of reference, as the bas-reliefs verify.

EXCERPTS FROM THE DEDICATIONS OF PTOLEMY VIII EUERGETES II, INSCRIBED ON THE DOOR OF KARNAK'S SECOND PYLON

Inscription on the northern doorjamb:

Thebes, site of origin and outlet of Nun, of the one whose name is hidden [Amun].

[The outlet of Nun is the place where the demiurge—Amun, in this instance—emerged from the primordial abyss of the waters.]

He made it [Thebes], he created it, he cooked it by the flame of his eye into marshland by the banks of the water. . . .

He heralded the things to come and they happened at once. He created what was uttered by his voice. . . .

He created Tatenen. He wrought the Eight. He formed his body like that of a sacred child who emerged from a lotus in the middle of Nun. He illuminated the lands with his two eyes.

He made men. He created the neters.

He organized the college of the Ennead. He instituted the Ogdoad.

The hillock of the sacred eye at the origin, until the earth had become the covering of Nun, that its height had become its height and that the heavens had absorbed the energy of the genii, so that the two uraei [the two eyes] were filled and the Eye of Horus was exalted.

Inscription on the southern doorjamb:

He has restored the great gate, without equal in Egypt—the portals that close it are of true cedar of Lebanon plated with copper from Asia; their modeling is perfect in beauty. Its total height is 53²⁄₃ cubits

Offering by Seti I of the "medjet unguent" with the "silver statue" to his father, Amun-Ra

and its width is 29½. One rejoices to see it in the light. The height of each of its two panels is 36 cubits, and that which it utilizes would be sufficient for two doors—in its name of magnificent doors illuminating the city-of-the-scepter-of-Amun-Ra, great of abodes in front of the Eye of Ra, lord of respect in Karnak, the queen of cities and nomes, the shore of the observatory of the demiurge, the right eye of universal lord [Harakhtes], and the sky of the one who has produced himself [Amun].

It came to pass, while His Majesty [Amun] was hiding his head in the presence of his borders, and while the earth was in the depths of inundation, that he set foot upon it. It banished his torpor completely when he came to rest upon its surface. This was the ground that became the solid hilllock that emerged in the beginning. (E. Drioton, "Les dédicaces de Ptolémée Evergète II sur le deuxieme pylône de Karnak," *Annales du Service des Antiquités de l'Egypte* 44 [1945])

The transcription of cubits into meters would give the following measures for the great door of the second pylon:

Total height	28.10 meters
Width	15.44 meters
Height of the door leaves	18.85 meters

The only measure taken in situ by Legrain was the height of the opening: 18.80 meters.

Farther on, the text mentions the distribution of ground between all the cities, praising the importance of Thebes, of the Nile's inundations, of the crops, and so forth.

And so the *north* doorpost speaks of the *principles and metaphysics of creation,* while the *south* doorpost recounts *material accomplishments,* in conformity with the teaching of the orientations.

ENTERING AND COMING FORTH

The inscriptions and sculpture that are carved in sunk relief signify *entering, penetrating,* while the same figures carved in relief denote *emerging,* or *coming forth.* This refers to the gesture of entering

Hieroglyphic group in sunk relief: sba, *"the gate"*

and emerging in general, as well as to the function of causing to penetrate or of causing to burst forth; as, for example, "opening and closing" may signify "to loose" and "to bind" with regard to the keys of Saint Peter.

All activity provokes a reaction, and life is phenomenal only by alternation. Action and reaction, entering and emerging, opening and closing: therein lies the entire esoteric story of the great temple of Amun.

This is exemplified in the great hypostyle hall of the temple of Amun, where all the figurations of the northern half are bas-reliefs in the name of Seti I, while those of the southern half are sunk reliefs in the name of Ramesses II.

On the inner face of the north wing wall of the second pylon, the barque Userhat of Amun, towed by the pilot barque, is making its way toward the south, toward the temple of Luxor (the Apet of the South): *the barques are carved in relief in that they are indicated as leaving the temple.*

On the inner face of the south wing wall of the same pylon, the barque Userhat of Amun and the pilot barque are making their way toward the north, returning from Luxor to Karnak: here *the barques are incised, in that they are entering the temple.*

On the inner face of the north wing of this pylon, only scenes of offering are represented on the second register: the silver statue, the milk vases, and the four calves, as well as the purification and ritual ascent to the sanctuary, and so on.

To the south, however, the second register unfolds the entire ritual of foundation of the temple.

To the *north,* then, the religious themes and principles are represented *in relief,* while to the *south,* the achievements are in *sunk relief.*

The red fire of Ra, enclosed in Atum, is still Sethian; the kings named Seti symbolize this state. By reaction, this fire provokes whiteness, which is evoked by the *nekhakha* scepter placed above Min's raised arm and by the silver statue offered to him. At its perfection, this whiteness will be the white crown, the South, which in turn will call forth redness, and this redness will be achieved by Ramesses.

SUMMARY

The original temple dates from the advent of the Amunian epoch of the constellation Aries under Sesostris I (Twelfth Dynasty). During the culminant lunar moment of the kings named Amenhotep and Tuthmosis, monumental works were added that, although ruined, are still to be seen today. The *sed*-festival sanctuary was shifted toward the east, and a tenth pylon opened its door upon a "back and forth" to the temple of Mut the Great, lady of Asheru (Asheru figures in Greek myth under the name of Acheron, the *river* of the infernal regions). Then the great Amunian colonnade was constructed, similar to that of Luxor.

All the temples surrounding the great temple of Amun participate in the opus that it teaches: they include the small temple of Ptah, reconstructed upon the site of the ancient sanctuary of Ptah from the epoch of Taurus, the Bull, and in relation to it, the temple of Mentu, reconstructed upon the ancient great sanctuary, also dedicated to Taurus. This Mentu-Ptah is the Greek Hephaestos, the Latin Vulcan "who forges metals." The most recent excavations have furnished proof that this site was indeed a strange and important laboratory.

The great temple of Mut—which is also the temple of Ptah's female aspect in the guise of the sanguinary Venus-Sekhmet sweetened by a bath in the waters of the Abaton at Aswan—is the site of the conception that *brings about the death of the seed* in order to gestate the new fruit. It is this

Hieroglyphic group in relief: "to appear gloriously"

phase of death that is represented by the temple of Mut, the maternal: it is the reversal of orienta-tions because with this death of the seed begins the materialization of its virtuality.

The temple of Khonsu, on the other hand, becomes the indispensable auxiliary to the Ramesside work. What was conceived through Mut is here gestated: the blackness of the eighth month, a renewal—for all beginning is a blackness, just as all conception is a requisite death of that which has given the impulse toward a new life. In this way, Khonsu plays a double role: one at the beginning, at first referred to by the Ramesside kings, and the other in the middle of the gestation of the "king."

THE ROYAL CARTOUCHES

THE MOST FREQUENTLY OCCURRING EXAMPLES AT KARNAK FROM THE EIGHTEENTH TO THE THIRTIETH DYNASTIES

All the cartouches have been drawn according to H. Gauthier's *Le Livre des Rois*, which provides their enumeration (which in almost all cases is horizontal).

The vertical arrangement of the cartouches has been made in accordance with the photos of the plates. For those cartouches that were hammered out or difficult to read, the depiction has been drawn in accordance with Champollion's *Notices descriptives*.

EIGHTEENTH DYNASTY

1. Nebpehtyre   Ahmose

2. Dejeserkare   Amenhotep I

3. Akheperkare   Tuthmosis I

4. Akheperenre   Tuthmosis II

5. Maātkare   Hatshepsut

6. Menkheperre   Tuthmosis III

7. Akheperure   Amenhotep II

8. Menkheperure   Tuthmosis IV

9. Nebmaātre   Amenhotep III

10. Neferkheperure   Akhenaten

12. Nebkheperure   Tutankhamun

14. Djeserkheperure   Horemheb

NINETEENTH DYNASTY

1. Menpehtyre   Ramesses I

2. Menmaātre   Seti I

3. Usermaātre   Ramesses II

4. Baenre   Merneptah

7. Userkheperure   Seti II

TWENTIETH DYNASTY

2. Usermaātre   Ramesses III

3. Heqamaātre   Ramesses IV

5. Nebmaātre   Ramesses VI

8. Neferhare	Ramesses IX	10. Menmaātre	Ramesses XI	1. "High Priest"	Herihor
1. Hedjkheperre	Sheshonk I	2. Sekhemkheperre	Osorkon I	4. Usermaātre	Osorkon II
8. Usermaātre	Sheshonk II	9. Usermaātre	Sheshonk III	3. Usermaātre	Osorkon III
3. Neferkare	Shabaka	5. Djedkare	Shabataka	6. Nefertumkhure	Taharka
3. Neferibre	Psamtik II	5. Khnemibre	Ahmose II	1. Kheperkare	Nectanebo I

TWENTY-FIRST DYNASTY

TWENTY-THIRD DYNASTY

THIRTIETH DYNASTY

TWENTY-SIXTH DYNASTY

3. Khakheperre — Pinedjem I
7. Hedjkeperre — Takelot II
4. Usermaātre — Takelot III
1. Wahibre — Psamtik I
3. Snedjemibre — Nectanebo II

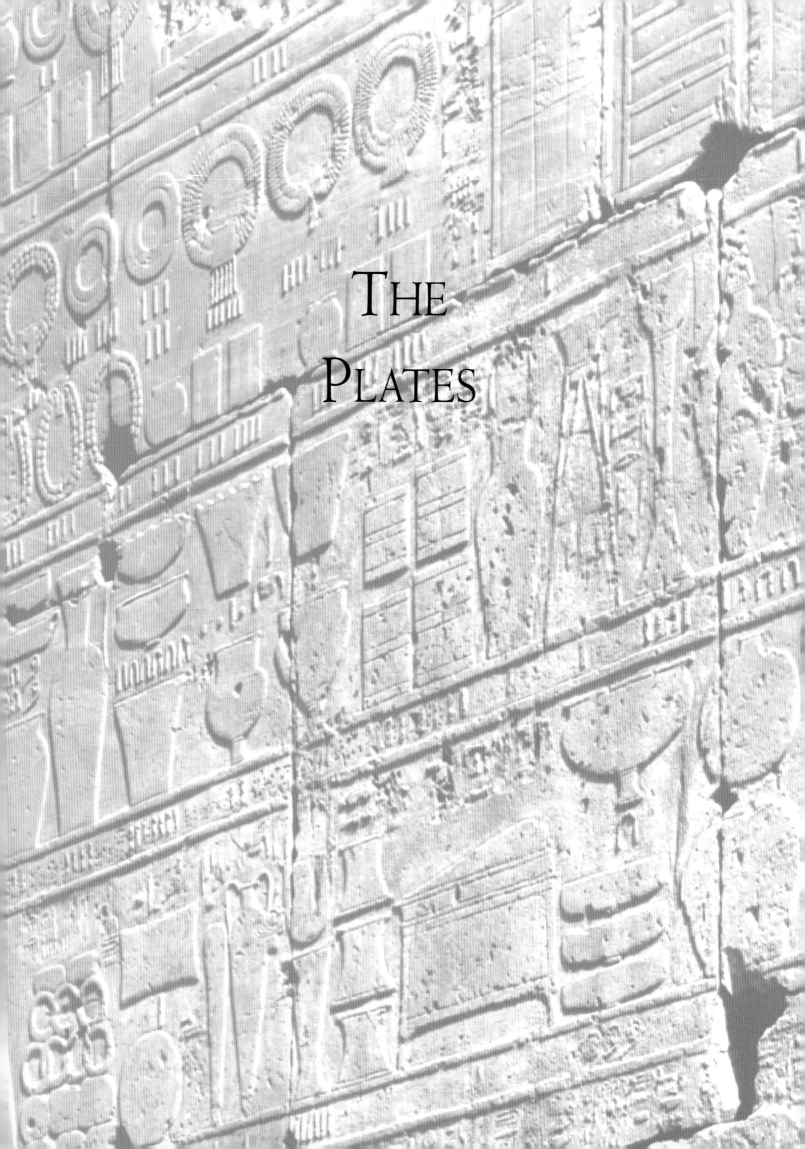

THE
PLATES

PLATE 1. *The Nile*

PLATE 2. *Boat Drawing Alongside*

PLATE 3. *Disembarking*

PLATE 4. *Goats*

PLATE 5. *Fountain in Front of the First Pylon*

PLATE 6. *The Wharf, the Avenue of the Sphinxes, the First Pylon*

PLATE 7. *Obelisk of Seti II, Southeast Corner of the Wharf*

PLATE 8. *First Pylon, Southern Wing: The Sphinxes*

PLATE 9. *First Pylon: General View from the South*

PLATE 10. *First Pylon, East Face of the South Wing: The Bubastite Portico*

PLATE 11. *First Pylon, East Face: The Bubastite Portico*

PLATE 12. *Bubastite Doorway, East Wall of the Temple of Ramesses III*

PLATE 13. *Bubastite Colonnade South of the First Courtyard*

PLATE 14. *Anta Pillar of the South Portico, Sphinx*

PLATE 15. *Ram-headed Sphinx*

PLATE 16. *Temple of Ramesses III, North Facade*

PLATE 17. *Temple of Ramesses III, Interior Doorpost of the North Doorway: Osirian Pillars*

PLATE 18. *Dorsal Face of the Osirian Pillars: The Wall Between the Pillars*

PLATE 19. *Temple of Ramesses III: Courtyard and Osirian Pillars, Taharka's Column*

PLATE 20. *Temple of Ramesses III: Portico with Columns*

PLATE 21. *Temple of Ramesses III: Hypostyle Chamber*

PLATE 22. *Repository of Seti II, South Facade: North Wing of the First Pylon*

PLATE 23. *Repository of Seti II, North Wing of the First Pylon: The Colonnade of Taharka*

PLATE 24. *Repository of Seti II: North Face, East Area*

PLATE 25. *Repository of Seti II, Southern Face: Doorway to the Chapel of Khonsu*

PLATE 26. *Repository of Seti II: North Face, West Area*

PLATE 27. *The So-called Magic Image of Amun, North Wall of the First Courtyard*

PLATE 28. *Taharka Column, Vestibule of the Second Pylon*

PLATE 29. *Southwest Corner of the Second Pylon: Anta Pillar, Bubastite Column*

PLATE 30–31. *Great Hypostyle Hall: Exterior North Facade, Western Half*

PLATE 32. *Taking of the Fortress of Pekanan*

PLATE 33. *Taking of Pekanan: New Version of the Lebanese Chieftains*

PLATE 34–35. *The Return of Seti I to Egypt with the Khetan Captives*

PLATE 36. *The Triumphal Return of Seti I with the Libyan Captives*

PLATE 37. *Harpagon Combat Against the Libyans*

PLATE 38. *Great Hypostyle Hall: North Entrance Doorway, West Jamb*

PLATE 39. *Great Hypostyle Hall: Embrasure of the North Doorway*

PLATE 40. *Great Hypostyle Hall, Eastern Interior Wall: Columns of the Northeast Section*

PLATE 41. *Columns of the Northeast Section*

PLATE 42. *North Edge of the West Wall, Torus of the Second Pylon: Transformed Bas-reliefs*

PLATE 43. *North Wall, Western Edge: The King Kneeling Before Mentu*

PLATE 44. *North Wall: The King Kneeling Before Amun*

PLATE 45. *North Wall: Naos of the Barque of Amun Carried by Priests*

PLATE 46. *North Wall, West Side: Seti I Offering a Papyrus Bouquet*

PLATE 47. *North Wall, East Side: The King "Giving the House to Its Master"*

PLATE 48. *Great Hypostyle Hall, Monostyle Column: Bas-reliefs from the Northeast Side*

PLATE 49. *North Wall, East Side: Seti I in the Persea Tree*

PLATE 50. *Seti I Kneeling Before Ra in his Naos, Followed by Sekhmet Holding the Palm of the Years*

PLATE 51. *East Wall, North End: Scene of Leaving the Sanctuary*

PLATE 52. *Vestibule of the Third Pylon, North Face*

PLATE 53. *The North-South Transverse Route of the Colonnade*

PLATE 54. *The First Two North Bays of the Northwest Group of Monostyle Columns*

PLATE 55. *Window of the First South Bay and Campaniform Columns*

PLATE 56. *First North Lateral Avenue and Hatshepsut's Obelisk*

PLATE 57. *Central Window Seen from the Northeast, Campaniform Columns*

PLATE 58. *North Aisle, Northeast Corner: Detail*

PLATE 59. *Grand North Colonnade, East End*

PLATE 60. *North Axial Window, Campaniform Columns*

PLATE 61. *Central Nave: Campaniform Columns, Obelisk of Tuthmosis I*

PLATE 62. *North Window: Campaniform Columns*

PLATE 63. *North Central Window: Campaniform Columns*

PLATE 64. *South Aisle: Obelisk of Tuthmosis I*

PLATE 65. *Group of Columns in the South Aisle*

PLATE 66. *Great Hypostyle Hall: Group of Columns on the Southeast Side*

PLATE 67. *Great Hypostyle Hall: Group of Columns on the South Side*

PLATE 68. *Transformed Cartouche*

PLATE 69. *South Aisle Seen from the East*

PLATE 70. *Second South Aisle: Claustra*

PLATE 71. *South Claustra*

PLATE 72. *Great Hypostyle Hall, South Wall, East Side: Ramesses II in the Persea Tree*

PLATE 73. *Great Hypostyle Hall, South Wall: Coronation of Ramesses II*

PLATE 74. *Great Hypostyle Hall, South Wall, East Side: The Race of the Apis Bull*

PLATE 75. *Great Hypostyle Hall, South Wall, East Side: Binding of the Two Lands*

PLATE 76. *Binding of the Two Lands, The Barque of Amun*

PLATE 77. *Great Hypostyle Hall, North–South Transverse Way: South Doorway*

PLATE 78. *South Wall, West Side: The Three Registers*

PLATE 79. *The Barque of Amun Carried by the Spirits of Pe and Nekhen*

PLATE 80. *The Barque of Amun Carried by the Spirits of Pe and Nekhen*

PLATE 81. *The Barque of Amun Carried by the Spirits of Pe and Nekhen*

PLATE 82–83. *Khnum, the King, and Horus Reclosing the Net for the Bird Hunt at Thoth's Signal*

PLATE 84. *Offering of Captured Birds by Ramesses II to Amun and Mut*

PLATE 85. *The Kneeling King Receives the Panegyrics*

PLATE 86. *Gift of the Panegyrics, Sacrifice of the Oryx*

PLATE 87. *Great Hypostyle Hall, West Wall, South Side: Bas-relief*

PLATE 88. *Great Hypostyle Hall, West Wall, South Side: The Theban Triad in its Naos*

PLATE 89. *Great Hypostyle Hall: North-South Colonnade*

PLATE 90–91. *Great Hypostyle Hall, South Wall: Exterior Facade*

PLATE 92. *West Wall of the Cachette Court, Outer Wall: Combat in Palestine*

PLATE 93. *Surrender of Askalon*

PLATE 94. *Great Hypostyle Hall, Southeast Corner: Presentation of the Prisoners to Amun*

PLATE 95. *Great Hypostyle Hall: Central Nave Seen from the East*

PLATE 96–97. *Third Pylon of Amenhotep III: Oarsmen of the Royal Barque*

PLATE 98–99. *Third Pylon of Amenhotep III: The Great Barque Userhat of Amun*

PLATE 100. *Obelisks of Hatshepsut and Tuthmosis I, Seen from the North*

PLATE 101. *Obelisks of Hatshepsut and Tuthmosis I, Seen from the West*

PLATE 102. *Obelisk of Tuthmosis I, Seen from the East*

PLATE 103. *The Royal Shooting of the Bow, Granite Block*

PLATE 104. *Obelisk of Tuthmosis I, Seen from the Northeast*

PLATE 105. *Upper Part of an Obelisk Inscribed by Tuthmosis III*

PLATE 106. *Cryptogram of Hatshepsut: Maātkare*

PLATE 107. *"Rearing" Cobra*

PLATE 108. *Obelisk of Hatshepsut, North Face and Northwest Corner*

PLATE 109. *Obelisk of Hatshepsut, North Face and Columns of the Ipet-sut Hypostyle Hall*

PLATE 110. *Osirian Pillar, Interior Surface of the Surrounding Wall South of the Temple of Ipet-sut*

PLATE 111. *Osirian Pillar and Column of the Southwest Corner of the Hypostyle Hall*

PLATE 112. *Columns from the Southwest Corner of the Hypostyle Hall*

PLATE 113. *Hatshepsut's Obelisk Seen from the East*

PLATE 114. *Fourth Pylon: Two Osirian Pillars*

PLATE 115. *Base of Hatshepsut's Obelisk, Southeast Corner*

PLATE 116. *Base of Hatshepsut's Obelisk, West Face*

PLATE 117. *South Wing of the Fourth Pylon: Osirian Pillars*

PLATE 118. *Base of Hatshepsut's Broken Southern Obelisk*

PLATE 119. *Pyramidion of Hatshepsut's Broken Southern Obelisk*

PLATE 120. *Statue of Tuthmosis III*

PLATE 121. *Statue of Tuthmosis III*

PLATE 122. *North Doorposts for the Doorways of the "Antechamber" and the Sixth Pylon*

PLATE 123. *South Doorposts for the Doorways of the "Antechamber" and the Sixth Pylon*

PLATE 124. *Northwest Corner of the Antechamber Preceding the Sixth Pylon*

PLATE 125. *Doorway of the Sixth Pylon, North Doorpost: Detail*

PLATE 126. *Antechamber of Tuthmosis III, South Doorway*

PLATE 127. *Offering of Maāt to Amun*

PLATE 128. *Detail of the Portal Name Hieroglyphs of the Fifth Pylon*

PLATE 129. *Antechamber and Vestibule of Tuthmosis III, Exterior Facade of the North Wall*

PLATE 130. *Doorway of the Sixth Pylon*

PLATE 131. *Doorway of the Sixth Pylon: Southern Granite Pillar, Naos of Philip Arrhidaeus*

PLATE 132. *Northern Granite Pillar, Naos of Philip Arrhidaeus*

PLATE 133. *Chamber of the Annals, South Doorway: Granite Pillars of Tuthmosis III*

PLATE 134. *Southeast Corner of the South Granite Pillar*

PLATE 135. *East Side of the North Pillar: Detail*

PLATE 136. *East Side of the North Pillar: Upper Section*

PLATE 137. *The Two Granite Pillars of Tuthmosis III, Seen from the North*

PLATE 138. *Peristyle Court of Tuthmosis III, Southwest Corner: Fasciculated Column*

PLATE 139. *Tuthmosis IV and his Mother, Queen Tiy*

PLATE 140. *South Wing of the Sixth Pylon: South Interior Wall*

PLATE 141. *Statue of Amun-Ra*

PLATE 142. *Statue of Amunet*

PLATE 143. *Dorsal Stela of Amunet's Statue*

PLATE 144. *North Chapels of Tuthmosis III: The King Offering the* Akh *Bird to Hathor*

PLATE 145. *North Chapels of Tuthmosis III: Doorway Lintel*

PLATE 146. *Statue of Senmut*

PLATE 147. *North Wall of the Sanctuary: Start of Tuthmosis III's Annals*

PLATE 148. *Bas-relief of Hatshepsut: The "Great Stride"*

PLATE 149. *Bas-relief of Hatshepsut: The Purification*

PLATE 150. *Granite North Doorway of the Sanctuary*

PLATE 151. *North Doorway of the Sanctuary and Naos of Philip Arrhidaeus*

PLATE 152. *North Exterior Wall*

PLATE 153. *Consecration of the Offerings, North Wall of the Naos*

PLATE 154. *Interior South Wall of the West Chamber*

PLATE 155. *Interior North Wall of the West Chamber*

PLATE 156. *Southwest Corner of the Naos*

PLATE 157. *Southern Outside Facade of the Naos*

PLATE 158. *The Departure and Return of the Sacred Barque*

PLATE 159. *Enthronement by Amun, Breast-feeding of the King by Amunet*

PLATE 160. *Presentation of the Four Calves to Amun-Ra Kamutef*

PLATE 161. *Example of "Squaring Up"*

PLATE 162. *Outer Wall South: Presentation of the Incense*

PLATE 163. *Granite Block of the East Wall of the Central Sanctuary*

PLATE 164. *Head of a Young King, Eighteenth Dynasty*

PLATE 165. *Chapels of Hatshepsut's Temple: Limestone Statue of Amenhotep II*

PLATE 166–167. *Overview of Hatshepsut's Temple from the Southeast*

PLATE 168. *Hatshepsut's Temple, South Wall, West End: Throne Detail*

PLATE 169. *South Wall, West End: "Text of the Youth" of Tuthmosis III*

PLATE 170. *"Text of the Youth" of Tuthmosis III*

PLATE 171. *East End of the Southern Outside Wall of Hatshepsut's Temple*

PLATE 172. *Temple of Amun, Seen from the Northeast*

PLATE 173. *Entry Doors of the North Chapels*

PLATE 174. *The Temple Foundation Ceremony*

PLATE 175. *Consecration of the Temple with Natron*

PLATE 176. *North Chapels: Feast of the White Hippopotamus*

PLATE 177. *North Chapels: Feast of the Erection of Min's Mast*

PLATE 178–179. *North Chapels: Feast of the Erection of Min's Mast*

PLATE 180–181. *North Chapels: The Net for the Bird Hunt*

PLATE 182–183. *Sed-Festival Temple*

PLATE 184. *Hall of Feasts: East Colonnade, South Section*

PLATE 185. *Hall of Feasts: Central Nave*

PLATE 186. *Hall of Feasts: Overall View*

PLATE 187. *Temple of Tuthmosis III: Detail of a Wall from the Chamber of the Kings*

PLATE 188. *Hall of Feasts: Capital of a Stake-Column*

PLATE 189. *Hall of Feasts, North End: Stairway of the "Chamber of the Clepsydras"*

PLATE 190. *Belt and Dagger of the Statue of Tuthmosis III: Detail*

PLATE 191. *Statue of Tuthmosis III: Detail*

PLATE 192. *Hall of Feasts: Square Pillar, Polygonal Columns*

PLATE 193. *South Hall: Polygonal Columns*

PLATE 194. *Polygonal Columns: South Hall*

PLATE 195. *Head from a Basalt Statue of Tuthmosis III*

PLATE 196. *Corridor Preceding the South Chapels*

PLATE 197. *Entrance Doorway to One of the South Chapels*

PLATE 198. *Amunet Holding the Was Scepter in Her Hands that Breaks a Line Demarcating a Line of Inscriptions*

PLATE 199. *Ritual Race of the King Wearing the Red Crown and Holding the Vessels of Purification in His Hands*

PLATE 200. *Outer South Wall of Alexander's Sanctuary*

PLATE 201. *The King Seated upon a Throne Placed on the Heb Symbol During the Sed Festival*

PLATE 202. *Sanctuary of Alexander: Entrance Doorway*

PLATE 203. *Sanctuary of Alexander: Back Wall*

PLATE 204. *Botanical Garden, Seen from the Northwest*

PLATE 205. *Botanical Garden, Seen from the Southeast*

PLATE 206. *Antechamber of the Axial Sanctuary: North Wall*

PLATE 207. *Capital from a Column of the Botanical Garden*

PLATE 208. *Botanical Garden: South Wall*

PLATE 209. *Botanical Garden: East Wall*

PLATE 210–211. *Botanical Garden: East Wall*

PLATE 212–213. *Botanical Garden: West Wall*

PLATE 214. *Botanical Garden: South Wall*

PLATE 215. *Botanical Garden: West Wall*

PLATE 216. *Botanical Garden: North Wall, West Section*

PLATE 217. *Block from the North Hall*

PLATE 218. *Eastern Sanctuary of Amun-Ra*

PLATE 219. *Tuthmosian Enclosing Wall of the Great Temple of Amun-Ra*

PLATE 220. *Monolithic Alabaster Naos of Tuthmosis III*

PLATE 221. *Alabaster Group from the Naos of Tuthmosis III*

PLATE 222. *Great Temple of Amun, East Facade: Original Location of the Obelisk of Saint John Lateran*

PLATE 223. *Eastern Temple of Ramesses II*

PLATE 224. *Column and Dorsal Face of the North Osirian Pillar*

PLATE 225. *North Osirian Pillar, Columns, and Ptolemaic Doorway*

PLATE 226. *South Osirian Pillar, Southwest Corner*

PLATE 227. *The Two Osirian Pillars, Doorpost of the South Doorway*

PLATE 228. *Ethiopian Colonnade that Precedes the "Upper Gate" of Ipet-sut of the Temple of Ramesses II*

PLATE 229. *Column and Osirian Pillars, Seen from the North Doorway*

PLATE 230. *Ethiopian Colonnade and the "Upper Gate" of Ipet-sut*

PLATE 231. *Eastern Temple of Ramesses II: Taharka's Colonnade, Gate of Nectanebo*

PLATE 232. *Baked Brick Enclosing Wall of the Great Temple of Amun*

PLATE 233. *Exterior Facade*

PLATE 234. *East Wall of the First Chamber*

PLATE 235. *The Seven Doorways and the "Reliquary of Osiris"*

PLATE 236. *East Wall of the Inner Chapel*

PLATE 237. *Doorway Leading to the Inner Chapels*

PLATE 238. *Alabaster Statue of the Divine Worshiper Amenirdis*

PLATE 239. *Chapel of the Divine Worshipers*

PLATE 240. *West Facade*

PLATE 241. *East Facade*

PLATE 242. *East Facade: Lintel*

PLATE 243. *East Facade: Unfinished Sculptures*

PLATE 244. *Nectanebo Gate, Site of the Temple of Akhenaten*

PLATE 245. *Head of One of the Statues of Akhenaten Found on the Site of the Eastern Temple*

PLATE 246. *Block of Akhenaten Found in the Second Pylon*

PLATE 247. *Bust of Akhenaten*

PLATE 248. *Block of Akhenaten Found in the Second Pylon*

PLATE 249. *Blocks of Akhenaten Found in the Second Pylon*

PLATE 250. *Block of Akhenaten Found in the Second Pylon*

PLATE 251. *Statue of Khonsu*

PLATE 252–253. *Pylon of the Temple of Khonsu*

PLATE 254. *Peristyle Court: Interior Facade of the Entrance Gate*

PLATE 255. *Peristyle Court: Colonnade of the West Portico*

PLATE 256. *Portico of the Peristyle Court, Northeast Corner*

PLATE 257. *Campaniform Columns from the Central Nave of the Hypostyle Hall*

PLATE 258. *Hypostyle Hall*

PLATE 259. *Hypostyle Hall, Northwest Corner: Base of a Monostyle Column*

PLATE 260. *Hall of the Barque: Doorway that Provides Access to the Pronaos*

PLATE 261. *Hall of the Barque: East Wall*

PLATE 262. *Hall of the Barque: Northeast Corner*

PLATE 263. *Khonsu*

PLATE 264. *Hall of the Barque: Bas-relief on the East Wall*

PLATE 265. *The Royal Offering of Ramesses IV*

PLATE 266. *West Wall of the Hall of the Barque*

PLATE 267. *West Doorpost of the Naos of the Barque, Outer North Wall*

PLATE 268. *Granite Block of Amenhotep II in the Temple of Khonsu*

PLATE 269. *Columns Northwest of the Pronaos*

PLATE 270. *Footprints on the Roof*

PLATE 271. *Overall View of the Eighth and Ninth Pylons Taken from the Roof of the Temple of Khonsu*

PLATE 272–273. *A Corner of Karnak Village and the Gate of Ptolemy III Euergetes: North Facade, Seen from the Pylon of the Temple of Khonsu*

PLATE 274. *Gate of Ptolemy III Euergetes: South Facade, Pylon of the Temple of Khonsu*

PLATE 275. *Gate of Ptolemy III Euergetes: Outer South Facade*

PLATE 276. *Gate of Ptolemy III Euergetes: North Facade and East Inside Splaying*

PLATE 277. *Interior Facade of the East Doorpost: Interior Splaying*

PLATE 278. *Eastern End of the Inner South Wall of the Great Gate*

PLATE 279. *Temple of Apet, East Facade: Entrance to the Lower Chapel*

PLATE 280. *East Facade: Entrance to the Lower Chapel*

PLATE 281. *East End of the Outer Wall North of the Pedestal*

PLATE 282. *Hathorian Abacus Surmounting the Composite Capital on One of Two Columns*

PLATE 283. *Doorways to the Holy of Holies and the North Lateral Sanctuary*

PLATE 284. *Doorway to the South Lateral Sanctuary*

PLATE 285. *South Chapel: Interior Facade of the Lintel*

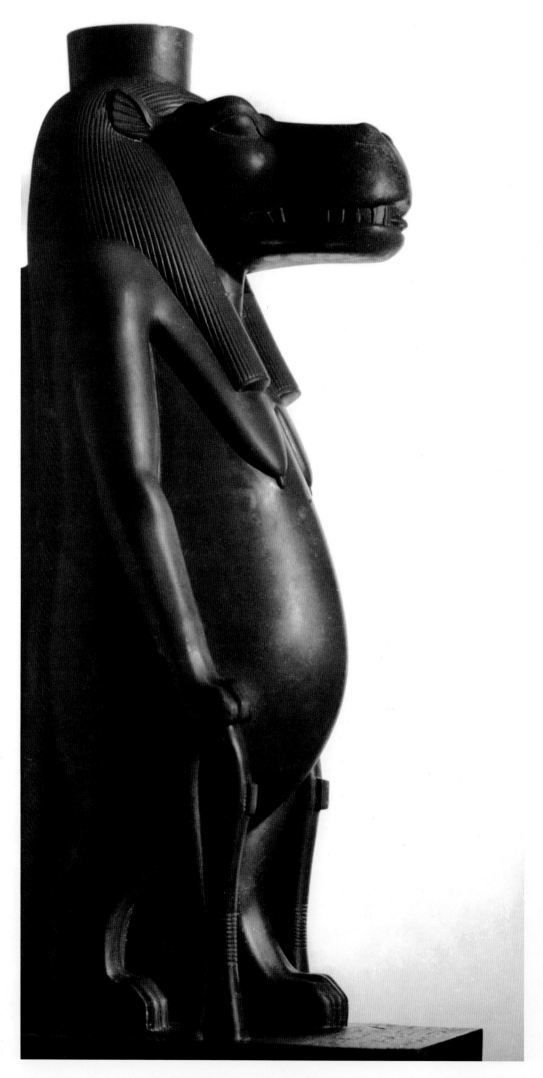

PLATE 286. *Statue of Apet-Tawaret*

PLATE 287. *West Wall of the North Lateral Sanctuary*

PLATE 288. *North Sanctuary: Door Detail*

PLATE 289. *North Chapel: The Resurrection of Osiris*

PLATE 290–291. *North Doorway of the Temple of Mentu and Overview of All the Temples of Karnak, Seen from the North*

PLATE 292. *Monumental Gate, South Facade*

PLATE 293. *Monumental Gate, North Facade*

PLATE 294. *Cornice and Lintel of the Monumental Gate, North Facade*

PLATE 295. *Two Statues of Amenhotep III*

PLATE 296. *Statue of Amun-Ra Protecting Amenhotep III*

PLATE 297. *North Doorway of the Enceinte of the Great Temple of Amun*

PLATE 298. *Statue of Djehuty, Chief of Amun's Granaries*

PLATE 299. *The Seven Doorways that Provide Access to the Sanctuary of Ptah*

PLATE 300. *East Facade and Splaying of the First Doorway*

PLATE 301. *Sandstone Block Found in the Enclosing Wall of Ptah's Temple*

PLATE 302. *Ptolemaic Portico*

PLATE 303. *South Wing of the Pylon: Ptolemaic Portico*

PLATE 304. *South Wall of the Portico: Tuthmosis III Making the Offering of Wine*

PLATE 305. *South Wall of the Portico: Amun, Ptah, Khonsu, and Mut*

PLATE 306. *South Wing of the Pylon, East Facade*

PLATE 307. *Doorway and North Wing of the Pylon, East Facade*

PLATE 308. *North Wing of the Pylon, East Facade*

PLATE 309. *North Wall of the Portico: Offering of Cosmetics to Ptah, Hathor, and Imhotep*

PLATE 310. *Column North of the Portico*

PLATE 311. *Statue of Ptah in Black Granite*

PLATE 312. *Sanctuary of Ptah: Entranceway, South Column of the Portico*

PLATE 313. *Black Granite Statue of Sekhmet*

PLATE 314. *East Wall: Imhotep, Son of Ptah and Amenhotep, Son of Hapu, Behind Hathor*

PLATE 315. *Small Temple of Ahmose: Outer Facade*

PLATE 316. *North Facade, East End*

PLATE 317. *Bas-relief on the Southeast Entry Pillar*

PLATE 318. *The King Introduced by Mentu*

PLATE 319. *The Horus Name of the King*

PLATE 320. *The King Introduced by Tum*

PLATE 321. *The King Introduced by Tum: Detail*

PLATE 322. *Hieroglyphs*

PLATE 323. *Sesostris Embraced by "Ptah-South-of-His-Wall"*

PLATE 324. *Sobekemsaf Making the Offering of Wine to Mentu*

PLATE 325. *Consecration of the White Bread Before Mentu by Sobekemsaf*

PLATE 326. *Interior South Wall: Amenhotep I "Worships the* Neter *Four Times"*

PLATE 327. *Outer North Wall: Consecration of the Offerings*

PLATE 328. *Outer North Wall: Amun-Ra*

PLATE 329. *The King, with the* Hes *Vases, Running the Ritual Race*

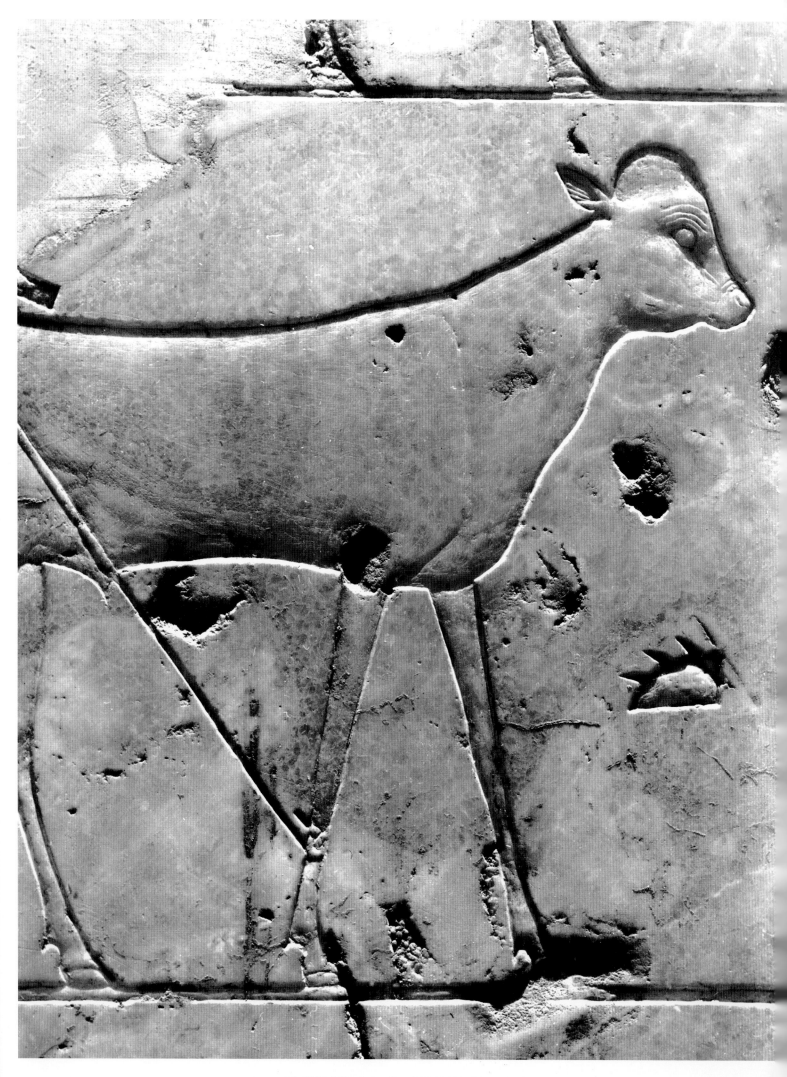

PLATE 330. *Outer South Wall: The Black Calf*

PLATE 331. *Outer North Wall: The King Girded by the Diadem*

PLATE 332. *The Barque Userhat Maneuvered by Tuthmosis III*

PLATE 333. *Censing of the Osiris Maātkare by Tuthmosis III*

PLATE 334. *Lapwings Perched on a Basket*

PLATE 335. *Race With the Hapu Bull in Front of the Sacred Barque*

PLATE 336–337. *Acrobatic Dancers, Harpist, and Sistrum Players*

PLATE 338. *Southeast Facade of the Scarab and its Pedestal*

PLATE 339. *Sacred Scarab of the Lake, Seen from Above*

PLATE 340. *Sacred Scarab of the Lake, Southern Facade*

PLATE 341. *The Temple of Amun: The Sacred Lake, Corridor of the Descent of Amun's Geese*

PLATE 342. *Outer Facade of the South Wall of the Third Tuthmosian Enclosing Wall of the Temple of Ipet-sut*

PLATE 343. *Monument of Taharka: Outer North Facade*

PLATE 344. *Offering of Incense to Tum*

PLATE 345. *Baboon Worshiping the Sun*

PLATE 346. *Worship of the Rising Sun by the King and Baboons*

PLATE 347. *Staircase Going Up to the Terrace*

PLATE 348. *Interior North Facade of the First Chamber: The Solar Barque*

PLATE 349. *Doorway of the Inner Chapel*

PLATE 350. *Limestone Bas-relief: Detail*

PLATE 351. *Statue of Amenemhet III*

PLATE 352. *The Queen Isis, Mother of Tuthmosis III*

PLATE 353. *Statue of Tuthmosis III*

PLATE 354. *Limestone (?) Head from the Eighteenth Dynasty*

PLATE 355. *Limestone (?) Head from the Eighteenth Dynasty*

PLATE 356. *Statue of Ramessesnakht, First Prophet of Amun, Twentieth Dynasty*

PLATE 357. *Statue of the Scribe Ahmose, Twenty-sixth Dynasty*

PLATE 358. *Statuette of Sheshonk, Son of Osorkon I, Twenty-second Dynasty*

PLATE 359. *Statuette of Sheshonk, Son of Osorkon I, Twenty-second Dynasty*

PLATE 360–361. *Overall View of the Sacred Lake and the Southern Pylons; In the Background, the Temple of Khonsu and the Gate of Euergetes*

PLATE 362. *The Sage Amenhotep, Son of Hapu*

PLATE 363. *Doorway of the Seventh Pylon, North Facade: Granite Statues*

PLATE 364. *Base of the Obelisk South of the East Wing of the Seventh Pylon*

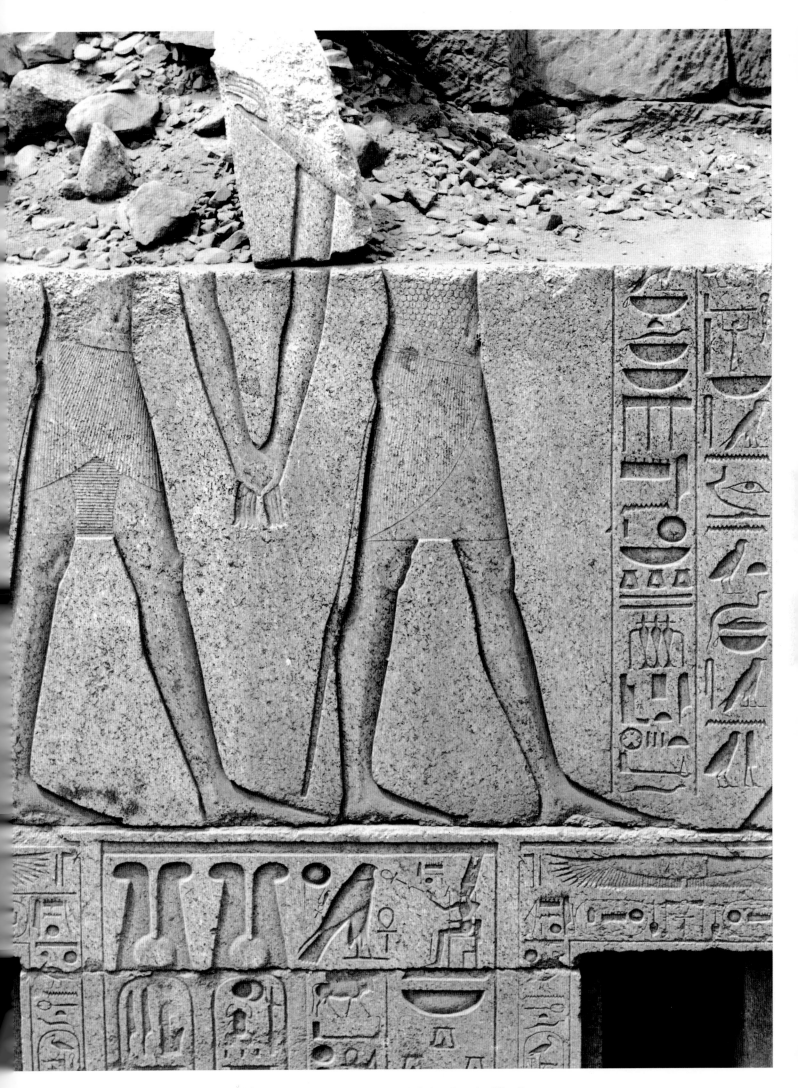

PLATE 365. *Doorway of the Seventh Pylon: Interior West Doorpost*

PLATE 366. *Owl Head from an Obelisk of Tuthmosis III*

PLATE 367. *Head of the "Sa" Bird from an Obelisk of Tuthmosis III*

PLATE 368. *Seventh Pylon, West Wing: South Facade*

PLATE 369. *Seventh Pylon, East Wing: Colossus of Tuthmosis III*

PLATE 370. *Seventh Pylon, West Doorpost: Colossus of Tuthmosis III*

PLATE 371. *Seventh Pylon, East Doorpost: Colossus of Tuthmosis III*

PLATE 372. *Alabaster Sanctuary of Tuthmosis III: Outside North Wall*

PLATE 373. *Alabaster Sanctuary of Tuthmosis III: Amun*

PLATE 374. *Inscription of Amenhotep: First Prophet of Amun*

PLATE 375. *Rome-Roy, First Prophet of Amun*

PLATE 376. *Royal Gift to the First High Priest Amenhotep*

PLATE 377. *Royal Gift to the First High Priest Amenhotep*

PLATE 378. *Eighth Pylon: East End*

PLATE 379. *Doorway Located to the West of the Eighth Pylon*

PLATE 380–381. *Eighth Pylon: North Facade*

PLATE 382–383. *Eighth Pylon: South Facade*

PLATE 384. *White Limestone Colossus of the Eighth Pylon's West Wing*

PLATE 385. *Interior Facade of the Passageway of the Eighth Pylon's Doorway*

PLATE 386. *Quartzite Colossus to the West of the Entrance of the Eighth Pylon*

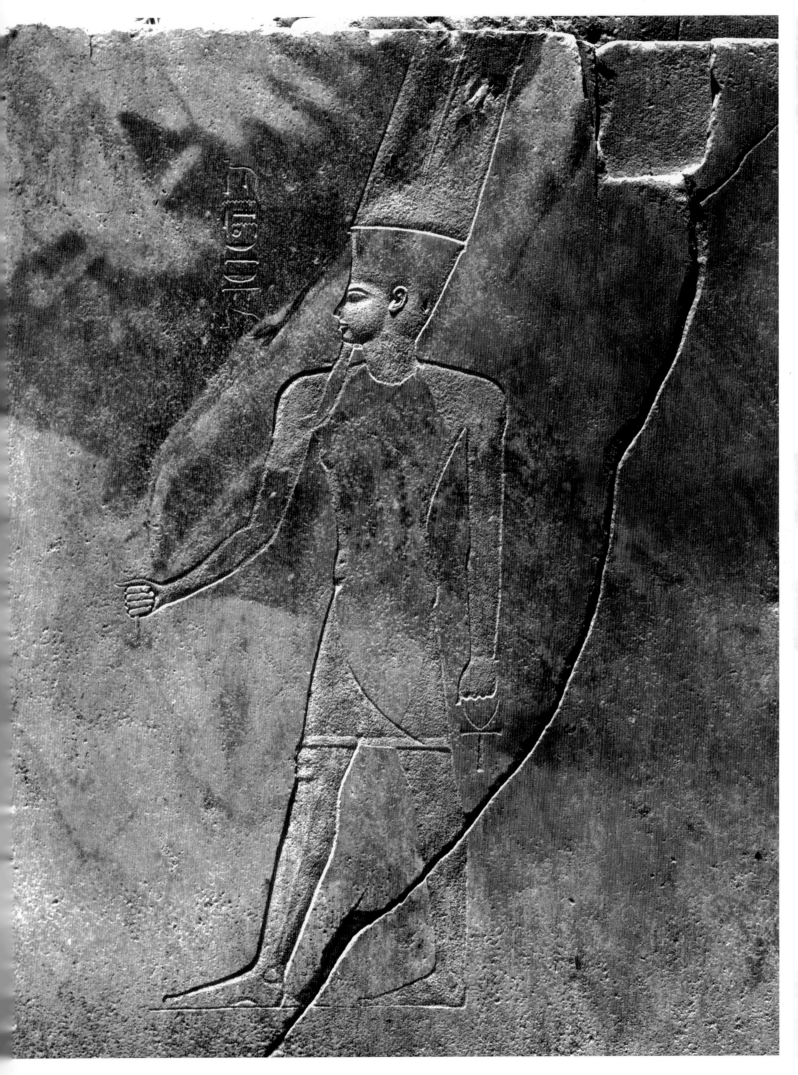

PLATE 387. *East Facade of the Quartzite Colossus's Pedestal*

PLATE 388. *Feet of the Quartzite Colossus*

PLATE 389. *West Doorpost of the Eighth Pylon's Doorway: Detail*

PLATE 390. *Ninth Pylon as Seen from the Doorway of the Eighth Pylon*

PLATE 391. *Ninth Pylon: West Wing, North Facade*

PLATE 392. *Ninth Pylon, Seen from the Southwest*

PLATE 393. *Ninth Pylon: West Wing; In the Background is the Temple of Khonsu*

PLATE 394. *Ninth Pylon: East Wing*

PLATE 395. *Interior Staircase of the Ninth Pylon*

PLATE 396. *Ninth Pylon: West Wing, South Facade*

PLATE 397. *The King in the Tree: Ramesside Block*

PLATE 398. *Ninth Pylon: Granite Pedestal*

PLATE 399. *Ninth Pylon: Overall View; In the Background is the First Pylon*

PLATE 400. *Monument of Amenhotep II: Overall View*

PLATE 401. *Monument of Amenhotep II: Southeast Corner*

PLATE 402. *Monument of Amenhotep II: Northeast Corner*

PLATE 403. *Monument of Amenhotep II: Northeast Corner*

PLATE 404. *Monument of Amenhotep II: Pillar "Raised Higher" With a Reused Block*

PLATE 405. *Amenhotep II Protected by the Serpent-Goddess Meretseger: Detail*

PLATE 406. *Tutankhamun*

PLATE 407. *Presentation of the Tributes from the Land of Punt*

PLATE 408. *Presentation of the Aegean and Syrian Tributes*

PLATE 409. *Tenth Pylon: Granite Gate*

PLATE 410. *Amun-Ra: Granite Block*

PLATE 411. *Gate, Seen from the North, and the West Colossus*

PLATE 412. *Northeast Colossus: Prisoners from the Southern Countries*

PLATE 413. *Northeast Colossus: Queen Mut-Nefertari*

PLATE 414. *The Two Colossi: West Doorpost of the Gate*

PLATE 415. *Western Colossus of the North Facade*

PLATE 416. *Granite Gate, Interior of the East Doorpost: Detail*

PLATE 417. *Granite Gate, Interior of the East Doorpost: Detail*

PLATE 418. *Tenth Pylon, Southern Facade: East Doorpost of the Granite Gate*

PLATE 419. *Tenth Pylon, Southern Facade, East Doorpost of the Granite Gate: Offering of the White Bread*

PLATE 420. *Pedestal of the Colossus of Amenhotep III*

PLATE 421. *Tenth Pylon: East Facade*

PLATE 422. *Double Pedestal of Amenhotep III*

PLATE 423. *Iunmutef Presenting the Protocol of Amenhotep III*

PLATE 424. *Quartzite Pedestal of the Colossus of Amenhotep III, West Facade*

PLATE 425. *Amenhotep Son of Hapu*

PLATE 426. *Tenth Pylon: South Facade*

PLATE 427. *Fist from the Colossus of Amenhotep III*

PLATE 428. *Fragment of the Black Granite Pedestal of Amenhotep III*

PLATE 429. *Fragment of the Black Granite Pedestal of Amenhotep III: Detail*

PLATE 430. *Musicians*

PLATE 431. *Ptolemaic Gate of the Enclosure: West Doorpost, South Facade*

PLATE 432. *Osirian Statue*

PLATE 433. *Osirian Statue*

PLATE 434. *Osirian Statue*

PLATE 435. *Circumcision Scene*

PLATE 436. *Sphinx*

PLATE 437. *Female Bust in Black Granite*

PLATE 438. *Ptolemaic Blocks from One of the Sanctuaries*

PLATE 439. *Overall View of the Ruins of the Temple of Mut and the Statues of Sekhmet*

PLATE 440. *Statue of Sekhmet*

PLATE 441. *Statue of Sekhmet: Detail*

PLATE 442. *Bust of Mentuemhet, Fourth Prophet of Amun*

PLATE 443. *Statue of Mentuemhet*

PLATE 444. *The Sacred Lake and the Temple of Mut*

PLATE 445. *The Two Colossi in Front of the Temple of Ramesses III Constructed near the Sacred Lake of Asheru*

PLATE 446. *The Sacred Lake of Asheru and the Temple of Ramesses III*

PLATE 447. *Plover in the Lake of Asheru in Spring*

PLATE 448–449. *Overall View of the Lake of Asheru*

PLATE 450. *Small Herd of Goats at the Edge of the Sacred Lake of Asheru*

PLATE 451. *Young Girl Fifteen Years Old*

PLATE 452. *Plover in the Lake of Asheru in Summer*

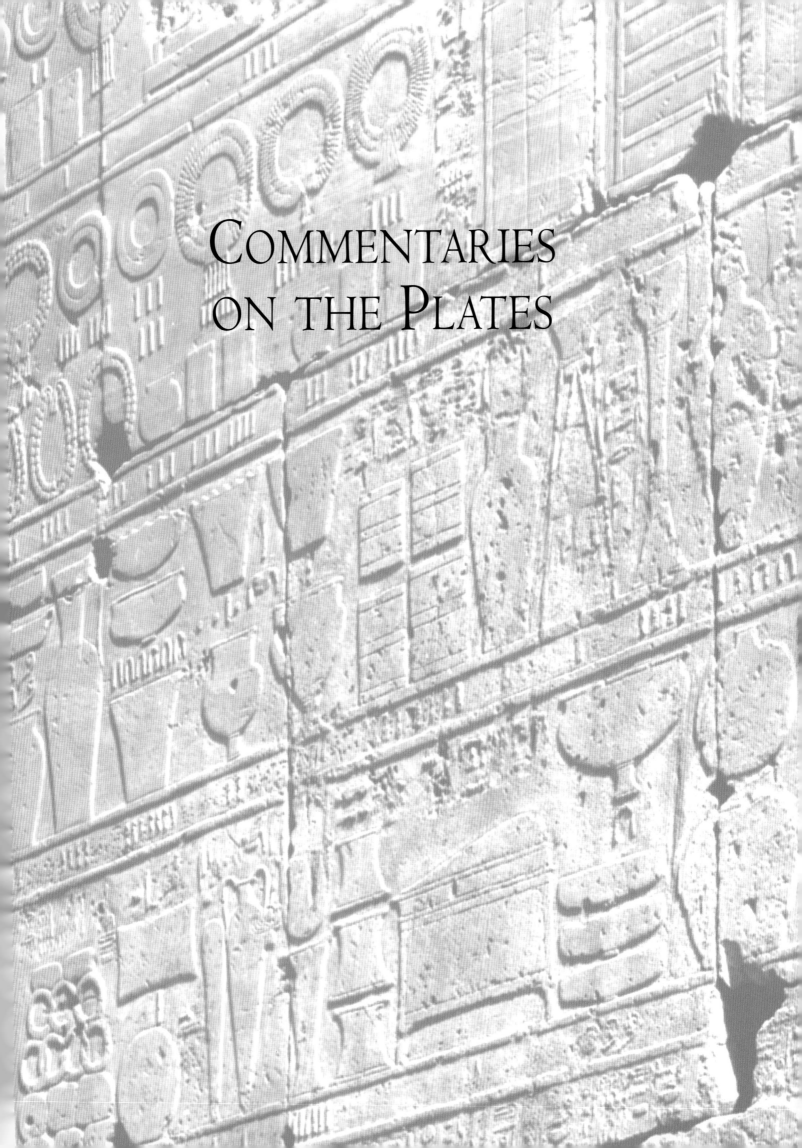

COMMENTARIES ON THE PLATES

Fig. 1. The Nile of the Theban nome

[They] who see Hapi shiver [when] he strikes [his waves], the sparkling ponds [of lotus and papyrus] whose flooded banks become green with the offerings from the falling *neters;* the faces of the people light up, the hearts of the *neters* are exalted.

(Pyramid Texts 1553–54)

Hail to thee, O Hapi, who emerges from this earth and comes forth to give life to Egypt. Thou who conceal thy arrival in the darkness on the very day that thy coming is celebrated, thou the wave that spreads over the orchards created by Ra to give life to all who thirst, and that refuses to water the desert with the overflow from the waters of heaven. From the moment of thy descent, Geb [the earth] becomes enamored of bread, Nepri [the neter *of seeds] presents his offering, and Ptah makes every workshop prosper. Are his fingers in pain, are they idle? Then all the millions of beings are miserable. Does he diminish in heaven? Then perish the* neters *themselves and man; the beasts are thrown into panic, and everyone in the world, great and small, is in agony. If, on the contrary, the prayers of humanity are granted when he rises and he takes to himself the name of Khnum [their creator] on his ascent, then the earth resounds with general rejoicing, all bellies are joyful, all backs shake with laughter, and all teeth are chewing.*

(*Hymn to the Nile,* from Maspero's translation of the Sallier II and Anastasi VII Papyri)

PLATES 1–3 • HAPI, THE NILE

The Nile surpasses all other rivers of the inhabited world in its benefactions to mankind. . . .

The rise of the Nile is a phenomenon that appears wonderful enough to those who have witnessed it, but to those who have only heard of it, quite incredible. For while all other rivers begin to fall at the summer solstice and grow steadily lower and lower during the course of the following summer, this one alone begins to rise at that time, and increases so greatly in volume day by day that it finally overflows practically all Egypt. . . .

And because of the anxiety occasioned by the rise of the river, the kings have constructed a Nilometer at Memphis, where those who are charged with the administration of it accurately measure the rise and despatch messages to the cities, and inform them exactly how many cubits or fingers the river has risen and when it has

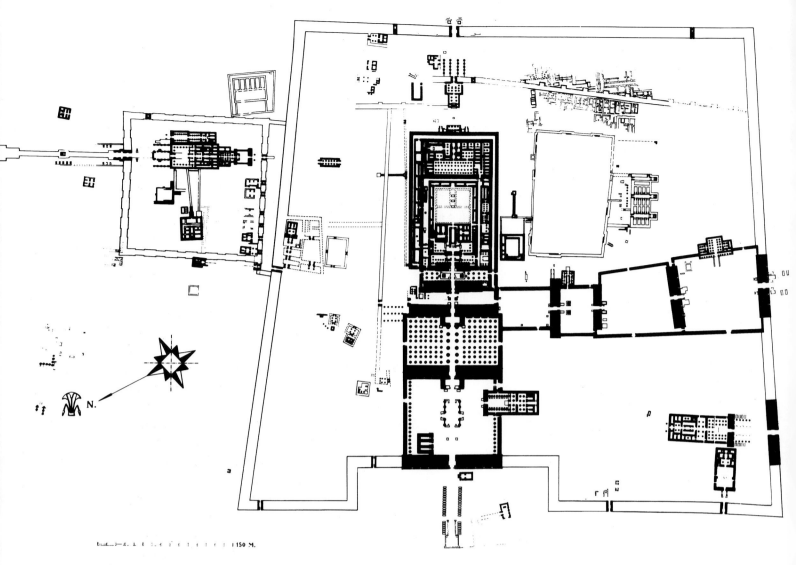

Diagram 1. Great temple of Amun; temple of Mentu to the north of the great wall

commenced to fall. In this manner the entire nation, when it has learned that the river has ceased rising and begun to fall, is relieved of its anxiety, while at the same time all immediately know in advance how large the next harvest will be, since the Egyptians have kept an accurate record of their observations of this kind for a great many years. (Diodorus Siculus, 1.36)

Anyone who has lived in Egypt is familiar with the agony provoked by an insufficient flooding or, on the other hand, the anguish caused by the slow and implacable rise of the waters. It is therefore understandable that the water levels have been carefully recorded each year since times of great antiquity.[1]

[1]For a note on the cubit measurement of floodwater levels recorded in Elephantine, Memphis, and the Delta, see Danielle Bonneau's *La Crue du Nil* (Paris: Klingsieck, 1964), p. 23. Also for songs and hymns to the Nile, ibid., pp. 361 and 406, 6.

The Palermo Stone gives evidence of this going back to the First Dynasty, and we will see, when passing in front of the wharf of Karnak, that these levels were noted not only in Memphis, as Diodorus spoke of, but also in numerous temples of Egypt and Nubia.

Hapi, the *neter* symbol of the Nile, is always represented under a male and female aspect, carrying all manner of fruits, birds, and so forth, in his arms. It is he who will unite the Two Lands under the royal throne; it is he who will serve as a prop to the symbols of the "nomes" (the geographical divisions of the country); it is again he who will pour forth the beneficial wave over all that lives on earth (fig. 1).

The temples of Karnak are located about 600 meters from the Nile on the east bank.

PLATE 1 • THE NILE

PLATE 2 • BOAT DRAWING ALONGSIDE

PLATE 3 • DISEMBARKING

PLATES 4–11 • THE TEMPLE OF AMUN: THE FIRST PYLON

We now enter a monumental grouping of structures, 25 hectares in size, enclosed within a thick wall of unbaked bricks. These constructions spread out over a span of more than two thousand years and present, at first sight, a complexity that we will strive to bring order to during the course of our excursion.

The great temple of Amun has its entrance on the west and its sanctuaries on the east. In the central part of the temple a transverse road leads to the temple of Mentu in the north and the temple of Mut in the south.

PLATE 4 • GOATS

PLATE 5 • FOUNTAIN IN FRONT OF THE FIRST PYLON

PLATE 6 • THE WHARF, THE AVENUE OF THE SPHINXES, THE FIRST PYLON

Wharf: Length:	14.70 meters
Width:	13.50 meters
Pedestals of the sphinxes:	1.35 meters by 1.70 meters over a distance of 0.95 meters.
Dromos:	Total length: 52 meters
Width between sphinxes:	13.10 meters
Total width:	20.50 meters

(Measurements given by Legrain)[2]

A canal dug out to the Nile terminates at a wharf located on the western extremity of an avenue bordered with two rows of ram-headed sphinxes leading to the great temple of Amun. This "dromos" comes to a halt 20 meters before the pylon. It is cut into two sections by the "royal highway," which went from Coptos to Syene by way of Thebes, and passes here between the seventh and eighth sphinxes.

Branching off from the royal highway, a slight ramp climbs toward the wharf. At the starting point

of this ramp were two human-headed sphinxes holding a ram-headed urn in their hands, of which nothing remains but the pedestals, which are 1.5 meters in height. (From Legrain, *Les Temples de Karnak*, chap. 1)

The different heights of the annual Nile floods that were marked during the time between the Twenty-second Dynasty (Sheshonk I, 950–929 B.C.) and the Twenty-sixth Dynasty (Psamtik III, 525 B.C.) can be seen on the western side of the wharf. As an example:

Year 3, first month of the third season, day 5 under the majesty of King Shabataka. When his majesty was crowned as king in the House of Amun, he granted him that he should splendidly appear as favorite of the Two Goddesses, like Horus upon the throne of Ra. [The Nile] which his father Amun the great, Hapi the great, great in Niles, granted him in his time: twenty (cubits), 2 palms. (Trans. Breasted, *Ancient Records*, vol. 4, § 887)*

These measurements are marked with regard to a horizontal line that must have formerly served as a reference for noting the augmentation of the average level of the flood over the course of the seasons.[3]

(According to the observations of Ventre Pasha, the elevation of the general depth of the Nile is 9.60 cm annually. From the beginning of the Eighteenth

---

[2]Precise dimensions of the dromos can be found in *Kemi* 21:79–106. The dromos was provided with channels intended for watering the plants and trees arranged before and behind the sphinxes (ibid., p. 114). The stylobate of a small Roman temple was unearthed on the border of the dromos right next to the south wing of the first pylon (ibid., p. 120).

*Brackets in citations from *Ancient Records* indicate Schwaller's insertions, parentheses indicate Breasted's own. Some spellings and punctuation have been altered to improve clarity—Trans.

[3]The comparison of the texts with the monument allows for the conclusion that the level of reference zero should correspond to that of the low-water mark and that the preferred flood level would be 21 cubits, 3⅓ palms in Aswan, reaching 11.25 m. This height corresponds almost exactly to Taharka's figure on the Karnak wharf, which is higher than all the others. The platform of the wharf, being 2 m above this inscription, is therefore 13 m above the low-water mark, making it unusable as a landing. This is the reason it is presumed to have served as a tribunal. Some very beautiful statues of the Twelfth Dynasty were found in its foundations. (See also *Karnak*, vol. 5, p. 58)

The excavations in the neighborhood of this tribunal have brought to light the elements of a real wharf alongside which the 68-m-long river barque of Amun would have come (see page 596), as well as its towing barque and the barques of Mut and Khonsu, a flotilla that brings to mind a pool that must have been more than a hundred meters long.

The small repository of Achoris, located at the crossings of the royal highway and the access ramp to the quay, must have been used for the maneuverings of the priests carrying the sacred barque (pl. 45) before its embarkation within the large barque Userhat of Amun (pl. 98–99). (See also *Karnak*, vol. 5, p. 3)

The Nile rises an additional 0.132 m every hundred years. (*Kemi* 21:78, 8)

Fig. 2. Temple of Psammuthis. This partition is adorned at its furthermost end by three stems held together by five bands. This image is represented here in the quite abnormal fashion of a very pronounced high relief. The profile of the king and the shape of his blue helmet already announce the Ptolemaic style.

Dynasty [about 1400 B.C.] to the present day, the level of the Nile, and consequently that of the farmlands, has risen by about 3.27 m.)

It is noteworthy that the wharf of Karnak does not bear any flood-level measurement from the first five years of Taharka's reign, which, moreover, is known to have been a period of drought. Thus Egypt found itself threatened anew as it had been already under Zoser (Third Dynasty), a fact that is recounted by the famous "Stela of the seven-year famine."

Once the flood finally occurred, Taharka had two stelae carved, one in Coptos, the other in Mataanah, which include the following texts:

Stela of the sixth year of King Taharka (696 B.C.):

Now a marvelous thing occurred in the time of His Majesty, in Khnt-hn-nfr. Never has such a thing been seen in all the time of his predecessors [and this] because his father, Amun-Ra, loved him. His Majesty had begged for an [abundant] Nile from his father Amun-Ra, master of the throne of the Two Lands, to prevent the misery of any person during his reign. Now all the things that emerged from the mouth of His Majesty, his father Amun made to be realized immediately. [Therefore] when the moment for the flooding of the Nile arrived, it began to swell greatly each day; when a number of days in which it grew had passed, it flooded the mountains of the southern land and the lowlands of the North. The country was similar to an inert, primordial ocean, without the sandbanks [being able] to be distinguished from the river. The flood had risen up to the city of Thebes; then His Majesty had the annals of the ancestors brought forth to see if such a Nile had been produced in their time, but nothing similar was to be found there. It was a rain shower from the Nubian skies that had made the mountains shine in all their glory. Every Nubian was rich in all things, and Egypt [was also] rich in all things, for each day. All gave thanks to the king; the king's heart was content over all else because of what his father Amun had done for him, by granting him the possibility [?] of presenting offerings to all the neters. (Jacques Vandier, La Famine dans l'Egypte ancienne, pp. 124–25)

Once and for all we are reinstating the Egyptian word *neter* in the place of its customary translation as "god."

Let's stress the fact that in Taharka's text, first, the Annals of the Ancestors are attested to by the Palermo Stone, which cites the height of the floods from the time of Menes. And second, it is "a rain shower from the Nubian skies" that provokes the flood, which runs counter to the symbolic affirmations that the "sources" of the Nile are in Elephantine. One must know to distinguish myth from fact.

PLATE 7 • OBELISK OF SETI II, SOUTHEAST CORNER OF THE WHARF

Height: 3.8 meters

On the northeast and southeast corners of the wharf, Seti II had two small obelisks erected. Nothing remains of the northern one except the pedestal, but the southern obelisk, which is almost intact, is interesting because it presents Seti II's complete titulary, which, reading from top to bottom, is as follows: his Horus name, his "Two Crowns" name, his Golden Horus name, his throne name as the king of the South and of the North, and finally his "Son of Ra" name, repeated in four vertical columns:

Solar Horus, mighty bull, beloved of Ra.

The Two Vulture-Cobra Mistresses, protector of the black [Egypt] that tames the foreign mountains.

Golden Horus, great with Victory in all the lands.

PLATE 8 • FIRST PYLON, SOUTHERN WING: THE SPHINXES

The sphinxes with lions' bodies and rams' heads (an animated symbol of Amun) are each protecting a royal effigy (Ramesses II) in the form of Osiris, who stands between their front paws. Around each pedestal an extra inscription was added during the Twenty-first Dynasty by the high priest Pinedjem, son of Piankhi.

With the wharf as its starting point, the avenue of the sphinxes terminates at the first pylon.

The first pylon, the current entranceway to the great temple of Amun, is composed of two massive blocks framing the large portal. On the west face of each block, four vertical grooves serve to house the poles, made from cedar of Lebanon and stitched with copper, *whose tips would reach the sky*. These poles, adorned with banners at their tops, went well beyond the height of the pylon. They were fixed against the walls by lines passed through the two rows of windows that were placed there for that purpose.

PLATE 9 • FIRST PYLON: GENERAL VIEW FROM THE SOUTH

In the foreground appear the remains of the encircling wall of unbaked bricks that have become attached to the southern face of the pylon's southern wing. This rests on a perfectly horizontal stone platform; the measurements taken with a level don't indicate even a centimeter's difference for its total length. On this pavement are drawn the essential

Fig 3. Doorway of the second pylon (photo by Maxime du Camp)

axes, notably those of the cornerstones, the foliated cusps of the poles, and so on.

The distance between the axes of the tori, corresponding to the total length of the mass of the two wings, is 111.37 meters, and the length between the tori is equal to 110.64 meters (measurements that we took ourselves in 1947 after the pylon was totally uncovered). These are the geodetic measurements:

Arc of 1° of the parallel (equator) at 0° = 111.324 meters,
Arc of 1° of meridian at 0° = 110.576 meters.

The pylon remains unfinished. The north wing has only thirty-two courses and measures 21.70 meters high, while the southern wing has forty-five courses and measures 31.65 meters high. Its thickness at the base is around 14.50 meters. (Measurements given by Legrain)

Its four faces have remained in an unfinished state, but examination of its masterly construction reveals the extreme care taken in the precision with which the slope of the monument is drawn on each of the blocks. For example, the ten lower courses and the upper courses marking the projection of the torus in the southwest corner bear a groove indicating its exact slant. Moreover, the upper face of each corner-stone bears drawings that define the thickness of the torus.

Thanks to these valuable marks, we have been able to measure by triangulation the average slope on a height of about 21 meters, at the southwest corner:

South face = 83°32′ × 83°34′,

West face = 81°36′ × 81°42′.[4]

The doorway of the pylon, on the other hand, presents an anomaly; all the blocks that constitute its jambs are carefully rejointed, not only on the west facade and the interior of the passageway (pls. 6, 9, and 11), but also on their face joined to the pylon, while the entire eastern facade has remained in a state of construction (pl. 11). This mode of abnormal construction makes this doorway an edifice that is totally independent of the pylon itself, which raises the questions: Why bring such careful workmanship to the invisible and concealed part of the edifice while leaving the rest in a state of incompletion? Why is the rough nature of the construction prominent in the east and its finished state prominent in the west?

This doorway has an interior width of 7.40 meters and a height of 19.36 meters. Its proportion when open would be 1 to 2.618 (the square of the golden number) to within a few centimeters.

Legrain remarks that the projection of the north vertical torus of the southern wing stops at the thirty-seventh foundation course, determining as well the probable height of the doorway, which would have

been around 26 meters. The door frame was 16.90 meters, which assumes a colossal lintel, and the splaying of 9.25 meters requires a door of two casements weighing more than eight and one-half tons.

On the inside of the doorway, to the upper right, the French scholars of the Bonaparte expedition carved the latitudes and longitudes of the principal Egyptian monuments that they had surveyed. Nouet corrected his calculations and gave these readings for Karnak:

30°20′34″ east longitude,

25°42′57″ north latitude.

In front of the southern wing of the first pylon there is a curious representation (fig. 2) on a small monument from the Twenty-ninth Dynasty. The two cartouches are scratched out; however, the Horus name allows these bas-reliefs to be attributed to Psammuthis (379–378 B.C.).

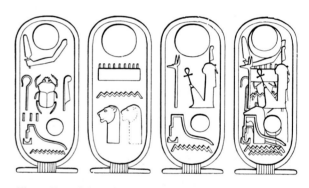

Fig. 4. From left to right: the three cartouches of Horemheb, Ramesses I, and Ramesses II superimposed on the fourth cartouche, which is alone depicted on the vestibule wall of the second pylon (at m, diagram 2)

PLATES 10–29 • THE FIRST COURTYARD

Depth: 82 meters
Width: 100 meters
(Measurements from Legrain)

The first courtyard includes edifices dating from a period that extends from the end of the Eighteenth Dynasty to the Ptolemaic Period (diagram 2).

The second pylon and the "vestibule" preceding it architecturally form one building. Now the western section of the vestibule preserves the vestiges of the tableaux carved in the name of Horemheb (last

---

[4]The construction date of the first pylon is still under debate (see *Kemi* 20, p. 110, 8). The width between the splayings is 9 m. The 19.36 m height of the bay comes from our own (unpublished) triangulations made in 1947. According to these the total height of the doorway would be (for thirty-seven courses) 25.83 m from the pedestal of the pylon and 26.25 m from the granite sill of the entrance.

king of the Eighteenth Dynasty or first king of the Nineteenth Dynasty), whose cartouches were subsequently added on to, some by Ramesses II and the others by Ramesses I and II, such as, for example, that which is found on the west face (at *m*, diagram 2). It is therefore obvious that the vestibule was erected by Horemheb and that the second pylon was at least begun by this pharaoh and only perhaps completed under Ramesses I.

Near the site of the future first pylon, Seti II (Nineteenth Dynasty) constructed a repository for the three sacred barques of Amun, Mut, and Khonsu, the Theban triad (pls. 22 and 26).

In front of the southern wing of the second

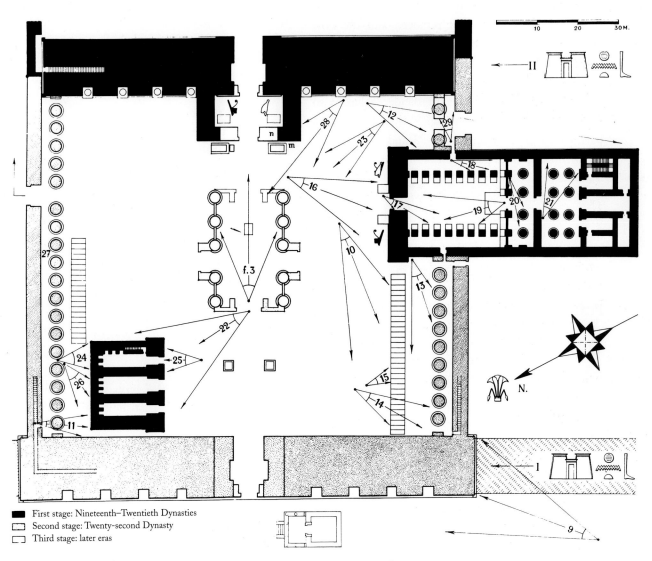

First stage: Nineteenth–Twentieth Dynasties
Second stage: Twenty-second Dynasty
Third stage: later eras

Diagram 2. The first courtyard

Please note: On the partial diagrams of the Karnak plan, the place from which a photograph was taken is indicated by a dot with a number corresponding to the plate. Numbers preceded by an *f* on certain diagrams refer to a related figure.

pylon Ramesses III (Twentieth Dynasty) erected the little temple bearing his name that is also consecrated to the three sacred barques (pls. 16–21).

Sheshonk I (Twenty-second Dynasty) next constructed the second pylon (a contestable assertion according to some) and closed the first courtyard by bordering it on the north and south with a portico that he left undecorated. At this time, the avenue of the sphinxes that originally led from the wharf to the second pylon was partially removed and the now extra sphinxes were stored on each side of the first courtyard (pls. 10–15 and 23).

Taharka, the Ethiopian king (Twenty-fifth Dynasty), next erected a portico of very slender columns in front of the second pylon (fig. 3), which framed a path paved in red granite (pls. 23 and 28, and figs. 8–10). This granite pavement is of a later date than Taharka.

Finally, the Ptolemies entirely reworked the large doorway of the second pylon (fig. 3) and added their name on the "dado" of Taharka's columns, whose shafts had already received the extra addition of Psamtik's cartouches (Twenty-sixth Dynasty) (fig. 8).

PLATE 10 • FIRST PYLON, EAST FACE OF THE SOUTH WING: THE BUBASTITE PORTICO

PLATE 11 • FIRST PYLON, EAST FACE: THE BUBASTITE PORTICO

Note the unbaked-brick constructions against the eastern face of the pylon, which, according to traditional opinion, were intended to serve as scaf-

folding for the construction of the building. Legrain observed that the arrangement of the brick underpinning of the north pier was different from that of the south pier; the first is made of layers of bricks arranged with the greatest of care, whereas the southern underpinning is formed of a dozen walls perpendicular to the pylon, the intervals of which are filled with earth and crushed stone.

To the bottom left the sphinxes are stored before the Bubastite portico that is made up of a single rank of columns with cylindrical shafts each capped by a capital in the shape of a closed bud. These sandstone columns bear no other decoration except the five standard bands indicating constriction, and which distinguish the shaft from the capital.

Above the anta pillar and the first column on the extreme southwest is a surviving fragment of an unfinished grooved cornice, in rough-hewn blocks (see detail pl. 13).

The date of the building of the pylon is disputed. Mariette attributes it to the Ptolemies, but Legrain asserts that it was constructed by Sheshonk before the colonnade and cites in support of this thesis an inscription at Silsila of the priest Heremsaf, the chief of works under Sheshonk:

His majesty gave stipulations for building a very great pylon . . . in order to brighten Thebes . . . in order to make a jubilee-court for the house of his father Amun-Ra, king of the gods, and to surround it with a colonnade. (Breasted, *Ancient Records*, vol. 4, § 707)

Legrain also noted that the cut of the stones for the antae pillars, unfinished *in the west as in the east* (pls. 14 and 29) is quite similar to that of the pylon itself.

Fig. 5. Bas-relief from the tomb of Ti, Saqqara, Fifth Dynasty

PLATE 12 • BUBASTITE DOORWAY, EAST WALL OF THE TEMPLE OF RAMESSES III

Between the second pylon and the temple of Ramesses III, the portico includes only two columns, which are in front of an open doorway to the south. The inscriptions on the architrave and pillars that frame this portico (pls. 12 and 29) are in the name of Sheshonk I and his successors (Twenty-second Dynasty).

Sheshonk I was a contemporary of Solomon. Upon the latter's death, profiting from the dissolution of the twelve tribes of Israel, he made an incursion into Palestine to regain the Egyptian sovereignty formerly exercised over the eastern lands. This expedition was crowned with success, and Sheshonk had carved in Karnak, not far from this portico, the list of the 156 conquered towns. (See 1 Kings 14, and 2 Chronicles 12 for the recounting of this expedition.)

Sheshonk is represented on the posts of this doorway, along with his son Iuput, high priest of Amun in Karnak, as was already noted by Champollion during his travels in Upper Egypt. It is indeed noteworthy that the kings of the Libyan Dynasty established their residence at Bubastis, in the Delta, and most often named their own sons as the high priests at the temple of Amun in Karnak. These latter individuals obtained the authorization to inscribe their names in a royal cartouche quite speedily, so that, in the image of the preceding dynasty, there were still two governments: one in the North and one in the South. Egypt was divided anew.

PLATE 13 • BUBASTITE COLONNADE SOUTH OF THE FIRST COURTYARD

PLATE 14 • ANTA PILLAR OF THE SOUTH PORTICO, SPHINX

PLATE 15 • RAM-HEADED SPHINX

Inside the temple we will often come across representations that are either rams or the depiction of a *neter*, or a royal figure wearing a crown supported by rams' horns.

These symbols are borrowed from two very distinct ovine breeds: one has horizontal horns that undergo a twisting movement and are slightly raised at the tip; the other has spiral-shaped horns whose tips come toward the front, almost reaching the chin.

Very ancient figurations are connected to the first species, and several skull fragments found in Neolithic deposits have confirmed their identification suggested by the bas-reliefs as being that of *Ovis longipes paleoaegyptiacus*. Khnum, the *neter* who fashions humanity on his potter's wheel, is also represented under the form of a ram-headed man with horizontal horns. Khnum is the great *neter* of Elephantine.

Amun's ram corresponds to the second species cited (pls. 14 and 15).

"Several bone spindles coming from the mummy crypts of Abusir are linked to this breed, as well as the skull preserved in the Cairo Museum as No. 29529." (Gaillard and Daressy, *La Faune momifiée de l'Antique Egypte* [Cairo, 1905], p. 31)

The study of this specimen has permitted the conclusion that "the structure of the bone of the skull as well as the horns conforms exactly to the *Ovis platyura* breed *(Aegyptica Fitz.)*, which provided the sheep with Amun horns known by the ancients." (Ibid., p. 30)

"This sheep has inhabited Egypt since long ago. It was probably brought there around the time of the Twelfth Dynasty, from when it has been found depicted on Egyptian monuments." (Ibid., p. 32)

Thus "Amun's Ram" appeared in Egypt only at the precessional age when the sun entered into the sign and constellation of Aries.

PLATES 16–21 • TEMPLE OF RAMESSES III

I made for thee a mysterious horizon in thy city of Thebes over against thy forecourt, O lord of gods (named): "House (pr)-of-Ramesses-Ruler-of-Heliopolis, L. P. H., in-the-House-of-Amun," abiding like the heavens bearing the sun. I built it, I laid it in sandstone, having great doors of fine gold. I filled its treasury with the things which my hands carried off, to bring them before thee every day. (Harris Papyrus, trans. Breasted, *Ancient Records*, vol. 4, § 195)

Thus Ramesses IV had his father speak in the renowned Harris Papyrus drawn up on the death of Ramesses III as a memorial to all the works he had accomplished on earth.

Fig. 6a. Bas-relief, Twenty-fifth Dynasty (Louvre Museum)

PLATE 16 • TEMPLE OF RAMESSES III, NORTH FACADE

"This edifice, which otherwise would be large, and only appears now as a small chapel, was preceded by a pylon whose upper portion is destroyed today. It is missing the cornice, the frieze, and the upper portion of the tableaux that decorated them," wrote Champollion. (*Notices descriptives*, vol. 2, p. 10)

Indeed, this building, which measures about 60 meters long, appears in the entire Karnak site only as an accessory chapel intended to shelter the three sacred barques when they went to the west bank or the temple of Luxor, during the times of the "beautiful feast of the valley" or the "great feast of Apet."

However, this repository is conceived as a temple complete in itself: a pylon, a courtyard bordered by eight Osirian pillars each on the east and west, and at a slightly elevated level, a portico opening onto the court and a hypostyle room preceding the three sanctuaries of the sacred barques.

The entire monument was crowned with a grooved cornice capping the standard torus that also bordered the corners of the pylon (pls. 12 and 16). In addition, the elevation of the "covered temple" corresponds to the stylobate torus on the exterior facades. (See H. Chevrier, *Le Temple Reposoir de Ramsès III à Karnak*, 1933, pls. VI and VII)

Champollion described the two underpinnings of this pylon in very precise terms:

"On the left underpinning, the king Ramesses Meryamun, wearing the *pschent* [the white crown

over the red], holds a group of begging prisoners by the hair as he massacres them with his white club. Facing him, Amun-Ra presents the harpagon to the pharaoh and holds with his left hand the bonds to which the captives with the coats of arms are attached. These are the people of the North and the Central regions."(*Notices descriptives*, vol. 2, p. 10)

On the right underpinning we see an identical scene, except that the king is wearing the red crown. We will frequently find this theme of "the massacre of prisoners" on the facades of pylons and the temple entranceways. It should be noted here that the red crown of the North is represented on the *west* wing of the pylon, just as, in the courtyard, the eight Osirises wearing the red crown of the North are in the west, while the other eight wearing the white crown of the South are in the east. Here the North is identified with the west and the South with the east.

Two heavy and squat 6-meter statues in red sandstone frame the gate, which has only one door. "The doorposts and the cornice are of gray speckled granite. This was the great doorway of the king of Upper and Lower Egypt, Usermaātre Meryamun. Hardly any of the blocks that composed it remain." (Legrain, *Les Temples de Karnak*, p. 89)

PLATE 17 • TEMPLE OF RAMESSES III, INTERIOR DOORPOST OF THE NORTH DOORWAY: OSIRIAN PILLARS

Fig. 6b. Cyrene coin

The splay on the right seen in the foreground is decorated with horizontal inscriptions of royal titles alternating with baskets crowned with three symbols: *was, ankh,* and *djed,* which mean prosperity, life, and stability.

In the background the Osirises on the west are wearing the red crown. Their two hands are crossed over their chest, with the left hand holding the *hek* scepter and the right hand the *nekhakha* scepter, which rest respectively on the left and right shoulders after a double crossing of hands and scepters (the symbol of resurrection).

The dedication of Ramesses III, written in two horizontal lines on the architrave supported by the square pillars against which the Osirises are leaning, gives the name of the temple mentioned in the Harris Papyrus in the upper line: *He has made the house of Ramesses, sovereign of Heliopolis in the house of Amun, in perfectly sound white stone [sandstone].* (See illustration below.)

PLATE 18 • DORSAL FACE OF THE OSIRIAN PILLARS: THE WALL BETWEEN THE PILLARS

On the right are the three pillars that support the architrave; in the back is the facade of the portico that opens out on the courtyard. The small lower wall that joins these pillars is capped with a torus, a cornice, and a uraeus frieze. One of the columns of this portico preceding the hypostyle can be seen through the window thus contrived. The step that conceals a part of the tableau on the wall between the columns is therefore a more recent addition.

PLATE 19 • TEMPLE OF RAMESSES III: COURTYARD AND OSIRIAN PILLARS, TAHARKA'S COLUMN

The row of eight Osirian pillars of the red crown on the left supports the architrave, which was once crowned by a grooved cornice. One of Taharka's columns and the northern Bubastite portico can be seen in the back, next to the entrance.

PLATE 20 • TEMPLE OF RAMESSES III: PORTICO WITH COLUMNS

The east face of the pillar in the foreground to the left of the entranceway offers a very beautiful example of the royal name of Ramesses III: Usermaätre Meryamun, under which is carved the name of Mut (the vulture), mistress of Heaven.

In the background are two of the four portico columns that support the architrave perpendicular to the axis of the monument.

The remains of two large statues of Sekhmet in black granite, similar to those in the temple of Ptah (pl. 313), were found on each side of the doorway that gives access to the room of the eight columns. "Around the pedestal the royal protocol of Ramesses III can be read. On the flat part of the pedestal for the statue on the left it says: 'Beloved of Mut-Sekhmet, lady of Asheru,' and written on the flat part of the right statue's pedestal is 'Beloved of Sekhmet-Menhit.' "(Ibid., p. 102)

(Thus the war goddess Sekhmet-Menhit is on the west, and her maternal aspect, Mut-Sekhmet, is on the east.)

PLATE 21 • TEMPLE OF RAMESSES III: HYPOSTYLE CHAMBER

The two rows of monostyle papyriform columns support the architraves erected in the axis of the temple. Above the pedestal the shaft emerges from eight leaves adorning the base. The two royal cartouches, flanked by two uraei crowned by the solar disk, are engraved in sunk relief between each leaf, in alternating fashion. Above them is a register of tableaux carved in light relief (an exceptional case with regard to the Ramessides), while the inscrip-

Fig 7. North face of the temple of Seti II

tions in the name of Ramesses III are deeply incised. Five bands under the capital mark the constriction of the shaft and retain the groupings of three vertical bands that go beyond the capital and the shaft. This motif is typically considered a vestige of the ancient "adventitious buds," which adorn this spot on fasciculate columns (see pl. 207). Finally, under the abacus, the top of the capital is capped by a frieze repeating the two cartouches (of which only one is flanked by uraei) crowned by solar disks. The width of the abacus is equal to the upper part of the capital and its height is generally half of that.

Note the massive style of these columns that are symbolic of an earlier foundation.

(Compare this decorative grouping with the columns of the same type in the great hypostyle hall of the temple of Amun, in which the classic adornment of the capitals' bases received the cartouches as additions.) (See also note to pl. 69.)

"The walls of the chamber of eight columns are adorned by two rows of large bas-reliefs representing several scenes from the daily worship of Amun. The king is about to enter the room, followed by his two acolytes, Mentu and Tum. Mentu will lead the king down the east side of the room, Tum will conduct him on the west side." (Ibid., p. 105)

PLATES 22–26 • THE REPOSITORY OF SETI II

The temple-repository of Seti II presents itself as a massive rectangle whose walls have a very emphatic slope and are capped by the standard torus and cornice. On its southern face three doorways traverse a thick wall that on the outside emphasizes a projection bordered by a torus, in the image of a pylon on the west and east (see diagram 2).

The foundations, the first course, and the doorways are made from quartzite that probably came from Gebel el-Ahmar near Cairo. All the rest is in ordinary sandstone from Gebel el-Silsila.

This monument is therefore composed of "beautiful white blocks of sandstone" coming from the South, placed on red stones coming from the North, and all buried in the black mud of a scaffolding of unbaked bricks.

It must again be noted that the quartzite blocks of the first course have a much more pronounced slope than the rest of the building (as is quite visible in pl. 26).

The temple of Seti II measures 7.10 meters above the level of its surrounding pavement. The

Fig. 8. Manuscript page from Notices descriptives *by Champollion the Younger (1829–30)*

central doorway measures 4.50 meters high, and the side doorways are each 3.79 meters. (Legrain)

PLATE 22 • REPOSITORY OF SETI II, SOUTH FACADE: NORTH WING OF THE FIRST PYLON

The three doorways give access to three long chambers, arranged parallel to one another with no communication between them. The west sanctuary is consecrated to Mut; it includes two niches in the back, and on its wall is the representation of the barque of Mut. The more important central sanctuary includes three niches in the back, and on its east and west walls are carved representations of the barque of Amun, on the naos of which is inscribed in anaglyph the name

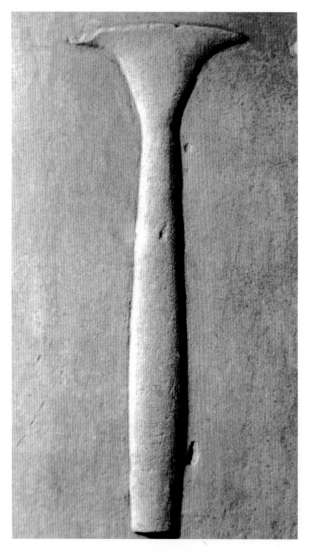

Fig. 9. Hieroglyph: wadj *symbol*

of Menmaātre (Seti I) and not Seti II (see commentaries for pls. 79–81). Finally the east sanctuary bears on its west wall the barque of Khonsu, on its north wall two niches, and on the east wall three niches and a doorway that provides access to a stairway that allows one to climb up to the roof (see diagram 2).

PLATE 23 • REPOSITORY OF SETI II, NORTH WING OF THE FIRST PYLON: THE COLONNADE OF TAHARKA

Twelve (?) columns, or rather twelve large-scale imitations of the *wadj* amulets that served as props for the sacred tokens of Amun and the king who inhabited this building, were once in the center of the large courtyard of the palace. It should in fact be noted that these constructions possess in no way the curve of a column but are lengthier and narrower below the bell of the capital....

It becomes obvious in view of this decoration that the author of the pillars is the king Taharka, who, after the expulsion of the Ethiopians under Psamtik, the first of the dynasty, has replaced the inscriptions left by the foreign king with those of the native king. However, the proper name of the former, although hammered out, is still quite visible on the second ring of the column of the first Bubastite portico. (Champollion, *Notices descriptives*, vol. 2, pp. 7–8)

There is very little to add to this description; the *wadj* symbol (fig. 9) represents a papyrus stem; it is generally used to designate a campaniform column (fig. 10). Taharka's columns are abnormally high, and the average diameter of the shaft is around one-seventh the size of the total height, whereas normally this proportion is hardly greater than one-sixth.

Legrain provides these measurements for the columns:

Diameter: 2.99 meters
Height: 21 meters, including capital, base, and dado
Width of the inner colonnade: 14 meters
Width of the outer colonnade: 20 meters

The total height with dado of one of Taharka's columns is 19.73 meters. The diameter at the curve is 2.75 meters and at the base 2.40 meters. The inter-columniation between the axes is 16.25 meters (See *Kemi* 20: 153). J. Lauffray thinks—like Champollion—that this "kiosk" is "hypaethral" (open to the sky). (Ibid., pp. 11–164) See also *Karnak*, vol. 5, p. 89.

General consensus deems that the intercolumniation (for a portico of about 17 meters between axes) is abnormally large, and is linked to Champollion's hypothesis that these columns were standard-holders.

PLATE 24 • REPOSITORY OF SETI II: NORTH FACE, EAST AREA

The posterior face of the building is adorned with two registers of tableaux representing Seti II's offerings to the Theban *neters*. On the lower register the *neters* are upright and walking; on the upper register they are seated on the cubic throne and holding the *was* scepter and the ankh (the key of life) in their hands.

The difference is clearly visible, here as in figure 7, between the first course, consisting of quartzite blocks, and the rest of the sandstone wall.

PLATE 25 • REPOSITORY OF SETI II, SOUTHERN FACE: DOORWAY TO THE CHAPEL OF KHONSU

The doorway to Khonsu's chapel, neither the lintel nor the jamb of which includes any decoration, is made of quartzite. Note the slope of the upper arris of the lintel, which climbs from west to east.

In the heart of the chapel of Khonsu are two niches that are presumed to have contained statues.

On the outside, on the sandstone partition to the right of the doorway, is a representation of Khonsu-in-Thebes-Neferhotep, Thoth who resides in Hermonthis, preceded by Amun.

PLATE 26 • REPOSITORY OF SETI II: NORTH FACE, WEST AREA

The posterior facade of the repository is divided lengthwise by a vertical column of text that corresponds to the median axis of the monument. The *neters* turn their backs from this point on, whereas the king on the left, facing west, clasps Amun-Ra

Fig. 10. Campaniform column of Taharka

Kamutef around the waist. The king on the right, turned toward the east, gives unction to his father, the ithyphallic Amun-Ra.

The northwest corner of this edifice is in rough-hewn blocks; the fourth scene over from the axis is cut in such a way by these unfinished blocks that it appears that they have been added later (fig. 7).

PLATE 27 • THE SO-CALLED MAGIC IMAGE OF AMUN, NORTH WALL OF THE FIRST COURTYARD

The pharaoh, *per-āa* (this is the name inscribed within the two cartouches), makes the libation and censes in the presence of a strange depiction: a head of Amun, wearing a mortier topped by a solar disk and two large feathers, which emerges from a goatskin bottle embraced by the extended wings of Maāt. This grouping sits on a pedestal crowned by a uraeus, in front of which is a lion whose chest comes up to the level of the shafts, which allows one to suppose that this "magic image of Amun" was paraded during processions. The whole affair rests on a see-through table behind which is an "ascending bouquet," or, more exactly, a series of lotuses, each of which is giving birth to a new lotus framed by two buds.

PLATE 28 • TAHARKA COLUMN, VESTIBULE OF THE SECOND PYLON

On the right is the south wall of the "vestibule," upon which is carved in relief the "massacre of the prisoners" in front of Amun, who is holding the scythe in his right hand and the *was* scepter in his left.

PLATE 29 • SOUTHWEST CORNER OF THE SECOND PYLON: ANTA PILLAR, BUBASTITE COLUMN

The anta pillar added above the original decoration of the second pylon has remained in an unfinished state on its southern surface and bears a depiction on the second register of its western face of Prince Osorkon I being breast-fed by Hathor.

PLATES 30–39 • GREAT HYPOSTYLE HALL: THE EXTERIOR NORTH WALL

PLATE 30–31 • GREAT HYPOSTYLE HALL: EXTERIOR NORTH FACADE, WESTERN HALF

Fig. 11. So-called magic image of Amun

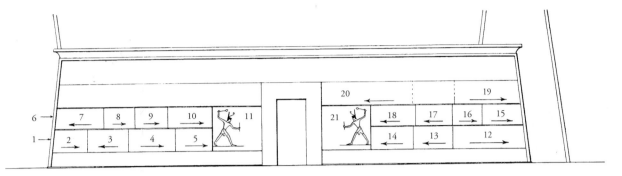

Fig. 12. Diagram of the location of the exterior north wall tableaux of the great hypostyle hall

East half:

1. The taking of the fortress of Pekanan (pls. 32 and 33)
2. The departure from Raphia for the desert road (fig. 13)
3. The Bedouins' ambush and the waterholes (fig. 13)
4. The return of Seti to the Egyptian border (figs. 15 and 19)
5. The offering of booty to Amun (fig. 19)
6. The new versions of the great chieftains of Lebanon (pl. 33 and fig. 17)
7. The capture of Yanoam (fig. 16)
8. The binding of the vanquished (fig. 18)
9. The capture of the prisoners (fig. 18)
10. The offering of booty to the Theban triad (fig. 19)
11. The ritual massacre of the vanquished

West half (overall view, pl. 30–31):

12. Archery battle against the Kheta (pl. 31)
13. The return to Egypt with the Khetan captives (pl. 34–35)
14. The offering of booty to Amun, Sekhmet-Mut, Khonsu, and Maāt (pl. 30)
15. Harpagon combat against the Libyans (pl. 37)
16. Javelin combat against the Libyans (pl. 31 and fig. 20)
17. The return with the Libyan captives (pl. 36)
18. The offering of booty to the Theban triad (pl. 30)
19. Archery combat at Kadesh, the land of Amor (pl. 37)
20. The tribute presentation to the temple (pl. 30)
21. The ritual massacre of the prisoners before Amun (pl. 30)

The tableaux here should be read starting from the northeast corner. The arrows indicate the direction the king is walking. At both ends of the partition are acts of combat; then the scenes converge toward the entranceway, indicating the return of the victorious king to the temple of Amun. On the right and left sides of this doorway, the scenes of the *massacre of the prisoners* (nos. 11 and 21) occupy the upper part of the two lower registers.

The Kheta are the Hittites that come from Turkey. Pekanan corresponds to the land of Canaan of the Bible. (See W. Helck, *Die Beziehungen Ägyptens zu Vonderasien im 3 und 2 Jahrtausend v. Chr.* [Wiesbaden, 1962])

EAST HALF

PLATE 32 • TAKING OF THE FORTRESS OF PEKANAN

PLATE 33 • TAKING OF PEKANAN: NEW VERSION OF THE LEBANESE CHIEFTAINS

I. Battle of Pekanan (plate 33, lower register, and plate 32, detail)

The text inscribed above the battle informs us:

Year 1. King of Upper and Lower Egypt, Menmare (Seti I). The destruction which the mighty sword of the Pharaoh L.P.H. made among the vanquished of the Shasu, from the Fortress of Tharu to Pekanan, when his majesty marched against them like a fierce-eyed lion, making them carcasses in their valleys, overturned in their blood like those that exist not. Everyone that escapes his fingers says: "His might toward distant countries is the might of his father Amun, who hath assigned to him a victorious valor in the countries."

Through this text it appears that this tableau sums up the entire history of battles led against the nomadic Bedouins, pillagers, rebels, the Shasu, who sowed disorder from the Egyptian frontier (Tharu) to the fort of Pekanan, which is here represented on a hill surrounded by trees.

Therefore it was at Pekanan (believed to be located in Palestine) that the decisive battle took place; above the king is the vulture Nekhebet, guardian of the South, and the guardian falcon of the North, assuring long life and protection to Seti-beloved-of-Ptah, endowed with life like the sun, the beloved of Menhit (the lion-headed goddess of war).

Standing in his chariot, Seti looses his arrows on the Bedouins, whose formations all fall in disarray. It should be noted that the representations of the vanquished avoids the *crossing* of the body without exception, and that even their limbs are only crossed on rare occasions. Among the rare fugitives who have managed to escape His Majesty's shafts, there are several who have reached the sanctuary of the fortress on the mountain. In the group of three that we see standing here (pl. 32), the first is raising his arms in a gesture of beseechment, and the man in the middle is breaking his lance as a sign of surrender. But here again, the artist's aversion to crossing is such that he has turned the iron head of the lance to the right and drawn it parallel to the arms of the man who is in front of him, in order to ensure that this iron tip doesn't pass above his body (observation of Wrezinski, *Atlas,* vol. 2, pl. 39).

From the ethnic point of view, the Shasu are characterized by thin bony faces with highly pronounced wrinkles, a vanishing forehead, a long arched nose, and a pointed beard. Their uniform consists of an apron gathered in by a belt and a long piece of cloth that they have wrapped around their chests for the battle. They are armed with spears and axes.

2. The departure from Raphia for the desert road (fig. 13)

At the foot of a hill on which sits a fortress whose name is lost but is generally presumed to be Raphia, dignitaries are presenting vessels and precious materials to the conqueror. Standing in his

chariot en route to the west, the king has turned back in a gesture of farewell toward the aediles of the city. He is named here: *Guardian King of the Black [Egypt] who causes the chiefs of Kharu [Palestine] to cease every contradiction of their mouths.*

This is the only known representation of the road across the desert.[5] Above and below the horses are mentions of fortified stations established at the waterholes indicated on the army's path. The first forts appear in the name of Menmaâtre, heir of Ra, Great from Victory, and so forth. But immediately after having breached the *sweet fountain,* the horses rear up before the fortress named Fountain of Seti-beloved-of-Ptah.

3. The Bedouins' ambush and the waterholes (fig. 13)

The Bedouins lying in ambush forced the king to turn back against them and engage them in a new battle. In this location it is the *Good God [Neternefer], Sun of Egypt [the Black], Moon of All Lands, Mentu in the foreign countries, irresistible, mighty-hearted like Baal . . . he has extended the boundaries of Egypt as far as the heavens on every side . . .* who puts the rebels to flight once more and exterminates the pillaging bands of Shasu under the protective Nekhebet that bears in its claws the symbol of the jubilee framed by the palm fronds of the years.

Under the horses' bellies are enumerated the wells and bastions that bear, most particularly in this location, the name of Seti-beloved-of-Ptah. Seti, like Baal, *neter* of war, is determined by the animal of Seth (generally hammered out in his cartouches; note the two royal names between the bow and the drawn bowstring).

Seti then passes near a spring whose name has been likened to that of the well where Hagar stopped when fleeing from Sarah. (Genesis 16:7, 14)

4. The return of Seti to the Egyptian border (fig. 15)

Once the battle was over, Seti returned to his westward march, bringing with him rows of prisoners whose hands and arms were bound in the most bizarre positions and attached to their necks by a

---

[5]This desert road is described on a papyrus by an officer surveying all the Middle Eastern regions subject to Egyptian authority. A. H. Gardiner, *Anastasi Papyrus,* 1.1.27–28. Helck, *Die Beziehungen Ägyptens,* pp. 323–27.

cord, the end of which was held by the king. Behind the royal chariot, in front of the feet of a small prince that has been almost completely destroyed, the fortress Wadjet (guardian divinity of the North) is placed near a crescent-shaped spring topped by a tree. (After the sketch by Champollion, *Notices descriptives*, vol. 2, p. 92) The next to last of the ten bastions has been compared to the Migdol of the Bible. (Exodus 14:2) Finally the king reaches the House of the Lion, the last stage of the journey before the border (the lion is the symbol of the bolt that opens and closes).

An inscription located above the king and his horses gives the reasons for this expedition in the year 1 of his reign. It is the sole inscription that is dated.

Year 1 of Uhem-mesut [renewal of birth], King of Upper and Lower Egypt, Lord of the Two Lands, Menmare, given Life.

One came to say to his majesty: "The vanquished Shasu, they plan (rebellion). Their tribal chiefs are gathered together, rising against [?] the Asians of Kharu. They have taken to cursing and quarreling, each of them slaying his neighbor, and they disregard the laws of the palace." The heart of his majesty L.P.H. was glad on account of it. Lo, as for the Good God [Neter-nefer], he rejoices to begin battle, he is delighted to enter into it, his heart is satisfied at seeing blood, he cuts off the heads of the rebellious-hearted, he loves an hour of battle more than a day of rejoicing. His majesty slays them at one time. He leaves not a limb among them, and he that escapes his hand as a living captive is carried off to Egypt.

Tharu, the Egyptian border town, is split in half by the canal that is bordered by reeds and inhabited by crocodiles, which is called the Water of the Cutting. This canal breaks off from the Nile near Daphne and flows southeast toward the lake of Talu, or Ballah, into which it spills. A bridge links the Asian side of Tharu—characterized by the cupola of its fortress—to the Egyptian side, where the constructions are in purely pharaonic style.

On the other side of the bank, the *prophets, nobles, and bureaucrats of the South and North have come to acclaim the return of the* Neter-nefer *on his return from Retenu with a great number of captives.*

The Water of the Cutting separates the disorder, expressed by the incoherent positions of the defeated prisoners who have transgressed the laws, from the respectful, orderly, and pious Egyptian dignitaries.

5. The offering of booty to Amun (fig. 19)

6. The new versions of the great chieftains of Lebanon (first tableau on the second register, pl. 33, upper register)

The king, facing south, listens to the speech of his fan bearer, who is assuring him of the surrender of the great chieftains of Retenu; *the fear is in their*

Fig. 13. Departure from Raphia for the desert road (scene 2); Bedouin ambush, waterholes (scene 3)

Fig. 14. North facade of the second pylon: outer north wall

limbs . . . it will be done according to his orders. Indeed, the great chiefs of R.mn.n (Lebanon), bowing or kneeling, are giving homage to the master of the Two Lands, whose power they exalt and whom they compare to his father Ra, the sun, the bestower of life.

(Among the numerous captives are the children of the chiefs of the foreign lands, as well. These children were reared in the pharaoh's court so that they would subsequently guide their countries' affairs in accordance with their overlord, the king of Egypt. (See A. Daumas, *La Civilisation de l'Egypte pharaonique* [Arthaud, 1965], p. 172)

In the forest are two great Lebanese chieftains chopping down a tree, whose fall is averted by ropes held by two men (fig. 17). These immense vertical trunks are destined for the construction of the *Great Barque of the River's Beginning* and the *Great masts bearing Amun's oriflammes.*

Under the horse's belly is a fortress that bears, inscribed between its two towers, the following: *City of Qadur in the Land of Hanuma,* which one assumes to be a fortified city located in the frontier mountain ranges of Lebanon.

Excavations and further exploration of various sites have gradually permitted the identification of several cities, for example: Qadur in Hanuma corresponds to Gadara or Um Queis, which is a little to the south of the Yarmuk, an eastern tributary of the Jordan River. (Helck, *Die Beziehungen Ägyptens,* p. 331)

7. The capture of Yanoam (fig. 16)

Located on a wooded hill, probably between two lakes, on one of the Lebanese watersheds, Yanoam (Tell el-Na'am, in the Sahel el-Ahma southwest of Lake Tiberias, 9 km south of Tiberias [Ibid., pp. 137–201]) plays an important role in pharaonic inscriptions. Already mentioned in the annals of Tuthmosis III among the towns conquered after his famous victory of Megiddo, Yanoam is later found in the numerous lists that enumerate the fortresses taken from the enemy. But these enumerations, which are made with no geographical order and appear as disorganized copies of older texts, have until now discouraged all efforts to situate precisely the regions cited.

Alone in his war chariot, Seti gallops into the swarming mass of the routed army composed of chariots and foot soldiers, the majority of whom have been struck by the arrows and javelins of the king. This latter is depicted in the midst of overcoming one of two chariot riders, whom he has seized by the throat and whom the artist has represented with his head completely turned around. This "drastic" figuration, when added to the extreme pains taken not to cross the bodies of those defeated or fleeing, except for limbs, has given rise to impossible positions.

The horseman, a very rare representation, is most likely a deserter on a suddenly unharnessed horse rather than the representative of a group of horsemen, since he is riding without a saddle.

Some of the fleeing soldiers, hiding behind trees and sorrowing over the fate of their companions, are represented full-faced.

Fig. 15. Return of Seti to the Egyptian frontier (scene 4)

8. The binding of the vanquished (fig. 18)

The king, on foot, is binding the vanquished by their elbows. Here he is named *Horthema, Lord . . . felling . . . his enemies.* It is therefore on the second register that we see the first appearance of the title Horthema, avenging Horus, carried by Horus in the myth when he was stabbing the Sethian animals with his spear to avenge his father Osiris, who was dismembered by Seth.

9. The capture of the prisoners and the return to Egypt (figs. 18 and 19)

The scene here merits description: the great chiefs of Retenu, bound together at the throat, wrists, or elbows, are ranked together in two rows behind the king. He is making the "great stride" in the direction of the west, but in the place of the customary symbols, he is holding four prisoners in his bent elbows, two on each side. His fists, clenched in the manner of an Osiris, are holding the harpagon (grappling iron), the whip, and the cords restraining the captives—who are called the "living ones struck down"—on the right side, and on the left side he is holding the bow and the reins of the horses, who are harnessed to the westward-facing chariot and are snorting with impatience.

10. The offering of booty to the Theban triad (fig. 19)

11. The ritual massacre of the vanquished (fig. 12)

The final scene is represented in almost identical fashion on each side of the doorway that divides these "warring" scenes into two distinct parts. We will come back to them later.

WEST HALF (PLATES 30–31, 34–35, 36 AND 37, 38 AND 39)

On the east half we have been able to establish that on the lower register the texts are almost sufficient on their own to explain the scenes represented, which gives them a credible historical character despite their problematical geographical sequencing. The nomadic Bedouins have been sowers of discord in all ages. Seti punished them, then described the route he traversed through the desert. This exceptional description can be considered historically valid, whereas on the second register the mythical character predominates, and the abnormal or impossible figurations take on a purely symbolic meaning.

On the lower register of the west half, the long texts inscribed above the king here have only remote connections with the subject depicted and simply contain a "long series of decorative names" that provide no information on the combats engaged in, which, moreover, are not dated and are arranged in an impossible geographical order. Because of this, historical interpretation is a difficult task at best.

Fig. 16. The capture of Yanoam (scene 7)

12. Archery battle against the Kheta (pl. 31, lower register, west end)

Crowned with the solar disk, the king, whose names and titles are inscribed in the open space of his bow, is standing in his war chariot in such manner that his legs appear. Seti looses his arrows on the routed army of the "vile Kheta," composed of chariots and foot soldiers, among which can be noticed some fugitives mounted on saddleless horses. This people is clearly distinguished from the Shasu,

Fig. 17. New version of the Lebanese chieftains and the chopping of the trees

Lebanese, and Palestinians represented on the east side of this partition. Probably originating from the high plateaus of Asia Minor, they had come down by means of the Taurus into northern Syria, and from the time of Tuthmosis III to Ramesses II the Egyptians fought with them without stop.

After having announced that the "vile Kheta" were reduced to dismembered corpses, a long text is introduced by the Horus name of Seti, which we see for the first time in this grouping. This is an extract of that text:

The most powerful of the powerful, like he who engendered him, illuminating the two lands like He of the horizon, great with strength like the son of Nut, victorious, the double Horus . . . strides the battlefield with great steps like the master of Ombos [Seth]. Great source of terror like Baal in all regions, uniting the Two Lands while still in the nest [sic]. His power protects the Black, Ra made his borders [tash] as far as his disk could shed light. Divine falcon with brilliant plumage, traversing the heavens like the majesty of Ra, wandering Jackal, encircling this earth at morning, Lion of the Piercing Eye, entering upon the inaccessible [shta] paths of every region. Powerful bull endowed with horns, sure of heart, who beats down the Setiu, crushes the Khetiu, massacres their chieftains, entering among them like a tongue of fire [kht] reducing them to nothingness.

PLATE 34–35 • THE RETURN OF SETI I TO EGYPT WITH THE KHETAN CAPTIVES

13. The return to Egypt with the Khetan captives

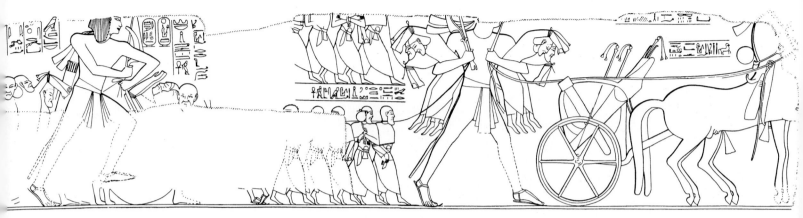

Fig. 18. The binding of the vanquished (scene 8); the capture of the prisoners (scene 9)

The king remounts his chariot, holding in his right hand the harpagon, the whip, and the reins of the horses, which have been harnessed in expectation of his departure. In his left hand he holds a bow and the ropes holding the chariots gained from his defeated enemies. The *greats of the mountains who ignored Egypt [the Black]*, arranged in two rows before him, *are brought by His Majesty as those captured alive bearing the choicest items their country has to offer.*

The text inscribed above the king repeats almost exactly what was said for the previous scene, except for the insertion of several phrases such as the following: *The archer conscious of his hand's placement, which places his glory [lit. "his souls"] like a copper mountain, which provides their noses with breath. The Retenu [Syrians] come to him, bowed down, the land of Tyhy [the Tehenu, Libyans], on their knees. Their chieftains fallen to his blade are transformed into nothingness. His bravery is among them like the fire when it destroys [?] their cities.*

(All the translations given here are taken from Wrezinski, *Atlas*, vol. 2, pls. 34–53a; and Breasted, *Ancient Records*, vol. 3, § 86–156.)

14. The offering of booty to Amun, Sekhmet-Mut (with the lion head), mistress of Asheru, Khonsu, and Maāt, daughter of Ra (pl. 30)

PLATE 36 • THE TRIUMPHAL RETURN OF SETI I WITH THE LIBYAN CAPTIVES

PLATE 37 • HARPAGON COMBAT AGAINST THE LIBYANS

15. Harpagon combat against the Libyans (pl. 37, middle register)

The king, under the name of Horthema, avenging Horus, is standing in his chariot with his left foot resting on the shaft. His left hand brandishes his harpagon, with which he threatens a Libyan chieftain, who is recognizable by the two feathers in his headdress, while the Libyans collapse in terror under his rearing horses.

16. Javelin combat against the Libyans (fig. 20 and plate 31)

Still under the name of Horthema the king is stepping upon a Libyan pinned to the ground with a spear and with one hand is restraining a chieftain of Tehenu (Libya). With his other hand he brandishes a javelin with which he is ready to strike his enemy.

Two princes were depicted on the right and the left who are presumed to have been the sons of Seti. The elder died before reigning and the second was the future Ramesses II. Their representation in this place has given rise to a historical problem by the fact that they have been reworked several times and are currently superimposed over two columns of text of which nothing remains but the words *like Ra* on the prince on the left (Ramesses).

17. The return with the Libyan captives (pl. 36)

Preceded by two rows of captive Libyans with bound arms, the standing king, reins in hand, conducts his victory chariot adorned with the heads of his victims. *He has forced them to cease standing upright on the plains, they are incapable of lifting their bows, they spend their days in caves, hidden like wolves.*

Fig. 19. Overview of the east part of the north wall of the great hypostyle hall

18. The offering of booty to the Theban triad (pl. 30)

19. The battle of Kadesh, the land of Amor (pl. 37, upper register)

Between the two towers of the fortress located on a hillside surrounded by various plants is the inscription: *land of Kadesh, land of Amor*. This should be distinguished from the famous Kadesh that is located on the Orontes, which is so often represented under Ramesses II and is always depicted in the loop of a river. [The following note that the author added later suggests second thoughts about this assertion. —Trans.] Despite the ethnic appearance of the combatants and the unusual representation of this fortress on a wooded hill, its mention in conjunction with the land of Amor suggests comparison with the Kadesh of the Orontes. (See also A. H. Gardiner, *Onom*, vol. 1, p. 140; and Helck, *Die Beziehungen Ägyptens*, p. 293)

At the foot of the hill a fleeing ox drover is pushing three buffalo with accented humped backs before him and begging for mercy. Seti's team of horses, at a full gallop, is rearing up before the enemy army composed of chariotry and foot soldiers in long robes with daggers in their belts.

All the combatants are transfixed by arrows or javelins, which are ordinarily kept in the pockets of the king's war chariot. They are all bearded, which distinguishes them from the beardless Kheta of the lower register, with their hair held by a band or clad in ovoid helmets that are reminiscent of the combatants of Yanoam.

20. The tribute presentation to the temple (pl. 30)

The several remaining vestiges of the final tableau of the third register show that it represented the offering of the vanquished by the king on foot, who is presenting himself before the pylon that is adorned with two times four masts.

21. The ritual massacre of the prisoners (pl. 30)

The final scene is represented once on each side of the doorway. Wearing the red crown of the North, the king is holding a dozen prisoners tied together by their hair with his right hand while he brandishes the white *hedj* club with his left. In front of him, Amun presents the harpagon in his right hand and with his left holds the key of life and the bonds of the prisoners with the escutcheons representing the conquered towns.

Is this "massacre of the prisoners" we encounter a ritual gesture that we also find in the consecration of "chests of cloths" as well as in that concerning already dead animals offered in the Holy of Holies during the conquest of the Eye of Horus, the ultimate goal of a religious service?

The words spoken by Amun are presented like a hymn:

O my son of my body . . .

I bring to thee the chiefs of the southern countries . . .

(I turn) my face to the north, I work a wonder (for thee), snaring the rebels in their nests . . .

I turn my face to the east, I work a wonder for thee, I bind them all for thee, gathered in thy grasp . . .

I turn my face to the west, I work a wonder for thee, consuming for thee every land of Tehenu . . .

I turn my face to heaven, I work a wonder for thee . . . the gods of the horizon of heaven acclaim to thee when Ra is born every morning . . .

I turn my face to the earth, (I work a wonder for thee, I appoint for thee victories in every country).

(Breasted, *Ancient Records*, vol. 3, § 116)

The enumeration of the conquered towns is, according to historians, "so jumbled up" that no historical conclusions can be drawn from it.

Fig. 20. Javelin combat against the Libyans (scene 16)

Fig. 21. Bas-relief of Sekhemkhet; Wadi Maghara

Here the *ka* placed behind the king is said to preside over the room of the *per-dwat*, in which the king must receive the baptism of life before being able to enter the sanctuaries. It certainly concerns a sacrifice that must be performed before entering the temple to officiate as priest-king.

One of the most ancient examples known of this "massacre of the prisoners" is carved 394 feet above the turquoise mines of Wadi Maghara, in the Sinai. Here the white-crowned king brandishes a club with which he threatens the Bedouin chief whom he has seized by the hair. This latter, who is kneeling, holds a feather in his hand that identifies him as a Libyan (fig. 21).

PLATE 38 • GREAT HYPOSTYLE HALL: NORTH ENTRANCE DOORWAY, WEST JAMB

On the upper register the king has removed his warrior attributes and is clad in a triangular apron and wears a diadem on his forehead. He is offering the sacred lettuce to Amun-Ra, the ithyphallic prince of Thebes (or *ferment* of *was.t*), who is followed by Isis, the great mistress of Heaven, the queen of the *neters*.

On the lower register the king, clad in a long linen robe, presents bouquets of lotus flowers to Amun, who is up and walking, followed by Ptah, swaddled in his naos. These tableaux are in sunk relief and done in the name of Ramesses II.

PLATE 39 • GREAT HYPOSTYLE HALL: EMBRASURE OF THE NORTH DOORWAY

The king wearing a blue helmet is going through the entrance door with the key of life in his left hand. With the right hand extended toward Amun, he *Gives the House to Its master*, as is described in the inscription to the left of the *was* scepter held by Amun.

The sculptures in relief have been reworked on several occasions, especially the king's legs (see pl. 47 for an analysis of a transformed figure).

PLATES 40–87 • GREAT HYPOSTYLE HALL

We are now entering the great hypostyle hall, which is considered one of the "Wonders of the World." It is bordered on the east by the third pylon,

erected by Amenhotep III, and on the west by the second pylon, which dates from the time of Horemheb or Ramesses I.

But during a period preceding the Ramesside era, this part of the temple didn't look like this. Architectural proofs indeed show that this room was originally conceived as a long "nave." Between the two pylons twelve campaniform columns were raised, perhaps by Amenhotep III or at the latest Horemheb. This room was then bordered on the north and south by two walls whose foundations have been rediscovered. At the beginning of the Nineteenth Dynasty the two walls of the original nave were removed, and on their foundations a front row of seven monostyle columns with closed buds

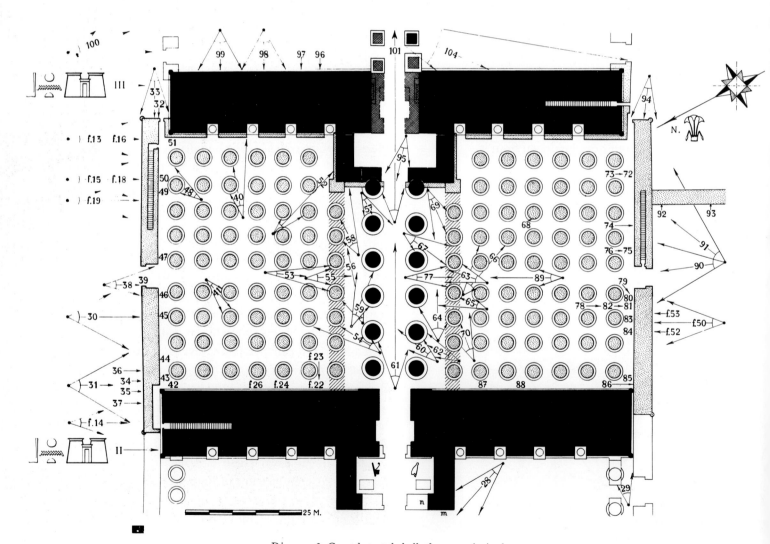

Diagram 3. Great hypostyle hall: the two principal stages

were erected. These were lower than those of the central bay. The hypostyle hall was then enlarged, and in order to support its roof 122 columns of this same type and size were constructed (see diagram 3).

This new room, which now measures about 52 meters by 101 meters, is closed at the north and south by two walls that, instead of taking support from the second and third pylons, embox these latter structures. This "boxing" or enclosing is characteristic of the constructions in the great temple of Karnak.

PLATE 40 • GREAT HYPOSTYLE HALL, EASTERN INTERIOR WALL: COLUMNS OF THE NORTHEAST SECTION

When the hypostyle hall was "closed," the west facade of the third pylon was re-covered by a vertical wall that corrected its slope but respected the grooves cut for holding the masts and maybe even these latter items as well. Five registers of tableaux, sculpted in relief under Seti I, are on this wall, where they are surmounted by a frieze of *khakeru* that represents the different phases of the Ritual of the Daily Divine Worship.

For example, on the lower register the king breaks the clay seals, draws back the bolt, then opens *the two sections of the door to heaven.*

On the second register, the kneeling king, after having "made the fire" (pl. 51), then the ritual censing, libation, and offerings, presents two torches to Amun (pl. 40); here he is said to *fill the dwelling.*

On the third register we see Seti, still kneeling, holding a torch before the generating Amun: *he lights with fire the first day of the year.*

On the fourth register the kneeling king, with a key of life in his hand, presents a list of offerings that are comparable to the Eye of Horus.

On the fifth register Seti kneels before Amun, who holds a rope rolled up like the hieroglyphic *h;* the caption says *he activates his fire.*[6]

[6]Listed from bottom to top:
Second register: Chapter on the lighting of the temple.
Third register: Chapter on the New Year's Day torch.
Fifth register: Chapter on the extinguishing of the torch. (Barguet, *La Structure du Temple Ipet-sout d'Amon à Karnak,* p. 75)

In front are two of the monostyle columns that were not originally decorated except by a ring of tableaux on the shaft and a frieze composed of two alternating cartouches of Seti I on the upper portion of the capital under the abacus. All the incised carvings are of later date (see also pls. 52–71, detail of the columns, fig. 43, and notes to pl. 69).

PLATE 41 • COLUMNS OF THE NORTHEAST SECTION

Fig. 22. Royal ascent of Seti I toward Amun-Ra (photo Banville 1864)

The tableau sculpted on the column in the foreground represents the king holding a vessel in the shape of the key of life in his hand and "making the offering" in the presence of Amun, *master of the thrones of all lands, master of Heaven,* who gives him *the Nine Bows joined under his sandals.*

PLATE 42 • NORTH EDGE OF THE WEST WALL, TORUS OF THE SECOND PYLON: TRANSFORMED BAS-RELIEFS

The west wall of the hypostyle hall consists of the interior eastern facade of the second pylon. Its northern section is divided into two essential parts:

1. The space included between the central doorway and the north face of the architraves of the second row of monostyle columns is occupied

> by an immense tableau whose figures are more than twenty feet high, sculpted in a very beautiful style of relief.
>
> Amun-Ra is seated on his throne; standing behind the god is the goddess Mut, who is ordinarily enfeoffed with him. A second enfeoffed goddess [out of whose horns the solar disk emerges] holds a [sistrum] and flowers in her right hand raised before Amun-Ra; with the left hand she holds the hand of the pharaoh with a scratched-out figure of enfeoffment, who is holding [the *hek* scepter and the *nekhakha* scepter] on his shoulder and is bowing as he approaches Amun-Ra . . . [fig. 22].
>
> Behind the king, the god [Khonsu] is standing, disk and crescent, the enfeoffment of the prince, necklace, body clad in a girdle, the one hand holding a panegyric scepter, the other designating a notch with the gnomon. He is performing the duties of Thoth here, for whom he is the prototype. (Champollion, *Notices descriptives*, vol. 2, pp. 45–46)

(See pl. 87, the scene in the southern section that is the counterpart to this one, in which Thoth takes the place of Khonsu.)

Above the face of Seti I, which bears the marks of three successive reworkings, is a great disk carved in sunk relief belonging to a previous decoration. Legrain, who observed "a large frieze of uraei similar to those that are normally depicted above the daises on which the barques sit in their repositories" above the architraves, presumes that this disk could be one of those that topped the heads of the rams adorning the prow and the stern of the barque of Amun.

Now this disk circumscribes the cartouche of Menmaätre and the name of Amun in such a way that it cuts the cartouche containing the name of Seti.

2. Starting from this colossal tableau, the height of the wall is actually divided into four registers of ritual scenes that preserve numerous traces of earlier reliefs that likely date from the time when the wings of the pylons were outside the monument and the hypostyle hall was no more than the central bay.

The principal scene in the original decoration occupied the entire length of the north wing and was as tall as the current second and third registers or more, probably even a portion of the fourth.

In the first scene of the fourth register, representing Ramesses I offering fire and water to Mentu, Tum, Shu, Tefnut, Geb, Nut, Osiris, and Isis, the sky cuts the figures of the previous decoration down to the waist. (See K. C. Seele, *The Coregency of Ramses II with Seti I and the Date of the Great Hypostyle Hall at Karnak* [Chicago, 1940])

The original scene, very similar to the representations of the east facade of the third pylon (pls. 96–99), represented Amun's great barque, Userhat, towed by another gigantic barque propelled by oars, heading toward the central doorway and the south—toward Luxor.

The arrangement of the tableaux was entirely modified at the time of the enlargement of the hypostyle hall; the colossal barque Userhat was replaced by a smaller one that was no longer towed by oarsmen but by the king and three *neters*. "The Userhat was towed by a fairy barque that moved forward by itself over the waters of the Nile. No mast, no sail, no oars nor oarsmen. Only the rudder oars that no pilot steered could be seen on the prow." (Legrain, *Les Templès de Karnak*, p. 196)

These barques retain traces of the oars of the previous barque.

Champollion describes the two barques of Seti I thus:

> A *bari* or barque. On the prow three standards are fixed [the Upwat, the falcon, the royal cartouche].

On the *bari* following, Upper Egypt, supplicating hands extend from the side of the prow *[sic]*. Four figures are pulling an immense *bari* with a rope behind the first barque. The head of the first towing figure is broken. He was jackal-headed [Upwat]. The second is the king Meneptah I in normal attire, the third is ram-headed, the fourth is falcon-headed.

"A fragment of text that is located in front of the god Aupuaitu in the towing barque indicates that it and the barque of Amun are going to Apitu of the South, that is, the temple of Luxor. That is why they are represented with their prows pointing south." (Legrain, *Les Temples de Karnak*, p. 194)

Next comes the great *bari* of Ammon-Ra; on the prow and on the stern [a ram's head bears the *atef* crown flanked by two uraei on the horns of Khnum]. In the middle stands a kind of temple or palace supported by two columns. Above the cornice is the anaglyph of the king's given name, which is repeated without variation for the entire length of this cornice. This palace contains a naos, a cornice crowned by a uraeus with a disk, a frieze [Isis knots and *djed* pillars] in which the *bari* of the god sits on a pedestal with the customary adornments. On the door or veil that closes the *kibotos* can be seen the anaglyph of the king's given name overshadowed by cherubs.

Behind the great *kibotos* [the palace] on the stern, the *bari* of Khons and that of Muth (destroyed) . . .

The great *kibotos* or palace, which encloses all the rest, is preceded by

1. masts of rejoicing *(a* and *b)* with floating streamers. The masts are attached to the frieze of the column *g;*

2. two obelisks *c* and *d;*

3. finally, four pseudo–lotus-flower columns *(e, f, g, h)* crowned with the king's inscription in alternation with sparrow hawks.

This explains the twelve *[sic]* columns in front of the second pylon, in the center of the first courtyard of this palace.

In front of the pseudo-columns:

1. On a small pedestal with an altar and

Fig. 23. Face of Seti I reworked three times

offerings is the small *bari*, covered by a veil of the queen [Ahmose-Nefertari];[7]

2. the king [Seti Meryenptah] wearing a helmet, throwing grains of incense into the Amschir;

3. a sphinx on a standard, enfeoffed with Sokaris, with tail turned up;

4. a goddess mother and Thmeï standing on the prow. Four jackal-headed figures make [*henu*] before the great *kibotos*. (Champollion, *Notices descriptives*, vol. 2, pp. 50–52. We have put the transcriptions

---

[7]Let us note that the queen Ahmose-Nefertari, wife of Ahmose (birth of the moon), first king of the Eighteenth Dynasty, is worshiped as a divinity. She represents the black feminine principle (which is reminiscent of the "black virgin" that is found in other cults); also, she is often represented with black skin and face even though as a "queen" she was of pure Egyptian blood and not of Negro descent.

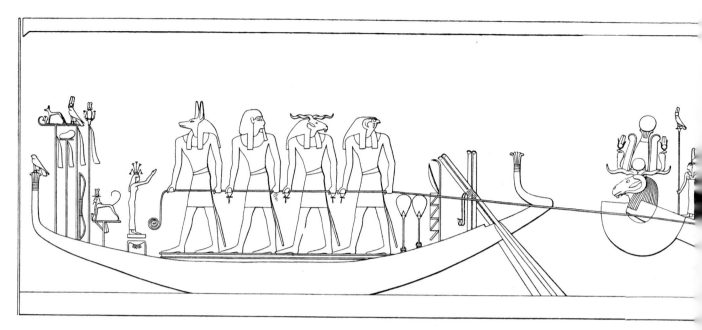

Fig. 24. The King and the neters *towing the barque Userhat of Amun (restored)*

of the hieroglyphic groups or original sketches in brackets.) (Figs. 24 and 26a.)

The *"bari"* of Amun described here is similar to that which originally occupied almost the entire north part of this wing of the pylon. At the time the transformations of this room took place, Seti I had his tableaux carved in such a way that the current

image of Amun seated upon his throne followed by Hathor (pl. 42) projects exactly onto the head of the ram wearing the *atef* crown that adorns the prow of the barque Userhat (fig. 26b and general diagram fig. 25).

PLATE 43 • NORTH WALL, WESTERN EDGE: THE KING KNEELING BEFORE MENTU

Fig. 25. Superimposition of the barques of Seti I (in black) over the previous bas-reliefs

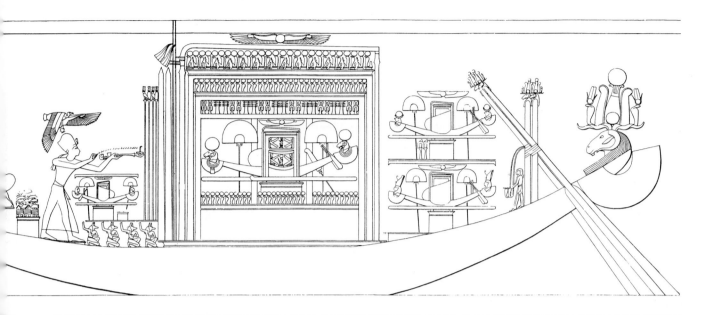

Fig. 26a. The barque Userhat of Amun (restored)

In the second register on the western end of the north wall, the king, on his knees and wearing a blue *khepresh* helmet, is offering to Mentu, who is in the heart of Thebes, three papyrus stems with his right hand, and with his left a bouquet of lotuses in bud and flower whose stems he keeps rolled up. Mentu is standing and holds the *was* scepter with his right hand and the ankh in his left.

The prow of the barque of Khonsu, adorned with the falcon head crowned by the disk in the crescent, can still be seen on the lower register; the rest of the barque has been hammered out. The barque of Mut is located below. On the right the upper corner of the naos crowned by a uraeus with disks contains the barque of Amun. We find here the same arrangement of barques as on the great *bari* (fig. 26a).

PLATE 44 • NORTH WALL: THE KING KNEELING BEFORE AMUN

The completion of the preceding tableau (pl. 43) can be seen behind the column in the foreground, then the king, overshadowed by the vulture Nekhebet, kneeling before Amun, to whom he is offering breads, plucked and trussed geese, and a bouquet of lotus buds and flowers on a platter. Amun gives him *all life, stability, strength, and all enlargement of the heart, as Ra.*

In the lower register is the upper part of a naos in which the sacred barque of Amun rests; this barque itself contains a small tabernacle.

(The lower part of this tableau is unfortunately in a very poor state.)

PLATE 45 • NORTH WALL: NAOS OF THE BARQUE OF AMUN CARRIED BY PRIESTS

The sacred barque of Amun is on the lower register of the north wall, followed by the two barques

Fig. 26b. Superimposition of Amun-Ra and the ram's head

of Khonsu and Mut. It is carried by the priests, who are heading east—toward the open north doorway. We see here the naos in detail, which is very suggestive of its contents:

Above: Amun-Ra, with a ram's head wearing the *atef* crown, rests on a lotus and is overshadowed by the wings of the two upright *neters* crowned with disks and holding in their hands the feather of Maāt and an ankh.

Below: A falcon-headed Ra crowned by a solar disk is seated on the *men* symbol and is holding a Maāt feather in his hand. This figure is the anaglyph of Seti I's royal given name, Menmaātre, which can be found repeated on the frieze above the naos. A female divinity (Maāt) with outstretched wings and crowned with disks kneels on either side of Ra on the *men* symbol. These divinities hold the ankh in one hand and a *djed* in the other, from which the ankh, then the *was,* is emerging, which signifies stability, life, and power.

Fig. 27. Seti I offers milk from the stables of Amun

In the front of the naos a wind-swollen sail is richly adorned by a frieze of anaglyphs, above which the white-crowned king offers Maāt, who is Justice; behind him, Maāt herself is kneeling on the *men* symbol; the feather she wears on her head is topped by the solar disk. This is another anaglyphical form of Menmaātre (fig. 29).

This symbolization of the royal name by mythical characters emphasizes the mystical nature of certain royal names.

PLATE 46 • NORTH WALL, WEST SIDE: SETI I OFFERING A PAPYRUS BOUQUET

Turned toward the west, the king is bowing while offering a lotus and papyrus bouquet. He wears a wig that is finely carved with lines radiating from the crown of his head and ending in curls. Two long, folded ribbons extend from the nape of his neck. The *user* necklace, composed of seven rows of semiprecious stones—lapis lazuli, carnelian, turquoise—and a row of pearls, separated by gold wire, covers a portion of his shoulders.

Note the Sethian animal used to write the name of Seti in the second cartouche, located above the king and after the name of Horus and the cartouche of Menmaātre.

PLATE 47 • NORTH WALL, EAST SIDE: THE KING "GIVING THE HOUSE TO ITS MASTER"

On the panel of the north doorway, the king is allegedly entering the temple and is heading east, that is, toward the sanctuaries. His first gesture here is to "Give the House to Its Master," as is said by the text inscribed under his right hand. The "house"— that is, the temple—is depicted by the sanctuary, above which he is holding an ankh in his left hand.

Amun-Ra, master of the thrones of the Two Lands, presiding in Ipet-sut (the name of the temple of Karnak), gives him all life, stability, power, and the assurance of *numerous years of Tum, as Ra.*

The royal figure has been modified three times. In the original figuration, the bearded king stands upright and his *nemes* headdress allows his ear to be seen; in the next figuration he is bowing, his beard has been removed, and the new headdress (similar to that of pl. 46) hides his ear. However, the ear of the original figuration remains visible behind his head, on the level of the cerebellum. Now, in the pharaonic canon the axis of equilibrium always passes tangentially to the front side of the ear.

E. Mackay, in "Proportion Squares on Tomb Walls in the Theban Necropolis" (*Journal of Egyptian Archaeology* 4 [1917]: 77), observes that in the Egyptian proportion squares a vertical line passes in front of the ear and the back knee and ends on the baseline at a point located at the first third of the back foot. Another important vertical line, immediately in front of the previous one, passes through the center of the iris of the eye and ends at the big toe of the back foot. When only one vertical line is drawn (for example, in the tomb of Perneb in Saqqara, Fifth Dynasty), it is the line that passes in front of the ear that is marked.

When the king wears the *nemes* headdress, this line coincides with the front edge of this headdress.

The transformation of this bas-relief would indicate a bowing movement (fig. 28). The ancient royal figure wore the *nemes* headdress, and the bowing king wears the curly-haired wig that is depicted in plate 46.

PLATE 48 • GREAT HYPOSTYLE HALL, MONOSTYLE COLUMN: BAS-RELIEFS FROM THE NORTHEAST SIDE

A vertical line on the monostyle column in the foreground separates two tableaux and marks the directional change of the *neters* represented: on the left Mut, lady of the Asheru, is sculpted in relief and is heading left, whereas on the right, Isis, the great mother, is carved in sunk relief, the same as the ithyphallic Amun that precedes her. This *neter*, with the swaddled body and one arm raising the *nekhakha* scepter, wears the headdress most often encountered, the mortier crowned by two long feathers that penetrate the heavens.

The seventh tableau over from the doorway can be seen on the second register on the bottom of the north wall. Here Amun-Ra Kamutef, prince (leaven) of the Great Ennead of the *neters*, wears a more particular headdress. His head is molded into a tight sheath above which can be seen the traces of two long feathers in very light relief that don't reach the heavens (see pls. 317 and 318 for more depictions of this headdress). His forehead is girded with a band that is extended in the back by a vertical stem that goes down to the pedestal.

More to the right, before the name of Horus of Seti supported by the *ka*, the kneeling king holds a basket of offerings above his head.

PLATE 49 • NORTH WALL, EAST SIDE: SETI I IN THE PERSEA TREE

This is the fourth tableau from the doorway on the second register. On his knees before the persea tree, the king, wearing a blue helmet, holds the *hek* scepter over his shoulder with his right hand and with his left holds one of the stylized fruits on which Thoth has just engraved his mystical name.

Fig. 28. Modified bas-relief

The ibis-headed Thoth has written with his gnomon the name of Menmaātre and is holding a shell in his left hand.

This king bears the traces of several reworkings in succession. Originally he was larger and wore a loincloth, the point of which touched his left elbow.

Above the tree (fig. 30), the anaglyph of the king is composed of the symbols for Maāt and *men,* crowned by thé solar disk Ra, from which are suspended two crowned uraei.

PLATE 50 • SETI I KNEELING BEFORE RA IN HIS NAOS, FOLLOWED BY SEKHMET HOLDING THE PALM OF THE YEARS

This tableau is the sequel to the previous one (see fig. 30). The kneeling king with his right leg stretched behind in the position of the "silver statue," which is very specific to Karnak, is bowing before Ra seated in his naos.

He is wearing a headband and the *atef* crown, which rests on the horns of Khnum and is flanked by two uraei on disks. He is holding the royal *hek* and *nekhakha* scepters in his right hand, and with his left he supports the symbols of the *sed* festival and longevity that are attached to the upper curved portion of the "palm of the years" that Ra holds with the *was* in his right hand, while his left hand grazes the front horn of the king's crown.

Behind Seti, lion-headed Sekhmet, named here "the great magician," raises her left hand in a gesture of benediction above the back horn and with her other hand holds the palm of the years, from which are hanging the same symbols. This palm is always terminated on its lower end by a "tadpole sitting on the *chen* buckle."

In one of the royal cartouches the Maāt of the name Menmaātre is surrounded by the *hek* and the *was* symbols, which are translated as the prince of Thebes.

Fig. 29. Detail of the sail on the sacred barque of Amun

Fig. 30. Overall view of plates 49 and 50

PLATE 51 • EAST WALL, NORTH END: SCENE OF LEAVING THE SANCTUARY

In the northeast corner of the hypostyle hall, on the upper register, the king, wearing a headband, a long, pleated linen robe, and a large scarf, is holding a key-of-life–shaped vessel in his right hand and a bundle of tied straws in his left, with which he is erasing the marks of his footprints while turning his back to the *neter*. The text of this tableau is lost, but its explanation can be discovered in the temple of Abydos and the Berlin Papyrus, which in sixty-six chapters describes the Ritual of the Daily Divine Worship.

The Royal Principle is always represented as officiating in the temple bas-reliefs, whereas in fact the ritual was performed by the *priest on his day*—for whom the name *wab* signifies pure—who is identified as the king. The statue of the *neter* is supposed to renew the Osirian passion each night. In the morning, the officiating priest, purified in mind and body, after having made his ablutions, starts with the purification by fire, which is a metaphor for the Eye of Horus, whose objective is driving back the power of Seth and annihilating the adversaries of the *neter*, as is done by the rising sun. On the bottom register of plate 51, to the left of Amun-Ra Kamutef, we find a text inscribed in five vertical columns, the first of which is entitled "Chapter on Making the Fire Each Day."

With respect to this the text includes a play on words between *tka*, the fire, and the *ka* of Amun-Ra.

After having *made the fire* (which, according to the inscription of Siut, was renewed on the day and night of the New Year), the priest-king proceeded to open the naos, which had been sealed for the night, and there perform all the gestures of the complete ritual.

Once the first part of the sacred ceremony is ended—the service is repeated twice—the officiating priest leaves the sanctuary while speaking the words, "I have left, with your great face behind me," which is all the Berlin Papyrus says.

The texts of Abydos, illustrated with figurations that are analogous to the ones we are looking at here, are more explicit:

Chapter of Retreating with the Papyrus Strip [hadn] into the Sanctuary of neter Ani. Thoth has arrived after having delivered the Eye of Horus from the hands of his adversaries. No male or female demon may enter this temple. It is Ptah who draws the door shut, it is Thoth who consolidates it. The door is consolidated with the bolt by the king Menmaātre. To be said four times. (A. Moret, *Rituel du divin culte journalier*, p. 103)

"To be said four times" means to be said toward the four directions.

Note the ankh-shaped vessel in the right hand of the king; his beak is a feather and only the front part is sculpted. He is cut in half, which signifies that only half of the worship ceremony has been completed.

Plate 52 • Vestibule of the Third Pylon, North Face

The "vestibule" that precedes the third pylon is currently almost totally destroyed. Nothing remains but the casing, which was erected during the modification of the hypostyle hall's layout (see diagram 3).

The tableaux on this casing are in flat relief in the name of Seti I, as on all the partitions of the north half of the hypostyle hall that we have just visited (pls. 40–51).

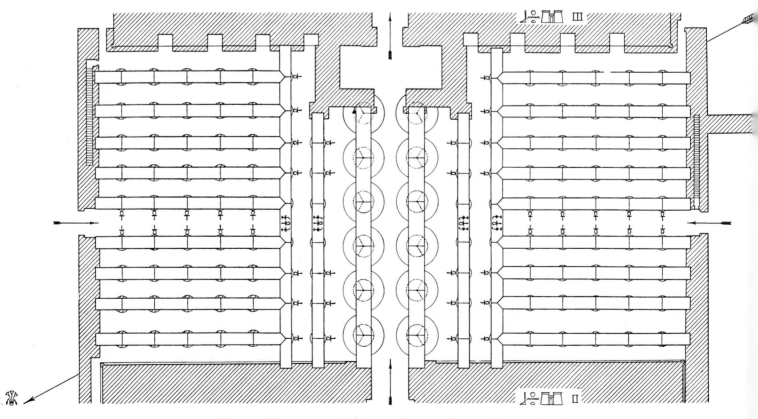

Diagram 4. Great hypostyle hall, the architraves: direction of the royal march

PLATES 53–71 • COLUMNS OF THE GREAT HYPOSTYLE HALL

The general layout of the great hypostyle hall includes four groups of columns, separated by the central "nave," which is oriented to the longitudinal axis of the temple, and by a transverse path perpendicular to this axis. The original layout, as has already been said, included only twelve columns in the nave (pl. 61 and diagrams 3 and 4), which measure about 21 meters high under the architrave and are recognizable by their capitals of blossoming papyrus flowers (pl. 53, in the background, and fig. 34).

The monostyle columns that were subsequently added are of the closed-bud style and their height is only around 13 meters under the architrave, so that the ceiling of the room has two levels. That of the central nave is 22.41 meters from the ground, and that of the lower sides is 14.74 meters (measurements taken by Legrain).

The two front rows of seven columns each support an architrave topped by a cornice above which are windows (or claustra) that correspond to each of the intercolumniations and reach again the height of the nave, contributing to the lighting of this room (pls. 53, 55, and 57, and fig. 35).

PLATE 53 • THE NORTH-SOUTH TRANSVERSE ROUTE OF THE COLONNADE

We can see one of the monostyle columns in the right foreground and in the background two large campaniform columns. Now, in addition to the general arrangement, there are quite a few nuances to be observed.

First there is the ankh symbol, framed by the bulrush of the South and the bee of the North, carved on the inside surface of the architrave located under the central window, which marks the axis of the transverse way (pls. 53, 56, and 89, and figs. 33, 35, and 38).

Then there is the ring encircling the base of the monostyle column (on the right); Ramesses II carved his cartouches in horizontal sunk relief in such a way that the figures and symbols are heading toward the ankh, which plays the role of an axis, perpendicular to the architraves (diagram 4, fig. 31, and pl. 40).

Next are the two bands of inscriptions, surrounding the shaft above the tableaux and under the base of the capital, of the horizontally placed cartouches of Ramesses IV, which are oriented in the same manner as the above (pls. 40, 52, 53, and 54, and fig. 33).

Finally, *neters* can be seen walking in both directions on the first campaniform column on the right, on both sides of a slender arris that extends the total height of the shaft. On one side Amun, followed by Khonsu, is heading toward the right; on the other side Mut is going in the opposite direction. This concerns one of the characteristics of these large columns: the shaft, which resembles a papyrus stalk, has three moldings that divide its cross-section into

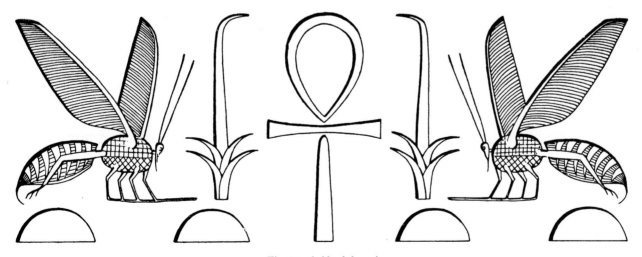

Fig. 31. Ankh of the axis

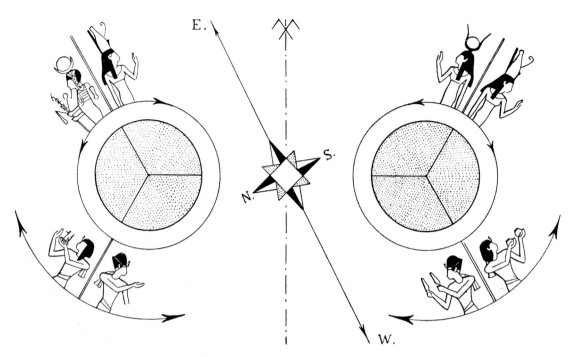

Fig. 32. The changing of the direction of the procession of the neters *and the king*

three sections of 120° that each correspond to one of the three tableaux represented on the periphery of the shaft. On all the tableaux of all the columns, the king is walking east toward the meeting with the *neters,* who are walking in the opposite direction.

Knowing that in certain temples the arrises of campaniform columns indicate a definite orientation, it is interesting to observe the following facts in Karnak: the general axis of the temple is around 27° north of the true east-west line; it so happens that one of the arrises of the campaniform columns is perpendicular to this axis, the axis of the changing direction of the *neters* is on the true east-west line (almost exactly 3°), on the east arris for the north colonnade. The directional change for the king is theoretically on the same true east-west line for the south colonnade, but on the western arris at almost exactly 3°.

PLATE 54 • THE FIRST TWO NORTH BAYS OF THE NORTHWEST GROUP OF MONOSTYLE COLUMNS

The columns of the first bay, surmounted by a torus and a cornice, bear on their abaci the cartouches of Ramesses II in sunk relief; the architrave is also carved in this fashion, but the upper portions of the capitals show signs of reworkings.

The inscriptions on the architrave, the abacus, and the top of the capital of the second row are in the name of Seti I, in light relief. Moreover, the six rows of columns carry the legends of Seti I, all in relief.

The sunk-relief inscriptions that were added to the base of the capitals and the top of the shaft are in the name of Ramesses IV (pl. 63 and fig. 33).

PLATE 55 • WINDOW OF THE FIRST SOUTH BAY AND CAMPANIFORM COLUMNS

The central window is formed by two enormous stones that each have twelve bars, "a renovation, giving passage to the light" (figs. 35 and 36).

The architrave of the campaniform columns of the row south of the nave bear two lines of inscriptions in relief dating from Seti I, whose cartouche has, however, been changed by Ramesses II. On the lower line he has inscribed the dedication of this part of the temple: *He has made a splendid sanctuary [akh] Ramesses Meryamun in the house of Amun before Ipet-sut.* This inscription is of major importance because it allows the hypostyle hall to be considered as existing previous to Ipet-sut, that is, the temple itself, properly speaking, for which the real entrance is located at the fourth pylon.

PLATE 56 • FIRST NORTH LATERAL AVENUE AND HATSHEPSUT'S OBELISK

On the left are four of the seven monostyle columns of the first north row that support the entablature and the windows. Note the cornice in the northeast corner, which turns at a right angle "enveloping" the greatly ruined original vestibule, which permits the obelisk of Hatshepsut to be seen in the background.

PLATE 57 • CENTRAL WINDOW SEEN FROM THE NORTHEAST, CAMPANIFORM COLUMNS

The lighting of the papyriform columns of the north row in the foreground demonstrates in striking fashion the characteristic moldings of these large columns, which separate Maāt (on the right) from Mut (on the left) and extend below the tableau on the lower rings, thus marking the change of the *neters'* direction to the east (see fig. 32 and note to pl. 53).

Fig. 33. The ankh of the axis of the north-south transverse way

In the background is the central window, recessed above the cornice of the first north bay. This cornice is formed from triglyphs separated by cartouches of Ramesses II in sunk relief and retains traces of color: alternating blue, red, and green on a yellow background (fig. 36).

PLATE 58 • NORTH AISLE, NORTHEAST CORNER: DETAIL

While the royal figures on these shafts are proceeding in the direction of the rising sun, that is to say, toward the sanctuary (pl. 56), those on the northeast corner have their faces turned toward the south and toward the *neters*.

Amun is seated on a throne that is carved in relief quite high up beneath the torus, while on the lower registers the tableaux are in sunk relief in the name of Ramesses II. Going from top to bottom, the first represents the king on his knees before Ptah, the second depicts the offering of the *medjet* paint to Thoth, and the third is of the offering of the white vessel to Amun (fig. 37).

Fig. 34. Campaniform capital of the north row

On the second tableau the king, his fist clenched with the little finger (consecrated to Mercury-Thoth) extended, is making the gesture of unction with the *medjet* unguent toward Thoth, master of the city of the Eight (that is, the eight primordial *neters*). His gesture is explained by the fact that the officiating priest always puts on a silver or gold fingerstall to anoint the sacred statue. This part of the Ritual of the Daily Divine Worship is extremely important.

The priest-king, after having entered the sanctuary, purifies it with incense, breaks the seal of sigillary earth sealing the doors of the naos, and uncovers the face of the *neter* by uttering the sanctioned words each time and making the *medjet* unguent offering. Let us recall that the *neter* is supposed to undergo the dismemberment of his body every night, in the image of Osiris dismembered by Seth. The unction on the forehead with the *medjet* paint *emerges from the Eye of Horus, puts his bones back in place, rejoins his limbs, reassembles his flesh, drives off the evil influences of Seth, and, subsequently, destroys all those who are in his retinue.* (Berlin Papyrus, chaps. 54–55)

The daily resurrection mirrors the annual cyclical resurrection. Osiris is the principle of nature's constant renewal, and reincarnations can occur only with the destruction of the mortal form (Seth). This resurrection or reanimation of the new form can be achieved only by the reconquest of the Eye of Horus (the living soul) imprisoned by Seth.

Crossing points of the hypostyle hall (fig. 36):

Above the first row of each quincunx of small columns extends a cornice that goes lengthwise in front of each row of large columns, which is formed of triglyphs separated by cartouches of Ramesses the Great in sunk relief (blue-red-green on yellow background).

And above this cornice, but recessed, are great pillars joined by an architrave that forms the crossing points of the hypostyle hall, formed by two enormous stones (*a* and *b*) that were cut with twelve bars to give passage to the light. On the pillars or jambs *A* are the tableaux of adoration of Ramesses the Great and this king welcoming and receiving life or gifts from Amun-Ra.

On the architraves or bands of cross points
B is the directory legend of the hypostyle hall.
(Champollion, *Notices descriptives*, vol. 2, p. 85)

PLATE 59 • GRAND NORTH COLONNADE, EAST END

This view is taken from the west. The viewer can also see the characteristic molding of the papyrus stalk (described in the notes to pl. 57), which no longer determines the directional change of the *neters* but that of the image of the officiating king, who, starting from this point, proceeds in the opposite direction. Note that this molding on the column in the foreground extends above the tableau up to the five bands under the capital.

PLATE 60 • NORTH AXIAL WINDOW, CAMPANIFORM COLUMNS

The central window of the first north bay is in the background, recognizable by the axial ankh carved under the architrave.

In the foreground, the molding of the southern campaniform column marks the king's directional change.

Note the enormous campaniform capitals that imitate the tuft of the blossoming papyrus above the encased folioles. In between these, plants of both the North and the South serve to frame and support alternating cartouches of Ramesses II (fig. 34).

PLATE 61 • CENTRAL NAVE: CAMPANIFORM COLUMNS, OBELISK OF TUTHMOSIS I

Height of the columns not including base or abacus: around 18.50 meters or 10 human fathoms.
Total height with base and abacus: around 21 meters or 40 royal cubits.
Height including the architrave: about 23 meters.
Large diameter of the shaft: around 3.50 meters.
Capital diameter: around 6.70 meters.
The circumference of the capital reaches about 21 meters and is equal to the height of the column, including the base and abacus.

In this impressive view of the great central nave, the viewer sees through the ruined doorways of the

Fig. 35. Claustra of the hypostyle hall

pylons to the granite sanctuary meant to shelter the sacred barque. The obelisk of Tuthmosis I is on the right.

The extraordinarily soaring allure of these columns draws one's eyes toward heaven. The tableaux, which represent the two forms of Amun alternating with one another, are placed quite high and surmount a ring on which the hieroglyphs of the Horus name of Ramesses II converge toward his vertically elevated, double cartouche.

PLATE 62 • NORTH WINDOW: CAMPANIFORM COLUMNS

The campaniform column described previously (pl. 60) is in the foreground, but seen from another

Croisées de la Salle Hypostyle

Au dessus du 1er Rang de chaque quinconce de petites colonnes dans le sens de la longueur et en face d'chaque file de grandes colonnes, s'élève une corniche formée de Tryglyphes séparés par des cartouches de Rhamsès le Grand en creux

Manuscrit dédic

et au dessus de cette corniche mais en retraite les Grands Piliers reunis par Architrave et formant les Croisées de la Salle Hypostyle, formés de deux Enorme pierres a. et b avec 12 barreaux taillés à jour donnant passage à la lumière sur ces Piliers ou Jambages A. des tableaux d'Adoration Rhamsès le Grand, ou ce Roi accueilli en recevant la Vie ou les dons d'Amon-Ra.

Sur les architraves ou bandeaux des croisées B legende dédicatoire de la Salle Hypostyle

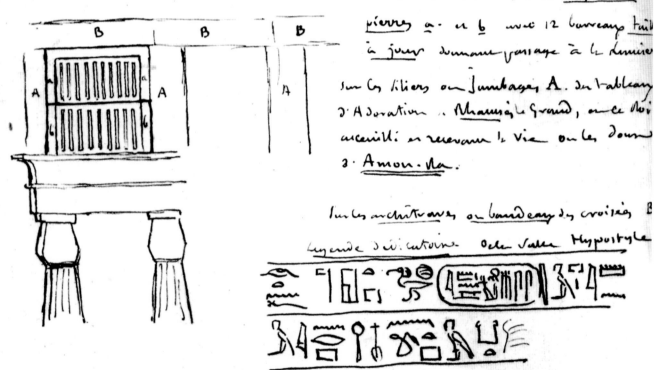

Fig. 36. Manuscript page from Notices descriptives *by Champollion the Younger (1829–30)*

angle. The first lateral window of the northwest section is in the background. The large column in the middle partially hides the text of the architrave of the first bay, which can be seen in its entirety (pl. 54).

PLATE 63 • NORTH CENTRAL WINDOW: CAMPANIFORM COLUMNS

The dedication inscription is located on the architrave of the great north colonnade. "On the second line, this dedication is originally of Merneptah I, and its admirably executed hieroglyphics are carved completely in relief. The full-relief cartouches of Merneptah I have been replaced by those of his successor Ramesses I carved in sunk relief." (Champollion, *Notices descriptives*, vol. 2, pp. 68–69; see also the "interesting portion" of this dedication)

Note the capital and the shaft of the column in the foreground, which show signs of being reworked on several different occasions.

PLATE 64 • SOUTH AISLE: OBELISK OF TUTHMOSIS I

The campaniform columns of the nave are seen on the left. On the right are the monostyle columns of the aisles. In the background are the remnants of the revetment wall for the "vestibule" of the third pylon, which originally closed off the east wall of this bay. Through the breech in this wall the obelisk of Tuthmosis I can be seen.

On the base of the first large column on the left, the solar disk in the royal cartouche has been replaced by a lozenge (pl. 65).

"Each large column is decorated by three tableaux that continue around the shaft to point *F* [fig. 39]. The largest portion represents worship and offerings made to the Theban triad. . . . But it is not always the same pharaoh presenting the offering. . . . The worshiper in the two tableaux that are visible when walking between the two rows of large columns is always the pharaoh Ramesses the Great. The third tableau, which covers the back part of the shaft on the side of the small columns, belongs to the reign of [Ramesses IV]." (Champollion, *Notices descriptives*, vol. 2, pp. 62–64)

Fig. 37. West face of the vestibule of the third pylon

Fig. 38. Claustra

PLATE 65 • GROUP OF COLUMNS IN THE SOUTH AISLE

The left of the two campaniform columns in the back is recognizable for the lozenge that is inscribed in the cartouche at its base (pl. 64). The monostyle column in the foreground bears the traces of several reworkings. The original decoration included only eight leaves, among which, above the three flowers of the South, is the plover resting on the basket who worships *Ramesses-beloved-of-Amun [Ramesses II] in the morning [dwa]*. Then Ramesses IV added his cartouches over the leaves. These cartouches are topped by a disk and feathers and flanked by crowned uraei. These were again added on to by Ramesses IV (see fig. 42).

PLATE 66 • GREAT HYPOSTYLE HALL: GROUP OF COLUMNS ON THE SOUTHEAST SIDE

The two monostyle columns in the foreground frame the transverse way. This is verifiable by the direction to which the hieroglyphs of the lower ring are oriented. They are heading toward the ankh that marks the axis of the columns perpendicular to the architraves (see diagram 4).

PLATE 67 • GREAT HYPOSTYLE HALL: GROUP OF COLUMNS ON THE SOUTH SIDE

In the right foreground is one of the campaniform columns of the nave. In the middle range are the monostyle columns of the first south bay. In the back on the right side there is a column of the second bay that belongs to the southwest sector, and on the left, a column of the same bay that belongs to the southeast sector (see note to plate 69).

PLATE 68 • TRANSFORMED CARTOUCHE

On the base of a column in the southeast sector can be found a beautiful example of the so-called usurped cartouche. Ramesses IV usurped it himself by reversing his own cartouche. He staggered the height of the hieroglyphs in such a manner that the larger disk forms a crescent around the smaller one (fig. 40).

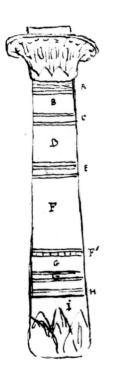

Au dessus des cordons (A) peint de diverses couleurs existe en B une série de cartouches unis en prénoms de Rhamsès le Grand ainsi décorés, et faisant le tour du fût.

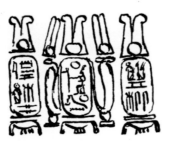

En D au dessous du cordon (C) des cartouches du même ainsi de plus grande proportion ainsi disposés

En F au dessous du cordon (E) = le pourtour du fût occupé par deux tableaux sculptés de relief dans lesquels représentant des actes d'Adoration.

En G au dessous du cordon (F') Grande Légende faisant ... outalement le tour de la colonne.

En H petite Légende en caractères plus petits faisant également le tour du fût.

enfin en I décoration du culot de la colonne ainsi composée ...

des fascicules du culot du papyrus entre lesquels s'épanouit un lotus au dessus du quel repose la légende de Rhamsès le Grand flanquée de deux Uraeus de la région supérieure et ... région inférieure ainsi qu'il suit

Fig. 39. Manuscript page from Notices descriptives, *by Champollion the Younger (1829–30)*

Fig. 40. The cartouche of Ramesses IV usurped by himself

PLATE 69 • SOUTH AISLE SEEN
FROM THE EAST

The three columns of the southeast sector of the first bay can be found in the front left. Toward the back are three of the four columns from the southwest sector of this same bay.

It is easy to see that all the capitals and the tops of the shafts of the eastern columns have received additional cartouches, while those on the west have retained their original decorations, at least in this first bay (pls. 67 and 70). Now, speaking of the "quincunx on the right" (that is, the south), Champollion noted when here in 1829:

"The decorations of the little columns on the right are of two kinds. Those of the first four rows (going across) seen on entering the hypostyle hall have retained their original decoration, which was that given to them under Ramesses the Great. The colors have in large part survived. With these we have an example of the first stage of all the little columns on the right and left of the hypostyle hall before the additions of Ramesses [Heqamaātre, throne name of Ramesses IV]. Here is this decoration that is extremely simple." (*Notices descriptives*, vol. 2, p. 81. See also the fig. 44 facsimile of Champollion's original notes. For the additions to the capitals in the south sector, a beautiful example can be found in pl. 63, in the foreground right.)

Usurpation has been the subject of much debate, and the additional cartouches added later pose problems that are quite awkward to resolve historically. Why, for example, do the capitals of the west columns retain their original decoration with no additions whatsoever, while those on the east have the addition of Ramesses IV's cartouches? This is not a question of an exception but of a system.

Fig. 41. South aisle: obelisk of Tuthmosis I

PLATE 70 • SECOND SOUTH AISLE: CLAUSTRA

From the roof, to which there is access by way of the stairways contrived in the thick walls of the hypostyle hall, the exterior of the southern claustra can be seen, as well as the posterior facade of the first row of seven monostyle columns. The latter three on the east have the addition of the Ramesses IV cartouches, while the four on the left have retained their original decoration (see pls. 67 and 69).

Plate 71 • South Claustra

Only the central window has kept its grill of recessed stone between the square pillars, which correspond to each column of the first bay. On the exterior face of these pillars, on two vertical columns of text, is the Horus name of Seti I, carved in sunk relief, facing the Amun-Ra that gives him life.

Above the claustra, the lintels are adorned by falcons that overshadow the two cartouches of Menmaātre Seti Meryenptah crowned by a disk and feathers and placed above the *nub* necklace, the symbol of gold.

Plates 72–86 • Great Hypostyle Hall: Bas-reliefs of the South Wall

Whereas all the walls of the north side of the hypostyle hall are sculpted in relief in the name of Seti I (pls. 40–52), all those of the south wall are carved in sunk relief in the name of Ramesses II. Certain historians find proof here of the fraudulent nature of Ramesside documents; others find here confirmation of the coregency of Seti I and his son Ramesses II. A proclamation addressed to Ramesses II on the Kubban stela lends support to this latter assumption:

You have drawn out the plans when you were still in the egg, in your position as child of a prince. Affairs of state were told to you as a child still wearing curly locks; not a monument was built that wasn't under your authority; there was no command made without your knowledge.

Fig. 42. Superimposition of the Ramesside cartouches

Fig. 43. Capital of a monostyle column from the north sector

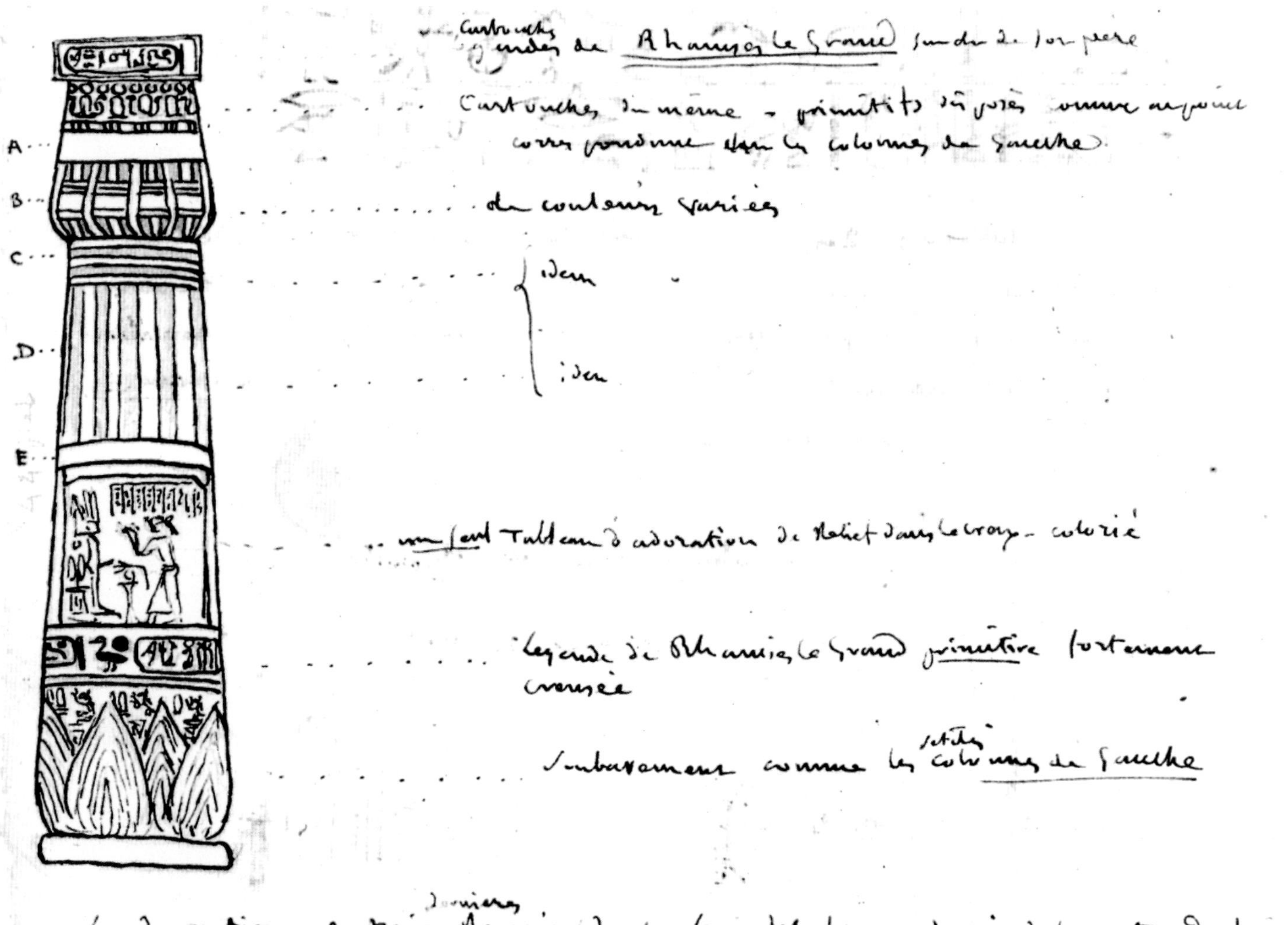

A

B

C

D

E

Fig. 44. *Manuscript page from* Notices descriptives, *by Champollion the Younger (1829–30)*

You were chief of the army when you were a ten-year-old child. (See Seele, *Coregency of Ramses II*, p. 27)

In regard to the first hypothesis, if by accepting the fact that Ramesses II "usurped" the bas-reliefs of his father, how then does one explain the worship that has made him the equal of a *neter*? (See pl. 74 and fig. 45.)

But those who adopt the second theory must ask themselves, for what mysterious reason did Seti I limit himself to the north side of the hypostyle hall and give his son responsibility for the entire south side? And, finally, why did Ramesses II have certain buildings adorned with sculpture carved in relief that he would later have razed to be replaced by those in sunk relief?

On the south partition of the hypostyle hall, for example, all the bas-reliefs on the west side were originally carved in relief and were subsequently entirely redone in sunk relief by Ramesses II (pls. 78–86), whereas the sunk bas-reliefs on the east bear no sign of being reworked (pls. 72–76). Moreover, the east and west sides are distinguished by variations of Ramesses' name. On the east he bears the royal "court" name Usermaätre, while on the west side he is called Usermaätre Setepenre (fig. 46).

(Observations made by Seele, who attributes the short forename to the period of coregency and the forename with the epithet Setepenre to the actual reign of Ramesses II.

The sole flaw in this historical version is that Seti I, actually depicted three times on the eastern portion, is referred to there as *maä kheru*, "vindicated," in other words deceased, which contradicts the idea of the coregency, but changes nothing as far as *facts* are concerned, facts meaning the nuances observed on this wall.)

Now, under the name Usermaätre the king is heading toward the *neters* proceeding from west to east, the direction of the nocturnal progress of the sun, and his bas-reliefs are carved once in sunk relief (pls. 72–76). Then he adds the label "elect of Ra" (Setepenre) to his name and goes from east to west, the direction the sun takes in the day. (The west-east progression by way of the sun is in apparent reverse direction to the course of the stars and therefore corresponds to the direction of the world's rotation.) These tableaux are first sculpted in relief, then sub-

Fig. 45. Ramesses II venerating his father Seti I

sequently hollowed into sunk relief (pls. 78–86).

PLATE 72 • GREAT HYPOSTYLE HALL, SOUTH WALL, EAST SIDE: RAMESSES II IN THE PERSEA TREE

After having been introduced toward the sanctuary of his father Amun by Tum, master of Heliopolis, and by Mentu, master of Thebes, the king, wearing a blue helmet, kneels in a persea tree. He holds the *hek* and *nekhakha* scepters in one hand over his shoulder and with the other props up the symbols of the *sed* festival extended to him by Amun seated in his naos (pl. 73). Behind him, Thoth, master of the Eight, the *neter* of writing, announces numerous renewals to him and inscribes the throne name on one of the oval fruits that he is holding up in his left hand. (Compare this with the same scene in relief on the north wall, east side, pl. 49).

Above the king, in the cartouche on the left crowned by the symbols of the kingdoms of the North and the South, the throne name of Ramesses II, Usermaätre, is inscribed. The winged disk with the multicolored plumage, the great *neter* of Behedet (Edfu), gives him life.

PLATE 73 • GREAT HYPOSTYLE HALL, SOUTH WALL: CORONATION OF RAMESSES II

Only three tableaux remain on this wall partition. On the bottom we recognize the king in the persea tree. Represented on the second register is the scene of the coronation of the king of Upper and Lower Egypt, Usermaātre, Son of Ra, Ramesses Meryamun, by the *neters*.

The king, seated on a throne, is wearing the double crown (the white in front of the red) and holds the two scepters in his fists, which are not crossed. He is framed by two seated feminine *neters* who are grasping his shoulders; on the east is Nekhebet the White, mistress of the South, who is assuring the king of her protection by "joining with his limbs" and of "his rejuvenation in the image of the Aten disk in heaven." Horus of Behedet is presenting the king with the white crown set on a basket, affirming to him that he will place *the white crown of the South and the red crown of the North* upon his head . . . and that he *will appear as Horus.*

On the west, behind Wadjet, mistress of the North, Thoth is presenting the red crown to the king, confirming his divine origin and the righteousness of his rule over the Two Lands, as his father Horus, son of Isis.

The three thrones are elevated on one pedestal, while Thoth and Horus walk on the ground.

On the third register, exactly above the coronation, can be found the scene of Chnuphis (Khnum) manufacturing the young king standing on a potter's-wheel altar. Here the royal infant is represented alone, whereas at Luxor he is depicted with his *ka*.

PLATE 74 • GREAT HYPOSTYLE HALL, SOUTH WALL, EAST SIDE: THE RACE OF THE APIS BULL

On the bottom register, behind the prows of the barques of Khonsu and Mut, a column of text informs us that "Menmaātre, *maā kheru*, accompanied his father Amun into the splendid temple Seti-beloved-of-Ptah in the house of Amun."

Seti I is indeed represented walking behind the sacred barques, in the same direction as the *neters*, and he is qualified as *maā kheru* (vindicated), which allows it to be understood that it concerns the king

after he was brought up to heaven and that he has rejoined He who had created him.

On the second register is a very curious scene that is often found on the lintels of doorways that provide access to the sanctuaries and that is still double in this case (pls. 90 and 132) but without a bull. The king, on one side wearing the red crown, on the other the white crown, makes the "great stride" holding sometimes the oar and the rudder *(hpt)* in his hands, sometimes the two libation vessels. Behind him the two symbols of heaven cut in half are crowning the symbols of the bull and the *ka* (homonym for bull).

During the inauguration of a monument, the sacred bull, Hap, sometimes accompanied the king during his race, as in this image. Sometimes the inscription specifies that *the king gives the land four times* (pl. 87), implying that this ritual race was made around the area of the temple, once for each direction. The symbols of the heavens cut in half, the scorpion, and the *ka* remain to be explained. The ritual of the cord and the race of Apis are already mentioned on the Palermo Stone in regard to several archaic kings, and indeed, we do find on a cylinder of Horus-den (fifth king of the First Dynasty) the first known testimony of the Apis race (fig. 47).

On the left, still on the second register, Usermaātre, wearing the curly locks of the crown prince and clad in a panther skin, holds the censer in one hand while he presents "food" to Menmaātre (Seti I) standing on a pedestal in a naos, as the equal of a *neter*: Ramesses II rendering homage to his father (fig. 45).

PLATE 75 • GREAT HYPOSTYLE HALL, SOUTH WALL, EAST SIDE: BINDING OF THE TWO LANDS

To the right and left sides of the king kneeling on the *sma* symbol, *Horus, great* neter, *master of Mesen.t and Thoth, master of the city of the Eight,* are joining the Two Lands of North and South for him, *under his feet,* assuring him the monarchy of the double Horus (Horus, master of the North, and Seth, master of the South).

The horizontal bar on which the king is kneeling always indicates a significant measurement.

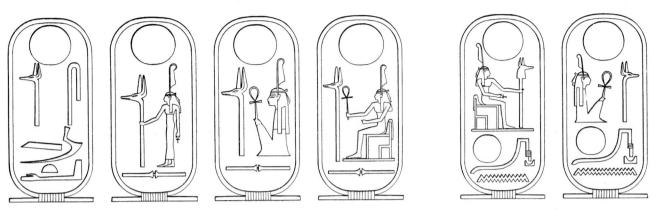

Fig. 46. West: Usermaātre Setepenre, East: Usermaātre.

PLATE 76 • BINDING OF THE TWO LANDS, THE BARQUE OF AMUN

The barque of Amun resting in a large naos (of which only a part of the uraei frieze of the dais can be seen) can be found on the lower register, in front of the barques of Khonsu and Mut (pl. 74). All the sculpture is in sunk relief, with the exception of the naos of the barque, whose representations, save for a few nuances, are the same as those in the naos of Seti I (pl. 45; see also the notes for pls. 79–81 and fig. 49).

PLATE 77 • GREAT HYPOSTYLE HALL, NORTH-SOUTH TRANSVERSE WAY: SOUTH DOORWAY

Note the arrangement of the architraves and the ankh of the axis (see diagram 4).

PLATE 78 • SOUTH WALL, WEST SIDE: THE THREE REGISTERS

On the bottom register is the barque of Amun followed by the barques of Khonsu and Mut carried by priests (pls. 79–81). On the second register, the king, framed by Tum and Mentu, who are holding his hand, is making the royal ascent toward the temple of Amun-Ra. He is preceded by the standards that are holding up Upwat, the opener of the ways, and the strange symbol of Khonsu that A. Moret has compared to the amniotic pouch containing the fetus, symbolizing birth or rebirth. Additionally, Seshat, mistress of writing, topped by the nine-pointed star, is holding the palm of the years in her hands with the eight symbols of the *sed* festival (renewal), while

Thoth inscribes the Horus name of the king and his renewals in his "annals" (fig. 48).

On the third register is the scene of bird hunting with the net (pls. 82–84).

PLATES 79–81 • THE BARQUE OF AMUN CARRIED BY THE SPIRITS OF PE AND NEKHEN

(Plate 79 forms the junction connecting plates 80 and 81.)

On the lower register of the west side of the south doorway, the king, wearing a blue helmet and a long coat, is censing the prow of the barque of Amun, which terminates in a ram's head crowned with a disk. This barque is resting on a stretcher that is carried on the shoulders of three groups of five falcon-headed figures in the front and thirteen jackal-headed figures in the back: the spirits of Pe and Nekhen, whom some have wished to see as priests wearing jackal and sparrow hawk masks. This interpretation was, rightfully, hotly contested:

"It is a singular reduction of the symbolic value and teaching of the walls of the Egyptian temples to want them at any cost to have only ever reproduced

Fig. 47. King Den's cylinder, First Dynasty (from W. B. Emery, The Tomb of Hemaka)

Fig. 48. The "royal ascent": Ramesses introduced by Mentu, Seshat, and Thoth

scenes from reality." (G. Foucart; *La Belle Fête de la Vallée*, p. 70)

Indeed, if the priests truly wore masks during the course of certain ceremonies, these must be categorically distinguished from the representations in the sanctuaries, where animal-headed figures are "functional principles" and not masked officiants.

In the center, the first prophet of Amun, the king Usermaātre Setepenre, clad in a panther skin, accompanies the barque.

Careful study of this tableau reveals that it was first entirely sculpted in relief—some say by Seti I, others by Ramesses II—then, with the exception of the naos and the king's face, it was entirely redone in sunk relief, preserving the traces of the original figuration.

In the upper part of the naos, the ram-headed Amun, placed on a lotus and the *mer* sign, is overshadowed by two winged Maāts placed on the *men* sign and holding the *user* symbol in their hands.

In the middle part, Ra, placed on the *men*, also is

holding the *user* symbol in his hand, instead of the feather of Maāt that he is holding in the north naos. (See pl. 45 and fig. 49.)

How should these strange anaglyphs be read? In the north the naos actually bears the name of Seti I, but in the south it is a question of the composition of the two names, Seti I and Ramesses II, which doesn't fit well at all with any idea of *usurpation* but confirms the mystical and symbolic meaning of the royal name.

"On the interior partitions of the walls of the south side of the hypostyle hall, inscriptions of Herihor tell of the restorations executed in his time:

"In examining the walls on which these inscriptions are carved, it was observed that Herihor's restoration consisted of repairing only the lower half of these same walls. Because of the invasion of nitric salts, the sandstone blocks of the bases were crumbling and deteriorating up to heights of a meter and more; the degradation had even reached the mid-leg level of the figures in the large tableaux." (Legrain, *Les Temples de Karnak*, p. 249) (For example, the legs of the barque bearers from pl. 80 were redrawn on the new blocks but the columns of hieroglyphs located between the king and the bearers were not recarved.)

PLATE 82–83 • KHNUM, THE KING, AND HORUS RECLOSING THE NET FOR THE BIRD HUNT AT THOTH'S SIGNAL

The image represents a pool in the midst of a papyrus thicket out of which seven ducks are flying. The two sides of the net, which had originally been held open on both sides of the pool, are now closed back over the captured birds, at the signal given by Thoth with his scarf. This is the explanation furnished by numerous analogous scenes depicted in the tombs of nobles, in which the net is held by peasants under the eye of the master of the tomb.

We have here an example of a "scene from private life" serving as the prop and symbol of a teaching, as is testified to by the accomplishment of an activity by the *neters* themselves.

Indeed, the texts accompanying Thoth designate him as "master of the city of the Eight," who presides in Hesret, at the heart of the "temple of the net," that is, a sanctuary located in Heliopolis and thus named in memory of the place where Seth was captured in a net by Horus. It thus concerns a scene that certainly has a relation to the myth.

Moreover, Thoth directs the "snaring" operation, and it is said that he extends his two arms like a bow in order to unfurl the strip of cloth. It so happens that Thoth, master of numbers, indicates the fathom by his height and by the distance between the two inside edges of his scarf: 2 meters.

It is written on this tableau that Thoth has crossed the swamp filled with birds, for whom he has set a trap in order to snare these aquatic fowl, destined to serve as offerings to the *neters*.

PLATE 84 • OFFERING OF CAPTURED BIRDS BY RAMESSES II TO AMUN AND MUT

The red-crowned king holds three birds in each hand that he is presenting to Amun, from whom he receives all life and "enlargement of heart."

PLATE 85 • THE KNEELING KING RECEIVES THE PANEGYRICS

While the king on the *sma* symbol had the face of a young man, he is represented as older here, and in the position that we find very often and most particularly in the great hypostyle hall in the temples of Karnak. (See also pl. 86.)

PLATE 86 • GIFT OF THE PANEGYRICS, SACRIFICE OF THE ORYX

A large naos on the lower register encloses the entire scene of the gift of the panegyrics. On the right a swaddled Khonsu-in-Thebes-Neferhotep is wearing the disk in the lunar crescent on his head and is holding all the scepters in his hands except for the *wadj*. Amun is seated in front of him holding the *was* scepter and the palm of the years in his left

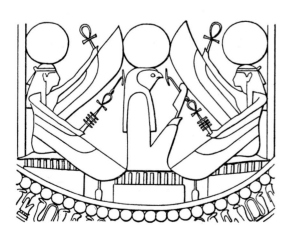

Fig. 49a. Anaglyph of the north barque

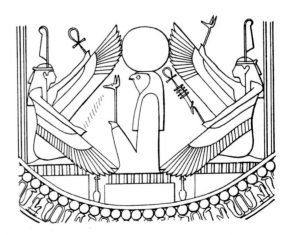

Fig. 49b. Anaglyph of the south barque

hand, while with the right hand he is giving the king the *hek* and *nekhakha* scepters, worth thousands of years of renewals as king of the North and South.

Mut, mistress of Asheru, is blessing the king and holding a double palm of the years in her right hand, from which are hanging eight *sed* renewal festival symbols. The king is kneeling on a pedestal that places him mid-height between the feet of Mut and Amun.

On the second register the king is sacrificing the oryx, which is placed on a table of offerings adorned with the *djed* pillar of Osiris and the knot of Isis, alternating with one another, in the presence of the Theban triad.

There are numerous passages in myths concerning the oryx, which, as one of the forms of Seth, is capable of devouring the Eye of Horus. The sacrifice of the Sethian oryx (which is white here) thus represents one of the last phases of the reconquest of the Eye of Horus, to which there is countless allusion in the Ritual of the Daily Divine Worship. The *djed* pillars of Osiris recall, in fact, his passion and resurrection through annual renewal.

The sacrifice of the oryx that has captured the Eye of Horus is indispensable to the signification of renewal (exaltation) by the rite of the *sed* festival.

PLATE 87 • GREAT HYPOSTYLE HALL, WEST WALL, SOUTH SIDE: BAS-RELIEF

On the lower register, the king wearing the red crown is making the "great stride" while giving the field four times to his father, Mentu, master of Thebes. He is carrying the seal in one hand and the *nekhakha* scepter in the other. Behind him are symbols for the scorpion and the *ka* (bull).

On the upper register is a colossal representation of Thoth inscribing the different titles of Ramesses II: his Horus name, his Golden Horus name, and his *nebti* name (master of the Two Crowns). This detail belongs to the large tableau found to the south of the entranceway and represents the king, followed by Hathor and Thoth, in the presence of a seated Amun behind whom Khonsu is standing. This is a counterpart of the large tableau to the north (fig. 22).

PLATE 88 • GREAT HYPOSTYLE HALL, WEST WALL, SOUTH SIDE: THE THEBAN TRIAD IN ITS NAOS

This tableau is the only one *in relief* in the entire southern half of the hypostyle hall. Here Amun-Ra, king of the *neters*, at the head of the Great Ennead, announces that he is giving a great increase to Hapi, the Nile. Now, in support of these words, the naos containing the Theban triad rests entirely on a band of water that is rising under the feet of Amun, replacing the pedestal of his throne. Moreover, the *was* scepter is framed by two wavy lines depicting water, a quite unusual drawing. The face of Amun is, quite exceptionally, bearing two ram's horns encircling his ears, and, in addition to his usual headdress, he is wearing a triple *atef* crown and two ostrich plumes placed on the horns of the Khnum.

"The band of water continues behind the naos containing the Theban triad, and the barque Userhat of Amun is sailing upon it going from south to north, towed by the five *neters* who are standing on the pilot barque. These two barques are the replicas in sunk relief of those of Seti I in relief on the north side of this same facade of the second pylon.

"Above the sacred barque, Amun's speech begins with these words: *Says Amun-Ra, master of the thrones of the Two Worlds, who is in the Nu [the primordial waters].*" (Legrain, *Les Temples de Karnak,* p. 214)

PLATE 89 • GREAT HYPOSTYLE HALL: NORTH-SOUTH COLONNADE

PLATE 90–91 • GREAT HYPOSTYLE HALL, SOUTH WALL: EXTERIOR FACADE

All of the exterior southern facade of the hypostyle hall "was formerly adorned with historical tableaux relative to the conquests of Ramesses the Great; but they are almost entirely effaced and one can hardly recognize the subject of the two registers still visible above the heaped-up piles of dirt and blocks." (Champollion, *Notices descriptives,* vol. 2, p. 120)

Wrezinski (*Atlas,* vol. 2, pl. 54) thinks that these bas-reliefs recount the military expeditions during year 8 of Ramesses II's reign. The sole surviving fortress name, Aya, is probably Kafer-Aya, 5 kilometers south of Homs on the Orontes. (Helck, *Die Beziehungen Ägyptens,* p. 142; *Journal of Egyptian Archaeology* 50: 48)

After being cleared, nothing remains today of this wall except three registers of tableaux, whose

Fig. 50. Exterior south facade of the hypostyle hall

arrangement, at first sight, is analogous to that of Seti I's north wall (pls. 30–39 and fig. 12), at least with regard to the western half.

The *two lower registers* begin at the western edge with acts of conquest, then the king begins his return route and heads toward the entrance of the temple, where he presents his defeated adversaries to Amun. The scene represented on each side of the doorway takes up a space equally as high as the first two registers and represents the "ritual massacre of the vanquished."

On the upper register everything changes; whereas on the north Seti I's tableaux converge toward the entrance of the temple, those of Ramesses on the south leave the temple in the direction of the outside.

It is quite remarkable that all the bas-reliefs of this partition describing the conquests of Ramesses II place an emphasis on duality: the binding of the two chieftains, the comparison of the king with the two *neters* Horus and Seth, the king trodding over

the two defeated enemies, and the reversion of two cities simultaneously, of which several are characterized by two rows of crenelations and two portals.

On the lower register the king brings back two rows of defeated enemies.

This double character is again stressed by the two lion heads supporting the two feathers of the disk adorning the heads of all the horses that are still visible. And to close this collection, the king is wearing the double crown, the white in front of the red, while he completes the "ritual massacre of the prisoners" (fig. 50).

It is therefore not surprising to observe the superimposition of the two tableaux, in which the current reliefs of the conquests in Palestine are sculpted over the previous bas-reliefs of the famous battle of Kadesh.

In Karnak, the narration of this battle is carved at the east end of the south wall of the hypostyle hall, in a long text of vertical columns below a large scene

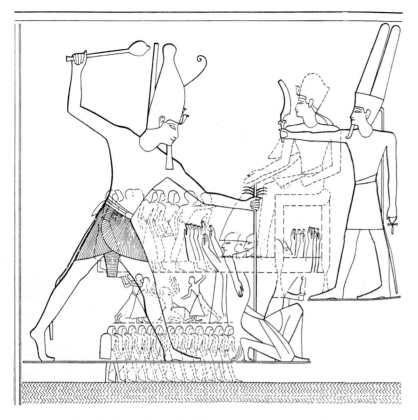

Fig. 51. Right-hand side of figure 50 with superimpositions

in which the king and the princes are bringing the bound group of prisoners before Amun (pl. 91, right).

Here are the essential phases that are relevant to the remnants of the original Karnak sculpture, which can be reconstituted thanks to the representations of analogous scenes on the pylons of the temple of Luxor, the Ramesseum, and the hypostyle of Abu Simbel.

Year 5, third month of the third season, day 9 [this period corresponds to our month of May]. When His Majesty appeared as the rising of Ra, he assumed the adornments of his father, Mentu. When the king proceeded northward, and His Majesty had arrived at the locality south of the town of Shabtuna, there came two Shasu to speak to His Majesty as follows: "Our brethren, who belong to the greatest of the families with the vanquished chief of the Kheta, have made us come to His Majesty, to say: 'We will be subjects of Pharaoh, L. P. H. [Life, Power, Health], and we will flee from the vanquished chief of the Kheta; for the vanquished chief of the

Kheta sits in the land of Aleppo, to the north of Tunip. He fears, because of Pharaoh L. P. H., to come southward.'" Now, these Shasu spake these words, which they spake to His Majesty falsely, (for) the vanquished chief of the Kheta made them come to spy where His Majesty was, in order to cause the army of His Majesty not to draw up for fighting him. . . .

In truth, the miserable chief of the Kheta is stationed, together with many countries . . . being every country which is in the districts of the land of Kheta, the land of Naharin, and all Kode. . . . More numerous are they than the sand of the shore. . . .

Then as His Majesty sat upon a throne of gold, there arrived a scout who was in the following of His Majesty, and he brought two scouts of the vanquished chief of the Kheta. They were conducted into the presence, and His Majesty said to them: "What are ye?" They said: "As for us, the vanquished chief of the Kheta has caused that we should come to spy out where His Majesty is." Said His Majesty to them: "He! Where is he, the vanquished chief of the Kheta? Behold, I have heard saying: 'He is in the land of Aleppo.'" Said they: "See, the vanquished chief of the Kheta is stationed, together with many countries which he has brought with him in force. . . . They are equipped with infantry and chariotry; more numerous are they than the sand of the shore. See, they are standing, drawn up for battle behind Kadesh the Deceitful." (Breasted, *Ancient Records*, vol. 3, §§ 317–21).

What the text doesn't specify but what serves as a caption to representations of this episode is that the two spies decided to reveal the exact position of the Kheta chieftain only after having been vigorously thrashed, a scene in Karnak over which the leg of the king has been superimposed. The king is making the gesture of striking down the vanquished before Amun, with his white club (figs. 51 and 53).

Then His Majesty called the princes into his presence to hear each word of the two spies.

It is a great fault, they said, *which the governors of the countries and the officials of Pharaoh, L. P. H., have committed in not informing that the vanquished chief of the Kheta was near the king.* (Ibid., § 323)

The situation was all the more serious as the king was alone there with his personal guard, his army, composed of the four divisions of Ra, Amun, Ptah, and Seth, slowly coming up behind him. Also, the vizier received the order to hasten the army, and, to go yet faster, this latter individual sent a horseman posthaste. But Ramesses was informed of this too late; the chief of the Kheta had already crossed the Orontes south of Kadesh and charged the army of His Majesty, who, taken by surprise, beat a hasty retreat. This was how the Kheta managed to surround the bodyguard of His Majesty while he was still seated, speaking with the princes.

Now, the king seated on his gold throne is currently outlined over the right arm of Amun, who is standing and holding the harpagon out to him (figs. 50 and 51), and this superimposition takes on its full value when one knows the prayer addressed by the king before going into battle:

I invoke you, O my father Amun! Here I am amidst numerous peoples unknown to me; all the nations have joined against me,[8] *I am alone, my numerous soldiers have abandoned me, none of my horsemen has cast a look my way, and when I have called upon them, not one has heard my voice. But I think that Amun is worth more to me than a million soldiers, one hundred thousand chariots, and myriad brothers or younger sons, were they all united together! The work of numerous men is nothing. Amun will sweep over them. . . .*

The voice has echoed all the way to Hermonthis, Amun comes at my invocation, he gives me his hand, I shout a cry of joy, he speaks behind me, I run to you, to you Ramesses Meryamun! I am with you. It is I your father, my hand is with yours and I am worth more to you than hundreds of thousands. I am the Lord of Strength who loves the valiant, I have found a courageous heart and I am satisfied. My will shall be done.

Similar to Month, on the right I hurl my lances, on the left I bowl them over. Before them I am as Baar in his hour. The two thousand five hundred chariots that surround me are broken into pieces by my mares. Not a one among them finds his hand for the combat; the heart is lacking in their chest and fear excites their limbs. They no longer know how to throw their darts and find no more strength with which to hold their lances. I precipitate them into the waters, as the crocodile falls there; they

Fig. 52. Superimposition of Amun and a scene of struggle

are lying face down, one upon the other, and I kill in their midst. (Sallier Papyrus, trans. E. de Rougé)

Who is speaking? The king or Amun? The superimposition of Amun and the king renders their identification with one another quite tangible.

All the defeated in the actual bas-relief can be seen quite distinctly, plunged to midbody in the waters of the Orontes of the preceding bas-relief, and, to complete the symbolic character of Amun seated and receiving the vanquished, an Egyptian soldier overcoming a Hittite on the original bas-relief is outlined over the leg of the *neter*, whereas the river entirely surrounds his throne (see fig. 52 and pl. 88).

---

[8] In accordance with the tale of this battle of Kadesh, it is true that the king of the Hittites had formed a coalition of almost all of Turkey against Ramesses II. (Helck, *Die Beziehungen Ägyptens*, p. 207)

Fig. 53. South wall of the hypostyle hall: superimpositions

PLATE 92 • WEST WALL OF THE CACHETTE COURT, OUTER WALL: COMBAT IN PALESTINE

On the upper register the royal chariot in full gallop charges the routed Palestinian army. Under the belly of the king's horse one of the fleeing soldiers can be seen mounted sidesaddle.

On the lower register, the king is treading on the vanquished enemy plunged into the water of an earlier representation that probably depicts the Orontes. With his right hand he is holding one of the fortress occupants by the hair and with his left hand he brandishes a harpagon. (The cartouches are in the name of Seti II.)

PLATE 93 • SURRENDER OF ASKALON

The defenders of the fortress of Askalon,[9] perched on a hill, are raising their hands in surrender while the pharaoh's soldiers are staving in the doors with axes and scaling it by means of ladders raised against the walls. On the hill Egyptian soldiers are exterminating the fleeing enemy; also, the gesture by one of the occupants of the fortress who has lifted at arm's length a child he is trying to save is readily understandable.

Not far from these bas-reliefs can be found one of the most remarkable documents preserved from

[9]Askalon is north of Gaza on the Mediterranean coast.

ancient Egypt: the famous peace treaty signed between Ramesses II and the Kheta chieftain. The oddity of this text has been commented upon by all the historians, who have difficulty accepting the fact that after sixteen years of victories, Ramesses II recognized the sovereignty of the enemy power over all the territories he had conquered!

The year 22, the twenty-first of the month of Tybi, the prince of the Kheta sent a messenger to the pharaoh Ramesses II bearing a silver tablet upon which his master had set down the conditions of the treaty between the two countries in order to bring a good peace and fraternity between them forever.

There shall be no hostilities between them, forever. . . . If another enemy come against the lands of Usermaātre Setepenre (Ramesses II), the great ruler of Egypt, and he shall send to the great chief of the Kheta, saying "Come with me as reinforcement against him," the great chief of the Kheta shall (come) and the great chief of the Kheta shall slay his enemy. But if it not be the desire of the great chief of the Kheta to come, he shall send his infantry and his chariotry, and shall slay his enemy. (Breasted, *Ancient Records*, vol. 3, §§ 376, 378)

In exchange, the great king of Egypt undertook the support of the prince of the Kheta in case of differences with his neighbors. Then the clauses relative to the maintenance of laws were established: the extradition of criminals and fugitives, the extradition of all emigrants, artisans, or peasants, but on the condition, for these latter three, of not touching their goods or family nor inflicting any punishment upon them.

"Such a document has an inappreciable value. It allows the evaluation of the development of these old Eastern civilizations that are too often represented as still steeped in barbarism." (J. Capart, *Thebes*, pp. 127–28)

PLATE 94 • GREAT HYPOSTYLE HALL, SOUTHEAST CORNER: PRESENTATION OF THE PRISONERS TO AMUN

On the right is the presentation of the booty taken from the vanquished to Amun in his naos. This includes precious vessels (fig. 54) and Asian prisoners arrayed in two lines.

On the left are the outside southeast corner of

the hypostyle hall, underlined by a torus, and the inside corner of the "cachette court," to the north of which is inscribed the narration of the battle of Kadesh.

PLATE 95 • GREAT HYPOSTYLE HALL: CENTRAL NAVE SEEN FROM THE EAST

The first two columns were part of the "vestibule" built by Amenhotep III. In the dismantling of the wall constructed by Seti I against its north partition, an unfinished bas-relief of Amenhotep IV, representing the ritual massacre of the defeated, was discovered. (*Kemi* 19: 250; 20: 187)

The foundations of the pedestals for the two obelisks unearthed on the inside of the wings of the third pylon could perhaps have supported the two

Fig. 54. Offering to Amun-Ra of the victory booty

obelisks of Amenhotep II, the existence of which is known by virtue of commemorative scarabs. The excavations in the passageway have revealed the existence of a pavement at the same depth, which dates, without doubt, from the time of the Middle Kingdom. On the border of this an oracular text was discovered carved on a re-used stela. This brings up the question: "Could this passageway be the site of the famous *silver floor* on which the sacred barque passed during oracular processions?" (*Kemi* 19: 251 and 271).

PLATE 96–97 • THIRD PYLON OF AMENHOTEP III: OARSMEN OF THE ROYAL BARQUE

PLATE 98–99 • THIRD PYLON OF AMENHOTEP III: THE GREAT BARQUE USERHAT OF AMUN

Each year, during the course of the Great Feast of Apet and the Feast of the Valley, the sacred barques of Amun, Mut, and Khonsu were led in a solemn procession to the temple of Luxor, Apet of the South, and the funerary temples of the west bank. They left Karnak on immense barques towed by boats propelled by oars.

The two boats of Amun and the king are represented on the east face of the north wing of the third pylon, of which they occupied almost the entire width. Now, the fact of encountering a representa-

tion on a monument whose description is provided by a contemporary stela is a stroke of chance so rare in archaeology it deserves to be mentioned.

Amenhotep III erected a stela of black granite in his western temple, behind the columns of Memnon, on which he described the principal monuments that he had built in honor of Amun and where he specified *making for him an august temple to the west of Thebes, preceded by a very large pylon called "Amun has received the divine barque," a place of repose for the lord of the neters at his "Feast of the Valley," from the time of Amun's voyage to the west, to see the neters of the west.*

Then after having described the temple of Luxor:

King of Upper and Lower Egypt: Nebmare, part of Ra, son of Ra: Amenhotep (III), ruler of Thebes. I made another monument for him who begat me, Amun-Ra, lord of Thebes, who established (me) upon his throne, making for him a great barque for the "Beginning-of-the-River," (named) "Amun-Ra-in-the-Sacred-Barque [Userhat]," of new cedar which His Majesty cut in the countries of God's-Land [the land of the neters]. It was dragged over the mountains of Retenu (Rtnw) by the princes of all countries. It was made very wide and large; there is no instance of doing the like. Its [hull] is adorned with silver, wrought with gold throughout. The great shrine [naos] is of electrum so that it fills the land with its (brightness).

Its bows, they repeat the (brightness). They bear great [atef] crowns, whose serpents twine along its two sides. . . . Flagstaves are set up before it wrought with

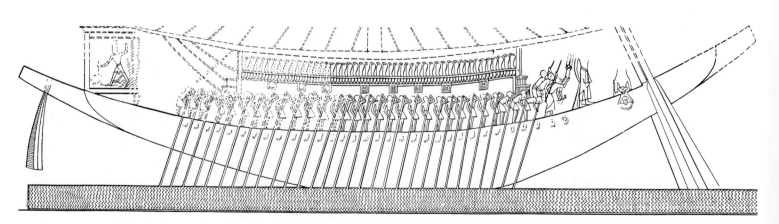

Fig. 55. Third pylon: restoration attempt of the barque of oarsmen

electrum, two great obelisks are between them; it is beautiful everywhere. The gods of Pe make jubilee to it; the gods of Nekhen praise it, the two Nile-gods of the South and North, they embrace its beauty, its bows make Nun to shine as when the sun rises in heaven, to make his beautiful voyage at his feast of Apet on his western voyage of a million years. (Breasted, *Ancient Records*, vol. 2, § 888, and Foucart, *La Belle Fête*, p. 49)

The description of the stela in no way exaggerates the splendor of the barque Userhat of Amun, whose representation we have seen on the third pylon (pl. 98–99). It even passes over in silence the delicate reliefs that adorned its hull and still retain some traces of the yellow paint that was meant to simulate the vessel's gold coating.

In the center, the naos containing the sacred barque of Amun is placed on a pedestal preceded by a staircase holding up the masts and the obelisks. In front of this pedestal are three worshiping jackal-headed figures and seven Niles. Behind the naos the king is navigating by holding the oar himself. In the front the king is making the gift of vegetables and the incense purification.

Perched on his roost, a human-headed sphinx with a cheetah body sits atop the *wedjat* eye that is always found on the prow of the barques. Between the sphinx and the king is a table of offerings. This entire bas-relief has been reworked by Amenhotep III himself.[10] Originally the two royal representations were smaller; traces of them remain on the prow, on the offering table, and toward the stern on the flabellum held by the ankh.

This transformation is difficult to explain, for if in the first stage there were, behind the naos of Amun, the two small barques of Khonsu and Mut (as in the barque of Seti I of the hypostyle hall, fig. 26), their traces were carefully effaced, whereas those of the two original kings were preserved.

Only the inside portion of the royal boat that towed the barque Userhat at the end of a rope has survived (pl. 96–97). Of the sixty oarsmen that pro-

pelled it, the only ones intact are those of the back section, who are profiled on the immense cabin with the double frieze of ovals and uraei.

It is curious to observe the "cinematic" development of the gesture formed by the progressive straightening of the oarsmen.

Between the first oarsman and the standing king, four priests are leaning with their faces turned toward the stern, looking toward the sacred barque. Two of them are holding the censers and flabellums.

On a little kiosk located toward the prow, the pharaoh was depicted striking down and treading upon the enemy peoples (the famous "ritual massacre").

To give an idea of the size of this barque Userhat, we know, through the Harris Papyrus, that it was 130 cubits on the river, that is, around 68 meters long.

On the east face of the south wing of the third pylon of Amenhotep III was carved a very long text of seventy-one vertical lines, of which only the lower portion survives. There remain only truncated phrases, of which here are several examples:

He is one who taketh thought, who maketh wise with knowledge . . . without his like, the good shepherd, vigilant for all people . . .

searching bodies, knowing that which is in the heart, whose fame apprehends the (evil) . . .

adorning the splendid Great House of him who begat him, with monuments of beauty and splendor forever. (Breasted, *Ancient Records*, vol. 2, § 900).

PLATES 100–151 • TEMPLE OF IPET-SUT OF AMUN

According to the inscription of the architrave of the campaniform colonnade of the great hypostyle hall (pl. 55 and commentary), the true entrance of the temple of Ipet-sut of Amun was the doorway of the fourth pylon, and the temple extended from there eastward. Schematically the plan of the temple of Ipet-sut properly speaking forms a vast rectangle (diagram 5, in black) that is boxed within a larger rectangle containing the jubilee buildings of Tuthmosis III (diagram 5, in crosshatch).

The temple itself underwent numerous reworkings. We will not describe them chronologically, but we will attempt to demonstrate the nature of their development as successive circles around a central "core."

---

[10] The two large depictions of the king are in their original location. The king was originally accompanied by a smaller figure that is presumed to have been Amenhotep IV, whose image would have been removed following the schism. (See P. Barguet, *La Structure du Temple Ipet-Sout d'Amon à Karnak* [B.I.F.A.O., 1953], p. 82; and *Kemi* 20: 193)

Fig. 56. Third pylon: the barque Userhat of Amun

In the square space that is completely destroyed today (diagram 5, *A* and *B*), it is thought there once existed a white limestone building of the Middle Kingdom that was still completely intact at the time of Hatshepsut. All that currently remains is three thresholds of rose-colored granite, indicative of the placement of the three chapels that were aligned to the temple's general axis; the one on the east would have been the original sanctuary (diagram 5, *A*).

"A high alabaster pedestal, carved in the name of Sesostris, upon which the divine naos rested, occupied most of it. Fragments of this have been rediscovered." (P. Barguet, *La Structure du Temple Ipet-sout d'Amon à Karnak*)

Two texts from Hatshepsut's time give one reason to suppose that there was a large feast chamber in front of the Holy of Holies (diagram 5, *B*), probably with columns.

In the westward extension of the Middle Kingdom structures is found a little rectangular temple attributed to Hatshepsut (diagram 5, in crossbars) that was first subdivided longitudinally into three groups of chambers. According to Borchardt, Tuthmosis III replaced the central chambers with a large room with four pillars, which were razed in their turn and replaced by the currently existing granite naos of Philip Arrhidaeus (diagram 5, *C*), which itself probably replaced a previous granite naos of Tuthmosis III.

The central sections *A, B,* and *C* constitute in some regard the "core" of the temple around which are built:

A first enclosure, bordered on three sides of the interior by a series of small chapels, which is terminated on the west side by the fourth pylon and the two walls that extend it and form a peristyle courtyard *(D, D')* in front of Hatshepsut's sanctuary. The sixth pylon and this enclosure of chapels were not built until Tuthmosis III, who considerably modified the original aspect of the temple with this addition.

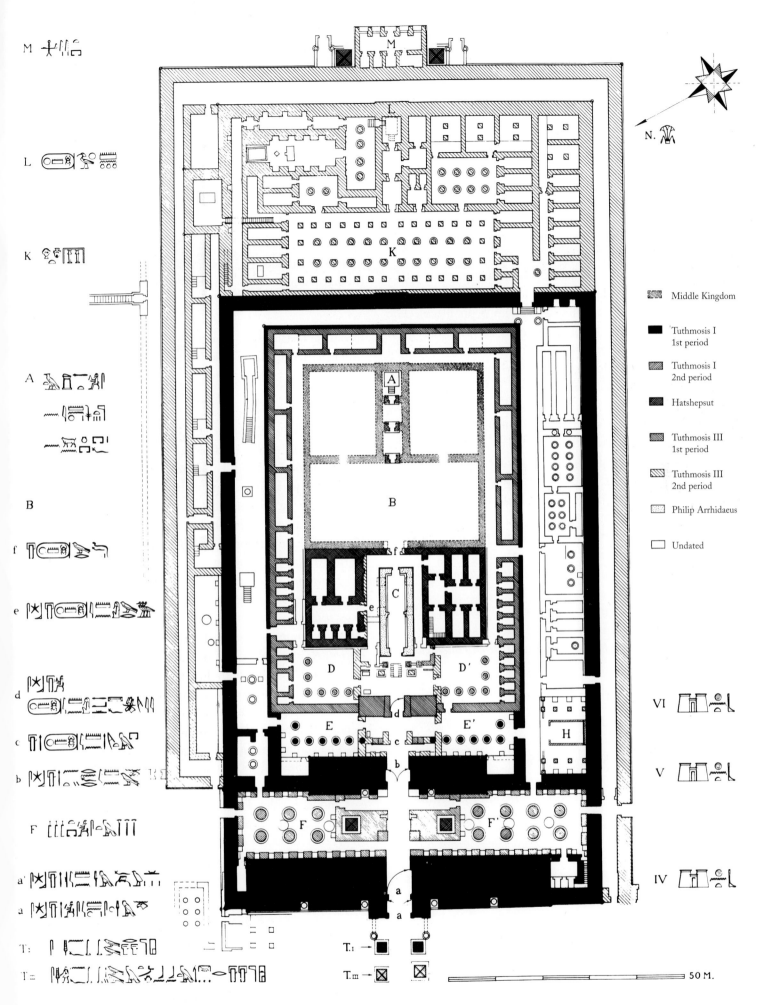

Diagram 5. Enclosures of the great temple of Ipet-sut: buildings of the sed *festival (according to the map from the Egyptian survey completed for the central sections after P. Barguet and Borchardt)*

Previously, a portico (according to Borchardt) was likely located at the emplacement of Tuthmosis III's chapels, whose four sides formed an immense open-air courtyard that extended westward to the fifth pylon. Nothing currently remains of this except the columns of the extreme west, in the name of Tuthmosis I *(E, E')*.

A second enclosure, terminated on the west by the fourth pylon attributed to Tuthmosis I, surrounds the previous buildings (diagram 5, in black). The "hypostyle hall" of the temple of Ipet-sut *(F, F')*, which itself underwent many alterations, is located between the fourth and fifth pylons. Hatshepsut had two obelisks erected within it.

Tuthmosis III added his jubilee buildings on the north and east *(K, L)* and surrounded this entire grouping anew with one final, large enclosure, on the outside of which he attached a small alabaster sanctuary that is open to the east *(M)*, while all the entrances to the temple of Ipet-sut are open to the west.

The greatest part of the study of the temple of Ipet-sut is drawn from the very interesting work of P. Barguet, *La Structure du Temple Ipet-sout d'Amon à Karnak.*

The diagrams are made from his map, plate II, and the different tonalities are taken from Borchardt's *Die Bauperioden des mittleren Hauptteiles des Amonstempels von Karnak.*

For the study of the doorway of the fourth pylon, see J. Leclant, "Les inscriptions 'ethiopiennes' sur la porte du IVᵉ pylône," in *Revue d'Egyptologie* (1951); and J. Yoyotte, "Un porche doré," in *Chronique d'Egypte* 55 (1953).

PLATE 100 • OBELISKS OF HATSHEPSUT AND TUTHMOSIS I, SEEN FROM THE NORTH

Between the obelisk of Hatshepsut (on the left) and that of Tuthmosis I rises an enormous mass of piled-up blocks, the lone vestiges of the north wing of the fourth pylon. Nothing remains of its revetment but several foundation courses of admirably cut and fitted white limestone blocks topped by sandstone blocks. The canted torus in its northwest corner is preserved up to a certain height; it is still visible in the

back of a niche containing an Osiris that was installed in the later revetment (pl. 100 and fig. 57).

PLATE 101 • OBELISKS OF HATSHEPSUT AND TUTHMOSIS I, SEEN FROM THE WEST

Obelisk of Tuthmosis I (from Jéquier)	Height: 19.60 meters Width at the base: 1.84 meters Width at the top: 1.65 meters
Obelisk of Hatshepsut (through triangulation)	Height: 28.58 meters Width at the base: 2.445 meters Width at the top: 1.77 meters Weight: 343 tons[11]

1. *Obelisk of Tuthmosis I.* Of the two obelisks erected by Tuthmosis I before the fourth pylon, only the southern one is still in place. The one in the north (left without inscription by Tuthmosis I and carved later by Tuthmosis III) was still standing in 1737 according to a report by the English traveler Pococke. Their erection is mentioned by the chief of all the works of Karnak, Ineni:

I inspected the erection of two obelisks . . . built the august boat of 120 cubits in length, 40 cubits in width, in order to transport these obelisks. (They) came in peace, safety, and prosperity, and landed at Karnak. (Breasted, *Ancient Records*, vol. 2, § 105)

Each side of the southern obelisk currently bears three columns of text; only the central inscription on the east is from Tuthmosis I; the lateral columns were by Ramesses IV and added on to by Ramesses VI. The central inscriptions of the north and south faces (figs. 58 and 59) provide the complete list of the king's titles; his dedication is inscribed on the east and west sides. Here (pl. 101), below the name of Horus and the royal cartouche, can be read:

He has raised as a memorial to his father Amun-Ra, chief of the Two Lands, two great obelisks at the double

---

[11]Obelisk of Tuthmosis I: total height 20.016 m, height of the pyramidion 2.23 m, width of the pyramidion's base 1.10 x 1.15 m, width of the base of the shaft 2.10 m. (Traunecker, *Karnak*, vol. 5, p. 32) The total height of Hatshepsut's obelisk, 28.56 m, corresponds to the 54 cubits mentioned on the Djehuty stela. The height of its pyramidion is 2.735 m. [Corrections made by author and supplied later—Trans.]

*doorways of the temple. . . . * (Diagram 5, T, I)

The mention of the double doorway of the temple on this obelisk (as on those of Tuthmosis II depicted on the "wall of the annals," pl. 147) is of the greatest importance.[12]

2. *Doorway of the fourth pylon.* Among the "great works" executed under Tuthmosis I in Karnak, Ineni mentions the great pylons (the fourth and fifth), the majestic masts of new cedar with electrum tips raised at the double doorways of the temple. Then, immediately afterward, he describes a door of one sole casement that, according to its name, could only be that of the fourth pylon (diagram 5, *a'*):

I have inspected the erection of the great doorway "Amun-mighty-with-strength"; its top casement is of Asian copper, whereon the divine shadow of Min is wrought in gold.

On the schematic plan, the door with one casement described by Ineni was fit into the large embrasure (around 4.50 meters wide) between the two wings of the pylon (diagram 5, *a'*). But between the two "jutting bodies" is a second embrasure for a double door that is considered as an addition of Tuthmosis IV, although it is architecturally connected to the very blocks of the jetties (diagram 5, *a*).

Indeed, on the jutting building section of the north (pl. 101 and fig. 60), three columns of dedicatory text of Tuthmosis IV are found on the left; on the right are found scenes of offerings in the name of Tuthmosis IV but of Ptolemaic work, and in the center a column of inscriptions in the name of Shabaka, of the same workmanship as the tableaux, copied without doubt from the original inscription. This text, which has incited much debate, says that Shabaka has executed:

. . . the restoration to new of the great and magnificent portal [called] "Amun-Ra-mighty-with-prestige"; it has been [re]done for him with a revetment of fine gold . . . as well as a large porch [or a grand ceiling] re-covered with fine gold; the two columns were worked with

Fig. 57. Fourth pylon: torus of the northwest corner

electrum, and the two bases supporting them with pure silver. (J. Yoyotte, *"Un porche doré,"* 34–35)

According to this text, illustrated by two contemporary representations of Tuthmosis IV, it is possible to imagine the principal entry of the temple of the Eighteenth Dynasty: a gold-coated sandstone portal, preceded by a roofed-in porch covered with gold and supported by two columns worked with electrum on silver-coated bases (of which only one still remains in place).

But on the occasion of festivals when the *two* sides of the *first* door were opened, could the profile of Min's shadow in gold still be seen on the large copper casement described by Ineni? Actually it would seem that *two* coexisting *doors*, one in front of the other, must be accepted here.

[12]The existence at the fourth pylon of a first doorway with double doors and a second doorway with a single door has been confirmed. (See Barguet, *La Structure du Temple*, p. 88) The door panels made from a single leaf of copper were intended for the doorway of the fifth pylon. (Ibid., p. 107)

Fig. 58. Obelisk of Tuthmosis I, north face

The hieroglyphic texts don't allow for the confusion of *casement* and *door*, as they are each determined by a specific sign. Ineni specifies that he has erected the masts at the *double door*, which leaves no doubt that it is a question of *two doors*—and not two casements—which could explain the two names: Amun-sekhem-fa-u, "Amun-mighty-with-strength," Ineni's single casement door (diagram 5, *a'*), and Amun-sekhem-shef.t, "Amun-mighty-with-prestige," the door with two casements (diagram 5, *a*).

Moreover, it is possible to conceive that the prestigious door with the one copper casement, bearing the golden silhouette of Min, was ordinarily hidden by the door with two casements that preceded it.

According to the inscription of Amenhotep I on the threshold of the limestone jubilee doorway discovered at Karnak, this pharaoh erected *a great door of 20 cubits at the double door of the temple*. A double door therefore already existed before Tuthmosis I, which, according to Barguet, must have served as an entrance to the brick enclosure that itself was "likely existing from the time of the Middle Kingdom."

A passage of Ineni concerning the works that he made for Amenhotep I says: *Its casements were fashioned from one sole sheet of copper*. If this concerns the casements intended for the above-mentioned limestone doorway, each sheet of copper should measure around 7.0 meters long by, probably, 1.5 meters wide!

3. *Obelisk of Hatshepsut*. All four sides carry a central column of inscriptions and, on the upper half, eight tableaux on which the king is directed toward Amun going from the northwest corner toward the southeast corner.

On its north face (pls. 100, 108, and 109), the central inscription begins with the Horus, the Two Goddesses, and the Golden Horus names, then continues under the royal cartouche with the following: *Her father*

Fig. 59. Obelisk of Tuthmosis I, south face
(photo by Banville)

Amun hath established her great name; Makere on the august Ished tree, her annals are myriads of years. . . . (When) she celebrated (for) him the first occurrence of the royal jubilee . . . [an allusion to the inscription of the royal name on the persea tree; see pls. 49 and 72]. (Breasted, *Ancient Records*, vol. 2, § 310)

On the west face (pl. 101), after the same title: *She made it as her monument for her father Amun-Ra, lord [of the Thrones] of the Two Lands, erecting for him two great obelisks at the august gate (named) "Amun-Great-in-Terror*[13] [shf.t], *wrought with very much electrum, which illuminates the Two Lands like the sun.* (Ibid., § 309)

It is therefore specified by the name of the door (diagram 5 in *b* and in pl. 128) that these obelisks were intended to be erected in front of the fifth pylon.

On the east facade (pl. 113 and fig. 61), the titles include only the Horus name of the queen, who affirms the building of these obelisks in the name of her father Tuthmosis I.

The text of the south facade, after the Horus name and the royal cartouche, confirms the royalty of Maātkare by the will of Amun and the Great Ennead.

Therefore the listings of titles are respectively the same on the west and north, and on the east and south.

PLATE 102 • OBELISK OF TUTHMOSIS I, SEEN FROM THE EAST

In the lateral columns of the text, the cartouches in the name of Ramesses IV have been added on to by Ramesses VI. The tableau on the base has been added by Ramesses II.

PLATE 103 • THE ROYAL SHOOTING OF THE BOW, GRANITE BLOCK

Amenhotep, under the title of Horthema (avenging Horus), achieved the execution of the royal shooting of the bow, *in the presence of the army and before the entire earth.*

Standing on his chariot, the reins of his horses looped around his waist, his left wrist protected by

Fig. 60. Obelisk of Hatshepsut, doorway of the fourth pylon

---

[13] De Lubicz has this as "prestige"—Trans.

Fig. 61. Obelisks of Hatshepsut and Tuthmosis I

the leather bracelet favored by archers, the king draws his bow and aims at a wooden post in front of him that is already transfixed by seventeen arrows. This is usually the first test.

Every wooden target having been riddled with arrows as if it were papyrus, the king completes the second test, described around the target of rectangular copper with concave sides placed upon the ground:

[It is] a large raw copper brick at which His Majesty has fired. Though three fingers thick, the very strong one has penetrated it with many arrows in such fashion that they extend three palms beyond the back of that target.

PLATE 104 • OBELISK OF TUTHMOSIS I, SEEN FROM THE NORTHEAST

PLATE 105 • UPPER PART OF AN OBELISK INSCRIBED BY TUTHMOSIS III

PLATE 106 • CRYPTOGRAM OF HATSHEPSUT: MAĀTKARE

The statuette of Setau (fig. 63) is the replica sculpted in the round of a fragment of Hatshepsut's cryptogram that we can see in plate 106, of which many examples exist in the temple of Deir el-Bahri. It represents a kneeling figure holding a gigantic uraeus between its hands, surmounted by a disk upheld by horns and resting on the *ka* sign.

"The symbol can be broken down into elements that are transposed in an equivalent manner, with the exception of the *ka* sign clearly expressed. The sun Ra is found in the disk placed between the horns, Maāt in the uraeus, with the cartouche enveloping the entire thing in the *chen* sign, which is its original form." (E. Drioton)

It is therefore read as Maātkare.

PLATE 107 • "REARING" COBRA

PLATE 108 • OBELISK OF HATSHEPSUT, NORTH FACE AND NORTHWEST CORNER

PLATE 109 • OBELISK OF HATSHEPSUT, NORTH FACE AND COLUMNS OF THE IPET-SUT HYPOSTYLE HALL

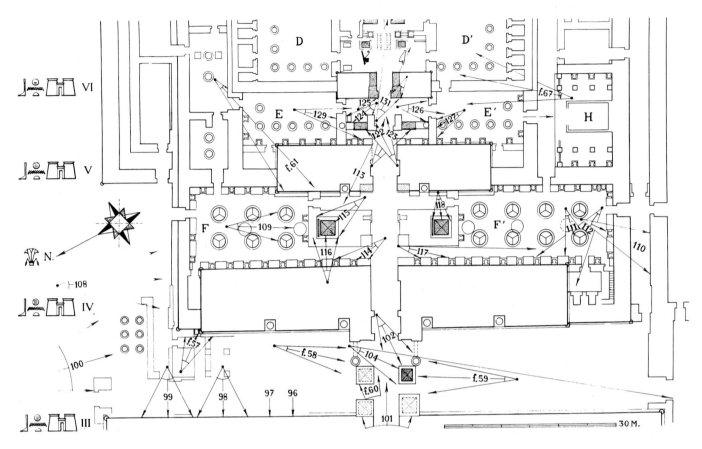

Diagram 6. Obelisks and building sections included between the third pylon and the sanctuary of the barque

The wall built by Tuthmosis III around the queen's obelisk went as high as the third tableau (starting from the base). On the five upper tableaux that emerged above it, the image of Amun was hammered out by Akhenaten and restored by Seti I.

At the foot of this wall is a limestone column pedestal that is presumed to have originally supported a cedar column. Sandstone papyriform columns are on each side (see diagram 5, *F*); the one in the background on the left bears, above the floral decoration, a ring of three lines of text that are of the greatest importance. Here Tuthmosis III recounts: *My Majesty had raised four columns in addition to the two columns of the north end, a total of six columns wrought with electrum . . . in solid sandstone . . . [of which] the height is 31 cubits (16.23 m) on the two sides of the august doorway.*

From this text and that of the two northern columns preserving the name of Tuthmosis I, Borchardt supposes that Tuthmosis I had already

replaced the two cedar columns in the north sector with two sandstone columns aligned on the sites of the two limestone pedestals. Two sandstone columns therefore existed when the queen raised her obelisks.[14]

PLATE 110 • OSIRIAN PILLAR, INTERIOR SURFACE OF THE SURROUNDING WALL SOUTH OF THE TEMPLE OF IPET-SUT

The surrounding wall was erected by Tuthmosis III but decorated at certain places on the inside by Ramesses II.

The Osirian statue carries an ankh in each of its two clenched fists. This is the symbol of the crossing of life, the time of death for the resurrection.

[14]The height of these columns was 31 cubits (16.23 m). (See *Urkunden*, vol. 4, p. 842) The pedestals of the previous columns were made of alabaster. The ceiling was probably wood.

PLATE 111 • OSIRIAN PILLAR AND COLUMN OF
THE SOUTHWEST CORNER OF THE
HYPOSTYLE HALL

PLATE 112 • COLUMNS FROM THE SOUTHWEST
CORNER OF THE HYPOSTYLE HALL

The obelisk of Tuthmosis I is in the background;
in the middle an Osirian pillar attached to the west
wall of the hypostyle hall forms the revetment on the
inside surface of the fourth pylon. The same column
that figures in plate 111 can be seen in the foreground, but from a different angle.

The base of the shaft is decorated by three series
of overlapping leaves. The outer three bear the characteristic ribbing of the campaniform order in their
centers, but without the diminution at the base that
customarily accompanies the column's decor (pl. 57),
and between the tips of each leaf is a lotus flower.

A three-line inscription forms a ring above the
leaves. It begins with Amenhotep II's protocol in the
axis of the second row of overlapping leaves, which is
probably perpendicular to the overall axis of this
room, then the text turns around the column, still in
the same direction, and continues the second line
above its own starting point.

An important passage can be found near the end
of the second line (pls. 111 and 112):

*He made (it) as his monument for his father
(Amun), making for him the august columns of the
southern hypostyle, wrought with electrum very plenti-
fully. . . . I increased that which was before; I surpassed
that which the ancestors made.* (Breasted, *Ancient
Records*, vol. 2, § 805)

There is still some question about the existence
of a golden adytum with silver paving stones and
numerous vessels that were more magnificent than
the bodies of the stars!

(It would be good to verify whether the ribbing
visible on the column of plate 112 wasn't oriented to
true north.)

PLATE 113 • HATSHEPSUT'S OBELISK SEEN FROM
THE EAST

Hatshepsut's obelisk can be seen through the
broken north splaying of the doorway to the fifth
pylon. In the foreground, right, is the interior north
casement of the doorway to the fifth pylon bearing
the cartouche of Tuthmosis I, to the right of which
can be seen the upper portion of an Osirian column
by this same pharaoh.

Fig. 62. Block with "Queen Hatshepsut's red naos" found in the third pylon

Plate 114 • Fourth Pylon: Two Osirian Pillars

Plate 115 • Base of Hatshepsut's Obelisk, Southeast Corner

Eight lines of inscriptions are carved horizontally on the four sides of the obelisk's base. The text begins with the top line of the southern facade with the titles of the queen and her recounting of the erection of two great obelisks of southern (Aswan) granite on the occasion of her first renewal: *Two great obelisks of enduring granite of the South, (their) summits [pyramidions] being of electrum of the best of every country.*

On the west (pl. 116), the queen affirms that she has acted under the command and supervision of Amun, recognizing his divinity. She has conceived of nothing without following his laws (of proportion) because her *heart was in sia* (wisdom). She knows that *Karnak is the horizon on earth [the first appearance], the August Ascent of the beginning, the sacred eye of the All-Lord, the place of his heart.* While she was sitting on the palace throne, she would commemorate He who had created her, her heart was guided to realize the erection of two electrum obelisks, *whose point(s) mingled with heaven, in the august colonnade between the two great pylons of the king, the mighty bull, Okheperkere (Tuthmosis I), the deceased [maā kheru] Horus.* (An affirmation that confirms that the fourth and fifth pylons were indeed built by Tuthmosis I.)

To the north (pl. 109, hidden by the wall), after a long oath of faith where the queen affirms that her power over the earth is due to divine kindness and that she will descend into the *amenti* and exist *in eternity as an "Undying One,"* she specifies that these two obelisks were extracted from the mountains and erected in seven months, during the fifteenth year of her reign.

On the east side the queen recounts how, following her desire to embellish the obelisk, she measured the best electrum by the *hekat, more than the entire Two Lands had (ever) seen. The ignorant, like the wise, knoweth it.* (Ibid., §§ 314–319)

Plate 116 • Base of Hatshepsut's Obelisk, West Face

One can admire the perfection of the carving of the hieroglyphics in the granite of this face of the obelisk. Each sign is in light relief within a hollow with sharp edges, cut exactly on a right angle to the flat surface of the obelisk. (See also pl. 118)

The revetment wall on the west is carved in sunken relief, while the north and east walls (pls. 109 and 115) are carved in relief.

Plate 117 • South Wing of the Fourth Pylon: Osirian Pillars

All these Osirises of the south sector are wearing the white crown and are fitted into the niches.

Plate 118 • Base of Hatshepsut's Broken Southern Obelisk

Fig. 63. Setau statuette (Louvre Museum)

Fig. 64. Karnak, as seen from the northeast by H. Béchard (around 1880)

PLATE 119 • PYRAMIDION OF HATSHEPSUT'S BROKEN SOUTHERN OBELISK

The upper portion of Hatshepsut's southern obelisk can be seen in fig. 64, a photograph taken around 1880. It is at the very spot where it was found, broken, on a mountain of debris; this photo places its fall at a relatively recent date.

PLATES 120 AND 121 • STATUE OF TUTHMOSIS III

Legrain catalog no. 42056. Statue of Tuthmosis III bearing flowers. Black granite. Actual height is 1.52 meters. Found in 1903 in the northeast corner of the block of masonry that surrounded the southern obelisk of Hatshepsut. Its base was right up against the east wall of the block, with the face turned toward the south.

The statue has been broken into numerous fragments, not all of which have been found.

Missing are the head, the torso, the arms, the table of offerings, a portion of the bouquets of wheat, and the front corners of the pedestal. (Log entry of the museum, 38.328.)

The left foot in front is set on five bows and the papyri of the North are represented above it. The right foot behind is set upon four bows, and the flowers of the South that are the counterpart to the papyrus have a form that is quite abnormal.

The king is very probably carrying, in the manner of a Nile (fig. 1), a platter of offerings from which are hanging sheaves of wheat, bouquets of papyrus, and braces of ducks with their heads down. On the left side two ducks have their heads turned up.

PLATE 122 • NORTH DOORPOSTS FOR THE DOORWAYS OF THE

"ANTECHAMBER" AND THE SIXTH PYLON

PLATE 123 • SOUTH DOORPOSTS FOR THE DOORWAYS OF THE "ANTECHAMBER" AND THE SIXTH PYLON

The interior of the portal of the fifth pylon can be seen in the extreme right foreground, then the sandstone doorposts[15] of the antechamber doorway that are in the name of Tuthmosis III but of Ptolemaic manufacture. These form a ledge in the rose granite wall. The king is wearing the red crown in the north and the white crown in the south.

In the middle are the red granite doorposts of the doorway to Tuthmosis III's sixth pylon, on which the king, wearing the white and red crowns in correspondence to the direction he faces, is worshiping the *neter* four times.

Tuthmosis III, as he wrote in his "Text of the Youth" (notes to pls. 166–169), made "an august pylon on the inside of the temple facing the sanctuaries"; this is in reference to the sixth pylon, erected between the fifth pylon and the "temple" of Hatshepsut.

Then Tuthmosis III divided anew the space between the fifth and sixth pylons in building upon the site of Tuthmosis I's colonnade, a wall made of granite blocks,[16] pierced by a doorway with sandstone doorposts (diagram 5, *c*). It thus forms a kind of "vestibule," closed on the north and south, that provides access to the preceding antechamber of the sixth pylon, which opens to the north and south by doorways (pls. 126 and 129).

The "royal ascent" is represented on the two granite doorposts that frame the vestibule door that provides access to the antechamber, but whereas ordinarily this depicts the king, framed by Mentu and Tum, going toward Amun, here this scene is sep-

arated into two tableaux. On the north the king, wearing the red crown, is led by Tum of Heliopolis. On the south he is wearing the white crown and being led to Amun by Mentu of Thebes. In addition these two half-scenes are directed toward the south instead of being oriented to the general axis of the temple.

The "royal ascent" toward the sanctuary is part of a group of ritual tableaux whose principal scenes, carved on the naos of Philip Arrhidaeus (pls. 157 and 159, and fig. 70) are as follows: the *purification* of the king (which took place without a doubt in front of the fourth pylon), the *imposition of the crowns*, which must have taken place in the hypostyle, the *royal ascent*, and, finally, the *enthronement*, or the embrace with the *neter*, which, at Karnak, took place in the little sanctuary marked H (diagram 5, pl. 126). (Pertaining to this problem, see Barguet, *La Structure du Temple*, pp. 147–148)

PLATE 124 • NORTHWEST CORNER OF THE ANTECHAMBER PRECEDING THE SIXTH PYLON

On the left is the advanced portion of the sandstone portal located between the "vestibule" and the "antechamber," on which Tuthmosis III dedicated this edifice to his father Tuthmosis I. On the right is the west doorpost of the north door to this antechamber, where the king wearing the red crown can be seen. There is a granite statue in the corner.

PLATE 125 • DOORWAY OF THE SIXTH PYLON, NORTH DOORPOST: DETAIL

Note the deeply carved line, "as if by a large knife blade in a soft material," in the corner of the monumental block of granite on the right.

PLATE 126 • ANTECHAMBER OF TUTHMOSIS III, SOUTH DOORWAY

Tuthmosis III is wearing the red crown on the west doorpost of the south doorway of the antechamber (north = west = red), while on the east doorpost he is wearing the white crown (south = east = white). The king is holding in one hand the *mākes* cane and the white *hedj* club and is extending the other toward the entranceway. In Luxor this double

---

[15]The dedication inscription of these doorposts declaring that they were plated with electrum is confirmed by the existence of small attachment holes at their bases.

[16]The granite blocks supporting the vestibule doorway are provided with corner tori on their north and south ends; they therefore represent the remnants of an ancient sanctuary that was originally built between the fifth pylon and the queen's buildings. See also Barguet, *La Structure du Temple*, pl. 15B.

Fig. 65. Doorway of the fifth pylon, which is in ruins today but still existed at the time of this photograph (1859)

scene is accompanied by a legend that indicates the chapter of "Entering toward the Sanctuaries" (Berlin Papyrus, chap. 22) from which here are several phrases:

Come to me Amun-Ra, for this embrace from which you will emerge this day and rise as king. . . .

Come to me Amun-Ra, and open the double doors of heaven and the double doors of earth. . . .

I enter with Maāt, so that Amun-Ra, lord of

Karnak, unites with the perfect Maāt of this day.

This doorway provides access to the peristyle court of Tuthmosis I (diagram 5, *E'*), of which several remnants of the shafts for sixteen-sided polygonal columns can be seen. In the background, against the wall of the second enclosure, was the site of the small *H* room, now destroyed, toward which the king directed himself during the course of his royal ascent, to be embraced by the *neter*. (See pl. 123 and

Barguet, *La Structure du Temple*)

All the names on the threshold were hollowed out and recarved in the name of Seti II.

PLATE 127 • OFFERING OF MAĀT TO AMUN

After going through the south doorway of the antechamber and entering the peristyle court of Tuthmosis I, one will note on the lone wall still standing (diagrams 6 and 7) a curious representation of Amun in light relief. The entire profile of the head is deeply carved, perhaps to receive the face and headdress of precious gems and metals (undoubtedly lapis lazuli and gold, Amun's face being most often painted blue and his headdress, yellow).

On the extension of the throne's pedestal, Queen Ahmose-Nefertari (wife of Ahmose), also sculpted in relief as she was "deified," is presenting the *neter* the sistrum and the *menat*. Behind her, Ramesses III, carved in sunk relief, is offering Maāt, the daughter of Ra who symbolizes justice, precision, measurement, truth, and conscience.

The outline of Amun and the queen in very light relief gives this great *neter* a phantom character, as if the character of the king were emphasized by opposing it to the spiritual nature of Amun.[17]

The offering to Maāt (chap. 42) that takes place in the second half of the sacred service (see pls. 51 and 58) in the Ritual of the Daily Divine Worship, is accompanied by a very long invocation to Amun-Ra of Karnak, "master of eternity, the ram who darts forth his rays, creator of all that exists." These are some brief extracts:

I am coming toward you, I am Thoth, the two hands rejoined to carry Maāt. . . .

Your daughter Maāt, you rejuvenate at the sight of her, you live on the perfume of her dew. Maāt places her-self like an amulet at your throat, she sits upon your chest. The neters *pay you tribute with Maāt, for they know her wisdom. . . .*

Your right eye [western] is Maāt, your left eye [east-

*Fig. 66. First peristyle courtyard of Tuthmosis I:
column engaged in the vestibule wall of Tuthmosis III*

ern] is Maāt . . . [Maāt is identical to the Eye of Horus, the sublime offering.]

The two halves of the earth come to you carrying Maāt, to give you the entire orb of the solar disk. O Amun-Ra, Maāt joins with your solar disk. . . .

You exist because Maāt exists, and Maāt exists reciprocally. [A. Moret, trans., *Annales du Service des Antiquités de l'Egypte* 40: 185–202]

---

[17]The sarcophagus of the queen Ahmose-Nefertari found in the cachette of Deir el-Bahri contained two mummies: that of the queen and that of Ramesses III. (See Gauthier, *Le Livre des Rois*, vol. 2, p. 185, 2) The high judges of the tribunals wore a jewel representing Maāt, the deity of truth and justice, over their chests, hung from a golden chain. (Moret, *Annales du Service des Antiquités de l'Egypte* 40: 185–202)

Fig. 67. Second peristyle court of Tuthmosis III: granite pillars

PLATE 128 • DETAIL OF THE PORTAL NAME
HIEROGLYPHS OF THE FIFTH PYLON

These two hieroglyphs, the ram's head with horizontal horns and the swallow, form the two titles of
Amun (whose name has been hammered out) in the
name of the portal to the fifth pylon: "Amun great
with prestige" (see pl. 101 and diagram 5, *b*).

PLATE 129 • ANTECHAMBER AND VESTIBULE OF
TUTHMOSIS III, EXTERIOR FACADE
OF THE NORTH WALL

When Tuthmosis III built the vestibule and
antechamber between the fifth and sixth pylons, he
included within the thickness of the walls of his new
construction two of Tuthmosis I's portico columns.
A sixteen-sided polygonal column of the northern
sector can be seen here. It carries the titles of
Tuthmosis I on the middle of the east side. (See fig.

66, the column of the southern sector.)

In the middle ground is the outer surface of the
antechamber's north doorway, beyond which the south
doorway can be recognized (see pl. 126 and fig. 66).

PLATE 130 • DOORWAY OF THE SIXTH PYLON

On each side of the granite doorposts of the
doorway to the sixth pylon, on sandstone curbing,
are carved five horizontal lines of prisoners with
coats of arms[18] mentioning the nineteen cities conquered during the course of the expeditions of

[18]The cartouche-escutcheons on the north wing are those of towns
conquered in Syria and Palestine; those on the south wing represent
the towns of Nubia and Sudan. (*Urkunden* 4, pp. 788–806)

An important piece of the lintel that had formed part of the doorway of the sixth pylon represents Tuthmosis III on its bottom facade.
The king is shown "'worshiping Amun-Ra in the ninth hour of the
day,' which emphasizes the cosmic nature of this temple." (Barguet, *La
Structure du Temple*, p. 112, pl. 16B)

Tuthmosis III recounted in the "chamber of the Annals." Above, the scene of the "ritual massacre" can be recognized.

In his "Text of the Youth," Tuthmosis III says that he built for this pylon:

A great panel fashioned from new cedar, worked with gold mounted in true black copper and . . . copper. The great name above it is in electrum, gold that has been twice refined, and black copper.

This "great name" is the "august-gate-Menkhe-Perre-beloved-of-Amun-mighty-with-prestige."

PLATE 131 • DOORWAY OF THE SIXTH PYLON: SOUTHERN GRANITE PILLAR, NAOS OF PHILIP ARRHIDAEUS

Beyond the sixth pylon's doorway, in the fore-sanctuary, Tuthmosis III erected two granite pillars that bear four tableaux on their east and west sides and symbolic flowers of the Two Lands on their north and south sides. These are the sole examples of this type known and their architectural role has been the subject of much discussion.

On the south pillar the king is wearing the white crown. On the upper tableau he is embraced by Amunet; on the one below, by Amun.

All the way in the back is the granite sanctuary of the barque of Philip Arrhidaeus, which replaced the ancient repository installed by Tuthmosis III. This had been fronted by a periptery whose square sandstone pillars were furnished with small holes at

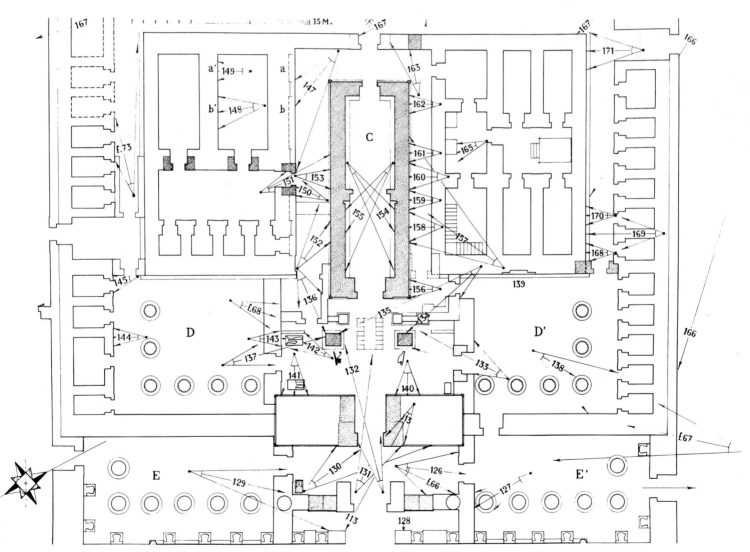

Diagram 7. Peristyle courtyard of Tuthmosis I and Tuthmosis III, sanctuaries of Hatshepsut, naos of Philip Arrhidaeus

their bases, suggesting that they were plated with either electrum or gold. Within this peripteral entrance, suggests P. Barguet, was the placement of the two obelisks "of clear electrum" (a blend of gold and silver) of 2,500 talents that Ashurbanipal was said to have brought away from Thebes (in 656 B.C.) "where they had been erected before the doorway of the sanctuary." The indication of their weight, the equivalent of 37,875 kilograms, permits their height to be estimated at about 6.9 meters. (See Desroches Noblecourt, *Revue d'Egyptologie* 8:47; and Barguet, *La Structure du Temple*, p. 130)

The "chamber of the Annals" was covered by a roof whose architraves rested on so-called heraldic pillars.

PLATE 132 • NORTHERN GRANITE PILLAR, NAOS OF PHILIP ARRHIDAEUS

On the north pillar the king wearing the red crown is embraced by Hathor, then by Amun, with the same gestures depicted on the southern pillar.

In the background, on the threshold of the doorway to the granite naos, can be seen the king of the North making "great strides" with his oar (see pl. 74). Between the naos and this pillar, the king worships the *neter* four times on the remains of a sandstone pillar.

PLATE 133 • CHAMBER OF THE ANNALS, SOUTH DOORWAY: GRANITE PILLARS OF TUTHMOSIS III

After the building of the sixth pylon, Tuthmosis III divided the peristyle court (diagrams 5 and 7, *D*, *D'*) into three sections, by two walls that formed a central chamber in front of the sanctuary. On the walls of this chamber, on the east facade of the sixth pylon, and on the walls of the sanctuary, he inscribed his twenty years of campaigns abroad, from which comes the name "chamber of the Annals" that is given to this part of the temple.

Through the southern doorway of the fore-sanctuary the three flowers of the South and the three papyri of the North can be seen on the granite pillars. The framing of this doorway, which was probably of granite, is currently missing. The inscriptions on the right are in the name of Seti II.

PLATE 134 • SOUTHEAST CORNER OF THE SOUTH GRANITE PILLAR

Note the admirable detail of the flowers of the South delicately carved on the base and surmounted by the cartouche of Tuthmosis Neferkhepru. On the upper tableau the king is embraced by Mut, the mistress of Asheru.

PLATE 135 • EAST SIDE OF THE NORTH PILLAR: DETAIL

Amun "embraces" the king in a strange position; he is holding his own arm passed over the royal shoulder.

PLATE 136 • EAST SIDE OF THE NORTH PILLAR: UPPER SECTION

Here the king is embraced by Mut, mistress of Heaven, and, as on all the other tableaux of these pillars, he is overshadowed by the vulture and not the falcon.

PLATE 137 • THE TWO GRANITE PILLARS OF TUTHMOSIS III, SEEN FROM THE NORTH

On the north pillar, above the papyrus, the stems of which are marked by the fine ribbing always indicated on the shaft of campaniform columns, is the cartouche of Menkheperre Setepenre.

In the background are the cornice and torus that crown the southern doorway of the fore-sanctuary. On the left is the naos of Philip Arrhidaeus; the hollow disk on its cornice contained, doubtlessly, the golden solar disk.

PLATE 138 • PERISTYLE COURT OF TUTHMOSIS III, SOUTHWEST CORNER: FASCICULATED COLUMN

Whereas Tuthmosis I surrounded his peristyle court with sixteen-sided polygonal columns (diagrams 5 and 7, *E*, *E'*), Tuthmosis III bordered his new inner courtyard with a portico of fasciculate columns with sixteen cusps, whose bases are very finely worked. On the north and south this portico fronted the chapels, today partially in ruins, that were built by Tuthmosis III on the site of Tuthmosis I's original enclosure wall.

The cartouche of Tuthmosis III alternated with that of Amenhotep I on the chapels' doorways.

PLATE 139 • TUTHMOSIS IV AND HIS MOTHER, QUEEN TIY

Legrain catalog no. 42080. Single statue of Tuthmosis IV and Queen Tiy together. Black granite. Height: 1.10 meters. Cairo Museum entry no. 36.336.

Found January 2, 1903, at Karnak, "in the room located to the south of the fore-sanctuary with the two granite pillars. It was buried, almost vertically, several centimeters below the normal level of the temple, near the east wall, in front of the stela that is carved in its center."

PLATE 140 • SOUTH WING OF THE SIXTH PYLON: SOUTH INTERIOR WALL

To the right are the remains of the granite doorpost of the sixth pylon's doorway. On the sandstone revetment seen on the left Amun is introducing the king. Behind Amun (modified) is a line of inscriptions on which Horemheb signs his restoration, then the two last lines of the famous text of the Annals inscribed by Tuthmosis III on the walls of the sanctuary and the fore-sanctuary, where he recounts the events pertaining to the construction of a fortress in Lebanon. His Majesty returned, disembarked at Thebes, and celebrated the victory feast for his first campaign of the year 23, on certain days selected according to Amun's etiquette. Then, *while the majesty of that august* neter *[Amun] navigated his way toward Ipet of the South [Luxor],* the king deposited very large offerings of all kinds at the entrance to this temple.

In a long enumeration of these gifts, consisting of slaves, livestock, precious metals, gemstones, and territories, there is mention of three cities, among which is Yanoam (see pls. 30–39), *flocks of geese for the sacred pool* (pl. 341), particular offerings for his new sed-festival temple (pls. 172–221), for his obelisks, for his statues, and for the feast of Min's emergence. Tuthmosis III speaks of the creation of a new garden *planted with all manner of pleasing trees* for the daily plant offerings.

Thus My Majesty has created all monuments, all laws, all regulations.... To my father Amun ... for great is my knowledge of his glory. I was instructed within his perfection, resting within his body....

The last two lines (pl. 140) provide a final list of offerings, among which are 318 white breads for the four obelisks (these are cakes that were in the shape of the pyramidion crowning the obelisk).

PLATE 141 • STATUE OF AMUN-RA

In the northwest corner of the fore-sanctuary is a statue of Amun in profile in front of the inner wall of the north wing of the sixth pylon. Behind it is the text relating the tributes received during the course

Fig. 68. Inscriptions of Osorkon II that have the image of an Ethiopian king (recognizable by his sandals) added to them

of the final campaigns of the year 39 and the year 42, which ends near the entrance to the pylon with these words:

Behold, His Majesty commanded the recounting of the victories he has won from the year 23 to the year 42, when this inscription was written upon his sanctuary. . . .

"There are two statues erected in front of the north doorway of the fore-sanctuary, on the east side one in the image of Amunet, on the west, Amun. These colossal statues measure around six meters in height. They are carved out of a deep-toned red sandstone." (Legrain, *Notes prises à Karnak, Rec. Trav.,* vol. 22, p. 20)

The statue of Amun was found broken into a great many pieces. Behind the feathers on the head-dress an inscription can be found that gives the Horus name of Tutankhamun and displays his cartouches overwritten by those of Horemheb.

PLATE 142 • STATUE OF AMUNET

"The statue of Amunet has also been very badly treated. We haven't yet been able to find the head. The body was broken into numerous pieces that I have been able to restore almost totally. . . . I discovered, under the spot where the statue's pedestal must have been set, a foundation stone [in the name of] Maātkare [Hatshepsut]. This, by the way, happened

often in many locations around the sanctuary. These stones were, in a manner of speaking, planted like seeds in the ground. (Ibid., p. 20)

PLATE 143 • DORSAL STELA OF AMUNET'S STATUE

There is a column of inscriptions on the dorsal stela of Amunet's statue that carries Horemheb's cartouche visibly added on to that of Tutankhamun (fig. 68), as on the statue of Amun.

Legrain notes that the name of Amun has not been hammered out on the two statues, which proves that they are certainly the work of Tutankhamun and not earlier than Amenhotep IV. But on the other hand, his study of the two dorsal inscriptions leads him to conclude: "In sum, the statues of Amun and Amunet teach us, since they have been remade anew, that Amenhotep IV had compelled the disappearance of the earlier statues, that Tutankhamun had the new ones carved in a red sandstone of admirable purity, that Horemheb usurped them from his predecessor, that they were overturned during the Roman or Coptic era, and that, finally, the statue of Amunet lay on the very ground where Hatshepsut had formerly buried foundation stones, perhaps under the previous statue destroyed by Akhenaten." (Ibid, p. 21)

Fig. 69. Figure whose feet are formed from duck heads

Note the peristyle court of Tuthmosis III (diagrams 5 and 7, *D'*) in the background, with its sixteen-cusped fasciculate columns.

PLATE 144 • NORTH CHAPELS OF TUTHMOSIS III: THE KING OFFERING THE *AKH* BIRD TO HATHOR

The king, holding the *akh* bird *(Ibis comata)* in one hand and four long stakes in the other (undoubtedly for holding the net for the bird hunt?), is making the "great stride" before Hathor, who is presenting him with the *menat* and holding the palm of the years. Hathor's son Ihy, completely nude, is in front of her, holding a sistrum toward the inscription that provides the name of the deity: House of Horus.

PLATE 145 • NORTH CHAPELS OF TUTHMOSIS III: DOORWAY LINTEL

Above the lintel of one of the northern chapels bordering the interior peristyle court of Tuthmosis III, a curious representation can be found of a small individual standing in the back of a papyrus barque, behind a person of greater height who is probably the king. In the temple of Luxor and the tomb of Ay there exist representations of the king alone in a similar skiff, harvesting papyrus.

The oddity of this representation stems from the fact that the legs and feet of the small individual are completely formed of duck heads (fig. 69), typical marsh fowl. In Abydos there is a *neter*, Hapi (the Nile), whose head has been replaced by two duck heads back-to-back.[19]

PLATE 146 • STATUE OF SENMUT

> Legrain catalog no. 42123. Statue of Senmut, architect of Hatshepsut and "foster-father" of her daughter, the princess Neferure. Black granite. Height: 0.6 meters. Found May 5, 1904, in the cachette court of Karnak (the head was found a

[19]This scene can be reconstructed thanks to an old photograph that shows the neighboring block, which has now disappeared. The king is sailing through the papyrus thickets and is carrying two genies in the back of his skiff. The one whose body is composed of duck heads is an ancient fishing deity whose name is Kheddw. (See Barguet, *La Structure du Temple*, p. 121 and pl. 21)

long way from the body). Date: Eighteenth Dynasty. Cairo Museum entry no. 37439.

Senmut was the most powerful nobleman in Hatshepsut's court. He directed all the works in the temples of Karnak, Luxor, and Deir el-Bahri himself, and left an inscription on the rocks of Aswan commemorating the extraction of two large obelisks, the work of which he led personally.

PLATE 147 • NORTH WALL OF THE SANCTUARY: START OF TUTHMOSIS III'S ANNALS

This is without a doubt the wall that has inspired the most commentary in the entire temple of Karnak. It depicts Tuthmosis III, who is holding the *mākes* cane and the white *hedj* club in one hand and the *sekhem* scepter in the other, consecrating the rich offerings in front of him on behalf of Amun. These are coffers, gold bracelets with precious stones, alabaster jars *filled with pure unguent for the divine rituals, a vessel of precious stone that His Majesty made following the intention of his own heart,* and all other manner of objects whose number and material is specified. Two large masts stand between the king and these offerings, each bearing a different inscription; on the one on the left Tuthmosis III declares that he has erected *two great granite obelisks with electrum pyramids at the double doorways of the temple* (the two obelisks that were in front of the fourth pylon and of which nothing currently remains but the bases. See pl. 101 and commentary).

On the mast on the right the king speaks of the erection of the *great granite obelisks with electrum pyramidions.* These are probably the two obelisks in front of the seventh pylon, of which one is presently in Istanbul (pl. 364 and fig. 124). Recall the mention in the Annals of offerings for the four obelisks (pl. 140).

Under this immense tableau that occupies the entire wall from the northeast corner to the granite doorway (diagram 5, *e*) are sixty-seven columns of text, reading from east to west, that recount the king's first campaign:

Tuthmosis III crossed the frontier at Tharu, in the year 22, to repress the rebellion of the Asians *each man [fighting] against [his neighbor].* In three weeks, after a brief stop in Gaza, the king arrived at Yehem and held a council of war, for he had just learned that the great chief of the Kadesh was gathering all the princes of Palestine and Syria, with their troops and horses, at Megiddo to fight the pharaoh.

Therefore His Majesty discussed with his general staff the plan of attack. Three roads were open to them; the first was the most direct but also dangerous because from Aruna on it went through a narrow gorge. The other two were more easily traveled but led either to the north or to the south of Megiddo. The officers implored the king to choose one of these latter routes rather than make them travel there by way of a road that was difficult *(shta):*

While they (come) and say that the enemy is there waiting, (holding) the way against a multitude. Will not horse come behind (horse and man behind) man likewise? Shall our (advance guard) be fighting while our (rear guard) is yet standing yonder in Aruna not having fought?

But the king flared up against their prudent counsel:

"I (swear) as Ra loves me, as my father Amun favors me . . . my majesty will proceed upon this road of Aruna! Let him who will among you go upon those roads ye have mentioned, and let him who will among you come in the following of my majesty! Shall they think among those enemies whom Ra detests: 'Does his majesty proceed upon another road? He begins to be fearful of us,' so will they think."

The officers called upon the protection of Amun and submitted.

He [the king] went forth at the head of his army himself, showing (the way) by his (own) footsteps, horse behind (horse), (His Majesty) being at the head of his army.

During this time the enemy had emerged, numerous and in order of battle, divided into two wings, one on the north road and one on the south road. Thus it happened that the foreguard had already filled the hollow of the valley while the pharaoh's rear guard was still in Aruna . . . but the enemy was not expecting them! *The shadow had turned*, camp was raised and orders given for an attack on the morning of the following day, "the day of the feast of the new moon."

His majesty went forth in a chariot of electrum,

arrayed in his weapons of war like Horus the Smiter [in the center of his divisions], [and when those leagued against him] saw his majesty prevailing against them, they fled . . . in fear. . . .

Then it was recorded upon a roll of leather in the temple of Amun this day.

(All the citations from the Annals are taken from Breasted, *Ancient Records*, vol. 2, §§ 421–33.)

PLATE 148 • BAS-RELIEF OF HATSHEPSUT: THE "GREAT STRIDE"

PLATE 149 • BAS-RELIEF OF HATSHEPSUT: THE PURIFICATION

These bas-reliefs, currently inside one of the north rooms of Hatshepsut's temple (diagram 7, *a'*, *b'*) were originally on the outside of the south wall of this same room (in *a* and *b*), but they were covered over by the "wall of the Annals" (pl. 147) when Tuthmosis III made the central portion of the temple into a single room with four pillars (diagram 5). Legrain removed Hatshepsut's reliefs, block by block, and remounted them in the location where they are found today.

In the scene of the "great stride" in front of Amun-Ra Kamutef, the queen and her cartouches have been hammered out, but with such care that the exact silhouette of her red crown, her two vessels, and the hieroglyphics of her name can still be seen. Neither the face nor name of Amun was hammered out by Akhenaten, as they were everywhere else, because at that time they were hidden by the wall of the Annals.

Note the joint of the stones that passes through at the level of the phallus of the generating Amun-Ra and the queen's navel (for the meaning of this scene see the commentary to pl. 74).

Thoth and Horus, standing on pedestals, are making the purification with the ankhs that fall from the two vessels and form a dome around the queen, who has been hammered out (for the meaning of this scene see pl. 157 and fig. 70). Only the scarabs have been spared in this hammered-out line of horizontal text.

These hammered-out effacements have given rise to a belief in a conflict between Tuthmosis III and Hatshepsut.

PLATE 150 • GRANITE NORTH DOORWAY OF THE SANCTUARY

This doorway, named Menkheperre-Amun-ur-bau (diagram 5, *e*), is the only one still in place of the three granite doorways mentioned by Tuthmosis III in his "Text of the Youth" (pls. 168–171).

PLATE 151 • NORTH DOORWAY OF THE SANCTUARY AND NAOS OF PHILIP ARRHIDAEUS

The north wall of the naos of Philip Arrhidaeus can be seen through the doorway; the king, wearing the red crown, is making the "great stride" while holding the two ritual vessels. (To see the counterpart of this scene, look at pl. 157: the king wearing the white crown on the south wall.)

PLATES 152–162 • GRANITE NAOS OF PHILIP ARRHIDAEUS

PLATE 152 • NORTH EXTERIOR WALL

Philip Arrhidaeus's naos is formed from two long chambers that correspond externally to two buildings of different heights placed end to end. This is clearly visible from the cornices and tori seen on this plate.

The western half is the highest, the exterior north face of which is occupied by an immense tableau representing Amun-Min Kamutef, sheathed in white. He is standing on a bulwark set on an altar, which is in turn supported by a staircase. Behind the statue is a large rectangle of red cloth, stretched between two falcon-headed stakes and surmounted by two words: *divine shadow*. The *neter* is preceded by twelve insignia, of which two are carrying his name: the bull *ka* and the vulture Mut perched on the *f* viper.

This tableau is evocative of one of the most ancient religious feasts, the emergence of Min, which is referred to from the very first dynasties.

PLATE 153 • CONSECRATION OF THE OFFERINGS, NORTH WALL OF THE NAOS

To the east, which is the lowest part of the sanctuary, the consecration of the offerings by the king with the *sekhem* scepter, *repeated four times*, can be found on the outside north wall.

The snake-headed vulture overshadowing the king is wadjet, the guardian spirit of the North.

Fig. 70. Naos of Philip Arrhidaeus: purification, imposition of the crowns, the royal ascent, enthronement

PLATE 154 • INTERIOR SOUTH WALL OF THE WEST CHAMBER

PLATE 155 • INTERIOR NORTH WALL OF THE WEST CHAMBER

The ceiling of this chamber, painted blue, is constellated with gold stars.

The walls are divided into four registers, on which the gestures for the "Daily Divine Worship" to Amun under his two different forms are represented in alternation. The "hunt with the net" (see pl. 82–83) can be recognized on the third register of the south wall near the entrance (pl. 154, on the right).

The walls are composed of three immense superimposed blocks,[20] but where in the north the joint separates the two upper registers from the two lower ones exactly, on the south it cuts through all the figures on the third register at the level of their sex organs.

PLATE 156 • SOUTHWEST CORNER OF THE NAOS

The jutting cornerstone that forms the pedestal on which the naos rests is a block of reused granite on which the Horus name of Tuthmosis II is carved. This reuse is strange; the stone is carved in such a way that the framing of the name is sloped with respect to the pedestal's horizontal and climbs toward the sanctuary.

This recalls two observations made by Champollion:

First, inside the sanctuary: Behind the king, and between him and the corner of the doorway [are] five columns of hieroglyphs that contain the dedication of the sanctuary as a restoration of that of Tuthmosis III; Philip Arrhidaeus indeed said that he reconstructed the sanctuary of Tuthmosis III, which was on the verge of falling into ruin.

Second, the granite sanctuary terrace is obviously composed of blocks that come from Tuthmosis III's

original sanctuary. One of these blocks still provides a great image, full length and of very fine workmanship, of the generating Amun, with remnants of an inscription containing the list of the gifts given to the god by the king, in gold and various other metals. (*Notices Descriptives*, vol. 2, pp. 149–52)

PLATE 157 • SOUTHERN OUTSIDE FACADE OF THE NAOS

The highest part of the building corresponds to the interior western chamber. It is divided into four registers topped by a torus and a cornice. The lowest part contains but one register, on which are drawn the offering of four calves (black, red, white, and spotted) and the race of the "great stride" by the king wearing the white crown carrying the oar and the rudder (for details see pls. 160 and 161).

The three registers on the left are very interesting. Above (fig. 70) can be found the entirety of the constituent scenes, which from left to right are: The purification of the king by Thoth and Horus, who spread in a dome around him the water poured from the two vessels. *Your purification is my purification and reciprocally* is the formula that is repeated four times.

Thoth and Horus crowning the king, for it is only after he has been purified and crowned that he can fulfill his sacred office.

Received by Thoth, the king is kneeling before Amun seated upon a throne, but he has turned his back and looks in the same direction, thus identifying himself with the *neter*. He receives life and the confirmation of his royalty; then, under the features of a "child with curly locks," he receives the divine milk (see pl. 159 and fig. 70).

On the middle register the sacred barque is leaving the sanctuary, borne on the shoulders of priests, then it is deposited in a chapel that marks one of the stations of the procession. They continue their march before reaching the second repository.

The return of the sacred barque is described on the bottom register, first by water, towed by the king himself standing in a skiff, then borne on the priests' shoulders as the barque is purified with incense by the king. The last scene describes the quadruple purification, with the *white vessels*, of the sacred barque

---

[20]These immense granite blocks probably come from obelisks that were broken, then carved into slabs. (See *Annales du Service des Antiquités de l'Egypte* 5:11) Those reused blocks depicted in plate 156 come from the upper part of an obelisk of Tuthmosis II (pl. 157). The western side of the building is divided into four registers, but the bottom register representing the scenes of foundation is almost completely destroyed.

returned to its sanctuary (pl. 158 and fig. 71).

The interesting assembly of these blocks, the junction between the highest and lowest sections, and the cutting of the figurations by the joints should be noted. For example, the entire royal ascent toward the naos (fig. 70) is drawn on a single block, without any cut, but by virtue of the cutting of the lower scenes that depict the naos on the barques, the royal ascent rests not on the earth but on the sky of these tableaux.

PLATE 158 • THE DEPARTURE AND RETURN OF THE SACRED BARQUE

PLATE 159 • ENTHRONEMENT BY AMUN, BREAST-FEEDING OF THE KING BY AMUNET

PLATE 160 • PRESENTATION OF THE FOUR CALVES TO AMUN-RA KAMUTEF

PLATE 161 • EXAMPLE OF "SQUARING-UP"

During the Ptolemaic era the "squaring-up" of the figures was established on twenty-two squares plus a fraction. The twenty-first square then passed through the level of the eyebrow; the twenty-second cut the fraction of the skullcap cut here by the joint.

Fig. 71. Naos of Philip Arrhidaeus: censing and purification with the white vessel

The known examples of the Ptolemaic canon place the navel at the level of the thirteenth square, which determines the ratio of the golden section with the twenty-first square. Now, on this figure, the division by squares places the upper edge of the sky at thirty-four units, which establishes the ratio of the golden section according to the Fibonacci series: 13, 21, 34.[21]

PLATE 162 • OUTER WALL SOUTH: PRESENTATION OF THE INCENSE

PLATE 163 • GRANITE BLOCK OF THE EAST WALL OF THE CENTRAL SANCTUARY

The east wall of the sanctuary opens on to the part of the temple, destroyed today, where buildings of the Middle Kingdom could still be found during the time of Hatshepsut (see diagrams 5 and 7, and commentaries to pls. 166 and 167).

PLATE 164 • HEAD OF A YOUNG KING; EIGHTEENTH DYNASTY

Head of an unidentified young king, in green igneous rock, found in the foundations of the third pylon at Karnak. Height: 0.21 meters. Dated Eighteenth Dynasty. His features are reminiscent of those of Amenhotep II (pl. 165).

PLATE 165 • CHAPELS OF HATSHEPSUT'S TEMPLE: LIMESTONE STATUE OF AMENHOTEP II

The king, seated, is holding a second figure by the shoulder, who today is totally destroyed. Above his *nemes* headdress he is wearing the *atef* crown. It is quite rare to encounter an example of sculpture in the round in such complete detail. Above the hori-

zontal horns of Khnum rises a bouquet of long, finely carved feathers, bound at the top and framed by two ostrich plumes.

PLATE 166–167 • OVERVIEW OF HATSHEPSUT'S TEMPLE FROM THE SOUTHEAST

On the right the foundation stones of the little chapels built by Tuthmosis III form the first enclosure around the central sanctuaries. On the left are vestiges of the chapels of the second enclosure wall.

In the center is Hatshepsut's temple, which is entirely closed on the north and south and opens on the west to the two peristyle courtyards of Tuthmosis III and Tuthmosis I. On the east it opens onto the totally destroyed portion of the Middle Kingdom temple, where one places the *great hall of feasts* mentioned in two texts that are contemporary to Hatshepsut. The one says that the queen *has ordered the creation [of a monument] in the best imported electrum in the great hall of feasts.* The other text mentioned the numerous offering tables she had installed there. Therefore a "hall of feasts" was already in existence during her era, and as it is not possible to place it within the hypostyle hall of the fourth pylon, which is designated as the *hall of columns*, its location, which is proved to have existed, must be in this site.[22] (from P. Barguet, *La Structure du Temple*)

At the western and eastern ends of the south wall of Hatshepsut's temple two seated kings are represented, turned toward the east; between them is one of the most curious texts of the entire temple (pls. 168–171 and diagram 7).

PLATE 168 • HATSHEPSUT'S TEMPLE, SOUTH WALL, WEST END: THRONE DETAIL

[21]The crown comes to the twenty-seventh square (pl. 163). The block of pink granite taken from the massive north wall of the second pylon currently erected at the entrance of the Middle Kingdom courtyard must be a fragment of the outer wall of the first room of Tuthmosis III's sanctuary of the barque. (See Barguet, *La Structure du Temple*, p. 140, 2; and *B.I.F.A.O.* 13: 15)

The magnificent black granite barque of Amenhotep III's mother that is presently in the British Museum was found in the sanctuary of Philip Arrhidaeus. (See Barguet, *La Structure du Temple*, p. 138, 5)

[22]A text from Edfu (2.11) describes the room sequence, which is certainly the traditional arrangement, starting from the sanctuary. The Holy of Holies opened into the *ḥrt-ib*, "the room of the heart," or the middle, also called "the place where the divine entities sojourn" (Edfu 7.15). This room of the heart, during the Middle Kingdom, must then have been located at *B* (diagram 5). Then comes the "room of offerings," which, at Karnak, could correspond to "the great dwelling of Maāt," cited by Tuthmosis III in his Annals text, that is at sections *C, D, E.* "The hall of feasts with its columns," cited next, can only correspond to hypostyle *F.* (See Barguet, *La Structure du Temple*, pp. 320–26)

PLATE 169 • SOUTH WALL, WEST END: "TEXT OF
THE YOUTH" OF TUTHMOSIS III

Behind the king, who is seated within a columned
building on a terraced pedestal, his Horus name,
"Mighty Bull Shining in Thebes," is written. The
royal throne is decorated with scales, and the plants
of the North and South, bound together around the
sign of union, *sma*, are carved in a square. On the
pedestal, just above, two Niles are linking the "Two
Lands." Behind them with their backs turned are
two opposing lions. The one on the left is projected
over an earlier figuration of Amun (recognizable by
the vertical band behind his back) dating from the
first stage of this building, before Tuthmosis III cut
the southwest corner to frame a doorpost there.

It was obviously intentional to leave the traces of
the ancient figuration of Amun penetrated by the
paw and jaw of the lion of the new sculpture.

In front of the "royal dais" are the first twelve
lines of the famous "Text of the Youth" of Tuthmosis
III (a retrograde text), of which the entire upper portion has been destroyed.

The king, after having made the recitation of his
ascension to the throne, describes the monuments
that he has built:

A divine abode of fine white sandstone for which
he performed the laying of the foundation rituals
himself. A Holy of Holies named *His-Great-Seat-is-
like-the-Horizon-of-Heaven, of sandstone of the Red
Mountain. Its interior was wrought with electrum.*
Three doorways that he named and of which one is
still in place (diagram 5, *e*). *An august pylon* inside the
temple (pls. 122 and 123), the sixth pylon, for which
he built a great cedar door (pls. 130 and 131). Three
other doorways. A sandstone chapel with doors of
cedarwood for his *fathers the kings (of Egypt)* who
were before him. . . . A monument for which he performed himself the ritual of "stretching the cord," at
the site of a brick monument that is completely
ruined. Finally *a splendid harp wrought with silver,
gold, lapis lazuli, malachite, and every splendid costly
stone, for the praise of the beauty of his majesty [the
neter] at his appearances.*

After all these extraordinary monuments, the
king then mentions the *harp of harmony*. (Cita-

tions from Breasted, *Ancient Records*, vol. 2,
§§ 138–66)

PLATE 170 • "TEXT OF THE YOUTH" OF
TUTHMOSIS III

Above the column bearing Tuthmosis III's cartouche a small graffito of Mut is carved.

PLATE 171 • EAST END OF THE SOUTHERN
OUTSIDE WALL OF HATSHEPSUT'S
TEMPLE

PLATE 172 • TEMPLE OF AMUN, SEEN FROM THE
NORTHEAST

PLATE 173 • ENTRY DOORS OF THE NORTH
CHAPELS

These two doorways provide access to the "north
chapels," where scenes of the ritual of laying the
foundation are represented. The third royal protocol
is inscribed on the lintel and the doorposts of the left
doorway, while the first is inscribed over that on the
right.

Tuthmosis III built a series of long chapels at the
north of the temple, east of the *sed*-festival chambers,
and surrounded the entire thing with a third enclosure (diagram 5).

On a large granite stela he provides specific
details on the monument he constructed on the site
of an older one, which he spoke of in his "Text of the
Youth":

*My majesty desired to make a monument to my
father Amun-Ra in Karnak [Ipet-sut], erecting a
dwelling [sanctuary], beautifying the horizon, adorning
for him Khaftet-hir-nebes, the favorite place of my father
from the beginning. . . . I made it for him upon this block
of enduring stone, exalting and magnifying greatly
[what was already at that site?] to the shrine [naos] of
Nun [the primordial waters]. . . .*

Tuthmosis III constructed *a shrine [naos] at the
east of this temple* (Ipet-sut), had the ruined portions
overturned and *removed the inclosure [of bricks] that
was by its side*, then he purified the site to erect on its
location a new sanctuary that was more beautiful and
bigger, then gave a command for the foundation
ceremony.

Fig. 72. North wall of the second enclosure of the temple of Ipet-sut: Ptolemaic bas-relief

PLATE 174 • THE TEMPLE FOUNDATION CEREMONY

The essential gestures of this laying of the foundation ceremony are as follows:

The king and Seshat, mistress of the divine books, bury a stake in the earth with a mallet. This scene is called *stretching the cord between the two stakes.*

The king hollows out a furrow by means of a hoe, then he refills it with the contents of a bushel basket.

The king molds a brick, then offers a series of briquettes, often of precious materials, *for the four corners of the temple.*

The first scene is missing here, but the inscription on the granite stela replaces it in some manner:

My majesty ordered that the foundation ceremony should be prepared at the approach of the day of the Feast of the New Moon . . . In the year 24,[23] *second month of the second season, the last day (of the month), on the day of the tenth feast of Amun . . . and Amun himself led*

[23]This information concerning the precise date of the foundation ceremony on the day of the feast of the new moon complements those given concerning the battle of Megiddo that also took place on a new moon feast day fifteen years after the coronation. These coordinates permit the enthronement of Tuthmosis III to be placed at May 1, 1490 B.C. (according to Mahler's tables, *A. Z.* 27: 104).

the first feast of stretching the cord with the king. (Breasted, *Ancient Records,* vol. 2, § 608)

The second scene represents the king wearing the *atef* crown and holding the hoe to hollow out the first furrow. The third shows the king kneeling to mold *(skht)* the first brick, which unites earth and water (pl. 174).

PLATE 175 • CONSECRATION OF THE TEMPLE WITH NATRON

The consecration of the temple also included a certain number of ritual gestures, including the one we see here of the king standing, cane in hand, encircling the temple with natron *(besen)*, stylized here in the form of a long ribbon but determined, under the caption, by a small vessel containing *besen* grains.

Fig. 73. Doorway to one of the north chapels

When the temple is finished, the king *"Gives the House to Its Master"* (pl. 47), and the inaugural ceremony is often accompanied by the ritual race with the Apis bull (pl. 74). The inauguration of the temple is in correspondence with the *sed* festival of royal renewal (see pl. 201).

PLATE 176 • NORTH CHAPELS: FEAST OF THE WHITE HIPPOPOTAMUS

Only two examples are known of this extremely rare scene: a fragment from the Saïte era currently in the Brussels Museum, and this tableau in the name of Tuthmosis III in one of the north chapels at Karnak.

The king, wearing the red crown, holds a baton and the white club in his hands. The long ribbon hanging from his left shoulder could be made from giraffe hide.

Behind the king are the two half-heavens that accompany the scene of the "great stride." In front of him, above the two small, dancing figures topped with the name of a city, is a hammered-out hippopotamus accompanied by the brief caption: *Feast of the White [Hippopotamus].*

The red, male, Sethien hippopotamus, the enemy of Horus, must be distinguished from the white, female hippopotamus that is the symbol of Apet. (See *Chronique d'Egypte* 65: 25–32 and pls. 177–179; P. Lacau and H. Chevrier, *Une Chapelle de Sésostris I à Karnak* [Cairo, 1956], pp. 113–18 and pl. 31.)

PLATES 177–179 • NORTH CHAPELS: FEAST OF THE ERECTION OF MIN'S MAST

This scene follows the preceding one. Numerous examples of it are known, but it is depicted here with several particular details.

The king wearing the white crown is holding the long cane and the white club in one hand, while with the other he is holding the *nehbit* scepter, with which he is making the gesture of consecration. The caption is not very explicit: *Erecting the* ka *of the* shn.t *for Amun, master of the Two Lands, dweller in Ipet-sut.*

In front of the king are two rows of men stretching ropes around a raised mast supported by four poles on which little figures, each with a feather on

its head, are climbing. This scene corresponds with those of the rituals in the preceding chapels.

PLATE 180–181 • NORTH CHAPELS: THE NET FOR THE BIRD HUNT

The word *sekht*, "to catch with a net," also designates the forming of the first brick.

PLATES 182–217 • TEMPLE OF MENKHEPERRE AKHMENU

This temple is the one that Tuthmosis III is said to have built upon the site of the brick enclosure of an older sanctuary for Nun (see pl. 173). Commonly referred to as the "hall of feasts," this east building is named temple of Menkeheperre Akhmenu.

PLATE 182–183 • SED-FESTIVAL TEMPLE

This exceptional overview allows several details of the previously described buildings to be seen on the ground. To the left the courses of the foundation outline the plan of the little chapels of Tuthmosis III forming the *first enclosure* around the central sanctuaries of the Middle Kingdom. In the foreground right are remnants of chapels attached to the *second enclosure*. In the background, on the right, are the buildings of the *sed* festival to which one gained access by means of the lateral stairway framed by two standing Osirises and preceded by two sixteen-sided polygonal columns.

This temple includes the great hall of feasts, the two-level ceiling of which was supported by twenty "stake-columns" and thirty-two smaller square pillars, which provided direct access to the three sanctuaries aligned to the temple's general axis, as well as to lateral chambers on the north and south.

PLATE 184 • HALL OF FEASTS: EAST COLONNADE, SOUTH SECTION

PLATE 185 • HALL OF FEASTS: CENTRAL NAVE

PLATE 186 • HALL OF FEASTS: OVERALL VIEW

The hall of feasts included three high naves oriented from south to north and entirely surrounded by an aisle of square pillars. The twenty pillars making up the central nave are a particular type, of which there are no other known examples. Their cylindrical shafts, painted bright red, thicken slightly going from bottom to top and then abruptly flare out above five bands painted yellow and blue, to support a kind of capital in the form of a flower adorned with large triangular leaflets, but reversed. These columns have, more massively, the silhouette of the "stakes" that support the dais of the double kiosk in which the king must alternately sit on two thrones back-to-back, on one side wearing the red crown and red court garments, then on the other the white crown and white garments, during the course of the ceremony of his renewal of the aisles. The paving stones of the ceiling, upheld on one side by a wall that is now destroyed (pl. 186) and on the other by square

pillars, creates a ledge on the inside of the hall (pls. 184–186 and fig. 74). Through the temple of Sahu-Ra (Fifth Dynasty) it is known that this style of entablature was used during the Old Kingdom, but by the Eighteenth Dynasty it is encountered only in Tuthmosis III's feast hall. By virtue of its archaic character this architectural detail assumes a great value.

It is this Hall of Feasts of Tuthmosis III that is going to provide us with the sufficient and necessary data to allow us to affirm that we have been correct in our impression of a concise restoration of the rooms of the "Middle Kingdom courtyard." It is indeed known, thanks to the texts of

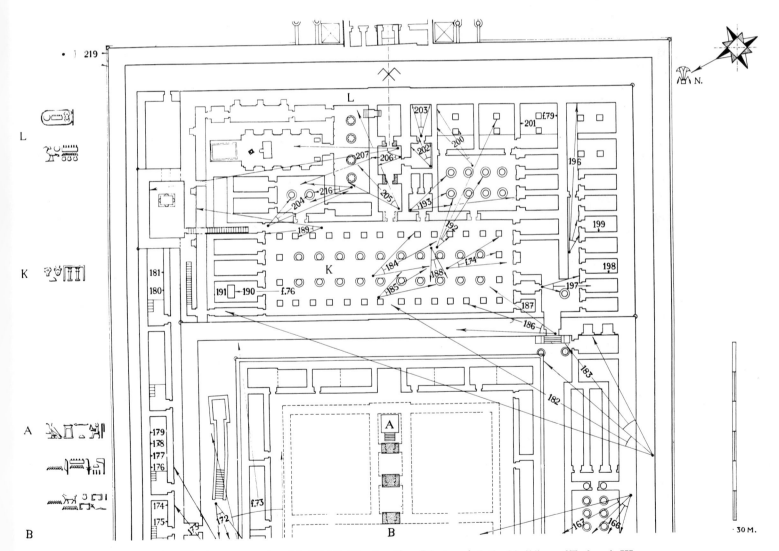

Diagram 8. The three sanctuaries of the Middle Kingdom (A to B), the sed-*festival buildings of Tuthmosis III*

Fig. 74. Stake-columns, square pillar, archaic entablature

the architraves supported by these stake-columns, that this hall was a *ḥrt-ib: [Tuthmosis III] he has created, as his memorial to his father Amun-Ra, master of the thrones of the two lands, the act of raising for him a* ḥrt-ib, *as something new, in beautiful white sandstone.*

Obviously the word *ḥrt-ib* must be emphasized here; though obscure until this point, its meaning is now made perfectly clear: Tuthmosis III reproduced the *ḥrt-ib* (and its rooms) almost on the same scale as the temple of Amun. The normal location of a *ḥrt-ib* is known to be behind the Holy of Holies that it serves as a vestibule, and behind the sanctuary of the barque (when one exists), from which its name "hall of the center" (lit., of the heart) is derived.

Therefore it is possible, without deceiving oneself, to transfer into the "Middle Kingdom courtyard" the general outline of the monumental eastern constructions of Tuthmosis III in their entirety. On the right of the Holy of Holies (therefore on the north), a solar chamber (corresponding to the rooms of Amun in the temple of Tuthmosis III) should be located, and to the left of the Holy of Holies should be an Osirian chamber (corresponding to the Sokarian rooms of this "temple"). (Barguet, *La Structure du Temple,* p. 154)

It can therefore be concluded that Tuthmosis III not only reproduced "almost to the same scale" this *ḥrt-ib* of the Middle Kingdom but emphasized this fact by the rare usage of the ancient entablature.[24]

PLATE 187 • TEMPLE OF TUTHMOSIS III: DETAIL OF A WALL FROM THE CHAMBER OF THE KINGS

The famous "chamber of the kings," where Tuthmosis had the kings of Upper and Lower Egypt from times of remote antiquity represented, existed in the southwest corner of the hall of feasts. The "royal list" that was seen in situ by Prisse d'Avennes (fig. 75) was transported to the Bibilothèque Nationale in Paris in 1843, and from there to the Louvre Museum.

[24]For the location of the hall of feasts see footnote 22, commentary for plate 166–167.

Lith. par Guesdon.   Imp. J. Rigo et Cⁱᵉ   Dess. par Prisse.

ÉTAT AVANT L'ENLÈVEMENT EN MAI 1845
de la chambre des rois à Karnac

Fig. 75. Lithograph made from a drawing by Prisse d'Avennes

Fig. 76. Remnants of a monument representing Tuthmosis III between Mut and Amun

PLATE 188 • HALL OF FEASTS: CAPITAL OF A STAKE-COLUMN

The Copts, probably at the dawning of Christianity, traced a circular motif reminiscent of the crown of thorns under the capital. This is, by the way, perfectly appropriate in this consecrated place.

See plate 184 also for an image of a haloed saint or Christ on the second column.

PLATE 189 • HALL OF FEASTS, NORTH END: STAIRWAY OF THE "CHAMBER OF THE CLEPSYDRAS"

The last square pillars of the hall of feasts can be seen on the left; on the right is the stairway leading to a high chamber where "a libation table with a drain," made of calcite on which the clepsydras (water clocks) were assumed to be placed, can still be found.

On the left pillar note the *mākes* cane that the king is holding in his hand just in front of the vertical axis of equilibrium of the female deity across from him whose name has been hammered out (see pl. 192).

PLATE 190 • BELT AND DAGGER OF THE STATUE OF TUTHMOSIS III: DETAIL

Three chapels can be found in the extension of the three naves of the hall of feasts. In the chapel on the left is a group of three very mutilated statues representing Tuthmosis III framed by entirely broken-off representations of Mut and Amun; nothing but the shoulders remain of these two *neters* (fig. 76). The pleated loincloth of the king is held up by a belt, the decorative motif of which was the object of a study on the style of "weaving from cartoons" that was likely used from the time of the very first dynasties. (See A. van Gennep and G. Jéquier, *Le Tissage aux cartons*)

PLATE 191 • STATUE OF TUTHMOSIS III: DETAIL

PLATE 192 • HALL OF FEASTS: SQUARE PILLAR, POLYGONAL COLUMNS

On this square pillar of the southeast sector of the hall of feasts, the king, wearing the white crown, is holding the white club and the ankh in one hand and with the other is raising the *mākes* cane exactly on the axis of equilibrium of Hathor, in the extension of the border of his headdress corresponding to the front ear lobe (see pls. 47 and 189).

PLATE 193 • SOUTH HALL: POLYGONAL COLUMNS

A hall that is 13.60 meters long by 9.38 meters wide provides access to three tiered chapels where the ceremonies particular to the *sed* festival are represented. Its eight sixteen-sided polygonal columns have a diameter of 1.35 meters at the base and 0.962 meters at the top. These are the measurements we took ourselves on one column:

Base height:	around 0.195 meters
Height of the shaft alone:	around 5.72 meters
Height of the abacus:	around 0.42 meters
Height of the architrave:	around 0.82 meters
Total:	around 7.155 meters

PLATE 194 • POLYGONAL COLUMNS: SOUTH HALL

PLATE 195 • HEAD FROM A BASALT STATUE OF TUTHMOSIS III

Legrain catalog no. 42053. Statue of Tuthmosis III in basalt. Actual height 2 meters. Found in the cachette court of Karnak broken into numerous pieces that were reassembled at the Cairo Museum. Museum entry no. 38234.

The king is wearing the white crown; his front foot is resting on five bows, his back foot upon four.

On the pedestal can be read:

Neter-nefer, master of the accomplishment of the rituals. Ramenkheper, endowed with life, beloved of Amun-Ra, who presides [in] the Akhmenu temple, that is, the temple of the *sed* festival for which this statue seemed to be intended (see fig. 121).

PLATE 196 • CORRIDOR PRECEDING THE SOUTH CHAPELS

As P. Barguet has emphasized (see also pl. 186), the entire north half of the buildings of Akhmenu have a solar aspect, while those of the southern half, for Osirian rituals, have a chthonic character, that is, one that is linked to terrestrial entities. The direction in which the figures are walking lends support to this distinction. On the one side they proceed from west to east by way of the north corridor (that is, in the same direction as the course of the stars) to reach the botanical garden and the solar chamber. On the other side they proceed from west to east by way of the south corridor (that is, in the direction of the earth), then turn back toward the north. On the north wall of this corridor the king, seated in the jubilee pavilion, is facing west, then, under the aegis of Seth and Horus, he fires his arrows toward the west, completing the circuit: west-south-east-north. In the *Culte d'Horus à Edfou* (Alliot, p. 523) this ritual takes place immediately after the flight of the four birds charged with announcing the royal advent toward the four cardinal points.

PLATE 197 • ENTRANCE DOORWAY TO ONE OF THE SOUTH CHAPELS

Fig. 77. "Sed festival": Narmer (First Dynasty)

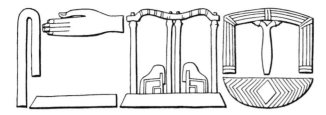

Fig. 78. Hieroglyph of the sed *festival*

Once over the stairway that leads to the entrance doorway of the *sed*-festival temple, one finds a small vestibule on the right whose roof was supported by a sixteen-sided polygonal column (pl. 197, on the right). This vestibule comes before a narrow corridor

Fig. 79. Bas-relief

that provides access to the nine small chapels attached to the thick wall constructed during the extension of the second enclosure of the temple of Amun (diagrams 5 and 8).

The king is wearing the white crown of the south on the bas-relief on the left, that is to say, the east.

PLATE 198 • AMUNET HOLDING THE *WAS* SCEPTER IN HER HANDS THAT BREAKS A LINE DEMARCATING A LINE OF INSCRIPTIONS

PLATE 199 • RITUAL RACE OF THE KING WEARING THE RED CROWN AND HOLDING THE VESSELS OF PURIFICATION IN HIS HANDS

Whereas on plate 198 the *was* scepter of Amunet breaks the line that demarcates the inscribed register, here this same scepter in the hand of Horus of Behedet serves to restrict the column of hieroglyphs inscribed before this *neter*.

PLATE 200 • OUTER SOUTH WALL OF ALEXANDER'S SANCTUARY

PLATE 201 • THE KING SEATED UPON A THRONE PLACED ON THE *HEB* SYMBOL DURING THE *SED* FESTIVAL

The *sed* or "renewal" festival is one of the most curious of all the pharaonic rituals.

Here the swaddled king is seated, in the position of Osiris, upon the throne placed on the *heb* basin.[25] He is preceded by the ensigns supporting the symbol of Khonsu (the formless skin) and Upwat, the opener of the paths, while being acclaimed by the souls of Pe. Behind him are two half-heavens and the signs of the scorpion and the *ka* that generally accompany the scene of the "great stride" (pl. 74).

One of this figure's characteristics is that the *hek* scepter, over the king's left shoulder, is extended on the bottom by a long cane (the shepherd's crook and the crozier of our bishops), which crosses the *nekhakha* resting on the right shoulder and joined in the

[25]The name for the throne and its accessories resting on the *heb* basin specific to the *sed*-festival ceremony, or royal jubilee, is *sepa*.

royal hand by a long *was* (key of the Nile) that goes down to the king's foot.

PLATE 202 • SANCTUARY OF ALEXANDER: ENTRANCE DOORWAY

This little sanctuary in the name of Tuthmosis III has been entirely done over in thicker reliefs by Alexander, who inscribed his cartouches on the inside. On the lintel of the doorway are the Nile bearing its offerings, the king wearing the white crown, and the king embraced by Hathor as he goes toward the north, because this room is not actually the axial sanctuary but is constructed on the south side of it (diagram 8). Above the lintel it is specified that the small *neters* seated facing the north are *the Great Ennead who are in Ipet-sut* (Karnak).

PLATE 203 • SANCTUARY OF ALEXANDER: BACK WALL

This wall is very curious because of the fact that it is assembled from reused blocks[26] in such a way that the drawings of any one scene lack continuity. For example, the fountain-of-purification water from the white vessel is broken and shifted, and ends on the bottom with a straight-line extension of its undulations. The sky is in relief, then simply drawn in; the *was* that Amun is holding is continued by the joint; and so forth. These are some typical examples of reused blocks for which it would make an interesting project to seek out the origins of their constituent elements.

In the foreground is a mass of white limestone that was once a splendid statue of the falcon Horus.

PLATES 204–217 • THE BOTANICAL GARDEN OF TUTHMOSIS III

PLATE 204 • BOTANICAL GARDEN, SEEN FROM THE NORTHWEST

In the foreground are the two sixteen-sided

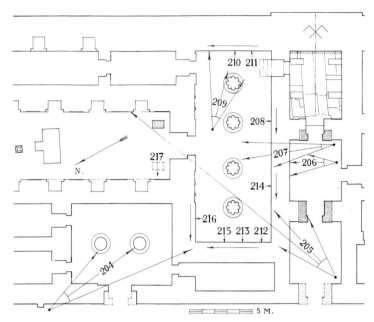

Diagram 9. Axial sanctuaries, botanical garden

columns of the room to which one gains access on the west by means of the hall of feasts. The titulary of Tuthmosis III is inscribed on the west sides of these columns; on the south column (to the right), is the second series of protocol names, and the third series is on the north column.

Behind this are the fascicule columns of the "botanical garden," and in the background are the axial sanctuaries and Alexander's sanctuary.

PLATE 205 • BOTANICAL GARDEN, SEEN FROM THE SOUTHEAST

The northeast corner of the first of three sanctuaries aligned on the axis of the temple can be seen in the foreground. In the background are the fasciculate, papyriform columns of the botanical garden. Sculpted on the architraves on both sides of the ankh are the second and fourth Horus name of Tuthmosis III, on the east and west respectively (see fig. 81).

PLATE 206 • ANTECHAMBER OF THE AXIAL SANCTUARY: NORTH WALL

To the right and under the cartouche of Menkheperre are two stands for offerings in the form of small columns with flowering capitals, then a "white vessel" on a stool, and then, farther to the

---

[26]As for the previous room, the officiant must enter from the west, pass by the south, then the east, and head toward the room's northeast corner. The fact that all these disparate blocks are dated from the time of Alexander excludes the reused-block hypothesis. These anomalies remain unexplained. (See Barguet, *La Structure du Temple,* p. 163, 3) [Note added by the author after completion of the book—Trans.]

left, under the cartouche of Tuthmosis, four *hesit* vessels—the first in the shape of a key of life—within a kind of see-through table under which is lying a "cubit of incense," adorned at one end with a falcon head and on the other with a small hand holding a basin where the incense in the small container attached to the middle of the cubit will be burned. These are all tools of ritual purification (see pls. 41, 80, 148, and 149). (Note the correspondence between the various elements of the cubit with the vessels placed above it.)

Plate 207 · Capital from a Column of the Botanical Garden

This column belongs to the papyriform style, of which the oldest specimen dates back to the Fifth Dynasty (temples of Neuserre and Sahure). The two styles, lotiform and papyriform, share a contemporary origin and are very similar in silhouette and in appearance. However, they can be distinguished by the following characteristics:

1. The shaft of the *lotiform* column is constituted of four or six lotus stems in circular sections that diminish slightly going from the base to the five bands that join them together. Above this collar the half-open buds of the lotus form the capital, properly speaking.

2. The shaft of the *papyriform* column consists of six or eight papyrus stems that each bear the characteristic ribbing of this cyperaceous plant. Moreover, at the start of the shaft, which is perceptibly narrower at the base, is a crown of leaves fastened to the stems (pl. 209). These three nuances clearly distinguish this style from the preceding one. Above the quintuple binding, "a new series of leaves similarly shaped to those of the foot of the shaft represents the calyx that encloses the inflorescence still closed up in buds." (G. Jéquier, *Manuel d'Archéologie égyptienne*, p. 213)

During the Eighteenth Dynasty three "adventitious buds," which were bound together and whose stems passed under the quintuple binding, were added between each large bud. Very stylized, these

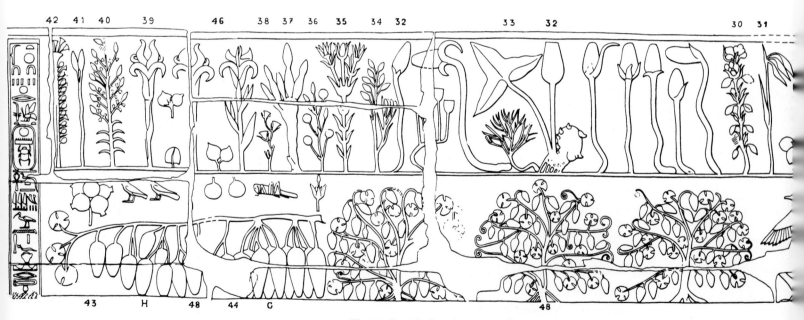

Fig. 80. Botanical garden, east wall

1. *Dracunculus vulg.* Schott *(Arum dracunculus). (a)* Entire plant with one flower and five leaves. *(b)* Entire plant with rhizome, two leaves, and a flower. 14. Type of *Calenchoe*, probably *Calenchoe deficiens* Forsk, or even *Calenchoe aegyptiaca.* 24 and 27. Composite flower on a long straight stem, probably a chrysanthemum? 25. Perhaps a *Dracunculus vulgaris* with the stem and rhizome after the fall of the sepals and petals? 32. *Arum italicum* Linné. 35 (and perhaps 31?). *Dipsacus.* 39. Flower of a type of iris.

adventitious buds filled the empty spaces at the base of the capital and the upper part of the shaft.

The royal titulary is inscribed on the southern lobes of these columns of the botanical garden and pointed in the same direction as on the architraves, thus demonstrating that the facade of the colonnade is to the south.

PLATE 208 • BOTANICAL GARDEN: SOUTH WALL

This room measures about 6 meters in width and 14.75 meters in length. Its columns are about 7.50 meters, measuring from the ground to the top of the architraves.

Beyond the south wall one can see the axial sanctuary that communicates with the garden by a "sort of window that is installed at 0.85 meters from the ground, and not by a door with an elevated sill, the stairs that provide access to this opening being modern.

"The pavement, where certain traces of the sanctuary's original walls and an axis can still be dis-

cerned, is formed from broken pieces of Queen Hatshepsut's sandstone architraves, painstakingly re-employed." (A. Varille, *Quelques notes sur le sanctuaire axial du grand temple d'Amon à Karnak*)

Thus the true entrance was on the north; however, the representations that survive on the lower registers of the east, south, and west walls depart from the "window" of the axial sanctuary in the direction of the northwest corner of the room, where they all meet (as can be seen by following the direction of the arrows in diagram 9).

On the south wall the birds are going toward the west. From right to left can be recognized:

The lapwing, *Vanellus cristatus*, remarkable for its alertness, its courage, and its acrobatic flight.

Casarka rutila, the red casarca. This "duck of the Brahmans" of the Indies was regarded as a sacred being by the Mongols. This is one of the only anatides that "pair" in the fields like geese.

The two others are not identified; however, the last presents the curved beak characteristic of the ibis.

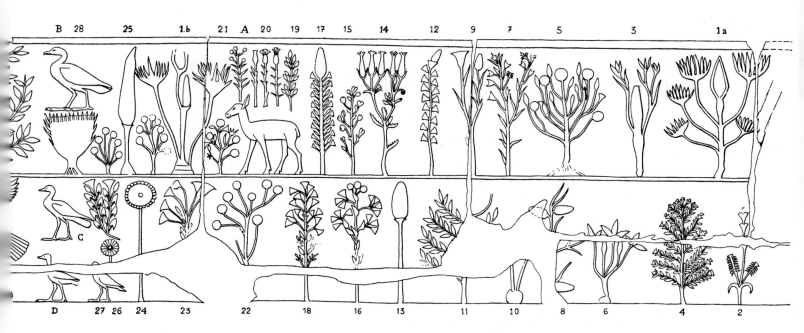

43. Fruits of *Punica granatum* (pomegranates). 48. *Vitis vinifera* (grapevines). (A). Female gazelle. (B). (spurred?) goose, *Plectoperus?* (C). Perhaps a bustard? (D). Perhaps the screeching oedicnemus, *Oedicnemus crepitans*. (E). Rock doves? (F). Spurred cuckoo or Egyptian cuckoo. (G). Migrating grasshopper. (H). Raven or Crow.

Fig. 81. Architrave of the botanical garden, south facade

The fruits above the birds are pomegranates *(Punica granatum)*.

PLATE 209 • BOTANICAL GARDEN: EAST WALL

PLATE 210–211 • BOTANICAL GARDEN: EAST WALL

The entire representation is introduced by this inscription carved on the northeast corner: *Year 25, under the majesty of the king of Upper and Lower Egypt, Menkheperre, forever living, plants that His Majesty has found in the land of Retenu* (Syria).

The identification of the plants in this room is due to Professor Schweinfurth and Dr. L. Keimer, that of the animals to Dr. Hilzheimer, and gathered together by Wrezinski (*Atlas*, vol. 2, pls. 26–33) in the German language. We have provided the translation in English and Latin in figure 80.

Note the *Arum italicum* Linnaeus (32): a flower enveloped in the sepal on a long twisted stem emerging from a rhizome consisting of five rootlets. The oval flower is cut off at the top for lack of space, the three-lobed triangular leaf with central veins in the three high lobes emerges from the same rhizome. (Wrezinski, *Atlas*, vol. 2)

The migrating grasshopper *(G)* is mentioned on

Fig. 82. Ash-colored crane, an example of lotus proliferation

the east wall; it so happens that it is well known that the clouds of locusts that devastated the plantations came from the east.

PLATE 212–213 • BOTANICAL GARDEN: WEST WALL

Among the birds that have been identified (fig. 83), the following should be noted:

The *ash-colored crane (D)*, characterized by its elegance, grace, and an intelligence that is comparable to that of parrots. Cautious and affectionate, it quickly establishes friendships with man. The Egyptians raised it in great quantity and thus had ample opportunity to study its recreational activities. The crane displays its joy by dances, notably at the rising of the sun, and by superb soaring flights, and it even amuses itself by tossing small objects in the air that it will catch in midair, always remaining full of grace and beauty.

The *anhinga of Levaillant (F)* is a frequent sight on both the White and Blue Niles. Inhabitants of rivers, lakes, and marshes, these birds are consummate swimmers and even more accomplished divers. Their name *bird with a serpent's neck* could not be any more appropriate, for not only does their neck sway like a snake's, but when this bird swims underwater, "it transforms itself into a serpent and when it prepares to defend itself, it projects its neck forward with such lightning-like speed that one cannot avoid the impression of being attacked by a viper." (H. E. Brehm, *La Vie des Animaux*, vol. 4, p. 848)

The *frigate eagle (K)* earns its name of "sea eagle" by the rapidity of its flight, the way it circles in the sky, its piercing vision, and the extraordinary speed with which it cuts off any retreat for its prey.

The *spiny hoplopterus* or *lapwing (M)* is called *siksak* by the Arabs because of its cry. It serves as a sentinel to other birds, which it alerts to the slightest danger by its piercing cry. This small bird even has the boldness to attack would-be predators by employing the spurs it carries at the starting point of the wing. The nuptial flight "in somersaults" of the male *Vanellus vanellus* is accompanied by a muted sound created by the configuration of the quill feathers. (See P. Grassé, *Traité de zoologie*, vol. 15, Masson, pp. 694–95)

The *ordinary plover (R)* is no less intrepid, courageous, and vigilant than the *siksak* when defending its offspring against kites, crows, and other nest raiders, but in the presence of a falcon it is terrified, emits anguished cries, and seeks to flee by any possible means, even to the point of drowning itself. It is very likely this terror before "Horus, king of the heavens" that has occasioned its choice as a symbol of a people submissive to the king. In this case it is depicted with its wings crossed (pl. 334).

The *Egyptian coucal (O)* lives in spiny bushes, among which it goes single file, glides, and climbs with as much agility as a rat.

The *hammered-out bird (P)* could have been the *Nile goose* (see pl. 213). The Akhenatenish removal is explained by the fact that this bird is the sacred goose of Amun. Bird *U* evokes as well the silhouette of the guinea fowl.

PLATE 214 • BOTANICAL GARDEN: SOUTH WALL

A detail of the calves and some plants from the south wall, none of which have been identified.

PLATE 215 • BOTANICAL GARDEN: WEST WALL

See figure 83.

PLATE 216 • BOTANICAL GARDEN: NORTH WALL, WEST SECTION

In the background the stairs leading to the "chamber of the clepsydras" can be seen, in the middle are the two columns of the neighboring room (pl. 204), and in the foreground is the western end of the north wall of the garden.

Blue lotuses *(Nymphea caerulea)* are represented in an abnormal fashion on the left: some have two flowers, others have a flower and a bud emerging from the same stem, or even a stem that divides in half to form one lone bud. There are also sycamore seedpods, pomegranates, and a desert raven (?).

On the right are the last lines of the text concerning the plants brought back from the "Divine Land":

All plants that grow, all flowers that are in God's-Land (which were found by) his majesty when his majesty proceeded to Upper Retenu, to subdue (all) the countrie(s), according to the command of his father,

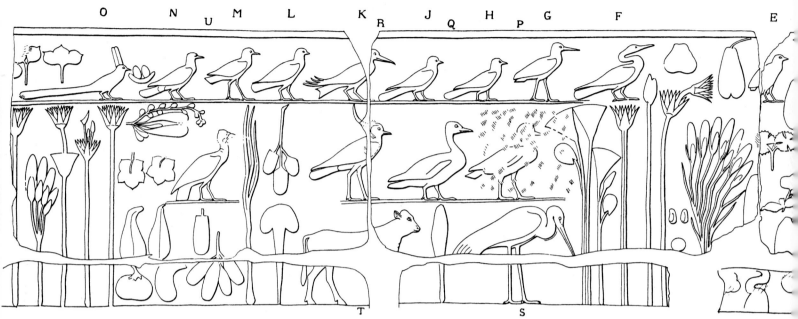

Fig. 83. Botanical garden: West wall

1. Blue lotus, *Nymphea caerulea* Savig. 2. Perhaps the medicinal Mandrake L.? (A, C, E, G, P, U). Undeterminable. (B). Probably the jackdaw of the towers, *Monedula turrium*. (D). Ash-colored crane, *Grus cinera*. (F). The anhinga of Levaillant, "bird with the serpent's neck," *Plotus levaillantii*.

Amun, who put them beneath his sandals from (the year 1) to myriads of years.

His majesty said: "I swear, as Ra (loves me) as my father, Amun, favors me, all these things happened in truth—I have not written fiction as that which really happened to my majesty. [The "spirits" of my majesty have caused their birth and growth to glorify his "foods."][27]

My majesty hath done this from desire to put them before my father Amun, in this great temple of Amun [Akhmenu], (as) a memorial forever and ever." (From Breasted, *Ancient Records*, vol. 2, §§ 451–52)

The depictions of a lotus stem that bears a leaf emerging from a blossoming flower, of a second stem with a bud, and a third bearing an open flower (fig. 84) are remarkable.

This concerns a rare phenomenon that seems to have escaped the notice of the naturalists who have addressed the subject of these abnormal representa-

tions of "fictional deformations." There actually exist examples of "proliferation" that are characteristic of this plant.

"There has been observed at the Paris Museum several years ago (in 1878) an extremely rare and quite interesting case of proliferation: floral peduncles developed within the axil of the petals of a flower of normal appearance; two of these peduncles were fused, but all bore at their tops another regular but smaller flower." (G. Nicholson, *Dictionnaire d'horticulture*, vol. 3, "*Nymphea Lotus*," p. 493; vol. 4, "Les differentes formes de prolifération," p. 344)

PLATE 217 • BLOCK FROM THE NORTH HALL

It seems that this hall, which was located to the north of the botanical garden and is today in ruins, was originally decorated in an analogous fashion. Nothing remains but several blocks. None of the birds or plants pictured on the block have been identified. However, the lower bird is depicted as a duck swimming among aquatic vegetation, of which some plants are being pulled by the current. This observa-

---

[27]This sentence is not in material cited and appears to have been Schwaller's addition—Trans.

(H). Rock dove, *Colomba livia.* (J). Turtledove, *turtur.* (K). Frigate eagle or "sea-eagle," *Tachypetes aquilus.* (L). Greek partridge, *Perdrix graeca.* (M). Spiny hoplopterous or "lapwing," *Hoplopterus.* (N). Gull. (O). Egyptian cuckoo, *Centropus aegyptus.* (Q). Wild goose. (R). Ordinary plover. (S). White egret, *Herodias alba.*

tion allows one to assume that in the botanical garden, certain animals and plants that are represented are not done so for uniquely decorative reasons. For example, shouldn't one seek, in the plants surrounding the gazelle (pl. 211), those that grow in its native habitat and serve as its food? It can be noted also that "the bird with the serpent's neck" (fig. 83, F), who lives in the water, is represented above aquatic plants, whereas all the other birds are placed on a line of earth.

The identified plants are typically Egyptian, and the majority of the birds are African; some are specifically Sudanese.

Wrezinski himself concludes: "The sycamore, the blue lotus, the grapevine, the palm trees, the melons, and the convolvulus are common in Egypt. The pomegranate tree, which comes, perhaps, from Syria, was already well known before Tuthmosis III. The dracunculus and the arum are not found in modern Syria, the calenchoe as well as the iris could come from southern Arabia; in short, these observations conform poorly with the text that announces that these plants come from the 'Divine Land,' which is generally assumed to have been Syria." (*Atlas,* vol. 2)

PLATE 218 • EASTERN SANCTUARY OF AMUN-RA

In the middle of the outer east wall of the third enclosure that encloses the temple of Amun and the *sed*-festival buildings, a small sanctuary is attached that is supported by the great temple but with which it has no communication.

In its current state this eastern sanctuary consists of an enormous alabaster monolith of Tuthmosis III, flanked by lateral chambers and preceded by a large hall that opens on the east and whose facade is adorned by quadrangular pillars decorated externally with "Osirian" statues that are joined together by walls of intercolumniation. The entire group of structures is framed by the bases of two broken obelisks of the queen Hatshepsut that are enclosed within two chapels of Nakhtnebef. These latter have been established in the face of two large images of Amun, undoubtedly highly venerated, that form the final point of two long series of tableaux depicting

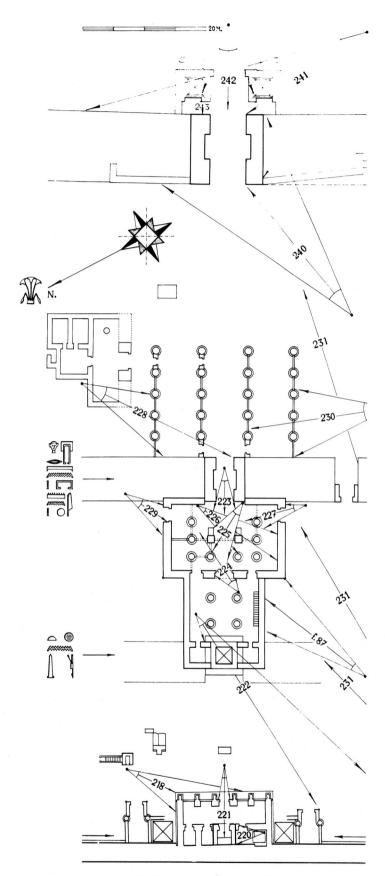

Diagram 10. East sanctuaries, gate of Nectanebo

Ramesses II before the divine principles of the temple. . . . The Ramesside scenes adorn the north, south, and east facades of the outer Tuthmosian walls of the great temple of Amun that terminate at the two sides of the eastern sanctuary. (A. Varille, *Description sommaire du sanctuaire oriental d'Amon-Râ à Karnak*)

PLATE 219 • TUTHMOSIAN ENCLOSING WALL OF THE GREAT TEMPLE OF AMUN-RA

The bas-reliefs of the north partition of the third Tuthmosian enclosure are in the name of Ramesses II. His Horus name is recognizable here carved in magnificent hieroglyphs, under Amun and Mut receiving the offerings. The spiral of Mut's double crown winds around within the body of a small, earlier figuration of Amun on which this inscription is outlined: *Mut, mistress of Heaven, queen of the neters.*

PLATE 220 • MONOLITHIC ALABASTER NAOS OF TUTHMOSIS III

Each of the two outer walls of the naos was occupied by a large scene in which Tuthmosis III presented the offerings to fifteen figures of Amun in sheaths, seated upon a throne and holding the *was* scepter with both hands. . . .

On the north wall, which is the best preserved, the king, holding the cane and the club in his left hand, is consecrating the offering with his right hand, "to Amun in each of his names."

PLATE 221 • ALABASTER GROUP FROM THE NAOS OF TUTHMOSIS III

"The naos and the two statues that it contains are carved in a monolith of alabaster. The monument presses directly against the back of the wall of the principal temple, which has been slightly hollowed for it to be built in. . . .

"The statue on the north represents Tuthmosis III, his waist girded by the *chendjit*, with a bull's tail between his legs. . . .

"The statue found to the right of the king is greatly damaged. The legs and thighs have been painstakingly chipped away with a hammer, and nothing remains but the attachment to the throne of

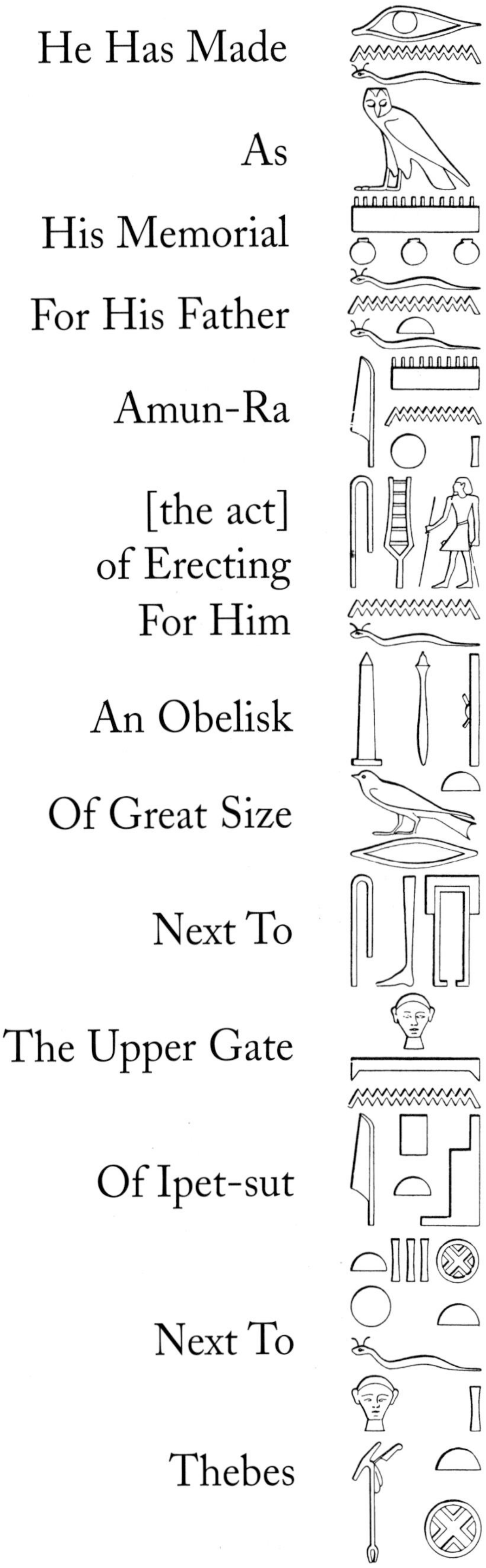

He Has Made

As

His Memorial

For His Father

Amun-Ra

[the act]
of Erecting
For Him

An Obelisk

Of Great Size

Next To

The Upper Gate

Of Ipet-sut

Next To

Thebes

Fig. 85. Text of Tuthmosis IV

the lower limbs. . . . In these conditions identification of the figure is difficult. Champollion suggested it was a Mut goddess, while Steindorff believed he recognized the queen Hatshepsut. Borchardt affirmed, to the contrary, that it was an image of Amun. . . . The clearly feminine nature of the figure compels me to definitively adopt a fourth solution; the companion of Tuthmosis III is very likely a Nekhebet. . . . It is a representation of Nekhebet's vulture that was 'reused' at the foot of this statue." (Ibid., pp. 143–44)

PLATE 222 • GREAT TEMPLE OF AMUN, EAST FACADE: ORIGINAL LOCATION OF THE OBELISK OF SAINT JOHN LATERAN

In the background is the southern portion of the east facade of the Tuthmosian wall encircling the great temple of Amun, on which the scenes, in Ramesses II's name, are oriented in the direction of the alabaster naos located in the temple's axis (pls. 218–221).

In the foreground, left, is the base of an obelisk removed from Karnak by the emperor Constantine around A.D. 330 and transported to Rome in 357 by his son Constantius II, who installed it in the Circus Maximus. This is where it was discovered, broken in three pieces, in 1587. The following year Pope Sixtus V had it raised in the square of Saint John Lateran, where it currently remains.

The four faces of this obelisk each bear three vertical lines of inscriptions; the central columns are of Tuthmosis III, and the lateral columns are of Tuthmosis IV.

In adopting the orientation provided by Breasted, the central columns carry the four titularies of Tuthmosis III in the following order: the first on the south, the second on the east, the third on the north, and the fourth on the west. (Compare this with the architrave of the botanical garden, fig. 81.)

On the southern face below his protocol Tuthmosis III specified that he had a single obelisk created, destined to be erected *in the forecourt of the temple of Ipet-sut,* and he emphasized the fact that this was the first time an obelisk was raised *alone,* which is entirely correct.[28]

[28]This single obelisk was intended for "the upper parvis of the temple neighboring Ipet-sut" according to P. Barguet, *L'obélisque de saint Jean de Latran dans le temple de Ramsés II á Karnak,* p. 241.

Fig. 86. Southern face

On this same southern face, Tuthmosis IV recounts that he finished this single obelisk, brought by his father Tuthmosis III, after it had remained resting on its sides in the hands of the engineers for thirty-five years. . . . He erected it in Karnak, making its pyramidion of electrum and acting in conformance with the instructions of his "father" himself (let us note that Tuthmosis IV is the grandson of Tuthmosis III).

On the western face Tuthmosis IV gives a precious indication by virtue of which it has been possible to find its original location: *He has made as His memorial for His Father Amun-Ra [the act] of erecting for him an obelisk of great size next to the upper gate of Ipet-sut next to Thebes*[29] (see pl. 228, the site of the "upper gate").

(For everything concerning this obelisk see P. Barguet, *L'obélisque de Saint Jean de Latran dans le temple de Ramesses II à Karnak*.)

PLATES 223–231 • EASTERN TEMPLE OF RAMESSES II

About fifty meters to the east of the great temple of Amun, a small building is found that was conceived as a peristyle court, with two Osirian pillars in the center, between which we can see today the central way that leads to the alabaster naos that, formerly, was directly across from the single obelisk. An offerings table is located between this naos and the temple of Ramesses II.

PLATE 223 • EASTERN TEMPLE OF RAMESSES II

PLATE 224 • COLUMN AND DORSAL FACE OF THE NORTH OSIRIAN PILLAR

PLATE 225 • NORTH OSIRIAN PILLAR, COLUMNS, AND PTOLEMAIC DOORWAY

All the columns of the temple of Ramesses II and the small room preceding the obelisk are made with the drums of ancient Tuthmosian polygonal

---

[29]It was erected "at the upper gate of Karnak, next to Thebes" according to Barguet, *L'obélisque de saint Jean de Latran dans le temple de Ramsés II á Karnak,* p. 241.

Fig. 87. Eastern temple of Ramesses II: Overall view

columns, re-covered with plaster and bearing the cartouches of Ramesses II (figs. 87 and 88).

The central doorway that currently provides communication between these two rooms was only opened under Ptolemy VII,[30] according to the dedication inscribed on the south doorpost by this pharaoh. Moreover, on the southern portion of the splaying of this new doorway is a depiction of worship of the "souls of the east" by four baboons; on the north it is the "souls of the west."

On all the columns the royal personage is going from east to west, in reverse of his steps in the great temple of Amun.

PLATE 226 • SOUTH OSIRIAN PILLAR, SOUTHWEST CORNER

Osiris's face is carved in a curious manner in an inlaid piece that gives it the aspect of a mask.

[30]The central door was only "opened" under Ptolemy VII at the probable site of a false door or niche. Barguet, *La Structure du Temple*, pp. 228, 234, 239.

PLATE 227 • THE TWO OSIRIAN PILLARS, DOORPOST OF THE SOUTH DOORWAY

PLATE 228 • ETHIOPIAN COLONNADE THAT PRECEDES THE "UPPER GATE" OF IPET-SUT OF THE TEMPLE OF RAMESSES II

The temple of Ramesses II is open on the east by a large portal that cuts through an enclosure of baked bricks laid on a winding bed.

The name of this portal is mentioned on its southern exterior doorpost in a tableau that depicts Ramesses II in the presence of Amun, who is making the same gesture as the king of "Giving the House to Its Master" above this text:

May all that enter by the upper gate of Amun's dwelling be purified two times. It so happens that "it is precisely the name of this gate that is mentioned on the obelisk of Saint John Lateran, in Tuthmosis IV's dedication. . . . This confirms our hypothesis in which the current gate of Ramesses II already existed

during the reign of Tuthmosis IV at the very least."
(Barguet, *l'obelisque de saint Jean de Latran*)

In conclusion: Not only is the original location of the Lateran obelisk confirmed, but also that of the "upper gate" and, subsequently, that of the brick enclosure that closed off the eastern access of the temple of Ipet-sut during the Tuthmosian era.

The Ethiopian colonnade consists of four rows of five columns each linked together by small walls of intercolumniation on which are represented the nomes and the characteristic scenes of the "royal ascent" to the temple. The central colonnade borders a red granite pavement analogous to that of the great colonnade west of the first court (pl. 23) and the Ethiopian colonnade that is north of the temple of Mentu. The remnants of a fourth colonnade of the same style remain between the temple of Khonsu and the gate of Ptolemy III Euergetes, to the south (pl. 252–253).

Karnak thus finds itself provided with Ethiopian colonnades at the four cardinal points.

PLATE 229 • COLUMN AND OSIRIAN PILLARS, SEEN FROM THE NORTH DOORWAY

On the outer as on the interior walls of the temple of Ramesses II, the king is oriented so that he is going from east to west, *toward Amun-Ra who hearkens to prayer,* a distinctive label that figures on this wall and on the Ptolemaic doorway.

PLATE 230 • ETHIOPIAN COLONNADE AND THE "UPPER GATE" OF IPET-SUT

PLATE 231 • EASTERN TEMPLE OF RAMESSES II: TAHARKA'S COLONNADE, GATE OF NECTANEBO

To the left in front of the two columns of Taharka is the outer south face of the temple of Ramesses II and its small southern doorway. To the right is the enclosure wall of baked brick laid on twisting beds, which was probably erected on the site of the old Tuthmosian enclosure wall. In the background is the gate of Nectanebo and the last thick wall that surrounds the entire great temple of Amun. (For the gate of Nectanebo see pls. 240 and 241.)

PLATE 232 • BAKED BRICK ENCLOSING WALL OF THE GREAT TEMPLE OF AMUN

Enclosed within this wall of baked bricks laid on twisting beds, which are more than 10 meters wide and 2 kilometers long, are not only the great temple of Amun but also those of Khonsu, Apet, and Ptah,

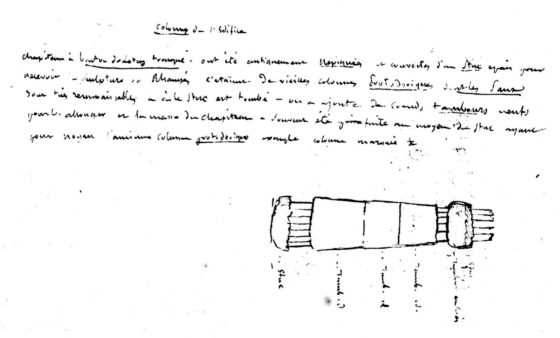

Fig. 88. Manuscript page from Notices descriptives, *Champollion the Younger (1829–30)*

the sacred lake, the "sacred wood," and numerous smaller buildings.

PLATES 233–237 • TEMPLE OF OSIRIS HEK-DJET

Already at the end of the Twentieth Dynasty the Egyptian empire had lost the eastern lands and Nubia. But while the "Asian people" started quarreling among one another again, the Nubians had formed a royal kingdom and built temples in which they claimed to preserve the pure pharaonic tradition.

During the Twenty-first Dynasty (1085–950 B.C.), there were three kings in Tanis, and the high priests of Thebes exercised authority over Upper Egypt.

At the time of the Twenty-second Dynasty (950–730 B.C.), the Libyan kings residing in Bubastis named their sons, more often than not, as the high priests of Thebes. These latter often even inscribed their names within a cartouche (see plate 12).

The Twenty-third Dynasty (817–730 B.C.) became tangled up with its predecessor; there were two parallel royal lines, and soon there appeared as many small kinglets as there were provinces. This period was the parceling out of Egypt when confusion reigned.

It was at this point, profiting from this disorder, that a prince of Saïs, Tefnakht, tried on two separate occasions to conquer the Delta and then the whole of Egypt. His son Bocchoris (Bakeurenef) was his successor, and both of them constitute the Twenty-fourth Dynasty (730–715 B.C.).

But the Ethiopian kings of the Twenty-fifth Dynasty (715–663 B.C.), who were extremely pious and peaceful, attempted the reunification of Egypt. Recognized as "kings of the Two Lands," they began again the works in the temples, using the purest archaic style for the texts and the bas-reliefs.

From 750 to 525 B.C., despite all the internal and external troubles, Thebes remained the protective, spiritual heart of the traditions, and the "divine worshipers of Amun," of royal blood, assumed spiritual authority there for more than two centuries and performed the ritual duties of the temple, a privilege formerly reserved for the kings, while the high priests apparently retained temporal power.

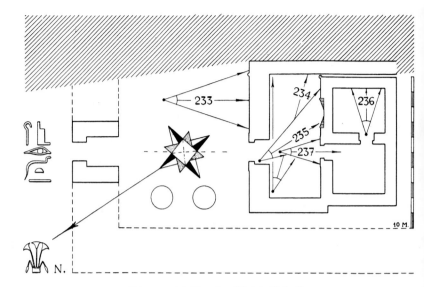

Diagram 11. Temple of Osiris Hek-djet

PLATE 233 • EXTERIOR FACADE

To the left of the entrance doorway, an Ethiopian king—whose cartouches have been hammered out but whose Horus name identifies as being Shabataka—receives from the hands of Amun the harpagon and the *sed*-festival symbols suspended from the palm of the years.

The figurations of the Ethiopian kings are remarkable for their wearing two uraei topped by two crowns, their powerful necks, their very distinctive hairstyle, the special form of the *user* necklace, and the details of the belt and the front panel of their aprons. One of these two uraei and the cartouches were subsequently hammered out.

PLATE 234 • EAST WALL OF THE FIRST CHAMBER

On the top register is the first of the divine worshipers, Shepenwepet, daughter of Osorkon III (Twenty-third Dynasty), who is presenting Maāt to Amun and receiving the *menat* from Isis-Hathor.

Below, Amenirdis, daughter of Kashta (the Kushite, the Ethiopian), holds the Hathorian sistrum on her shoulder and receives in her left hand the three keys of life given to her by Amun. Her titles are inscribed above the two cartouches: Divine Worshiper, Divine Wife. In a column of text to the left can be read: *The divine wife, Amenirdis, endowed with life, has made hek djet as a memorial to her father Osiris.*

Fig. 89. Postern of the east

Behind Amun, Mut the Great is holding in her hand an ankh symbol that is combined in a curious fashion with the symbols of the *sed* festival.

PLATE 235 • THE SEVEN DOORWAYS AND THE "RELIQUARY OF OSIRIS"

In the south wall of this same chamber the seven Osirian doorways are all boxed within one another. To the left of the scenes in which Shepenwepet is being breast-fed by a Hathorian deity with a curious hairstyle (on top), then embraced by Amun, there is

a representation of the symbol of the nome of Abydos that is worshiped in the temple of Osiris, in which it is thought the "reliquary" containing the head of Osiris, one of sixteen (or twenty-one) parts of this *neter*'s body that was dismembered by Seth and placed all over Egypt, can be seen.

PLATE 236 • EAST WALL OF THE INNER CHAPEL

The cartouches on this curious representation reveal that these two kings kneeling back to back in two perseas bear two distinct names:

On the left, Usermaātre Osorkon is wearing the white crown of the South. Amun is inscribing his name on a fruit of the tree.

On the right Usermaātre Takelot is wearing the red crown of the North and it is Tum who carves his name.

This probably refers to Osorkon III, father of Shepenwepet, and Takelot III. It so happens that "on a statue found in the cachette court of Karnak, the names of the king Osorkon and the king Takelot appear arranged in a strange manner; the king of Upper and Lower Egypt Miamon Siese Takelot, Master of the Two Lands, the son of Ra Miamon Siese Osorkon, master of the diadems. A more perfect union could hardly be dreamed of: the name of *nesut-bit* is attributed to one king and the name of *sa-Ra* is attributed to the other king. This strange titulary certainly applies to Osorkon III . . . and consequently Takelot III who was perhaps the high priest before being associated (?) with the throne for which no information is available." (Drioton and Vandier, *L'Egypte*, p. 511)

A singular Osirian grouping can be found on the lower register: two arms extended (the fathom) measure a curve (the cycle) on which a kneeling individual is turning his head behind him and holding the *seshed* skin of Osiris, the falcon Horus perched on a kind of vessel between two horns with a feather (symbol of the west), then the symbol of the "followers—or companions—of Horus," on which a leopard climbs,[31] and finally the *sekhem* scepter.

---

[31]The feline carnivore "with sharp claws" that climbs up the symbol of Horus's companions is called *mafdet*. This entity, well known since prehistoric times, "leaps on the napes" of venomous serpents, throws them over, tramples them, pulls out their hearts, and "tears off their heads."

Fig. 90. Akhenaten block

This small, purely Osirian temple is therefore speaking of what occurs in the Dwat, that is to say, the nocturnal aspect of the solar cycle in which midnight separates day's end from the rebeginning. Allusion is made here to a resurrection, a renewal, which eventually provides an explanation for the apparent bifurcation of one same state of being.

Another characteristic is that the scarab dominating this tableau is placed, in quite atypical fashion, under the winged disk, a new allusion to the transformations undergone by the sun in the Dwat.

PLATE 237 • DOORWAY LEADING TO THE INNER CHAPELS

On the left doorpost of this doorway the Hathorian character nursing Shepenwepet (pl. 235) can be recognized. On the lintel two kings are seated back-to-back on two thrones resting on a long pedestal, at the ends of which two Niles link the Two Lands. In front of the king on the left the vulture

Nekhebet, on a basket, surmounts the symbolic flowers of the South that rise up from the head of the Nile. Before the king on the right the flowers of the North are supporting the serpent Wadjet.

The dual character of all the representations in this little building, from the double uraei of the Ethiopian king to the most recent depictions, should be emphasized.

PLATE 238 • ALABASTER STATUE OF THE DIVINE WORSHIPER AMENIRDIS

Statue found at Karnak. Height: 1.67 meters. Twenty-fifth Dynasty.

PLATE 239 • CHAPEL OF THE DIVINE WORSHIPERS

On the doorposts of this chapel's doorway, Amun is "embraced" on the left by Amenirdis and on the right by the divine wife Shepenwepet. In the background is the Nectanebo gate.

PLATES 240–243 • THE NECTANEBO GATE

The enclosure wall (pl. 232) is constructed on beds of bricks that are alternately convex and concave,

---

Some see this as a member of the Felidae family, others a viverrid: a genet or, more likely, a mongoose. Note the reversal of the north-south orientations.

thus forming an undulation whose impetus is provided by the east gate of Nectanebo. "It seems that the enclosure wall, whose bricks undulate like waves, represents the primordial waters that surround, on all sides, the sacred mound." (Barguet, *La Structure du Temple*, p. 32; see also the dedication of the gate of the second pylon, p. 74)

PLATE 240 • WEST FACADE

PLATE 241 • EAST FACADE

The great propylon of the east (gate of Nectanebo).

This immense gate, for which the upper portion is made of enormous blocks and the doorposts from smaller stones but assembled with a great deal of care, provides entrance into the great enclosure of Oph (Karnak) on the east side. The large enclosure of baked bricks touches on both the left and right side of this propylon, which has never been adorned with any sculpture, either on its top or jambs, on the inside as well as outside of the enclosure, except that toward the back on the left side (when exiting) there are two tableaux of worshiping carved in the thickness of the doorway. (Champollion, *Notices descriptives*, vol. 2, pp. 261–62)

To the west (pl. 240), the lintel is formed of two enormous monolithic blocks, with a third from which the mold of the torus has been cut out. On the stone monolith of the cornice's first course, a large rectangle facing the setting sun is worked in relief, at the site of the uraei-flanked disk. On the east side (pl. 241), the arrangement of the lintel's blocks is analogous, but the torus, the disk facing the rising sun, and the uraei are sculpted.

PLATE 242 • EAST FACADE: LINTEL

On this facade the distance between the blocks indicates an intentional break between the sculpted portions and the missing portions of the figurations.

On the left side only the upper part of Ptolemy II Philadelphus offering Maāt is carved. Amun has only his feathers, his lower limbs, and his throne.

Behind him the upper portion of Mut's body is carved in sunk relief, while the lower part is simply marked out. Aside from her crown, Queen Arsinoe is entirely drawn out in dots, while in the next figuration only her forearms and her right hand are thus marked. On the right, the king, Amun, and Khonsu are sculpted down to the waist and cut in half by the joint. The lower portions of their bodies are entirely missing. The inscriptions on the top are complete.

PLATE 243 • EAST FACADE: UNFINISHED SCULPTURES

Here only the lower parts of the figures are sculpted.

This entire solar gate is nothing but an immense symbol that demands careful study, for it obviously isn't a question of accidentally unfinished sculptures; these anomalies answer to a symbolic intent.

On the other hand, the installation of the doorposts sticks out on the right and the left, forming an immense disk that is built into the wall of the baked-brick enclosure (pl. 240).

PLATES 244–250 • AKHENATEN

PLATE 244 • NECTANEBO GATE, SITE OF THE TEMPLE OF AKHENATEN

The temple of Amenhotep IV is located to the east of the great temple of Amun. This king changed his former name of Amenhotep, "Peace of Amun," into Akhenaten, "Glorification of the Solar Disk" (*akh* can be translated as "beneficial," "glorious," "splendid," and a thousand other like qualities).

The transitory period of Akhenaten has been found quite intriguing, for it departs completely from the normal rhythm of Egyptian history, by virtue of the fact that this king repudiated Amun to replace him by Aten, the visible solar disk. It follows the Tuthmosian era during which a queen, Hatshepsut, assumed the role of king, and Akhenaten's reign took on a feminine character (pl. 247).

The faces on the statues as well as the bas-reliefs generally present a caricature of sensuality that is totally absent in all the rest of the pharaonic works.

PLATE 245 • HEAD OF ONE OF THE STATUES OF AKHENATEN FOUND ON THE SITE OF THE EASTERN TEMPLE

PLATE 246 • BLOCK OF AKHENATEN FOUND IN THE SECOND PYLON

PLATE 247 • BUST OF AKHENATEN

In his two crossed fists the king is holding the *hek* and *nekhakha* scepters, which are crossed in turn. On his right wrist he is wearing the two cartouches of his titulary from the so-called Amarnian period.

Note the exceptionally elongated neck, the thick-lipped and sensual mouth, the faunlike eyes, the very pronounced waist, and the feminine breasts.

PLATE 248 • BLOCK OF AKHENATEN FOUND IN THE SECOND PYLON

The king's profile is outlined over the sun's rays that terminate in little hands from many of which the ankh symbol is escaping.

PLATE 249 • BLOCKS OF AKHENATEN FOUND IN THE SECOND PYLON

The similarity of the two faces can give rise to the notion that the feminine crown and wig are resting on the king's head and not on that of the queen.

PLATE 250 • BLOCK OF AKHENATEN FOUND IN THE SECOND PYLON

This scene illustrates the famous Egyptian formulation "sniffing the earth." It is of a gripping realism, typical of Akhenaten.

It is remarkable that thousands of Akhenaten's blocks have been found that came from his eastern temple and were reused on the inside of the second pylon of the temple of Amun, for which they constitute the foundation on the yellow desert sand.

"We have found a small bed of several *talatats* still bound together by mortar that constitutes one of the corners of a small building, perhaps an altar with the torus, but lacking the cornice." (H. Chevrier, *Annales du Service des Antiquités de l'Egypte* 44: 244–45)

If the desertion of Amun had not been part of a foreseen order and Akhenaten had simply been a destroyer, the elements of his work would *certainly*

not have been respected; it would certainly have been easy enough to suppress them. Given the care and love that went into the construction of monuments, from the foundations to their finishing touches, these stones would *certainly not* have been buried as "seeds" in an Amunian edifice if they had been considered unhealthy or malefic.

General Orientation of the Principal Sanctuaries

The great temple of Amun has its sanctuary on the east and its entrance on the west. For almost half of its total length it is traversed by a perpendicular path that leads to the temple of Mentu in the north and the temple of Mut in the south.

The temple of Mentu's entrance is on the north side and its sanctuary is to the south; similarly, the temple of Mut has its entrance on the north and its sanctuary on the south.

These provisional orientations can be compared with those of the successive temples of Medamud in which two original mounds, constructed on perpendicular axes, have served as a foundation for the following: *(a)* the temple of Mentu and its sacred bull is laid out on a north-south axis, with the sanctuary in the south; *(b)* the temple of Amun and its sacred ram is laid out on the east-west axis, with the sanctuary in the east.

It is even possible to put the temple of Mut in Karnak in relation to the temple of Hathor in Dendera, since both have the choir in the south.

The temple of Khonsu[32] has its sanctuaries in the north and is reminiscent of the temple of Horus in Edfu, which also has a north-south orientation.

The temple of Apet is perpendicular to that of Khonsu; its choir is on the east.

Finally, the little temple of Ptah-to-the-south-

---

[32]The temple of Khonsu-who-governs-in-Thebes, in which Champollion discovered the so-called Bakhtan stela, is about 100 m east of the northeast corner of the enclosing wall. The Bactrian capital Balkh is moreover renowned for the region of Badakhshān, from which the most beautiful lapis lazuli is mined. The trip there would thus take 515 days, but the distance between Thebes and Balkh must be taken into consideration, which is, as the crow flies, and going north of the Zagros Mountains (which separate Iraq from Iran) around 6,225 km, or, winding round this mountain chain as did Alexander, 7,850 km. The average day's march is therefore a minimum of 12 to 15 km, to which still must be added all the meandering imposed on the traveler by the high mountains of Afghanistan.

of-his-wall is actually to the south of the enclosure wall that separates Amun's domain from that of Mentu. His sanctuary is to the east.

PLATE 251 • STATUE OF KHONSU

Statue of Khonsu in gray granite, found in Karnak, dating from the Eighteenth Dynasty. Actual height: 2.6 meters.

This *neter* is the object of a famous story, carved in hieroglyphs on a stela discovered by Champollion in a small Greco-Roman temple neighboring the temple of Khonsu. This tale, dating from the Ptolemaic era, affects the form of an official document supposedly taken down under Ramesses II, but, says G. Lefebvre in his *Romans et contes égyptiens:*

"It is a counterfeit, executed, moreover, with no great skill, since the author naively gives Ramesses II part of Tuthmosis IV's protocol; what's more, he is as

mediocre a grammarian as he is uninformed a historian, he didn't succeed in creating a pastiche of the style of the official inscriptions of the Nineteenth Dynasty; on the other hand, his writing honestly has the character and allure of stories from the Rammeside era."

Following the royal protocol and praises to the sovereign the *story of the princess of Bakhtan* begins:

His Majesty was in Naharin, as was his custom each year, the great from all the foreign lands came to him in bowed and peaceable attitude.... The prince of Bakhtan [he too] had his presents brought, at the head of which he had placed his eldest daughter. Glorifying His Majesty [who loved her] more than any other. Thus she was given the titulary, to wit, "Great Royal Wife Neferure." And when His Majesty arrived in Egypt [with her] she fulfilled all the duties of a royal wife.

Then when His Majesty was in Thebes the

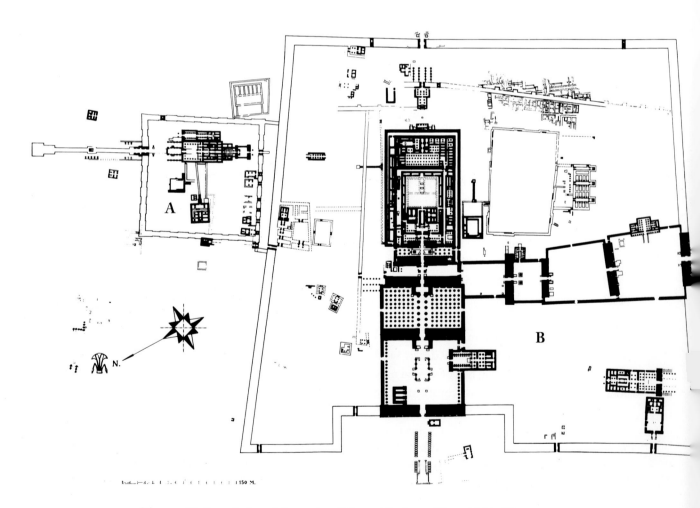

Diagram 12. Overall view of the temples of Mentu (A), Amun (B), and Mut (C)

Victorious, [it happened that] someone came to His Majesty and said: "A messenger from the prince of Bakhtan has arrived, bearing gifts for the royal wife. . . ." He said, while kissing the earth before His Majesty, and then repeated to Her Majesty: "I come to you, my lord and master, concerning Bentrech, the younger sister of the royal wife Neferure; an illness has invaded her body. May it please Your Majesty to delegate a scholar to see her." Then His Majesty said, "Have the staff of the House of Life and the officials of the court brought forth." They were brought forth immediately into the presence of His Majesty and he said: "See thou [I] have had you called forth so that you may hear my words, to wit, bring me one of your company who is skilled and who [knows] how to write with his fingers." The royal scribe Djehutyemheb came before His Majesty and His Majesty commanded him to go to Bakhtan with this messenger.

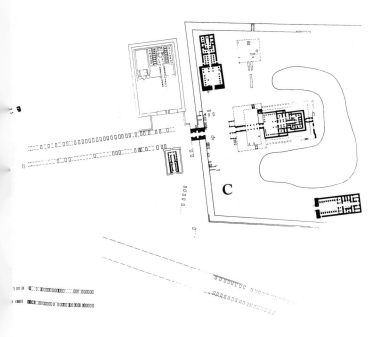

C

When the scholar arrived in Bakhtan he found Bentrech in the state of [someone] who is possessed by a spirit; he found as well that [it was] an enemy who must be combated. Then the prince of Bakhtan sent anew [a message] before His Majesty couched in these terms: "O my lord and master, may it please His Majesty to order the transport of a neter *[to Bakhtan." This message came] to His Majesty in the year 26, the [first] month of summer during the feast of Amun, while His Majesty was in Thebes.*

Then His Majesty spoke before Khonsu-in-Thebes-Neferhotep saying: "My good lord, I speak before you concerning the daughter of the prince of Bakhtan." Then Khonsu-in-Thebes-Neferhotep was led before Khonsu-who-governs-in-Thebes, the great neter *who drives off the evil spirits [lit., "the lurkers"]. Then His Majesty said before Khonsu-in-Thebes-Neferhotep: "My good Lord, if you turn your face toward Khonsu-who-governs-in-Thebes, the great* neter *who drives off the evil spirits, he will be made to go to Bakhtan." He shook his head violently two times. Then His Majesty said: "Provide him with your magic fluid that I can make His Majesty go to Bakhtan to save the daughter of the prince of Bakhtan." Khonsu-in-Thebes-Neferhotep shook his head violently two times. Then he had the magic fluid passed into Khonsu-who-governs-in-Thebes, four times.*

His Majesty ordered that Khonsu-who-governs-in-Thebes be led toward the large sacred barque [and to have him accompanied by] five transport vessels, chariots, and numerous horses, [to the] right and [to the] left. This neter *arrived in Bakhtan in the space of one year and five months. Then the prince of Bakhtan came with his soldiers and the great ones of his realm before Khonsu-who-governs-in-Thebes. He went down flat upon his belly saying, "You come to us that you may show your friendship for us, by order of the king Usermaātre Setepenre."*

Then this neter *made his way to the place where Bentrech was. He had the magic fluid passed into the daughter of the prince of Bakhtan; she immediately felt better. Then this spirit that was within her said before Khonsu-who-governs-in-Thebes: "Be welcome in peace, great* neter *who drives off the evil spirits! Bakhtan is your city, its inhabitants are your servants, I myself am your servant. I will return to the place from which I have come, so to alleviate your heart entirely concerning that*

Fig. 91. Statue of Khonsu photographed by Legrain at the time of its discovery (1903)

for which you have come. May Your Majesty command the making of a feast day with me and with the prince of Bakhtan." Then this neter *nodded his head to his priest while saying: "May the prince of Bakhtan make a great offering to this spirit."*

Now, during the time that this was going on between Khonsu-who-governs-in-Thebes and the spirit, the prince of Bakhtan was standing there with his soldiers and [he] had great fear. Then he made a large offering before Khonsu-who-governs-in-Thebes and before the spirit of the prince of Bakhtan, all while creating a feast day in their honor. Then the spirit went peacefully to the place where it pleased him to go, by the command of Khonsu-who-governs-in-Thebes, and the prince of

Bakhtan greatly rejoiced. . . .

Then he thought to himself, saying: "I will make it so that this neter *remains here in Bakhtan, and I will not let him return to Egypt." And this* neter *remained three years and nine months in Bakhtan.*

[One day while] the prince of Bakhtan was sleeping on his bed, he saw [in a dream] this neter, *who had left his chapel in the form of a golden falcon and soared off into the sky, taking flight toward Egypt. He awoke in anguish, then he said to the priest of Khonsu-who-governs-in-Thebes: "This* neter *is still here with us; let him return to Egypt, have his chariot returned to Egypt!" Then the prince of Bakhtan arranged for the*

departure of this neter *for Egypt; he gave [to him] a great number of presents, consisting of all kinds of good things, as well as soldiers and horses in very great quantity.*

They arrived peacefully in Thebes, and then Khonsu-who-governs-in-Thebes made his way to the temple of Khonsu-in-Thebes-Neferhotep. He placed the presents given to him by the prince of Bakhtan, consisting of all kinds of good things, before Khonsu-in-Thebes-Neferhotep, without saving anything for his [own] temple. Khonsu-who-governs-in-Thebes arrived peacefully at his temple in the year 33, day 19 of the second month of winter, of the king Usermaātre Setepenre, may he be gratified with life, like Ra, forever. (Lefebvre, *Romans et contes égyptiens*, 1949, pp. 221–232)

PLATES 252–271 • TEMPLE OF KHONSU

A brief passage from the Harris Papyrus informs us that the temple of Khonsu was built by Ramesses III:

I built a house for thy son, Khonsu in Thebes, of good sandstone, red gritstone, and black stone (granite). I overlaid its doorposts and doors with gold, (with) inlay-figures of electrum like the horizon of heaven. (Breasted, *Ancient Records*, vol. 4, § 214)

Apart, however, from the seven small chapels that surround the four-columned hall located behind the sanctuary of the barques, the bas-reliefs of this temple don't bear the cartouches of Ramesses III but those of Ramesses IV, Ramesses XI or XII, the high priest–king Herihor, and Pinedjem, who, according to their dedication, would seem to have constructed the first court and the pylon.

The temple of Khonsu consists of a peristyle court bordered by a portico of twenty-eight mono-style columns divided into four groups: two groups of eight that border the court and two groups of six on a small, slightly elevated platform, and a hypostyle hall with four campaniform columns in the middle and two monostyle columns on each side. From this room one enters the sanctuary of the barque, in which chapels open to the left and right and where, to the east, a staircase leads to the roof.

From the sanctuary of the barque one enters into a kind of pronaos that provides access to three sanctuaries located to the north and four small lateral sanctuaries. The one in the northeast corner contains a representation of the dead Osiris, lying on a stretcher, between Isis and Nephthys.

PLATE 252–253 • PYLON OF THE TEMPLE OF KHONSU

In front of the temple of Khonsu's pylon are remnants of an Ethiopian colonnade of the type similar to that preceding the "upper gate" of the great temple of Amun (pls. 228–230), bordered on the outside by a row of sphinxes.

This pylon measures 34.5 meters long by 7 meters wide and 18 meters high. Its facade has four grooves that are intended to house masts with banners.

Under the torus of each wing is a dedication that specifies that *the first high priest of Amun, master of the rites, Pinedjem, son of the first high priest of Amun, Piankh, has made this very great and august pylon for his father Khonsu-in-Thebes-Neferhotep on the front of his temple.*

The bas-reliefs that cover the two wings of the pylon represent ritual scenes of worship performed by the first high priest, Pinedjem. On the east wing the divine worshiper, divine wife of Amun, Maātkare—who is presumed to be the daughter of Psusennes I—is represented alone, whereas on the west wing Maātkare and Henuttawy, worshiper of Hathor, are depicted (fig. 94).

PLATE 254 • PERISTYLE COURT: INTERIOR FACADE OF THE ENTRANCE GATE

Champollion noted everything that was above-ground in his time (fig. 92), and he observed that the antae pillars of the portico bore the inscription of the high priest–king Herihor. He remarks, concerning the interior facade of this doorway:

"Cornice decorated by an anaglyph bearing under the curve of the 'annary' scepter the captions of Ptolemy. This portion of the doorway is therefore modern and replaces a more ancient doorway cap from which two end stones remain. These, being employed under the tori of the two massifs of the pylon, could not be disengaged without danger. It is there in the curve of the annary scepters that the *first high priest of Amun, Pinedjem maā kheru* can still be read, in the place of the Ptolemaic inscriptions.

The rest of the cornice bears more modern inscriptions because the stones have been renewed." (Champollion, *Notices descriptives*, vol. 2, pp. 219–24)

Plate 255 • Peristyle Court: Colonnade of the West Portico

The architraves, the abaci, the capitals, and the shafts of the monostyle columns bear the complete royal titulary: the Horus, the Two Goddesses, and the Golden Horus names of the first high priest of Amun, Herihor, who inscribed within the two royal cartouches both his name and his priestly title. He is also represented officiating with the headdress and other royal attributes and not with the shaven head and robes of the priest.

On the architraves to the east and west of this court, the Horus name of the high priest is put into relationship with Amun, his Two Goddesses name with that of Mut, lady of Asheru, and finally his Golden Horus name with Khonsu. It is again speci-

fied there that he created this large columned hall as a work for eternity, *with the hand of Ptah who provided the blueprint.*

Plate 256 • Portico of the Peristyle Court: Northeast Corner

In the foreground is the slightly elevated north portico, followed by the doorway of Ptolemy IV Philopator that opens onto the hypostyle for which two of the campaniform columns can be seen. The sanctuary of the barque is visible in the background.

Note the columns on the right that are made from the drums of fasciculate columns that are presumed to have been furnished by the great funerary temple of Amenhotep III on the west bank. Knowing that the high priests religiously safeguarded the royal tombs and mummies from the thefts and depredations that went unchecked during the Twentieth Dynasty, the real reason for this reuse should be sought out.

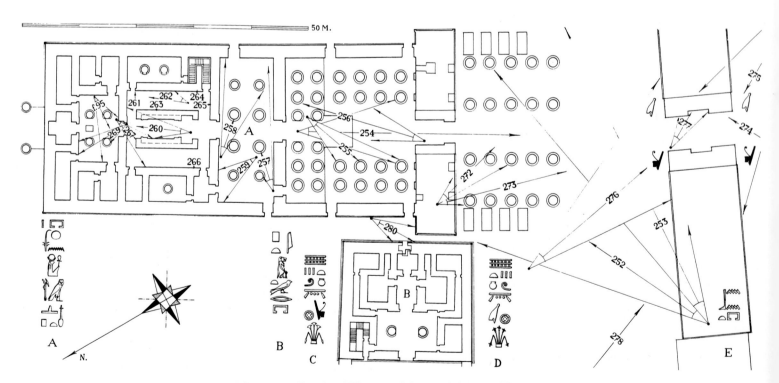

Diagram 13. Temples of Khonsu and Apet, and the gate of Euergetes

(A) Temple of Khonsu-in-Thebes-Neferhotep; (B) Temple of Apet the Great; (C) nome of the land of the north; (D) nome of the land of the south; (E) name of the spot consecrated to Khonsu

PLATE 257 • CAMPANIFORM COLUMNS FROM THE CENTRAL NAVE OF THE HYPOSTYLE HALL

The hypostyle hall consists of three naves and two aisles. The central nave is configured of four quite massive campaniform columns that are around 7 meters tall; the two lateral bays are supported on one side by the campaniform columns and on the other by the monostyle columns that are 5.5 meters tall, topped by an architrave, torus, cornice, and claustra similar to that of the great hypostyle hall of the Nineteenth Dynasty temple of Amun (pls. 40–87).

PLATE 258 • HYPOSTYLE HALL

The dedicatory texts on the architraves of both the large and small columns are in the name of Menmaātre Setepenamun (Ramesses XI or XII), who is said to have built this hall called *"Wearer-of-Diadems"... Live the Good God* [Neter-nefer] ... *the monument builder, plentiful in wonders, whose every design comes to pass (immediately) like his father Ptah-South-of-His-Wall.* (Breasted, *Ancient Records*, vol. 4, §§ 602–3)

At the base of the wall of the hypostyle, *the high priest of Amun-Ra, commander in chief of the armies of North and South, Herihor,* inscribes that he worked at the enlargement of the *house of Khonsu,* exalting it with electrum, precious stones, and offering tables in silver and gold.

Toward the doorway that provides access on the court, Herihor bears a new title: *Overseer of the granaries and viceroy of Kush* (the black country). A very interesting inscription that is unfortunately in very fragmentary condition tells of a miracle produced by Khonsu for him with the approval of Amun. Would this concern his ascension to the throne? Only the fact that in the court he bears the royal titulary and attributes, whereas in the hypostyle he is still only the viceroy of Kush, permits this supposition.

PLATE 259 • HYPOSTYLE HALL, NORTHWEST CORNER: BASE OF A MONOSTYLE COLUMN

On the north wall the prows of the barques of Mut and Khonsu can be seen followed by the great *bari* of Amun.

PLATE 260 • HALL OF THE BARQUE: DOORWAY THAT PROVIDES ACCESS TO THE PRONAOS

The jambs and double lintel of this doorway that leads to the pronaos are of Ptolemaic manufacture. On the upper lintel two groups of eight *neters* are worshiping the disk set within a thin crescent, the symbol of Khonsu; on the lower lintel the king is presenting two vessels of wine to a hieracocephalic (falcon-headed) Khonsu who wears a headdress of the disk in the crescent, then he is shown making the offering of Maāt to Amun followed by Khonsu, who is wearing the braid denoting a crown prince (on the right), and to Amun followed by Mut (on the left).

The upper block and walls of this room are in the throne name of Ramesses IV, Heqamaātre Setepenamun, carved in very deep sunk relief.

In the foreground right are the remains of a barque sanctuary that is almost completely destroyed.

PLATE 261 • HALL OF THE BARQUE: EAST WALL

On the lower register, to the right, the hand of the king can be seen offering his anaglyph Heqamaātre to Amun-Ra and Mut, who are both standing.

On both sides of the cartouche on the lintel the king, wearing a blue helmet, is offering this same anaglyph to a seated hieracocephalic Khonsu, topped by a disk within a crescent.

Above the lintel (second register), Khonsu is offering the palm tree of the years and the *sed*-festival symbol, while Isis breast-feeds the young king-prince wearing the white crown. On the right is the *neter* Shu, who is wearing the ostrich plume that is his symbol on his head and receiving two vessels from the hands of the king.

The frieze that surmounts this tableau is composed of the anaglyph of Ramesses IV's royal name: Heqamaātre Setepenamun, and his Son of Ra name: Ramesses Maātmeryamun, in which the hieroglyph *mes* is replaced by the king wearing the braid of the crown prince (the word *mes* signifies, according to its determinative, "to be born," "birth," or "born of," in other words, the child).

PLATE 262 • HALL OF THE BARQUE: NORTHEAST CORNER

To the right, on the bottom register of the east wall, the king is purified by Thoth and Horus, then he achieves the "royal ascent" between Tum and Mentu and makes the offering of Maāt in the form of his anaglyph (pl. 261).

In the back, on the bottom register of the north wall, the king, blessed by a lion-headed Mut, makes an offering of a vessel crowned with a falcon head and the disk within a crescent to a standing Khonsu-in-Thebes-Neferhotep, who is bearing the disk of Ra encircled by a serpent. The offering vessel bears the same symbol as that of the *neter* to whom it is offered. Here, for example, the vessel has a falcon head crowned by a disk within a crescent for Khonsu, whereas for Amun it would have a ram's head.

On the top the king protected by Isis makes the

Fig. 92. Peristyle court of the temple of Khonsu

offering of his anaglyph to Khonsu wearing the feathers that are a characteristic of Mentu. These two registers are surmounted by the frieze of anaglyphs (pl. 261).

PLATE 263 • KHONSU

Khonsu, wrapped in white linen over which cross two ribbons (most commonly painted red), is holding all the scepters in his hands save one: the *wadj*. The *hek* and *nekhakha* scepters frame the *djed* scepter, from which the ankh and *was* emerge, characteristic of Khonsu (see pl. 251).

The top of his chest is encircled by a large necklace made up of multiple rows of pearls, on which is hanging the *menat* necklace of Hathor, which is terminated by its characteristic counterweight that falls back over the spinal column. He is wearing the blue headband of Ptah, and the braid of the crown prince passes under the royal band, from which also emerges the uraeus crowned with a disk in a crescent.

PLATE 264 • HALL OF THE BARQUE: BAS-RELIEF ON THE EAST WALL

Ramesses IV offers the first fruits of the season to a falcon-headed Khonsu.

PLATE 265 • THE ROYAL OFFERING OF RAMESSES IV

The king, who is holding the censer, presents the table of offerings to the Theban triad: Amun, Mut, and Khonsu.

This scene is superimposed over an older one. The original line of the ground can be found at the level of the existing king's knees, and the older figuration of the king, which has been hammered out, is outlined in silhouette on the table of offerings; his feet are resting on the heads of the ducks, and his head is over the fifth and sixth lines of the ten-line text inscribed above. This text reads as follows:

1. *Offering that the king gives to Geb, to the Great Ennead, to the Small Ennead, to the* neters *of the* itr.t *of the South*
2. *and of the* itr.t *of the North and of all the* neters, *presented by your son whom you love, the master of the Two Lands, Heqamaātre Setepenamun,*

Fig. 93. Superimposition

3. *the master of the crowns, Ramesses-shu-Maāti-mri-Imn; ten hundredweight of bread, ten hundredweight of pitchers of beer, ten hundredweight of beef, ten hundredweight of fowl, ten hundredweight of alabaster vessels,*

4. *ten hundredweight of vestments, ten hundredweight of resins, ten hundredweight of jars of oil, ten hundredweight of bouquets of flowers, ten hundredweight of viands, ten hundredweight of everything good and pure,*

5. *ten hundredweight of everything good and sweet, that is to say, what the sky provides for you, what the earth creates for you, what the Nile brings for you*

6. *from its cavern. May the hand give, the flood purify,*

7. *and the master of the Two Lands, Heqamaātre Setepenre, the master of the Crowns, Ramesses-shu-Maāti-mri-Imn, make an offering to his father,*

8. *Amun-Ra, the master of the thrones of the Two Lands. I know [the gods] who are in the sky, I know [the gods] who are on the earth, I know*

9. *[the gods] who surround Horus; I know [the gods] who neighbor Seth. I satisfy Horus by returning his eyes to him,*

10. *I satisfy Seth by returning his testicles to him. It is I, Thoth, he who satisfies the gods and puts things in their proper place.*

(Trans. L. Christophe)

The superimposition of the two tableaux is a complete teaching; the king offers himself as the totality of the gifts of the sky and of all creatures (5). Furthermore he is identified with the Nile's gift (6), and the feet of the king from the first tableau are resting on the heads of the ducks in the second, recalling one of the representations of the Nile *neter* at Abydos, who has human form but whose head is replaced by two duck heads.

The last three lines identify the king with Thoth, asserting his knowledge of everything that exists in heaven and earth, in Horus and Seth, and makes an allusion to the myth of the struggle between these two gods in which Seth gouged out the eye of Horus, who in turn tore off Seth's testicles. It was

Thoth who reconciled the two adversaries and *put things back into their proper places.*

Here the king is identified with Thoth, whereas in Abydos it is Thoth who speaks the first part of this text in the presence of the king.

In the original scene the Theban triad was seated and can still be seen under the existing tableau's representation of the triad, which is, however, upright and in movement.

PLATE 266 • WEST WALL OF THE HALL OF THE BARQUE

The entire lower part of this wall has remained free of any bas-relief; only the dedicatory frieze is carved, in the name of Ramesses IV, beloved of Khonsu-Neferhotep. On the fourth course a Coptic cross can be seen.

PLATE 267 • WEST DOORPOST OF THE NAOS OF THE BARQUE OUTER NORTH WALL

Ramesses IV, his face turned toward the naos entrance, is offering to a hieracocephalic Khonsu a small king in the "silver statue" position that is holding his name in its hand: the king is offering himself in the form of Maāt bearing the *hek* and crowned with the Ra disk.

The stone that forms the foundation of this pillar is a reused block that has been overturned and upon which the last line can still be read: *sanctuary of perfect stone. . . .* It is therefore the image of the sanctuary itself that serves as a course in the sanctuary of the barque!

PLATE 268 • GRANITE BLOCK OF AMENHOTEP II IN THE TEMPLE OF KHONSU

The king Amenhotep II, Akheperure, wearing the white crown, is here presenting the *nehbit* scepter in the shape of a rounded cone supported by a lotus flower (the word *nehb.t* designates the lotus flower and the nape of the neck).

In front of this scepter is a vertical shaft whose forked end is reminiscent of the lower part of a *was* scepter, upside-down. We are dealing here with the upper portion of the well-known scene of the erection of the mast of Min (pl. 178–179). In Luxor, in a scene similar to that of the hypostyle hall, the king is

holding the *mākes* cane in one hand and raises the *nehbit* scepter in the other, before the mast of Min, which consists of a vertical shaft that is terminated at its top by a fork and upheld by four forked batons on which four people are climbing. They are recognizable as Libyans by the feathers they are wearing on their heads.

PLATE 269 • COLUMNS NORTHWEST OF THE PRONAOS

The four columns of the pronaos are of the polygonal type but slightly "fluted" on the top sections except at their perfectly cylindrical bottoms. The base and start of the shaft are carved from one block. The four central sides bear the royal legend: on the first to the left the cartouche carved above is of *Ptah the Great, south of his wall* (south face) and of *Mut the Great, mistress of Asheru . . .* (east face and south face on the second column). (See also fig. 95.)

PLATE 270 • FOOTPRINTS ON THE ROOF

Pilgrims have often traced the contour of their feet to piously mark their journey to a sanctuary. Often, too, they scraped the stone of the temple's outer walls to take with them a tiny bit of the sanctuary's substance, a gesture that is still made today.

PLATE 271 • OVERALL VIEW OF THE EIGHTH AND NINTH PYLONS TAKEN FROM THE ROOF OF THE TEMPLE OF KHONSU

Taharka's two columns before the temple of Ramesses II and the great gate of the east are recognizable beyond the lake (pls. 231, 240, and 241).

PLATES 272–277 • GATE OF PTOLEMY III EUERGETES

Discovered on either side of the Euergetes gate is the existence of three strong foundation courses that are the same width as the gate and 28.2 meters long. They seem to have been intended to support a pylon whose entire length, including the gate, would have been 68.6 meters. (See Traunecker, *Karnak*, vol. 5, p. 24 and fig. 11. Surveys of the gate by P. Clère in *Mémoires publiés par les membres de l'Institut Français d'Archéologie Orientale*, 84.)

PLATE 272–273 • A CORNER OF KARNAK
VILLAGE AND THE GATE OF
PTOLEMY III EUERGETES,
NORTH FACADE, SEEN FROM
THE PYLON OF THE TEMPLE OF
KHONSU

This monumental gate serves as a "propylon" to the temple of Khonsu and crosses through the baked-brick wall of the enclosure that surrounds all the temples of Karnak.

Each doorpost bears five tableaux on which the king offers in succession the scepter of the prefect,

Fig. 94. Papyrus of Queen "Henuttawy-Hathor-Dwaït, royal wife, royal mother, and divine worshiper"

Fig. 95. Twenty-sided polygonal columns

the incense, the sistra and the *menat,* the unguents, the necklace and the pectoral jewelry, each time to two different *neters:* for example, Amun and Mut, or Amun and Khonsu, on the bottom register. Khonsu is represented here in all his guises: wrapped, in human shape, with a falcon head, then with an ibis head. All, however, show him wearing the disk in the crescent.

Four tableaux created as opposing two-by-twos are on the lintel. On the two ends the king is making the "great stride"; on the right (west) he is wearing the red crown of the North and is holding the oar and rudder in his hands. On the left (east) he is wearing the white crown of the South and holding the two *hes* vessels (same crowns on the bottom registers).

On the second register and on the lintel, behind

Khonsu, Hathor is wearing a naos on her head, from which radiates a bouquet of papyrus (fig. 97 and pl. 276).

On the palmette-adorned cornice (these were most often painted in alternating stripes of blue-green-blue-red over a yellow base) the winged disk stands out flanked by two uraei. Under the torus, in the center, is the disk of Khonsu, toward which two friezes of very small figures direct themselves.

PLATE 274 • GATE OF PTOLEMY III EUERGETES: SOUTH FACADE, PYLON OF THE TEMPLE OF KHONSU

PLATE 275 • GATE OF PTOLEMY III EUERGETES: OUTER SOUTH FACADE

The arrangement is the same as on the interior facade, but the tableaux and the direction in which the king is walking are different. Here the king is directed toward the entrance, whereas on the inside he had already entered and had turned his back toward the gate.

On the bottom register of the left doorpost and the lintel, the same feminine deity is wearing a naos on her head from which papyri are radiating (fig. 97 and pl. 274); this is *Hathor the Great who is in the heart of Bennt*, the place consecrated to Khonsu, toward whom she is extending her right hand.

The interior doorpost is decorated with five tableaux.

PLATE 276 • GATE OF PTOLEMY III EUERGETES: NORTH FACADE AND EAST INSIDE SPLAYING

This gate consists of two door frames with an interior splaying, entirely decorated, and meant to receive doors that were attached, on the top, to the cavity that is visible in the inside southeast corner and, on the bottom, by gudgeons normally made of basalt or copper. (A small copper gudgeon has been found in situ at the temple of Luxor.)

PLATE 277 • INTERIOR FACADE OF THE EAST DOORPOST: INTERIOR SPLAYING

Within the splaying of the gate, the horizontal lines on which are inscribed the royal titulary separate friezes of ankhs with two little arms holding the *was* scepter from friezes where vertical cartouches flanked by uraei alternate with a human figure signifying the "thousands," who is holding the palm of the years with the *sed*-festival symbol, resting on baskets, in each hand.

On the inner doorpost, on the left, the king is offering Khonsu the Hathor-headed sistrum and the *menat* necklace with the counterweight. This necklace, which is most often offered by Hathor or Mut, is also one of Khonsu's attributes when he is wrapped in a manner similar to Ptah (pl. 263).

It so happens that in two of the rooms of the temple of Dendera, palace of the *menat*, the counterweight is represented as animated: "Placed horizontally on a pedestal, it appears to us, in reality, in its original form of a feminine torso; the top of the body is modeled after Hathor, and the goddess is presenting the infant Horus with both arms. The king, who is standing behind the divine emblem, is favored with adjectives characteristic of 'the infant engendered of Tatenen, the divine seed of Ptah, he who has fashioned the golden *menat* of the Golden One.'" (P. Barguet, "L'Origine et la signification du contrepoids de collier menat")

Therefore the "regenerative" quality of the *menat* necklace is affirmed, whose counterweight also takes on, at least on one occasion, the appearance of a scarab, signifying the "transformation," and the "becoming."

PLATES 278–289 • THE TEMPLE OF APET

This study of the Temple of Apet is based on the article by A. Varille, "La grande porte du temple d'Apet à Karnak."

PLATE 278 • EASTERN END OF THE INNER SOUTH WALL OF THE GREAT GATE

The great gate of Apet opens in the western section of the baked-brick enclosure wall surrounding the temples of Karnak. It is 6.60 meters wide at its outer framing and its passageway is 12.55 meters long. Its arrangement was similar to that of the gate of Euergetes. The interior facades north and south of the passageway, of which nothing remains but the lower courses, each included five tableaux representing King Nakhtnebef making an offering to a male and female *neter* in alternation.

On this plate the king is presenting the vessels of wine *to his mother Apet the Great*. The royal titulary seen behind the king is in Nakhtnebef's name, but all these bas-reliefs have been retouched by Ptolemy II and Ptolemy III, who mention their "renewal" in the splaying and the western portion of this gate.

The single door leaf was closed by a bolt that is gone today. . . . A text of five columns allows us to confirm that the piece that bolted the gate was one of those moving bars in the form of a lion, of which several examples can be seen in museums. The working principle of these bolts, whether made of wood, bronze, or stone, is always the same: a small lion slide-bolt partially emerges from the housing encased within the doorpost so that it may be used to block the door proper . . . , pulled by a small chain of seven double links from the last of which hangs a heart. . . .

The perfection of the symbolism behind these bolts is astounding. The heart that causes the lion to emerge is therefore the bolt's "motor." Now, the heart is the organ that, through contraction and dilation, "opens" and "closes," prompting the vital flow of blood through diastole and systole.

Inscription on the bolt of Apet:

I am the wife of he who appears in gold, the wife of Ka Nefer. I am the bolt of the great gate to the dwelling of my lord. I drive off whoever approaches him. I am the great uraeus, the terrifying mistress, who repels the unprovided, who represses the opposition. I attack the vile enemy by knife. I . . . his companions. I eat their hearts. I devour their livers in this name of Sekhmet-Menhit. I swallow their blood and I do not let them climb into this temple of eternal life.

"The lion is frequently used as a symbolic guardian of the temple; statues of lions before a gate, images of lions on doorjambs and pillars, a lion figurine like the bar of a bolt." (Varille, "La grande porte")

It should be recalled that the "handcuffs" of Seti I's prisoners also had a bolt in the shape of a lion (pls. 30–39).

Fig. 96. Bolt

PLATE 279 • TEMPLE OF APET, EAST FACADE: ENTRANCE TO THE LOWER CHAPEL

The temple of Apet is constructed on a two-tiered pedestal or "tank" in which crypts that make allusion to the tomb of Osiris have been installed. On the east facade a door can be seen that provides access to a small Osirian chapel that is completely independent, but the main entrance to the temple is on the west.

The cornice of the pedestal corresponds approximately to the floor level of the temple of Apet and to the torus of the doorway to the Osirian chapel.

PLATE 280 • EAST FACADE: ENTRANCE TO THE LOWER CHAPEL

A narrow corridor separates the east facade of Apet's temple from the temple of Khonsu. On the left is the northeast corner of the pylon of Khonsu, on the right, in the name of Ptolemy XIII, is the doorway to the Osirian chapel. The bas-reliefs on the wall are in the name of Augustus. Below, on each side of the doorway, is the king, wearing the red crown on the right and the white crown on the left, who is presenting a platter to Osiris-un-nefer, filled with vases and vegetables. Behind him is a kneeling Nile, who is wearing on his head the symbolic flowers relative to his orientation: the reed on the South and the papyrus on the North.

PLATE 281 • EAST END OF THE OUTER WALL NORTH OF THE PEDESTAL

The list of the nomes of Upper Egypt is carved on the two tiers of the pedestal, starting from the northeast corner: the list is introduced by King Augustus—wearing a blue helmet on top and wearing the crown of the North on the bottom—who is presenting the offerings to Osiris-un-nefer (fig. 98).

On the top register each nome emblem is preceded by its particular *neter*. On the lower register a Nile and a kneeling female figure bear the emblems of "flooded land" and "agricultural territory" for the corresponding nome.

The first *neter, Ptah-handsome-in-countenance*, is upright and walking. His principal temple is in Memphis, or *the place preeminent*, also called *the scales of the Two Lands*, for here is the dividing line between Upper and Lower Egypt. A female figure behind Ptah is carrying on her head the symbol of the first nome of Lower Egypt, *the White Wall* where the triad Ptah-Sekhmet-Nefertum and the great deified sage Imhotep, son of Ptah, are worshiped.

Exactly below is a Nile that carries the symbol of the basin on its head, which signifies flooded land, designated here as *chen-ur*, "the great loop," and the female figure is crowned with the name of agricultural territory, *the field of Ra*.

On the upper register (pl. 281), *Horus-who-rules-with-two-eyes* preceded the symbol of the second nome of Lower Egypt, the nome Letopolis (or Khens) where the nape of Osiris's neck is preserved. The different portions of Osiris's body, dismembered by Seth, were worshiped in each nome's representative Serapeum. The relic of the second nome of Lower Egypt is the scapula, that of the third nome is the right leg.

Coming next is Hathor, mistress of the city of date trees, capital of the third nome, the Libyan nome where was guarded the right femur of Osiris in the "temple of the Thigh." From the time of greatest antiquity this nome was renowned for the quality of its wines. Its emblems are the falcon and the feather of the west, and its agricultural territory is called *the field of Amun*.

PLATE 282 • HATHORIAN ABACUS SURMOUNTING THE COMPOSITE CAPITAL ON ONE OF TWO COLUMNS

From the Twelfth Dynasty have been found almost completely cubical capitals that bear a monumental Hathor head on two sides. In the Ptolemaic temple of Hathor in Dendera, the columns are suggestive of the sistrum: the cylindrical shaft depicts the neck and the capital is replaced by the four faces of Hathor surmounted with a naos framed in scrollwork, forming an abacus.

In the temple of Apet (one of the forms of Hathor), the four faces of Hathor are carved on the abacus placed upon the composite capital consisting of four umbels, eight palm leaves, and sixteen buds.

The cartouche on the cornice of the doorway to the sanctuaries is in the name of Ptolemy VIII Euergetes II.

Fig. 97. "Hathor the Great who is at the heart of Bennt"

PLATE 283 • DOORWAYS TO THE HOLY OF
HOLIES AND THE NORTH LATERAL
SANCTUARY

To the left is the door that provides access to the north lateral sanctuary, *the dwelling of User-menu*, where the resurrection of Osiris is depicted (pl. 289). To the right is the entrance to the axial sanctuary

Fig. 98. Temple of Apet: east end of the north wall

called the *dwelling of the Golden One,* located above the Osirian chapel that connects to the court of the temple of Khonsu (pls. 279 and 280), and whose paving opens over a well. All the way in the back is a niche, on the walls of which are depicted two forms of Apet.

PLATE 284 • DOORWAY TO THE SOUTH LATERAL SANCTUARY

On the lintel of the doorway to this sanctuary is written its name: *The dwelling s.st. bau,* which Varille translates as "the high seat of the linked souls."

Crypts have been worked into the thickness of the north and south walls of the sanctuary. The examination of their partitions with the aid of an ultra-violet light has revealed the existence of figures and texts that are totally invisible to the naked eye. (See Traunecker, *Kemi* 21: 73)

PLATE 285 • SOUTH CHAPEL: INTERIOR FACADE OF THE LINTEL

The female hippopotamus on the left is holding two knives in her paw, which is resting on the *sa* sign. This sign is reminiscent of gestation in the womb, which is the preeminent symbol for the *protection* of life, from which the meaning currently attributed to this symbol is derived. Above it is the guardian deity of the North, Wadjet, who has a cobra head on a vulture's body, with its wings extended.

On the right is the lioness beneath the vulture Nekhebet, the guardian of the South.

In the center is the falcon, Horus, son of Isis, wearing the two crowns—the red over the white—emerging from a brake of papyrus that recalls the marsh of Buto in which Isis secretly reared her son Horus to hide him from the pursuit of Seth.

Horus is standing on the *sma* sign (to link or bind), around which are knotted the papyrus of the North and the reeds of the South.

PLATE 286 • STATUE OF APET-TAWARET

Statue found in the temple of Apet, Twenty-fifth Dynasty (Cairo Museum).

PLATE 287 • WEST WALL OF THE NORTH LATERAL SANCTUARY

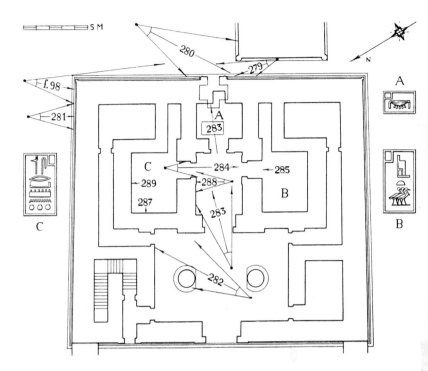

Diagram 14. Temple of Apet

Ptolemy VII is offering the royal bandage to Osiris who resides in Thebes, followed by the feminine principle of Amun wearing the red crown.

PLATE 288 • NORTH SANCTUARY: DOOR DETAIL

Isis is on the left coiffed with a vulture crowned by the disk between two horns.

On the right is one end of the lintel and the left doorpost of the doorway to the north sanctuary, on

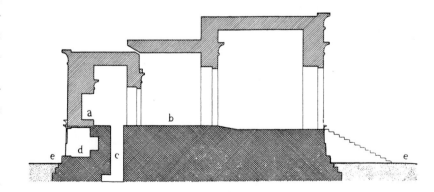

Diagram 15. Longitudinal cross-section of the temple of Apet

(a) niche of Apet; *(b)* ground level of Apet; *(c)* wells; *(d)* niche of Osiris; *(e)* ground level of Khonsu

which the cartouches of Ptolemy VIII Euergetes II and Cleopatra III are carved. The Horus name receives life from a seated Amun above the cartouche of *Un-nefer-maā-kheru* (Osiris Triumphant).

PLATE 289 • NORTH CHAPEL: THE RESURRECTION OF OSIRIS

A famous scene from the north lateral sanctuary represents *Osiris who is at the heart of Waset* in the guise of a young man, stretched out on a bed in the form of a lion, and who is in the midst of waking. The *neter* is beginning to move, bending the right arm and lifting the left foot, below the bed's lion tail, which is very long and curved in a peculiar fashion. The horizontal legend specifies that this concerns *this day of the bull Neg, regenerated* (wab) *in the marsh, brought to life by Mut, the Osiris who is within the temple of the Great Apet, on the west side of the temple of Khonsu.* . . . This Osiris reborn is overshadowed, at the area of his thigh, by a composite bird that has the shape of the soul *ba* with the vulture body of Mut, the

talons of the bird of the flood, and a bearded Amunian head with feathers. A counterweighted necklace *(mny.t)* goes around its neck. This flying creature is named *Amun-Ra, sublime soul of Osiris, that perches on his cadaver in the dwelling of his delivery.* It should be noted that the bird is endowed with a phallus, which gives this soul the power to emit a seed. As for the prone Osiris, presented as the counterpart of the bird, it appears very much to be an abstract of Khonsu who has been issued from the western darkness toward which the sanctuary of Apet opens, and who must be resuscitated in the east. The Ptolemaic temple of Apet therefore reveals, at the moment when Egypt is at its peak of initiation, the final phase of the generation of the Theban Khonsu, the son of Amun in Mut, Ptah become the royal man, in complete equilibrium.

The decoration of the temple of Apet sums up all the principles of the natural work, from the times of the primordial ones to royal Khonsu. (Varille, "La grand porte")

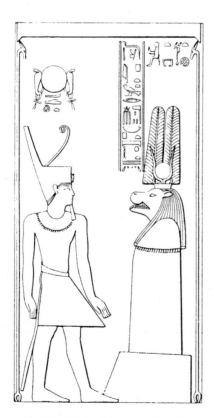

Fig. 99a. Niche of Apet; north wall

Fig. 99b. Niche of Apet; south wall

In fact, the complete scene shows the four "primordial" couples, represented in the shapes of frogs and serpents, behind Isis and Nephthys, who are standing on either side of the sleeping Osiris: to the east are Nun and Nunet, Amun and Amunet, behind Isis; to the west are Heh and Hehet, Kek and Keket, behind Nephthys.

On the north facade of the niche (A), the king wearing the red crown is standing before a bust of a hippopotamus on a pedestal of Maāt: *The Great Apet [Universal Apet], who brings to life the Principles, mistress of Heaven, the vessel of the Two Lands, she who sublimes in Waset.*

On the south facade (B), the king wearing the white crown is offering the clepsydra to a head of Hathor supported by a small column on a cubic pedestal, with the legend: *The Universal Apet who brings to life the Principles, the vessel of the Neters, she who sublimes in Waset.*

The Apet on the north is therefore the vessel-matrix *(hnwt)* of the Two Lands, whereas the Apet on the south presents the character of a celestial Hathor, as the vessel-matrix of the Principles. (Ibid., pp. 112–13)

PLATES 290–297 • THE TEMPLE OF MENTU

To the north of the great enclosure of Karnak, a quadrangular enclosure surrounds the buildings consecrated to the triad Mentu-Rattawï, and Harpra.

All that remains of the temple of Mentu that was built by Amenhotep III is the foundations. Its sanctuary was in the south attached to a small temple of Maāt that was oriented in the opposite direction. Its main doorway was preceded by an Ethiopian portico of twenty columns that enclosed Amenhotep III's two obelisks, and by a ramp that went down toward the northern monumental gate. The temple of Harpra, attached to that of Mentu, is preceded by a hypostyle hall, with Hathorian columns that date from Achoris.

A "high temple" and the sacred pool can be found to the west, and to the north is the monumental gate from which comes the dromos with rams that leads to the wharf. This group of structures forms a complex in and of itself independent of the temple of Amun.

The temple of Mentu at Karnak was probably built on the site of a much older sanctuary. One of the blocks of Amenhotep I and Amenhotep II that was reused in the foundations by Amenhotep III retains the mention of Mentu with the determinative of a bull.

"A stela of Ptolemy III (246–221 B.C.) mentions the construction of a *large brick wall that measures 300 cubits in length by 300 cubits in width.* These dimensions could only be applicable to the enclosure of the temple of Mentu at Karnak and therefore designate its creator." (Traunecker, *Karnak*, vol. 5, p. 156)

Toward the end of the Middle Kingdom, Mentu-Ra was the supreme deity of Upper Egypt, where his four bulls were worshiped in his sanctuaries of Karnak, Medamud, Tod, and Ermant.

PLATE 290–291 • NORTH DOORWAY OF THE TEMPLE OF MENTU AND OVERVIEW OF ALL THE TEMPLES OF KARNAK, SEEN FROM THE NORTH

Between the palm trees and the ruins of the temple, women come seeking the water of the Nile. What rumors and legends circulate among these people. . . .

North of the temple of Mentu stands the Gate of the Slave. Once I was told how in the evening a large Negro would stand there waiting for passersby to whom he would offer access to an underground domain full of fabulous treasure. The entrance was located in the west part of the gate's frame, exactly under the spot where the sculptor Castex carved his name in the year VII of the French Republic. Those invited would enter confidently and return laden with gold, but suddenly, the black slave would rise up in their path and demand, as in the tale of Ali Baba, that the secret word be spoken immediately. If this wasn't done, the wall would close back up and crush the treasure hunter, while the Negro would burst into laughter, revealing all his large white teeth. (Legrain, *Louqsor sans les Pharaons*, p. 103)

This legend of a fabulous treasure belonging to the temple of Mentu, transmitted across the ages, is all the more strange since there actually existed, during the time of Amenhotep III, a considerable quantity of gold dedicated to this temple, as is spoken of in the dedication of his stylobate:

The King of Upper and Lower Egypt, Nebmaātre . . . has erected as foundation for his father from him . . . a restored temple, in beautiful white stone, rudjt, *unshakably located in Waset with no prejudice to the previous construction. . . . It was purified in its totality with* djām *gold. Its doors are in* djām maā *gold, and adorned with all kinds of precious substances, by virtue of the contribution from the mountains of the South. All its paving is of* sa-uy *gold. The leaves of the doors are in pine and* setet *copper by virtue of the contribution from the mountains of the North. It resembles the eastern horizon of the sky. It is a masterpiece of silver and a golden vessel; it holds all precious stones. It is a place of peace for the Lord of the Powers, for it has been made in the image of his Sedia that is in the sky. Its perfect name established in the scriptures is "Nebmaātre, heir of Ra, Khaemmaāt."*

Its total wealth in pounds is:

djām gold	31,485	⅔ *dbn*	(2,865.196 kg)
sa-uy gold	25,182	¾ *dbn*	(2,291.630 kg)
black copper	4,620	⅔ *dbn*	(420.480 kg)
lapis lazuli	6,406	*dbn*	(582.946 kg)
carnelian	1,731	⅔ *dbn*	(157.582 kg)
turquoise	1,075	⅔ *dbn*	(97.886 kg)
bronze	14,342	*dbn*	(1,305.122 kg)

A pool is dug, favoring the development of a garden, so that all manner of flowers resplendently render. (Varille, *Karnak*, vol. 1, p. 12)

PLATE 292 • MONUMENTAL GATE, SOUTH FACADE

The cartouches of Ptolemy III and Ptolemy IV are carved on this double-doored gate, which is 18.75 meters high by 10.96 meters wide and conceived on the same model as the propylon of Khonsu. The excavations have permitted the rediscovery, inside this gate, of the foundations for a smaller gate, probably from the Eighteenth Dynasty, which wouldn't be suitable for the baked-brick enclosure that crosses there now. This enclosure is presumed to be from the time of Nectanebo.

Whereas the facade of the propylon of Khonsu was divided into five registers, that of Mentu consisted of only four (four is the characteristic number of Mentu). On the bottom register the king is wearing the white crown of the South on the east and the red crown of the North on the west.

Represented in the center of the lintel is the triad to whom this temple is consecrated: Mentu, Rattawï (Ra.t tawï, feminine principle of Ra and of the Two Lands), and Harpra (Hor-pa-ra, "Horus the sun").

PLATE 293 • MONUMENTAL GATE, NORTH FACADE

The height of the jambs of this gate is divided, as on the inner facade, into four tableaux. Going

Fig. 100. Monumental gate of the temple of Mentu: condition at an earlier time

from bottom to top, they are arranged as follows: the king offers land to Amun-Ra; then Maāt, on a basket, to Khonsu, and the sistra to Mut. On the third register, Ptolemy III, followed by Berenice, offers water and salt to Mentu, and, on top, the king transfixes a serpent and a turtle (two Sethian creatures) with his spear.

Two bays equal the height of two lower registers; the one on the right is in the form of an obelisk and the one on the left takes the form of a stela, crowned by a winged disk. According to Champollion's description, two colossi of yellowish, crystalline sandstone from the Ramesside era, which are broken today, leaned up against these bays.

PLATE 294 · CORNICE AND LINTEL OF THE MONUMENTAL GATE, NORTH FACADE

Depicted in the center of the lintel, leaning on portions of two columns of text, are Amun and Mut, and Amun and Khonsu, to whom the king is offering Maāt. On the extreme left (east) the king wearing the white crown is offering the vessels of wine to Mentu.

PLATE 295 · TWO STATUES OF AMENHOTEP III

To the north of the monumental gate there is a dromos lined with sphinxes that heads toward the wharf. Excavations 60 meters from the gate revealed the existence of a small chapel containing the remnants of two statues facing south. On the west was one of Seti II in sandstone and on the east an alabaster statue of Horemheb. In front of them and buried 1.3 meters deep were thousands of fragments of two statues of Amenhotep III, painstakingly arranged in two separate tanks.

Fig. 101. Temple of Mentu of Amenhotep III: gate foundation

These forty thousand pieces were so carefully reassembled by C. Robichon that he was able to totally reconstruct the two statues of Amenhotep III, which measure about 3 meters high, including the pedestal.

The king on the left is holding the "divine post" with the ram's head of Amun and "places his sandals on the Nine Bows" that are carved on the pedestal, which is square on the west side and rounded on the east. (See C. Robichon, P. Barguet, and J. Leclant, *Karnak-Nord*, vol. 4)

PLATE 296 • STATUE OF AMUN-RA PROTECTING AMENHOTEP III

This statue was found in one of the two chapels of the temple of Mentu; the kneeling king is wearing the short shirt of the *sed* festival and holding in his two crossed fists two *nekhakha* scepters, which cross back over each other. This magnificent statue of mutilated black granite represents the king protected by Amun-Ra.

PLATE 297 • NORTH DOORWAY OF THE ENCLOSING WALL OF THE GREAT TEMPLE OF AMUN

The enclosing wall of the temple of Mentu is opened to the south of the seven doorways that open onto a narrow corridor that separates it from the large enclosure of the temple of Amun, the inside of which can be entered through this small, unadorned doorway.

Remnants of an earlier monument can be seen in the foreground.

PLATES 298–314 • THE TEMPLE OF PTAH

The temple of Ptah consists of three interconnecting sanctuaries that are consecrated to the Memphite triad Ptah-Sekhmet-Nefertum, preceded by a small portico of two columns and a pylon in the name of Tuthmosis III.

Five doorways were later added to this very small building. A large granite stela in the name of Tuthmosis III was found between the fourth and fifth doorways. On it was carved the following:

My majesty commands that there be built the temple of Ptah-south-of-his-wall, in Thebes, which is a station

. . . of my father Amun-Ra, lord of Thebes. . . . Lo, my majesty found this temple built of brick and wooden columns, and its doorway of wood, beginning to go to ruin. My majesty commands to stretch the cord upon this temple anew, erected of fine white sandstone, and the walls around it of brick, as a work enduring for eternity. My majesty erected for it doors of new cedar of the best of the terraces [Lebanon], mounted with Asiatic copper. . . .

I overlaid for him his great seat with electrum of the best of the countries. All vessels were of gold and silver, and every splendid costly stone, clothing of fine linen, white linen . . . to perform his pleasing ceremonies at the feasts of the beginning of the seasons. (Breasted, *Ancient Records*, vol. 2, §§ 614–15)

PLATE 298 • STATUE OF DJEHUTY, CHIEF OF AMUN'S GRANARIES

Black granite. Height: 0.84 meters. Found in situ in 1900 in the northeast corner of the Theban temple of Ptah. It was flush with the north wall, facing east. Reign of Tuthmosis III. Legrain catalog no. 42123.

This statue has a history. In 1900 when G. Legrain undertook the excavation of the temple of Ptah, he ran into the reluctance of the workers, who feared this place where seven small children had been swallowed up by a cave-in, hence its name of "infants' grave." This was the den of the ghoul, the ogress that must have eaten them, for their bodies were never recovered. Now, to attack the ogress in her lair was a foolhardy venture, for she was said to be guarded in the north of the temple by a row of Negroes who protected her from any who came near. It was precisely in that spot where the black granite statue of Djehuty was found.

The transportation of this statue to Cairo was another adventure. It was first placed facing the prow, but the boat kept running aground. "The sailors had no hesitation in discovering the cause of these multiple halts: the statue of Djehuty was turned around, facing the back, and everything went smoothly from thereon.

"In Karnak confidence was restored with the departure of Djehuty. In the opinion of the peasants, by discovering the black statue I had quite simply made the guardian genie of the temple of Ptah my prisoner, and what's more, by copying and translating the few lines of hieroglyphs carved there, I had made myself the master of the magic grimoire, which would compel the surrender of the children-eater." (Legrain, *Louqsor sans les Pharaons*, pp. 110–11)

This popular legend is all the more curious as, in the myth, Sekhmet is actually the sated devourer of blood who would destroy all humanity in her devastating fury.

PLATE 299 • THE SEVEN DOORWAYS THAT PROVIDE ACCESS TO THE SANCTUARY OF PTAH

On the exterior and interior facades of the first doorway that crosses an enclosure of baked bricks, the cartouches of Ptolemy VI are carved, and on the interior facades of the passage are those of Ptolemy XI and Ptolemy XIII (pl. 300).

The second and fourth doorways are in the name of Shabaka, which has been hammered out. While the first two are constructed to have a lintel, the following three that precede the pylon are of the "broken lintel" variety topped by a cornice and a torus.

The third, of Ptolemy XIII, consists of two engaged columns. Lastly, the fifth serves as an entrance to a pretty portico of four composite columns of Ptolemy III (pls. 302 and 303).

All the way in the back is the sixth doorway, which crosses through the pylon, and beyond a small altar is the seventh doorway, which opens directly onto the central sanctuary where the statue of Ptah is located (pl. 311).

PLATE 300 • EAST FACADE AND SPLAYING OF THE FIRST DOORWAY

To the left, on the inside jambs, is a depiction of Nefertum bearing a lotus feather topped with two long feathers on her head. Two *menat* counterweights (fig. 102) also fall out of this. This *neter* is connected to the creation myth:

"In primordial times the 'children of the weak' rose up against Ra and sought to make him perish in the morning, when he himself was no more than an

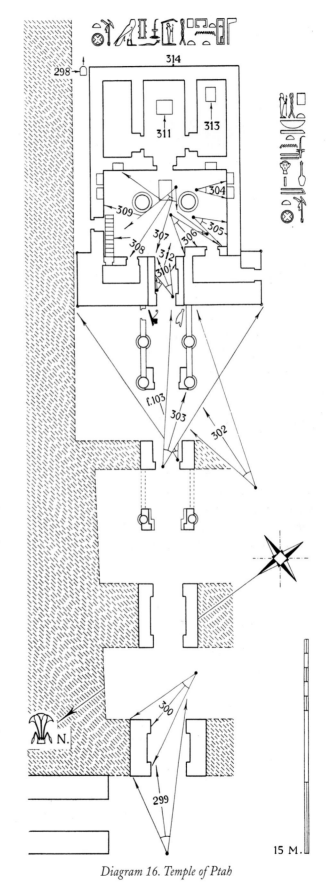

Diagram 16. Temple of Ptah

Fig. 102. Nefertum (Louvre)

infant emerging from a lotus flower. 'There was combat in the entire universe, *in the sky and on the earth,* but the sun god emerged victorious and his enemies were delivered up to him on the flaming isle of Schmun. . . .' When Ra thus triumphed over his enemies and put law in the place of injustice, he bore a lotus flower at his nostrils. This was Nefertum, little god of the temple of Memphis." (A. Erman, *Religion égyptienne,* p. 88)

PLATE 301 • SANDSTONE BLOCK FOUND IN THE ENCLOSING WALL OF PTAH'S TEMPLE

This reused block bears the depiction of a royal personage (probably Ramesside judging from the distinctive shape of his apron's front panel) that is standing before a swaddled Ptah. The entire undecorated portion of this block is outlined with dots, and the king is cut off. This allows us to presume that the image of Ptah was intentionally reused in a building dedicated to him.

PLATE 302 • PTOLEMAIC PORTICO

The total height of these very elegant columns is 10 royal cubits (5.25 m or so), while the space between the tori framing the doorway measures half of this.

In the center is the entrance doorway, whose lintel bears the titulary of Tuthmosis III, and in the background is the north wing of the pylon, which has no other decoration but its torus.

PLATE 303 • SOUTH WING OF THE PYLON: PTOLEMAIC PORTICO

On the south doorpost of the pylon doorway and the gate of Ptolemy III with the broken lintel, the king is wearing the white crown and making the ritual gesture of entering the sanctuary after being purified four times. On the north the king is wearing the red crown.

PLATE 304 • SOUTH WALL OF THE PORTICO: TUTHMOSIS III MAKING THE OFFERING OF WINE

On the inside south wall of the portico the king, wearing the blue helmet, is making the offering of

0

two vessels of wine. He is followed by his *ka* wearing his Horus name on his head, which is *Mighty Bull Appearing in Thebes*. The *ka* is also holding in his left hand, which is placed on his right arm, the long cane topped by the pharaoh's head, and with his right hand at the end of his left arm, he is holding the key of life and the feather of Maāt.

PLATE 305 • SOUTH WALL OF THE PORTICO: AMUN, PTAH, KHONSU, AND MUT

This tableau, which is sculpted in light sunk relief, is located on the south wall of the portico. On the right, above the *was* scepter of Amun, are four vertical lines of an inscription that Mariette saw in its complete state and of which Legrain found nothing but the bottom half. The portion that is lost today had allowed historians to date the Ptah feast mentioned here as having taken place two months after Horemheb's coronation, coinciding with the Beautiful Feast of Apet at Luxor.

Immediately after his coronation, Horemheb undertook the restoration of the worship that had been abolished during the Akhenaten schism, but the oddity here in this text is that the cartouche seems to have been usurped by Horemheb and the bas-reliefs in no way resemble his style.

Behind Amun, *Ptah, lord of Maāt, king of the Two Lands, beautiful of countenance in Thebes . . .* is standing on the pedestal of Maāt, with his head tightly wrapped in a blue lapis lazuli headdress. His two hands emerge from his wrapped body holding the sheath that ends in the *djed* pillar, from which the *was* scepter emerges, and two *mankhet* counterweights of the *hadr.t* pectoral hang from his neck by two ribbons.

The name of this counterweight, *to live*, can be understood when it is seen emerging from the last cervical vertebra and protecting the first thoracic vertebrae, where the nervous ganglia are found that react on the heart, which is covered by the pectoral (here broken, but most often found adorned with a winged scarab, the sun).

Behind Ptah, Khonsu-in-Thebes-Neferhotep is wearing the crown-prince's braid, which passes under his diadem, and is holding in his hands all the scepters but the *wadj*: the *djed* pillar, the *was* scepter,

the ankh, the *hek* crosier, and the *nekhakha* scepter, from which the triple stream appears below Ptah's counterweight. He is wearing the *menat* necklace with its distinctive counterweight, the Hathorian symbol of regeneration on which Mut-who-rules-in-the-house-of-Ptah is resting her hand.

PLATE 306 • SOUTH WING OF THE PYLON, EAST FACADE

On the left is the door leading to a little chamber that has been contrived in the south wing of the pylon, in which a doorway opens to the south. The cartouches on the jambs are in the name of Ptolemy IV, *heir of the god Euergetes*. On the lintel the king is making offerings to a seated Ptah.

Fig. 103. Ptolemaic portico: north wing of the pylon

Compare the two titularies of Ptah on the north and south jambs of this doorway with the similar arrangement of Hathor's titles in the niche of Apet (fig. 99).

On the large tableau to the right, Ptolemy IV is advancing toward a Hathor. Compare the Ptolemaic style of this scene with the pure lines of the previous bas-relief (pl. 305).

PLATE 307 • DOORWAY AND NORTH WING OF THE PYLON, EAST FACADE

On the interior of the doorway the restorations done by Ptolemy III in this part of the building are mentioned.

Fig. 104a. Imhotep, son of Ptah

The interior facade of the doorway is sloped and its cartouches are of Tuthmosis III, whereas the wall of the north wing of the pylon is vertical and holds the cartouches of Ptolemy IV.

To the back left is a row of five doorways preceding the pylon.

PLATE 308 • NORTH WING OF THE PYLON, EAST FACADE

Above the small doorway of the inner chamber of the north wing of the pylon are found two tableaux of worship in the name of Ptolemy IV. On the bottom register the king, followed by Arsinoe, *worships the* neter *four times* in front of a swaddled Ptah, who is standing in his naos followed by Hathor (for whom Sekhmet, the lion, is the other aspect). On the upper register the king is offering Maāt to the Theban triad, Amun, Mut, and Khonsu.

To the right are the stairs leading to the roof of the pylon and the corner of the north wall. Under the corbelled construction, which follows the entablature of the portico, a single tableau is located, surmounted by a frieze of *khakeru:* the king makes an offering to Ptah, Hathor, and Imhotep (pl. 309).

PLATE 309 • NORTH WALL OF THE PORTICO: OFFERING OF COSMETICS TO PTAH, HATHOR, AND IMHOTEP

On the north wall of the portico Ptolemy IV is offering the statuette of the "sphinx bearing the cosmetics" to Ptah, who is standing in his naos and holding the *was,* the ankh, and the *djed* in his hands. Behind him, Hathor is followed by *Imhotep, son of Ptah,* who was deified in the Ptolemaic era and merged with the Greek Asclepios. As is known, Imhotep was the great sage to whom is attributed the majority of texts, mathematical as well as medical, that have come down from the Third Dynasty (Zoser). He was also the "great patron" of architects, and they would never formulate any temple plan without his help or that of the *neters.*

Behind Imhotep, under the portico's architrave, is a text of three vertical lines in the name of Tuthmosis III:

To his father Ptah, beautiful of countenance, lord of the Two Lands. . . . He built the House of Ptah anew in fine white sandstone, the door panels of cedar from the best of terraces [Lebanon], more beautiful than it was before. . . . When My Majesty found this house built of bricks.

This text is almost exactly the same as that on the granite stela found between the fourth and fifth doors of this temple.

Under the portico, above a small niche, is a bas-relief, similar to that located on the opposite south facade (pl. 304), representing Tuthmosis III followed by his *ka*.

In the foreground is one of the two columns of the portico in front of the sanctuary of Ptah. Its base diameter is 106 centimeters, the height of the shaft is around 3.50 meters, so that the diameter is contained almost exactly 3.30 times in the length of the shaft alone, and a little less than four times in the total height of the column, including the base and abacus, which is 4.02 meters. This proportion is quite specific to the temple of Ptah and from its original character, as the ancient entablature still emphasizes. In the Eighteenth Dynasty this is found only in the feast rooms of Tuthmosis III (pl. 186).

PLATE 310 • COLUMN NORTH OF THE PORTICO

In the left foreground is the inner jamb of the doorway, on which is a representation of Ptah that has been hammered out and redone on several different occasions. Below is a dedication from Ptolemy III, who says he has restored this monument. In the middle of the photo is the north column of Tuthmosis III's portico, and in the back is one of the niches that has been installed into the east wall.

PLATE 311 • STATUE OF PTAH IN BLACK GRANITE

This splendid statue of Ptah is carved in a monolithic block of black granite in such a way that a pink vein of stone starts from the right hand and crosses the chest. Ptah is holding in his hands the same scepters as in his representations in the bas-reliefs: the *was* emerging from the long sheath ending in the *djed*. Note the massive shape of the swaddled feet and the painstaking detail of the *user* necklace. In front of him, on the same pedestal, is the bottom portion of a kneeling figure.

The most ancient text known concerning Ptah is a copy on black granite of an "old text destroyed by the worms," made in the Twenty-fifth Dynasty by Shabaka, the black king:

This is Ptah, who is called by the great name [Tatenen]. . . . He is [the binder] of the lands of Upper and Lower Egypt, its unifier. . . ." He who engenders himself," said Tum, "He who gave birth to the company of the nine neters."

It was Ptah, finally, who founded the cities and provinces, determined the site for each sanctuary, and put each *neter* in its place of worship, and it is Imhotep, son of Ptah, who transmits the plans of these sacred places to humans.

PLATE 312 • SANCTUARY OF PTAH: ENTRANCEWAY, SOUTH COLUMN OF THE PORTICO

In the back is the entrance to the central sanctuary, where Ptah's statue is located (pl. 311), and a small, pink-granite offering altar in the name of Tuthmosis III. The sixteen-sided polygonal south column on the right partially conceals one of the niches in the east wall.

PLATE 313 • BLACK GRANITE STATUE OF SEKHMET

Found in numerous pieces in the sanctuaries of the temple of Ptah by G. Legrain during his excavations in 1900, the statue was reerected in its original site in the south chapel, just below a small orifice installed in a paving stone of the roof, through which moonlight filters on certain nights directly on its head. There is a striking contrast between the slender body with its narrow thighs and the massive head wearing a flattened disk with raised uraeus, bound to the shoulders by the heavy, lined hairstyle falling over the breasts. Sekhmet is holding the *wadj* scepter with the flowering lotus and the ankh of life in her hands.

Sekhmet, the lion-headed female deity, is one of Hathor's two aspects. Bloodthirsty and cruel, she is the one bid by Ra to destroy rebellious humanity, but as Hathor, the House of Hor, she realizes "the broadening aspect" symbolized by the *wadj* scepter she holds before her.

Fig. 104b. Amenhotep, son of Hapu

PLATE 314 • EAST WALL: IMHOTEP, SON OF PTAH AND AMENHOTEP, SON OF HAPU, BEHIND HATHOR

Located on the outer east facade of the temple of Ptah, at two different levels going from left to right, are a representation of Ptah in light relief, whose head must have been sculpted on an added "piece" or stone that is now missing, and one of Hathor-at-the-heart-of-Thebes, followed by two deified scribes from the Old and New Kingdoms: Imhotep, son of Ptah (the Fire), and Amenhotep, son of Hapi (the Water). Imhotep, clad only in a short loincloth and a pectoral, is holding the *was* of the *neters* in his hand. Amenhotep, clad in a long robe held up by a suspender, is holding the palette and scroll of the scribe.

The very small *neter* wearing the disk in the crescent on his head, in front of Hathor, is Horus the child, the Harpocrates of the Greeks, already mentioned in the Pyramid Texts (633): *The sandal of*

Horus treads upon the serpent, the serpent of Horus-the-child-with-the-finger-in-his-mouth.

Here the child Horus also bears the title of *sma-tawi*, "binding of the Two Lands."

PLATE 315 • SMALL TEMPLE OF AHMOSE: OUTER FACADE

A Nile wearing a bouquet of papyrus (symbol of the North) on its head can be found on the bottom register of the left doorpost of the entranceway. Under the platter of offerings is a cartouche of Ahmose. On the upper register is a coiled, lion-headed cobra that wears the symbol of Neith on its chest.

Behind the Nile, Sefekht, the *neter* of writing, crowned with the seven-pointed star, is marking the first notch of the palm of the years with a long staff.

Ahmose (Twenty-sixth Dynasty) plays a great historical role. An ancient Saïte general, he profited from a revolt of the Egyptians against Apries "allowing himself to be crowned" king. (Herodotus, 2.162) An able diplomat and wise administrator, he was quite good at clearing up the misunderstandings caused by the incessant influx of Greeks seeking to relocate to Libya as well as Egypt and annoying the inhabitants of both lands.

Ahmose was a great friend of Polycrates, the tyrant of Samos, with whom he broke his alliance following the curious tale of the emerald. (Herodotus, 3.50, 120)

Herodotus also speaks of a "coat of arms that Ahmose, king of Egypt," sent to Greece as a present: "a remarkable work of linen cloth whose weaving represented various figures. It was moreover adorned with gold embroideries and cotton fringe; and what was most marvelous in this work is that each of the threads forming the weave of the coat of arms, although extremely fine, was itself composed of three hundred sixty quite visible strands." (Herodotus, 3.47)

PLATES 316–322 • *SED*-FESTIVAL TEMPLE OF SESOSTRIS I

This white limestone building with admirable sculptures has been entirely reerected by H. Chevrier with the blocks of Sesostris I (Twelfth Dynasty, 2200 B.C.) extracted from the foundations of the third pylon of Karnak, where they were reemployed by Amenhotep III.

The two access ramps are in response to the intention of this *sed*-festival monument, which had two thrones upon which the king would be seated during the ceremony—in one, to the south, wearing the white crown and in the other, to the north, wearing the red.

PLATE 316 • NORTH FACADE, EAST END

The complete list of nomes is carved on the foundations of the north and south facades of this "white chapel"; on the south are the twenty-two of Upper Egypt, and on the north are the sixteen of Lower Egypt. This has allowed for the determination of this monument's orientation and informs us that under the Twelfth Dynasty Lower Egypt was divided into only sixteen nomes, whereas there were seventeen during the Eighteenth Dynasty and twenty during the later period of Egypt's decline.

Above each nome name the following bits of information are inscribed: *(a)* the surface area of the nome indicated in *atour*, miles, and *sta.t*; *(b)* the calculation of the surface unit, the *sta.t*, which can vary with each nome. The unit thus found permits the calculation of the surface area inscribed below the name of each nome; this is an overall cadastral register of all of Egypt.

On the north side of the foundations a series of supplementary measurements are enumerated: (1) the flood level at Elephantine, Rhoda, and Behdet, written in cubits; (2) the height of the water above the ground in Upper and Lower Egypt; (3) the length of Egypt from Elephantine to Behdet, in *atour* of length. All these measurements are located on the votive cubits. They were consecrated in the temple under the protection of the god. (Lacau and Chevrier, *Chapelle de Sésostris*, p. 251)

PLATE 317 • BAS-RELIEF ON THE SOUTHEAST ENTRY PILLAR

The king, wearing the white crown over the red, is introduced by Mentu, master of Thebes, who gives him life and leads him toward Amun-Ra to celebrate

Fig. 105. Hieroglyph of the "sed-festival" pavilion

his *sed* festival.

Above the king is his cartouche and Horus name.

PLATE 318 • THE KING INTRODUCED BY MENTU

PLATE 319 • THE HORUS NAME OF THE KING

The falcon of Sesostris I's Horus name is wearing

Fig. 106. "Khnum"

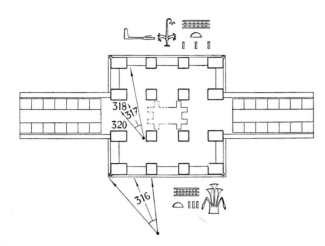

Diagram 17. White chapel of Sesostris I

the white crown of the South, as this scene is comparable to the portion of the "royal ascent" in which the king is introduced by Mentu, the *neter* of the South. Under the rectangle in which the Horus name is inscribed is the representation of a temple facade in whose center can be seen a gateway complete with its door leaves.

Note the meticulous manner with which each detail of these hieroglyphs has been engraved.

PLATE 320 • THE KING INTRODUCED BY TUM

This scene completes the introduction by Mentu. Here the king, wearing the red crown, is led by Tum of Heliopolis (the Innu of the North) toward the ithyphallic Amun-Ra Kamutef, who will confirm his kingship over the Two Lands.

PLATE 321 • THE KING INTRODUCED BY TUM: DETAIL

PLATE 322 • HIEROGLYPHS

PLATE 323 • SESOSTRIS EMBRACED BY "PTAH-SOUTH-OF-HIS-WALL"

This scene can be found on a pillar that is currently located at the Cairo Museum and came from Karnak, where it formed part of another building of Sesostris I. The fact that the king is being embraced by Ptah-south-of-his-wall allows one to conclude that the worship of Ptah in Thebes goes back at least as far as the Twelfth Dynasty.

PLATE 324 • SOBEKEMSAF MAKING THE OFFERING OF WINE TO MENTU

PLATE 325 • CONSECRATION OF THE WHITE BREAD BEFORE MENTU BY SOBEKEMSAF

These Fourteenth Dynasty bas-reliefs come from Medamud, one of the four sanctuaries consecrated to Mentu in Upper Egypt.

Behind the king consecrating the bread is Amun wearing a mortier with two feathers (each of these is divided into fourteen), who is giving the king life with the ankh placed at the nape of his neck. Mentu, wearing the feathered disk and the double uraeus, is called *Mentu master of the nome of Thebes at the heart of Ma(du)* (Medamud).

Note the emphasis placed on the lateral peroneal muscles.

PLATES 326–331 • REPOSITORY OF THE BARQUE OF AMENHOTEP I

This repository, in the shape of a naos open at both ends, was intended to shelter the sacred barque. It is composed of four courses of alabaster blocks found in the third pylon and rebuilt by Chevrier.

On the outer doorposts of the doorways are vertical bands of inscriptions of admirably stylized hieroglyphs (figs. 107 and 108).

PLATE 326 • INTERIOR SOUTH WALL: AMENHOTEP I "WORSHIPS THE *NETER* FOUR TIMES"

The raised arms of Min can be seen above the characteristic flower of this *neter* emerging from a *chen* and topping a sanctuary behind the king. Amun-Ra is facing the king and handing him the key of life at the end of the *chen* attached to his *was* scepter.

PLATE 327 • OUTER NORTH WALL: CONSECRATION OF THE OFFERINGS

In his left hand Amenhotep I is holding the cane and the white *hedj* club that ends in a kind of ball formed from scales, which resembles the *aïchta*, or *crêma*, a typical fruit of Egypt that contains a kind of white cream.

Fig. 107. "M"

PLATE 328 • OUTER NORTH WALL: AMUN-RA

PLATE 329 • THE KING, WITH THE *HES* VASES,
RUNNING THE RITUAL RACE

On the left is the pure and impersonal countenance of the *neter,* while on the right are the pronounced features and curved nose of the king.

PLATE 330 • OUTER SOUTH WALL: THE BLACK
CALF

This little calf with the astonished expression and knitted brow is part of the ritual offering of the four calves: black, red, white, and spotted. These calves are held by cords, in the king's hand, that are attached to the beasts' right front legs and whose ends are usually four keys of life. The hieroglyph in front of the left foot means "black" *(kem).*

PLATE 331 • OUTER NORTH WALL: THE KING
GIRDED BY THE DIADEM

PLATES 332–337 • SANCTUARY OF THE BARQUE
OF HATSHEPSUT

When G. Legrain excavated the north wing of the third pylon in 1901, he discovered a doorway in the name of Ramesses III, of which the left doorpost encompassed the pylon's northeast torus. His attention was drawn to the diversity of materials employed in its construction: limestone, Silsila sandstone, quartzite from Gebel el-Ahmar, and so on. Giving this curious combination a closer look, he saw that all the quartzite blocks bore the cartouches of Tuthmosis III and Hatshepsut. One of these was a representation of the two obelisks of the queen (fig. 62); others bore depictions of barques. The meaning behind this reuse becomes clear on seeing that they were found precisely at the corner of the pylon on which there is a representation of the barque Userhat of Amun, maneuvered by the king himself (compare pl. 98–99 with pl. 332) not far from the obelisks (pls. 100 and 101).

Now, the systematic excavation of the third pylon by Chevrier has allowed for the unearthing of several hundred blocks belonging to this same red quartzite edifice, which was intended to serve as a repository for the sacred barque. Even though the complete number of blocks has not yet been reassembled, it is possible to get an idea of the monument.

This building consists of two long rooms (somewhat like the naos of Philip Arrhidaeus); it was bordered at the four corners by the standard torus and

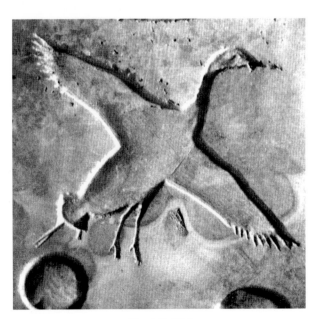

Fig. 108. "Pa"

Fig. 109. Procession and repository of the sacred barque

topped by a grooved cornice. The cornice consisted of nine courses of stone in all. The bottom course was composed of a row of black granite blocks on the outside that form a pedestal at their base and whose upper section bears the list of the nomes. On the inside this bottom course is composed of a row of red quartzite bearing several decorative motifs, among which is the *rekhyt* (pl. 334).

Certain blocks of the upper courses were decorated on the two opposite sides, thus establishing a link between the inner and the outer scene. This carries precious information about the contingent "transparencies" of the ritual. Other blocks are decorated only on the one side (the majority of the barques, for example), specifying that there is no transparency but only a link created by the dovetails.

It must still be noted that all the decorated surfaces constitute a complete tableau, from ground level to the sky, and for the majority an entire scene, in such a way that, according to the scene to be represented, the blocks were measurably shorter or longer (fig. 109), which lends support to the hypothesis that the blocks were cut in the quarry according to exact predetermined measurements. This presumes the existence of a *master blueprint* of the arrangement of all the tableaux intended to cover the monument, inside and out, including the desired "transparencies."

The outer decoration therefore consists of as many registers as there are courses—minus the cornice, the frieze of *khakeru,* and the base—which are six in number, on which the barques and the ritual were depicted. The interior decoration covered seven registers.

PLATE 332 • THE BARQUE USERHAT MANEUVERED BY TUTHMOSIS III

The long barque glides through the water. The head of the Amun ram emerges from a *user* necklace on the prow and on the stern. In a baldachin at the center is a naos decorated with Isis knots and *djed* pillars that has two masts with two ensigns in front. Facing the naos, Queen Maātkare (Hatshepsut) *worships the* neter *four times.* In the back, Menkheperre (Tuthmosis III) is said to *descend into the great barque Userhat of Amun and sail four times.*

A rope fixed to the front of the Userhat ties it to another boat that is towing it, represented on a contiguous block, where two immobile, royal figures are seated within a naos and holding the other end of the rope. How are they capable of propelling this small boat? "A fairy boat," Legrain would say. This is positive proof that this is a symbol demonstrating that it is a question of a "principle" and not a realistic event.

PLATE 333 • CENSING OF THE OSIRIS MAĀTKARE BY TUTHMOSIS III

On the left, Queen Maātkare is wearing the red crown, a beard, and all the masculine attributes. However, in her inscriptions she is sometimes designated in the masculine and sometimes in the feminine.

On the right Tuthmosis III is said to be making the censing to Amun-Ra, but the queen's cartouche is the one inscribed above Osiris.

The bound Osiris, standing at the front of the naos containing the barque of Amun placed on its pedestal, is wearing the double crown. In his two crossed hands he is holding the *hek* and *was* scepters that in turn cross with the ankh and the *nekhakha*: a double crossing that symbolizes resurrection. He is wearing a scarf, moreover, like Seshat.

The pavilion where the barque was stored is called wahet, *which I translate as "station." It is probable in fact that these were constructions made for the occasion, like those still erected in our time for certain religious feasts. The text informs us that there were at least three. . . . It isn't the queen who officiates; she is represented in a quite unusual form that gives this scene its particular character. She is seen from the two sides of the pavilion as a statue of Osiris; this would seem to prove that she was dead. . . .*

The barque of Amun stops in this first pavilion, which has a statue of the queen at both its entrance and its exit. This is the first act of the ceremony, whose objective must be the union of the queen with Amun. . . .

Thus in these sculptures from the temple of Karnak, we see Tuthmosis III giving worship to the dead queen. Therefore it is he who must have built this edifice after the death of Hatshepsut. It is also clear from these inscriptions that it was not he who erased the queen's depiction and names. If he is still to be held accountable for a portion of the destruction accomplished at the expense of this queen,

which I find highly dubious, it is certain that the era of the "persecutions" didn't begin until much later and not at the beginning of his reign. (G. Legrain, *L'aile nord du pylône d'Aménophis III à Karnak*, pp. 19–21)

PLATE 334 • LAPWINGS PERCHED ON A BASKET

These birds, *rekhyt*, signify "the people." They have one wing crossed over the other in a sign of submission, following the standard version. They are lifting two little arms in a sign of adoration, a meaning that is made specific by the star located below, which means *to worship in the morning*, dwa. For more on why the lapwing was chosen to symbolize the people, see the commentary on pl. 213.

PLATE 335 • RACE WITH THE HAPU BULL IN FRONT OF THE SACRED BARQUE

The queen Maātkare, wearing the red crown, is taking "the great stride." She is holding the *nekhakha* scepter over her right shoulder and the seal in her right hand. Behind her an ankh is holding a small flabellum.

Accompanied by the Hapu bull, the queen is *giving the ground four times.* This is the ritual race whose origin goes back to the first dynasties (pl. 74

Fig. 110. The Apis bull race in front of the naos of the barque

and fig. 47), which is run for the inauguration of a monument and in the event of a *sed* festival (of renewal), which amounts to the same thing.

PLATE 336–337 • ACROBATIC DANCES, HARPIST, AND SISTRUM PLAYERS

The *dance* (khbt) *by the female dancers* somer-saulting backward is seen on the top; below are the *dances* (ib.ou) *by the male dancers*. The acrobats are preceded by the blind harpist, the male dancers by men who provide rhythm by clapping their hands and by female sistrum players who are holding *menat* necklaces in their hands. It is said that these songs and dances were performed on the occasion of the sailing of Amun-Ra.

In the temple of Luxor the dancers and sistrum players did, in fact, greet the sacred barques on their arrival during the great feast of Apet.

Note the emphasis placed here on the female dancers' hair.

PLATES 338–340 • THE SACRED SCARAB ON THE NORTHWEST CORNER OF THE LAKE

Currently located at the northwest corner of the sacred lake is a stylized scarab sculpture in the round that is resting on a granite pedestal. The front face of

this cylindrical pedestal has been flattened to form a stela, carved entirely in sunk relief, in the name of Amenhotep III. The kneeling king is making the offering of two *nu* vessels to Tum of Heliopolis. The solar disk, left in relief between the two extended wings that crown the text, forms part of the name of Nebmaātre that is inscribed in the vertical axis of this stela. This disk, the symbol of Ra, is the sole element in relief within this entire work sculpted in sunk relief.

This monolith, by virtue of its location near the sacred lake and its representations, is a synthesis of the Heliopolitan myth that teaches of the birth of Ra, emergent from the Nu, the primordial waters. The winged disk, Ra; the *kheperr* scarab; and Tum of Heliopolis symbolize the threefold nature of the creation, which serves as a symbol for the course of the sun.

Kheperr is the name of the scarab. *Kheper* is also the verb "to become," "to transform." *Khepri* is the name of the sun at its rising or its setting, whereas *Ra* is more specifically the name of the sun at its culmination at noon. Tum, the third name of the sun, at either its rising or its setting, is connected to the Heliopolitan myth of *He who does not yet exist*.

An insect is chosen to represent this phenomenon, and it is one that in its becoming obeys the

Fig. 111. Race of the Apis bull

prompting of a mysterious functionality that thought can barely grasp, which is the becoming without comprehensible cause. In the evolutionary chain of living beings, the insect is not biologically situable. In fact, it is the living *subterranean* form, that which becomes what it is through metamorphic stages of worm and nymph before appearing in a form ready to live under the sun.

The *kheperr* scarab is the sole animal known on earth that makes the gesture of "rolling" a perfect sphere that it manufactures itself, a gesture that can perhaps be compared to the diurnal movement of the solar sphere as it moves through the sky from its rising to its setting. It is the sole creature to bury a ball in the earth in which to lay its eggs. The transformations that then take place occur in total obscurity. This sphere rests underground for several lunar cycles, with birth finally occurring in a damp environment. This is a strong summary of the Heliopolitan myth recalled by certain phrases from the hymns to the sun:

Hail to thee who art Ra perfect with each day, who rises in the morning without respite, who is Khepri overloaded with work. . . . Carver who has carved thyself, thou have cast thy own body, O sculptor who has never been sculpted. . . . Thou who travels the uppermost eternity . . . thou wander as well under the earth. . . .

He who hastens, he who runs, he who achieves his revolutions, Khepri of illustrious birth.

PLATE 338 • SOUTHEAST FACADE OF THE SCARAB AND ITS PEDESTAL

PLATE 339 • SACRED SCARAB OF THE LAKE, SEEN FROM ABOVE

PLATE 340 • SACRED SCARAB OF THE LAKE, SOUTHERN FACADE

A. Varille assumed that this monolith came from the funerary temple of Amenhotep III on the west bank of the Nile. Actually "the monumental scarab came from Kom el-Heitan where the funerary temple of Amenhotep III was built. The text carved on the side of the stela explicitly states that it concerns: *Khepri who rises from the earth.* (P. Barguet, *La Structure du Temple,* p. 17)

Fig. 112. "Son of Ra"

PLATE 341 • THE TEMPLE OF AMUN: THE SACRED LAKE, CORRIDOR OF THE DESCENT OF AMUN'S GEESE

In the background are the columns of the great hypostyle hall, the obelisks of Tuthmosis I and Hatshepsut, the top of the queen's broken southern obelisk (fig. 115), and the granite scarab at the northwest corner of the sacred lake, of which two stairways can be seen facing an Osirian structure in the form of a mastaba. In the foreground is the drum of a sixteen-sided column of the same style as those of the temple of Khonsu, which was part of a small peristyle that was in front of the dwelling places of the sacred geese and the "descentery" from which the birds glided directly into the water.

Some have expressed their belief that the priests of Karnak purified themselves in the water of the sacred lake, but it is highly unlikely given the fact that the lake, used by the ducks and geese that sported in its muddy waters, was not of the necessary purity for this purpose. On the other hand, lake water exposed all day to a burning sun cannot in any case be called *fresh water,* which is the term used regarding these ablutions on a bas-relief found on a block of Hatshepsut at Karnak.

Fig. 113. The sacred "kheperr" scarab

The offering lists provide several names for geese: *r.*, *gb*, *trp*, and *smn*. For another thing, the famous Maidum fresco has allowed identification of the *Anser cinerus* (greylag goose), the *Anser albifrons*, and the *Branta rufficolis* (barnacle goose).

Trp is the common goose. The *Anser cinerus* or greylag, *r.*, is the domesticated wild goose. This bird takes only one mate, to whom it remains very faithful. It has been observed, in the course of migrations, that a male goose would rather die from the cold with its wounded mate rather than abandon her and continue his flight with the other migratory birds. The greylag, *r.*, was fattened to the point that *it could walk on its stomach*. As for the *smn* goose, consecrated to Amun, this is the *Chenalopex aegyptiaca*, the Nile goose.

In the aviary of the sacred lake there were also all kinds of ducks, such as the whistling duck, *ushat* (fig. 114), which was specially fattened and served, in this regard, to designate offerings of food, *djefau*. The pintail duck, *sa*, served as a symbol to designate the "son" in the title *Son of Ra*.

The main purpose of these immense bird reserves was not only to supply the offering tables on

Herodotus informs us that the Egyptian priests wash themselves twice daily in cold water and twice at night.

On his statue the priest Hor himself says, I presented myself before the neter, *being an excellent young man, while another was ushering me into the horizon of heaven. . . . I have emerged from the Nun and I have been freed of what evil was in me; I have removed my clothing and unguents just as Horus and Seth in purifying themselves, I have advanced toward the* neter *in the Holy of Holies, whereas I felt fear in the presence of his power.* (Erman, *La Religion des Egyptiens*, p. 223)

The kings had a great interest in maintaining and stocking the aviaries as is shown by the following extract.

My majesty formed [Kheper] *for him flocks of geese* [r.] *to fill the (sacred) pool, for the offerings of every day. Behold my majesty gave to him 2 fattened geese* [r.] *each day, as fixed dues forever, for my father Amon.* (Annals of Tuthmosis III, Breasted, *Ancient Records*, vol. 2, § 559)

Fig. 114. Fattened duck above the pool

a daily basis but also, if one uses the choice of the symbols to form a judgment, to allow for the study of the nature and habits of these creatures.

Why, for example, call the *Chenalopex* dedicated to Amun *smn*, "establishment," "to establish?" This bird, one of the most despotic creatures alive, is ferociously jealous, combative, and violent. At mating periods the males join in protracted and even fatal battles with one another. In this creature the aquatic nature of the divers is joined with the aerial nature of the flying birds. The *Chenalopex* is, moreover, very intelligent. Was it capable, like the common gander, of feeling friendship for a specific human being and even following him around like a dog? This is something only the breeder would know, and that individual will understand the real reasons behind the choice of this bird.

(During the twenty-seven- to twenty-eight-day incubation period that takes place in March, in Egypt, only the female lies on the eggs, under the vigilant protection of the male, who warns her with his cries in the event of danger.)

The tomb of Pahemneter reveals "a series of storerooms flown over by birds and arranged on both sides of a long vestibule, at the end of which a chapel is erected that is apparently dedicated to Ernutet, as the coiled serpents with feathered headdresses framing the door would seem to indicate." P. Barguet (*La*

Structure du Temple, pp. 18, 39; and *Journal of Egyptian Archaeology* 25: 154; 18–19) is tempted to see in this a representation of the structures built south of the lake. These were erected by Psammuthis, probably on the site of buildings going back to the Eighteenth Dynasty.

PLATE 342 • OUTER FACADE OF THE SOUTH WALL OF THE THIRD TUTHMOSIAN ENCLOSING WALL OF THE TEMPLE OF IPET-SUT

Although built by Tuthmosis III, the wall of the third enclosure is entirely re-covered with tableaux in the name of Ramesses II carved in very deep sunk relief.

On the left the king is consecrating with the *sekhem* scepter in his right hand the "boxes" that presumably contain the four cloths: the white, the green, the red, and the *idmi* cloth.

On the right the king is offering the medjet cosmetic to *Mehiit*, a lioness deity who is the wife of Onuris, worshiped in This (Upper Egypt) and in Sebennytos (Lower Egypt).

PLATES 343–349 • OSIRIAN TEMPLE OF TAHARKA, NORTHWEST CORNER OF THE SACRED LAKE

Fig. 115. Upper portion of Hatshepsut's southern obelisk

Fig. 116. Head of Taharka, black granite (Cairo Museum)

This small building comes across as a kind of almost-square "mastaba" that has a torus at each corner but no door on any of its outer walls. The study of the east wall, composed of blocks that are sometimes unfinished and sometimes scored, has suggested the existence at this location of an access ramp leading to the terrace. One would then have had to traverse the terrace from east to west to reach the staircase descending into the chambers located in the northwest corner of the monument. The direction of the walk from east to west is in conformance with that of the king represented on the north facade of this monument (pls. 343 and 344), but opposite to the general advance of the king in the temple (pl. 342).

The entire building's interior, except for the northwest rooms, was only a dirt fill, the walls of the facade being duplicated on the inside, to around 1.5 meters, by other support walls containing a large number of reused stones from the Ethiopian period, of which several still retain the cartouche and the

two uraei, not hammered out, of Shabaka.

The excavations of 1949–50 have brought to light two walls of unbaked bricks attached to the north and south ends of the east wall. These two walls constitute a sort of "courtyard" preceding the "pure wells" from which the water for the purifications of the daily worship service were drawn. The southern brick wall is interrupted by the opening of a staircase descending to the sacred lake perpendicularly to its border wall. (See J. Leclant, *Orientalia*, 19–20: 1950–51)

The study of the cartouches and the hammering out of the double uraeus on the blocks belonging to this structure has allowed it to be established that it was constructed by Taharka with blocks from his predecessor Shabaka and his cartouches were subsequently added on to by Psamtik II.

The following observations result: this Ethiopian (black) building has its largest section filled with black soil; it has a courtyard that links a "pure well" on one side and the sacred lake on the other, which can be seen as a symbol demonstrating *pure* water and *life-giving* water.

PLATE 343 • MONUMENT OF TAHARKA: OUTER NORTH FACADE

The king is purified by a double stream made up of the *ankh* and the *was* (Life and Power) that falls in a dome around him. His two open hands show the palm of one and the back of the other. Two falcons cross their wings over his chest under his three-row *user* necklace. The musculature of the legs is drawn with a vigorous hand; this is the Ethiopian style. Taharka's cartouche has been scratched out and replaced by that of Psamtik II. The king is going from east to west, but from the north, therefore in the reverse direction of the sun's diurnal course.

PLATE 344 • OFFERING OF INCENSE TO TUM

The king, clad in a pleated loincloth with a triangular front panel, is *giving incense to his father Tum.* He is holding the "cubit of incense" and sprinkling grains of it into the fire.

PLATE 345 • BABOON WORSHIPING THE SUN

This baboon is carved on an Ethiopian block

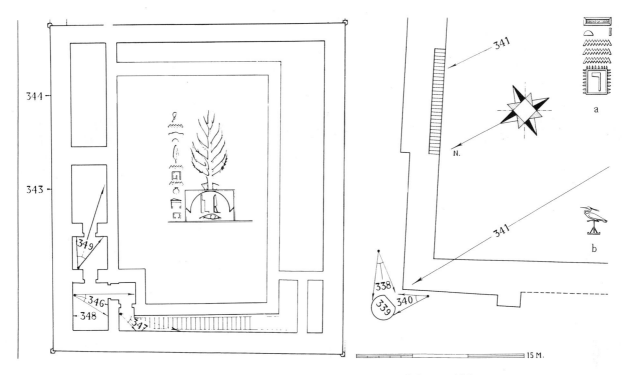

Diagram 18. Osirian temple of Taharka, northwest corner of the sacred lake:
(a) hieroglyphic grouping signifying "sacred lake" (b) presumed name of Karnak's sacred lake

found on the west wall of Taharka's small building. Under his arms, raised in worship, is the hieroglyphic grouping of the three storks—or *jabirus*—signifying the souls, *bau*, also translated as "spirits," which A. Varille translated as "linked souls." (See fig. 118, "The souls of Heliopolis.")

PLATE 346 • WORSHIP OF THE RISING SUN BY THE KING AND BABOONS

Behind the king are six baboons, turned toward the east, that are called *the eastern souls who worship Ra* when he rises. There were probably two groups of four baboons each facing east, as necessary.

The classic texts say: *To worship the sun and cause it to rise, by the spirits of the east. The spirits of the east are the four* neters *who worship the sun. It is they who make the sun to rise and who open the doors of the four gates of the sky's eastern horizon.* (A. Piankoff, *Le Livre du Jour et de la Nuit*, p. 4)

If the baboon has been chosen for this gesture of worship toward the rising sun, and also as a symbol of the clepsydra (which measures time), it is because it alone, of all animals, gives a howl at *every hour* and

urinates *twelve times during the day and twelve at night* during the equinox. (Horapollo, 16) It is also said that when the sun enters into conjunction with the moon, the male baboon loses his vision and his appetite. (Horapollo, 14)

PLATE 347 • STAIRCASE GOING UP TO THE TERRACE

On the wall next to this staircase, which is located on the inside of the west wall, are representations of androcephalic figures and mummified baboons, each corresponding to a stair, climbing from north to south above a solar disk.

Now, in the tombs The Book of Night is to be found on the west and The Book of Day to the east. Thus the ascension of the figures here very probably corresponds to the last hours of the night, where it is said:

To emerge from the Dwat, to rest in the barque of the morning and sail over the Nun until Ra's hour, "He who sees the beauty of his Master" [twelfth hour of the night] transforms into Khepri, rises toward the horizon, to enter the mouth and emerge from the vulva, to loom

Fig. 117. Ethiopian block

up within the opening of the gate [with its double door] of the horizon at the hour of "He-who-raises-the-beauty-of-Ra" [first hour of the day] to give life to humanity. (Piankoff, *Le Livre du Jour*)

This is the summary of the myth behind the sun's course, which provides the meaning behind this monument erected by a black king.

PLATE 348 • INTERIOR NORTH FACADE OF THE FIRST CHAMBER: THE SOLAR BARQUE

Fig. 118. "The souls of Heliopolis"

This bas-relief is sculpted on a flattened surface, after the removal of the base of a dozen columns of hieroglyphs from which the cartouches have been visibly removed or cut away. The cartouche that should be under the reed and the bee is completely missing, and the base of the hammered-out cartouche under *Son of Ra* has been cut away.

The solar barque is proceeding from east to west, in the direction of the sun's daily path. In the middle is Tum in his naos, who is topped by the single word *iuf,* "flesh."

The east-west progression of the solar barque on the north wall and its eventual exit by the staircase where the litanies to the sun are carved is strange, because it appears from the perspective of the southern hemisphere, where everything is reversed. This is also the character of "the Dwat," "the otherworld," which is evoked here by the Osirian mound.

PLATE 349 • DOORWAY OF THE INNER CHAPEL

A strange and extremely rare representation is carved on the lintel of the doorway to the inner chapel. On one side a female figure is drawing a bow, with her left arm pulled behind her back, to let fly the arrows at the targets in the form of round breads. On the other side a male figure is making the "great stride," brandishing his right arm aloft behind and holding the white club in his left hand. This is Taharka and his mother.

In the center a tree is jutting up from a hemispheric mound drawn within a rectangle. The text is brief: *the* shndt *tree* [spiny acacia] *of the chest,* and the name of Osiris is on the mound. A similar representation on a Saïte sarcophagus explains: *This is the mound that hides what it holds; this is the hill of Osiris.*

Numerous Ptolemaic texts speak of mounds on which sacred trees were planted.

PLATE 350 • LIMESTONE BAS-RELIEF: DETAIL

This bas-relief of an incomparable purity is of early–Eighteenth Dynasty manufacture. It belongs to a group (fig. 119) that unfortunately doesn't include any cartouche that would permit one to date it. However, in the Louvre storerooms there is a small block of the same limestone representing Queen Ahmose-Nefertari, the wife of Ahmose I, first of the Eighteenth Dynasty. Taking into account that the king depicted here cannot be Amenhotep I, whose distinctive face (pls. 329, 331) is well known, there is every reason to assume that this block represents Ahmose (birth of the moon).

PLATES 351–359 • STATUES FOUND IN THE CACHETTE COURT

Between the outer south wall of the great hypostyle hall, upon which is carved the "Poem of Pentaur" (the battle of Kadesh, pl. 90–91), and the seventh pylon is the courtyard known as the "cachette court" because the excavations have allowed the recovery of a great number of buried blocks and statuary in the ground, of which we shall provide several examples here.

Around 751 statues and 17,000 bronzes as well as fragments of basalt cubits were found in the excavations, which reach 14 meters in depth in the whole western side of the courtyard. Under the surface were also found numerous architectural elements that had belonged to Middle and New Kingdom buildings. On the southwest periphery of the courtyard are square pillars of Sesostris I, of which some are still in situ. This would seem to indicate that there was once a Twelfth Dynasty peristyle court here.

PLATE 351 • STATUE OF AMENEMHET III

Black granite. Discovered May 3, 1904, in the cachette court of Karnak. Height: 1.1 meters. Legrain catalog no. 42014. Twelfth Dynasty.

Fig. 119. Limestone block, early Eighteenth Dynasty

King Amenemhet III has his arms extended and his fingers lengthened to the base of his triangular apron, from whose corners rays are emerging, leaving no doubt as to the trigonometric nature of this symbol. The sad and calm authority of this royal countenance comes across through the granite.

PLATE 352 • THE QUEEN ISIS, MOTHER OF TUTHMOSIS III

Black granite. Height: 0.98 meters. Karnak, cachette court. Found broken in numerous fragments and reassembled at the Cairo Museum. Eighteenth Dynasty. Legrain catalog no. 42072.

This seated statue bears the dedicatory inscription of Tuthmosis III: *He has made, as his memorial to his mother, the royal mother, Isis, who has been found righteous.*

Historically Isis is not considered the queen of Tuthmosis II but his concubine. However, on this statue, as on a stela in Tuthmosis III's funerary temple in Gurnah, the name of Isis is inscribed within a cartouche.

In his "Text of the Youth," Tuthmosis III compares himself to the young Horus raised in the marsh of Khemmis—consequently the *son* of Isis—and in his tomb he bears the name of his *mother* Isis on his shroud.

Note the lunar nature of the face and the excessive importance given to the wig; the short chin, the bulging eyes, and similar length of the nose can be seen again in the face of Tuthmosis III. The queen wears the two uraei, one is topped by the white crown, the other by the red crown.

PLATE 353 • STATUE OF TUTHMOSIS III

Gray basalt. Current height: .9 meters. Found May 8, 1904, in the cachette court of Karnak. The legs are missing. Eighteenth Dynasty.

Tuthmosis III is wearing a uraeus on his forehead whose body winds serpentlike over his head, dividing it in two, just as the falx cerebri divides the brains into two hemispheres.

Note the fine carving of the false beard, which is held on by the chin strap passing before the ears,

which in turn is held in place by the royal headband.

PLATE 354 • LIMESTONE (?) HEAD FROM THE EIGHTEENTH DYNASTY

PLATE 355 • LIMESTONE (?) HEAD FROM THE EIGHTEENTH DYNASTY

Head of Amenhotep III (?), Eighteenth Dynasty. cachette court of Karnak. Catalogued as "limestone," but surely this is terra-cotta? Statue no. 38597 of the Cairo Museum.

This young king is wearing the blue *khepresh* helmet, which has been finely sculpted. The uraeus, the body of which divides the helmet in half, rises above the golden headband girding his forehead and passes under the pleat of the coif to hold up the nape of the neck.

The young profile, huge eyes, smile, and small chin bring to mind Amenhotep III whose bas-reliefs are known for their refreshing simplicity and purity. A same-sized head of Amenhotep III, in black granite (fig. 122), currently in the Louvre, leaves no doubt about this identification.

PLATE 356 • STATUE OF RAMESSESNAKHT, FIRST PROPHET OF AMUN, TWENTIETH DYNASTY

Gray granite. Height: 0.8 meters. Discovered January 21, 1904, in the cachette court of Karnak. Legrain catalog no. 42162.

With his left hand Ramessesnakht is holding one end of a papyrus that is unrolled over his knees, upon which he is writing. A baboon, an animal consecrated to Thoth, is kneeling on his shoulders and resting its two hands on his head: the scribe is directly inspired by Thoth, the master of the *neter-medu*, the divine scripture.

This high priest is well known by one of the two stelae that Ramesses IV had carved on the rocks of Wadi Hammamat, located between Coptos and the Red Sea.

On the first stela the king relates how, *excellent with wisdom like Thoth, he perceived the words of the*

Fig. 120. Mask of Tuthmosis III (?): obsidian, eyes and eyebrows originally inlaid with precious stones,
found in the cachette court on July 5, 1905

House of the Sacred Scriptures . . . to visit the quarries of Wadi Hammamat.

On the second the king says that in obedience to the desire of the *neter* he commanded *the scribe of the House of the Sacred Scriptures, the scribe of the posses-* *sions of the crown and the prophet of the House of Min [in Coptos] to seek, in the mountain of Bekhen, the [material] for the "Place of Truth," which had to be of great and marvelous monuments.*

The expedition was commanded by the first

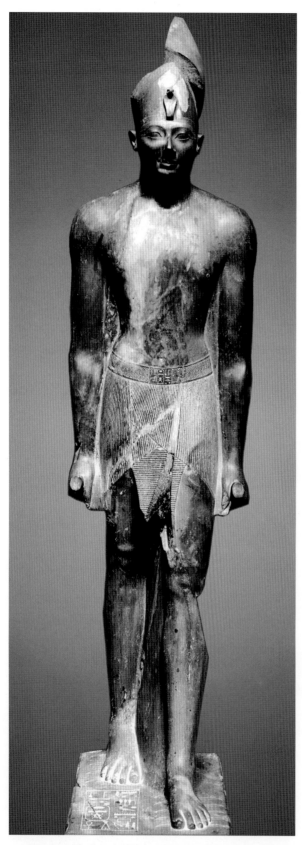

Fig. 121. Tuthmosis III, basalt statue (Cairo Museum)
(Photo: Brugsch Pasha)

prophet of Amun, chief of works, Ramessesnakht, who had under his direction numerous stewards, nobles and scribes, army commanders and numerous soldiers: in all, 8,368 men, allowance made for the 900 people who lost their lives in the course of this expedition.

There is mention made of a chief *artisan, three master builders for the quarry works, one hundred and thirty quarrymen and stone carvers, two draughtsmen, and four sculptors,* in addition to the large amount of manpower furnished by the army. This precise detail is of the highest importance, for it lends support to the hypothesis that the blocks were cut in the quarry to strict measurements arrived at beforehand and explains the discovery of some remains of working drawings—of Hathorian columns for example—in certain quarries.

PLATE 357 • STATUE OF THE SCRIBE AHMOSE, TWENTY-SIXTH DYNASTY

This magnificent "statue-cube" dating from the Twenty-sixth Dynasty is a good example of Saïte sculpture, representing the scribe of the divine scriptures, *Ahmose, high priest of Amun in Ipet-sut, "purified" priest of Khonsu and Mut, great lady of Asheru,* the Theban triad. (The purpose of these statue-cubes has always been to provide measurements: the head, the cubit, the height of the bust, the foot.)

PLATES 358 AND 359 • STATUETTE OF SHESHONK, SON OF OSORKON I, TWENTY-SECOND DYNASTY

White-veined green breccia. Height: 0.48 meters. Found in the cachette court of Karnak on April 17, 1904. Legrain catalog no. 42194.

"A piece has been put back in place on the right shoulder. This has been done with singular meticulousness, since to fix it to the statuette a dovetailed tenon has been contrived that joins the two pieces extremely well." (Legrain)

The inscription of this statuette makes clear that it concerns the *first high priest of Amun-Ra, king of the neters, the great chief of the armies, Sheshonk, found righteous, royal son of the Master of the Two Lands,*

Fig. 122. Amenhotep III; black granite (Cairo Museum)

Osorkon I, and of Maātkare, prophetess of Hathor in Dendera, "divine mother" of Hor-sma-tawi, royal daughter of the master of the Two Lands Psusennes II.

The first high priest of Amun, Sheshonk, is therefore son of the second king of the Twenty-second Dynasty (Bubastite) and grandson, on his mother's side, of the last king of the Twenty-first (Tanite) Dynasty, Psusennes II.

The information provided on this statue concerning its identity is completed by a statue of the Nile, also found at Karnak and presently in the British Museum, on which this same high priest defines his titles: . . . *master of the South and North, great chief of the troops of all Egypt. . . .* He inscribes his name in a cartouche and asks for . . . *omnipotent valor in order to take his land captive.*

It is thought, historically, that this is not a matter of a usurper of the royal title but that the king, reigning from Bubastis, actually placed all authority in the hands of the high priest, at least for Upper Egypt. The high priests maintained order in Thebes while the king kept an eye on the ever threatening maneuvers of the Near East countries from the Delta. The son of this high priest would be, moreover, the fifth king of this Harsiesis (Horus son of Isis) dynasty.

General Sheshonk is wearing the representation of Amun on his chest and that of the mummified Osiris on his pleated robe. He is clasping a stake crowned with a Hathor head in his left arm.

The curious white vein surrounding his head is reminiscent of a chin strap, and the shoulder piece denotes the articulation of the right arm, that of action, while the left is consecrated to divinity—a peculiar method of emphasizing the double role of priest and general. This "piece" on the shoulder is not a unique case.

On the outside of Ramesses II's court at the temple of Luxor is a black granite statue in the name of Merneptah, whose left shoulder and left wrist have similar pieces embedded by means of a dovetailed tenon.

PLATES 360–427 • THE SOUTHERN PYLONS

PLATE 360–361 • OVERALL VIEW OF THE SACRED LAKE AND THE SOUTHERN PYLONS; IN THE BACKGROUND, THE TEMPLE OF KHONSU AND THE GATE OF EUERGETES

Like all the monuments of Karnak, the lake, too, has its legend:

On certain nights, a golden barque emerges from the waters of the lake, as resplendent as in days of yore, and the king who steers it is in pure gold, and his sailors are of silver. And when the moon shines, the barque sails, leaving behind a long wake of precious stones. At times it comes to the dock, as well, and then if some brave soul with a heart thrice bound in bronze comes forth to dare the great adventure, he climbs aboard the phantom ship, then, victorious, returns to his home laden with fabulous treasure; but everyone knows that if he makes the slightest sound, the merest sigh, the fairy barque, the gold king, and the silver sailors will sink immediately below the waves of the lake, which will engulf the foolhardy one forever. . . .

However, the appearances of the mysterious boat are becoming more and more rare; for more than thirty years no one can boast of truly seeing it. . . . It is not, alas! soon to reappear, for my storyteller added that it would not be seen again until there was no longer a liar or a thief within the country. (Legrain, *Louqsor sans les Pharaons,* pp. 97, 99)

PLATE 362 • THE SAGE AMENHOTEP, SON OF HAPU

Gray granite. Height 1.42 meters. Legrain catalog no. 42127.

Fig. 123. Amenhotep II protected by Meretseger;

black granite (Cairo Museum)

Found at Karnak on October 24, 1904, in front of the north facade of the seventh pylon. "It was overturned, face against the ground, the head turned toward the east. It was not buried beneath the ground. Its ancient location shouldn't have been far from the spot where it was found. Date: Eighteenth Dynasty, and touched up during the Ptolemaic era." (Legrain)

PLATE 363 • DOORWAY OF THE SEVENTH PYLON, NORTH FACADE: GRANITE STATUES

On the belt of the colossus on the right, who is upright and walking, the cartouche of Tuthmosis III has been carved; on his left shoulder is the name of Ramesses, and on his right is that of Heqamaātre (Ramesses IV).

The Osirian colossus on the left bears the same cartouches on its shoulders and the name of Usermaātre Setepenamun (Ramesses IV) on the vertical band. These two statues, erected in front of the east doorpost, are wearing the white crown.

In the background is the inside west facade of the passageway, on which the "royal ascent" (pl. 365) is represented, above the niches. The inside east facade of this passageway includes a long inscription, of which only scattered fragments remain. On one of these fragments Tuthmosis III, on returning from his conquests, mentions the construction of a great barque *Userhat of the river's beginning.*

Indeed, the scene of the "ritual massacre of the prisoners," accompanied, as always, by the list of conquered towns (pl. 368), is located on the two north and south wings of this pylon.

On the north facade of the east wing of the seventh pylon is a list of 119 Palestinian towns that are reminiscent of the towns conquered during the first campaigns; the 240 following names refer to sites between Lebanon and the Euphrates that Tuthmosis III overran in the year 33 of his reign during his eighth campaign, in the course of which he overthrew Mesopotamia (Mitanni and Naharin). On the east post of the doorway a text recalls the coronation date.

PLATE 364 • BASE OF THE OBELISK SOUTH OF THE EAST WING OF THE SEVENTH PYLON

In the foreground is the pedestal for one of the two red granite colossi that framed the entrance of the seventh pylon, bearing on its lateral facades the "vanquished with escutcheons."

The pedestal of the eastern colossus of Tuthmosis III represents Nubian prisoners, whereas the western pedestal depicts Asian prisoners. The base of the shaft of the eastern obelisk (fig. 126) is 3.125 meters wide. In basing his conjectures on the erroneous measurements of the north obelisk of Hatshepsut, G. Legrain (*Annales du Service des Antiquités de l'Egypte* 5: 12) restored its height to 37.70 meters, whereas it was only 36.50 meters according to its exact dimensions, or even only 28.35 meters if one uses the proportions of the obelisk of Tuthmosis III currently in New York. Traunecker proposes to resolve this problem in the following manner: On the one hand the portion of the obelisk currently in Istanbul measures 19.59 meters, of which 2.67 meters is the height of the pyramidion. Its base measurement is 1.69 meters, and that of the shaft at its section is 2.30 meters. On the other hand, the representation of the obelisk of the seventh pylon on the north wall of the sanctuary (pl. 147) shows that the upper tiers of the dedication are identical to the inscription on the south face of the obelisk fragment in Istanbul, which would allow the total height of this monument to be restored to 28.98 meters. (See Traunecker, *Karnak*, vol. 7)

In the middle is the pedestal and broken base of one of the two obelisks that were in front of this pylon. In his Annals (pls. 140 and 147), Tuthmosis III mentions the erection of four obelisks on the occasion of his renewal feasts. Two of these were intended for the doorway of the sixth pylon, and the other two were for the seventh pylon.

A fragment of the sphinx found next to the seventh pylon in fact bears this inscription: *He presented two obelisks of stone, one on each side of it.*

The upper section of one of these two obelisks was carried off to Constantinople by Emperor Theodosius. According to the orientations provided by Breasted, the first and second protocols would be on the south and east facades, pointed toward the northeast corner, the third and fourth would be on the north and west facades, pointed toward the same corner, which permits one to believe that the obelisk of Istanbul was that of the west.

On the south: the first complete protocol, then: *[Ramenkheper] (Tuthmosis III); he made (it) as his monument for his father Amun-Ra, lord of Thebes; erecting (for him very great obelisks of red granite, the pyramidions of electrum).*

On the east: the second Horus name and the Two Crowns, then: *[Menkheperre, Fraction of Ra] (Tuthmosis III), lord of victory, binder of every land, who makes his boundary as far as the Horns of the Earth, the marshes as far as Naharin.*

On the north: the third Horus name only, then: *[Menkheperre, who exalts the grandeur of Ra], whom Atum reared as a child, in the arms of Neith, Divine Mother, to be king; who has taken all lands, the extent of time, lord of jubilees.*

On the west: the fourth Horus name only, then: *[Menkheperre, Work of Ra] (Tuthmosis III), who crossed [by sailing] the "Great Bend" of Naharin . . . with might and with victory at the head of his army, making a great slaughter (among them).* (Breasted, *Ancient Records*, vol. 2, §§ 630–31)

PLATE 365 • DOORWAY OF THE SEVENTH PYLON: INTERIOR WEST DOORPOST

This interior doorpost west of the passage of the granite doorway includes a stylobate with niches topped by cartouches of Tuthmosis III and the winged disk. Between the niches is Amun-Ra, who is seated on a throne and extending the key of life to the falcon of the royal Horus name. The two cartouches crowned with feathers have been reworked in the name of Seti II. It is notable that the lintels of the two niches and the gap between them are made from one sole block.

On the top register the king, likely accompanied by Tum and Mentu, is completing the *great stride toward the sanctuary* while walking from south to north (see also pl. 157 and fig. 70).

Note the delicate nature of the carving and the perfection of the draftsmanship in this extremely durable crystalline granite.

PLATE 366 • OWL HEAD FROM AN OBELISK OF TUTHMOSIS III

This bird is the letter *m* of the hieroglyphs, which plays a very important role in Egyptian grammar.

PLATE 367 • HEAD OF THE *SA* BIRD FROM AN
OBELISK OF TUTHMOSIS III

This hieroglyph belongs to the vertical legend
that is on one of the currently broken obelisks of the
seventh pylon. (The little circle is one of the three
"seeds" carved under the cubit, fig. 125.)

PLATE 368 • SEVENTH PYLON, WEST WING:
SOUTH FACADE

On this west wing the king is wearing the red
crown of the North. He is brandishing the white
club *to strike down the great of Retenu [from] all the
mountains, [from] all the inaccessible [mysterious] lands*
joined together under his fist.

These vanquished, who are raising their arms
and kneeling in three superimposed rows, are Asian
warriors, recognizable by their beards and counte-
nances. The five in the middle are represented facing

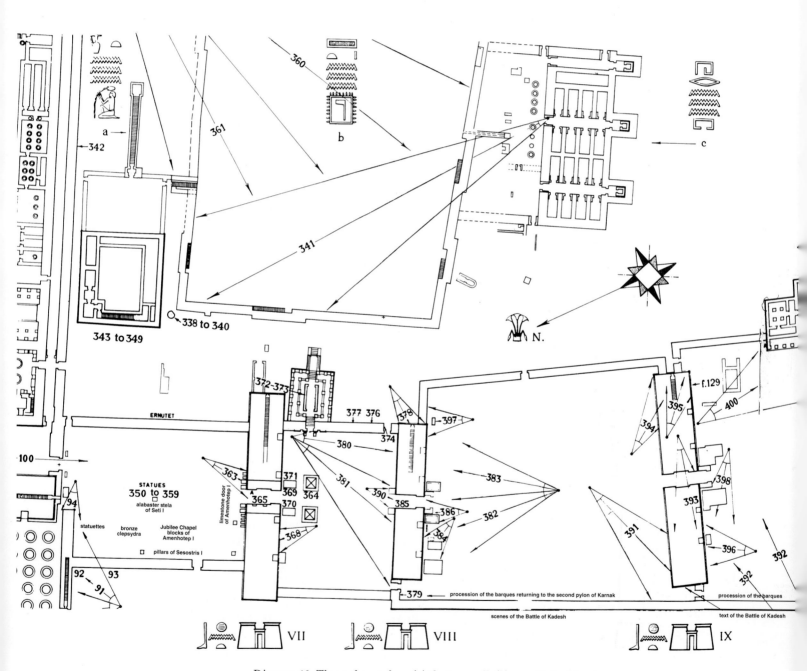

Diagram 19. The southern pylons: (a) the pure well; (b) sacred lake; (c) aviary

forward. The *mākes* baton held in the king's hand separates them into two groups vis-à-vis each other but with their heads facing opposite directions. Their posture is made clear by that of the two front figures: the Asian on the left, facing forward, is raising his right hand and holding a dagger in his left while clasping the body of the prisoner on the right, who is raising his left hand and with his right resting an ax over his shoulder.

Under this scene are the "prisoners with escutcheons" indicating conquered cities. This list, presented by the god of the west, includes only the Palestinian cities already depicted on the north facade of the eastern wing (pl. 363).

PLATE 369 • SEVENTH PYLON, EAST WING: COLOSSUS OF TUTHMOSIS III

In the foreground is one of the two colossi that front the entrance of the seventh pylon. They are broken, unfortunately.

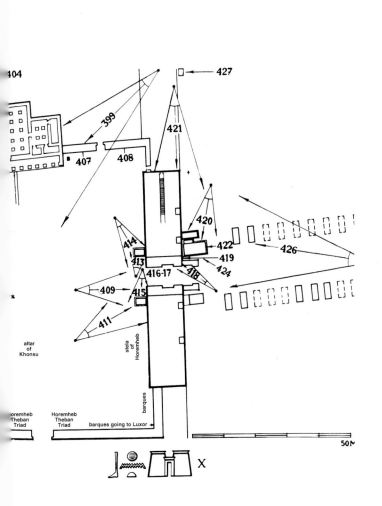

Fig. 124. Obelisk of Istanbul, top section

Fig. 125. Fragment of one of the two obelisks of Tuthmosis III

Behind this colossus, to the left, is the southern facade of the doorpost where *the doorway Menkheperre-Amun-Ra-great-in-appearance* is horizontally inscribed on the uppermost of the two bottom lines.

The cartouche on the lower line has been modified in the name of Heqamaātre Meryamun Ramesses (Ramesses IV), who has already added his name upon the statues of the north facade.

Above, the king, wearing the white crown of the South and holding the white club, is standing before Amun-Ra. The vertical inscription is in the name of Menmaātre (Seti I), who is said to have "renewed" this monument in the temple of Amun.

Toward the right is the partially destroyed scene of the massacre of the defeated that is the counterpart to that of the west wing. The "prisoners with escutcheons" are here presented by a *neter* from the black countries: *Dudun, the First of the Land of the Bow* (probably Nubia and Sudan).

Dudun was also cited in the Pyramid Texts as being the *child of the South who gives the purifying incense with which the* neters *are perfumed.*

PLATE 370 • SEVENTH PYLON, WEST DOORPOST: COLOSSUS OF TUTHMOSIS III

PLATE 371 • SEVENTH PYLON, EAST DOORPOST: COLOSSUS OF TUTHMOSIS III

These colossi, carved in red Aswan granite, are remarkable for the crisp lines of the loincloth pleats, for the detail of the musculature of the knees and the lateral peroneal muscles, for the lifelike way the fist lies along the body. This is a technical masterpiece in a material that is extremely hard and difficult to work.

Great quantities of granite powder have been discovered in the sculptors' studios, which was used, presumably, to polish the statues; but for carving, the sole tools known are made of bronze, and this metal must undergo special preparation to be able to attack granite. But the procedure remains unknown at the present time.

Under the left leg of the colossus, Ramesses II is carved in sunk relief, standing and wearing the *nemes* headdress, with the *hek* and *nekhakha* over his right shoulder. He is heading, as is the colossus, toward the south (pl. 370).

PLATE 372 • ALABASTER SANCTUARY OF TUTHMOSIS III: OUTSIDE NORTH WALL

As is written at the entrance of this small sanctuary, each wall is made of a single alabaster stone close to 8 meters long. This is a naos that was probably intended to shelter the sacred barque, quite similar in arrangement to that of Amenhotep I and covered with similar decorations.

The alabaster repository of Tuthmosis III was originally a simple peripteral kiosk, built during the first royal jubilee, subsequently enlarged and endowed with a second row of pillars. In front of its facade depicting a miniature pylon were two statues of Sesostris I in pink granite. (See J. Vandier, *Manuel d'Archéologie égyptienne,* vol. 2, p. 804 and fig. 392)

PLATE 373 • ALABASTER SANCTUARY OF TUTHMOSIS III: AMUN

Compare this sculpture of Amun with the basreliefs on the tenth pylon of Horemheb.

On the central tableau the king is making the "great stride," holding the oar and rudder in his hands, in the presence of Amun wearing a mortier crowned by two feathers that are each divided into fourteen sections.

PLATE 374 • INSCRIPTION OF AMENHOTEP: FIRST PROPHET OF AMUN

Amenhotep, son of the high priest Ramesses-nakht, a contemporary of Ramesses II, was the immediate predecessor of the future priest-king Herihor. The inscriptions carved on the inside of the gateway that connects the courtyard of the seventh and eighth pylons with the sacred lake represents this high priest entering from east to west toward the king Ramesses IX.

The high priest Amenhotep had carved on the inner facade of the east wall, near the eighth pylon, a text recalling "that he reconstructed the dwellings of the high priests formerly raised by Sesostris I" in the domain of Amun. (See G. Lefebvre, *Histoire des Grands prêtres d'Amon dans Karnak*, p. 187) These buildings, also evoked by Rome-Roy (pl. 378) very probably correspond to the remnants of the ancient dwellings recently unearthed east of the lake, near the enclosure with bastions attributed to Tuthmosis III. The deepest levels passing beneath this wall go back to the Middle Kingdom, and certain objects even date back to the Old Kingdom. (See *Kemi* 21: 217–37; *Karnak*, vol. 5, p. 26)

PLATE 375 • ROME-ROY, FIRST PROPHET OF AMUN

Gray granite. Height: 1.08 meters. Found in the cachette court of Karnak on February 15, 1904. Legrain catalog no. 42186.

Fig. 126. Base of the east obelisk

Rome-Roy, named first prophet of Amun toward the end of the reign of Ramesses II, remained at the head of the clergy of Thebes for about twenty-five years, until the reign of Seti II.

On the anterior facade of this statue-cube is an inscription of five vertical lines that provides his name and titles: *Chief of heaven's mysteries, on the earth, in the hells, sacrificer of Kamutef, director [of the treasure] of Amun, director of the double granary of Amun, chief of the prophets of all the neters, first prophet of Amun, Rome.* (Trans. G. Lefebvre, *Inscriptions concernant les grands-prêtres d'Amon Rome-Roy and Amenhotep*, p. 19)

On the left side of the statue, the inscription begins with the title and name of the first prophet, Roy, who therefore bears a double name. This name: Rome and Roy, was a source of confusion for quite some time. Roy describes his works in the house of Amun: *. . . of statues in silver and gold worked with embossed gold . . . of great doors in gold (encrusted) entire with precious stones . . . of barques [going] on the river for Amun, Mut, and Khonsu.*

On the right side his history is recounted: how through his worth and spirit he was promoted from a simple "*wab* priest" to the rank of *divine father*, and finally elevated to the dignity of *first prophet of Amun* in his temple laden with rewards and loaded with favors.

On his back is a prayer to *those who will come later* that they may honor his statue and his *ka*.

Thus, in front the offerings to Amun-Ra Horakhty Atum and the titles of the high priest Rome are inscribed; to his left are the works of Roy, to his right his personal history and ascension to the high priesthood, and on the back is the prayer to those who will come later.

(See plate 378 for Rome-Roy's inscriptions on the east wing of the seventh pylon.)

PLATE 376 • ROYAL GIFT TO THE FIRST HIGH PRIEST AMENHOTEP

On the eastern outside facade of the wall linking the seventh and eighth pylons are two tableaux representing the very important gifts of gold, silver, and all manner of precious things, made by Ramesses IX to the first high priest of Amun, Amenhotep.

On the left tableau, the high priest, facing the king, is raising his arms and looking toward the north. Two smaller officiants frame him, resting their hands upon his linen robe. His name and title are inscribed in front of his face: *The vizier, great confidante of his master, first prophet of Amunresonther, Amenhotep,* maā-kheru *[righteous of voice].*

Behind the nape of his neck is his ancestry: *. . . on the throne of his father, the first prophet of Amunresonther, Ramesesnakht.*

The king calls down the benediction of Amun and the *neters* on the high priest for his numerous acts of bravery and the countless good deeds he has accomplished in the temple.

PLATE 377 • ROYAL GIFT TO THE FIRST HIGH PRIEST AMENHOTEP

On the tableau to the right, the high priest is turned toward the south and the two officiants are behind his robe, whereas on the left tableau one was in front and one was behind.

The king in person said to the great and to his companions that were at his side, "Give numerous tributes, countless rewards in fine gold and silver and thousands of good things to the first prophet of Amunresonther, Amenhotep . . . because of the numerous and perfect monuments that he has made in the house of Amunresonther [inscribed] in the great name of neter-nefer.*"*

These depictions and this inscription can be compared with stela C213 in the Louvre (fig. 127), on which Seti I can be seen giving a similar gift.

PLATE 378 • EIGHTH PYLON: EAST END

On the lintel of the doorway that opens onto the stairway of the east wing of the seventh pylon is the depiction of two kneeling priests facing each other with their hands raised in gestures of adoration toward the erased royal cartouches. To the left (therefore to the south), the priest is called Roy, and to the right (the north) he is called Rome. This is one and the same individual, as is also made evident by his statue (pl. 375).[33]

---

[33]Rome-Roy lived between the end of the reign of Ramesses II and the beginning of that of Seti II and therefore "passed through the troubled times during the reigns of Amenmesses and Siptah." (Lefebvre, *Inscriptions concernant les grand-prêtres*, p. 148)

To the right of the doorway, in front of two shaven-headed priests wearing formal linen robes—Rome-Roy and his son Beknekhonsu—is a long inscription dating from the reign of Seti II. The first six lines of it consist of an adoration by Amun's first prophet, Rome.

I come to you, master of the neter, *Amun, who was at the beginning,* neter *of* neters, *creator of all that exists, master of* neters *and men, chief of Heliopolis, prince of Thebes, great bearer of the crown in Het-Berber [temple of the sun in Heliopolis]; when the eyes of men gaze upon you, the breath comes forth from your mouth toward every nostril. . . .*

Thou didst grant me long life carrying thy image, while my eye beheld thy two uraei every day, and my body was endowed with health, being without sorrow and free from all fear, O powerful king of eternity, thy food is with me, thy favors come due, thy name is protection for me.

Starting with the seventh line another text begins that apparently, this time, is in the name of Roy.

Greatest of Ra-Atum's seers in Thebes, second prophet of Amun, first prophet of Amun, Roy . . . he says, "O wab priests, scribes of the house of Amun, excellent servants of the divine offerings, bakers, mixers, confectioners, makers of loaves . . . performing all their duties (?) for their lord, thou who enter this workshop each day that is within the house of Amun, (may all of you) utter my name each day and remember me with good thoughts. . . .

I found this room in complete ruins, its walls falling, the woodwork rotted, the doorposts of wood perishing (as well as) the paint of the bas-reliefs. I restored it in its entirety, more vast than it had been, heightening, widening . . . excellently (?); and I made its doorposts of sandstone, and mounted upon them doors of true pine; (I made) a (comfortable) workshop (for) the bakers and mixers who are in it. I made it in work that was better than before, for the protection (of the personnel?) of my neter *Amun, master of* neters. (Quotes from ibid., pp. 34–35)[34]

Rome is on the north = mystical nature (inspiration) and Roy is on the south = physical nature (realization).

PLATE 379 • DOORWAY LOCATED TO THE WEST OF THE EIGHTH PYLON

Three registers can be found to the left of the postern located on the west side of the eighth pylon. Depicted there are the presentation of fat cows, crowned and bedecked with ribbons such as can be seen in the court of Ramesses II at Luxor, which are proceeding toward the pylon; the procession of the priests laden with flowers; and on the top register, a pylon with four flagpoles that seems to be preceded by a vestibule or provided with a double doorway (?).[35]

This wall was cut on a bias according to the carvings of the bas-reliefs.

PLATES 380–389 • THE EIGHTH PYLON

PLATE 380–381 • EIGHTH PYLON: NORTH FACADE

The eighth pylon, which is the best preserved, was constructed by Hatshepsut, according to historians. On the bottom register of the east wing's north facade is a depiction of Tuthmosis I presenting a twenty-line text to the Theban triad. This inscription, set down by the queen herself in homage to her father, confirms her as "king."

The sacred barque is on the top register, carried on the shoulders of priests in an easterly direction preceded by the king, who is introduced by the great lion-headed magician followed by Hathor. Next the king wearing the white crown presents himself before Amun in front of fifteen *neters* in three rows.[36]

Tuthmosis II's titulary is carved on the west doorpost. On the east doorpost is the titulary of

---

[34] This is also quite similar to Breasted's translation in *Ancient Records* vol. 3, §§ 621–25—Trans.

[35] These representations go back to the time of Ramesses II and are related to the second pylon of the temple of Amun at Karnak. (Barguet, *La Structure du Temple*, p. 258)

[36] On the extreme east of the bottom register Amun is followed by the "Small Ennead of Karnak" consisting of fifteen sacred entities arranged in three rows. The fifteen entities of the top register are the "Great Ennead of Karnak."

Tuthmosis III but with a combination of his cartouche and that of Queen Menkheperkare.

PLATE 382–383 • EIGHTH PYLON: SOUTH FACADE

The south facade of the eighth pylon was fronted by seated colossi made from different materials: two of limestone and one of quartzite on the west; on the east only one, made from white limestone, remains.

On each wing, one lone tableau representing the massacre of the prisoners occupies the entire portion located between the two flagpoles. The king has the characteristic curly hairstyle and titulary of Amenhotep II. He is brandishing the white club outfitted with a curved blade to strike down the defeated prisoners, who are represented as *standing*, which is quite exceptional.[37]

On the west doorpost are the cartouches and titulary of Tuthmosis II. On the east doorpost are those of Tuthmosis III associated with the queen, as on the north facade, and arranged in similar fashion.

PLATE 384 • WHITE LIMESTONE COLOSSUS OF THE EIGHTH PYLON'S WEST WING

This colossal statue is carved from a single block of white limestone. This is King Amenhotep I, who is seated with his right hand closed and his left hand open, resting upon his knees. Note the emphasis that has been placed on the carving of the breasts.

To his left is a small statue of a seated female figure.

PLATE 385 • INTERIOR FACADE OF THE PASSAGEWAY OF THE EIGHTH PYLON'S DOORWAY

Ramesses II, who is holding the *hek* and *nek-hakha* scepters over his shoulder, receives the panegyrics from a seated Amun.

---

[37]Leaning against south facade of the eighth pylon's west wing, between the quartzite colossus of Tuthmosis II (pls. 386–388) and the limestone colossus of Amenhotep I (pl. 384) is a stela of Amenhotep II that recounts this sovereign's campaigns in Syria during years 7 and 9 of his reign. A fragment of a similar stela is currently propped up against the east doorpost of the pylon's doorway.

PLATE 386 • QUARTZITE COLOSSUS TO THE WEST OF THE ENTRANCE OF THE EIGHTH PYLON

This admirable statue is carved of red quartzite from Gebel el-Ahmar. On the belt and side of the throne are cartouches of Tuthmosis II, who is said to have had this colossus created for the temple of Ipet-sut.

The fore-doorway is made of small sandstone blocks and is in the name of Ramesses IX, who has the same Horus name as Tuthmosis III.

PLATE 387 • EAST FACADE OF THE QUARTZITE COLOSSUS'S PEDESTAL

This delicate unfinished image of Amun, whose headdress is cut short, has for its legend only this: *Words spoken by Amun-Ra, master of Heaven, master of Earth.*

The scepter emerging from Amun's hand is barely outlined.

PLATE 388 • FEET OF THE QUARTZITE COLOSSUS

The finely sculpted feet of the colossus are one with the pedestal on which they rest.

In the background is the east doorpost of the doorway that has the cartouche of Tuthmosis III combined with that of the queen (pl. 383).

PLATE 389 • WEST DOORPOST OF THE EIGHTH PYLON'S DOORWAY: DETAIL

To the right is the cartouche of Tuthmosis II, Akheperenre. At the location of his Son of Ra name on the left, a niche has been hollowed out—probably by the Copts—in which the sky is in the form of a seashell.

PLATES 390–399 • NINTH PYLON

The ninth pylon is built within the axis of and perpendicularly to the avenue of the sphinxes that leads to the temple of Mut. The fact that the latter was constructed by Amenhotep III suggests that the ninth pylon, constructed by Horemheb, could have replaced an older, probably brick, pylon of Amenhotep III. (See Barguet, *La Structure du Temple*, p. 253)

Fig. 127. "Stela of the necklaces": Seti I (Louvre)

PLATE 390 • NINTH PYLON AS SEEN FROM THE DOORWAY OF THE EIGHTH PYLON

In the right foreground, within the splaying of the eighth pylon's doorway, the king is introduced by Mentu-Ra and Mut, great lady of Asheru (who replaces Atum here), before Amun, who gives him the panegyrics (pl. 385). These tableaux are from Ramesses II, but the horizontal legend of the stylobate is from Ramesses III. The small square and rectangular cavities were intended to hold ceramic plates, of which several were found intact and in place.

PLATE 391 • NINTH PYLON: WEST WING, NORTH FACADE

The bottom part of this pylon was covered by two registers of tableaux on which the king is proceeding from east to west, that is to say, "entering the temple." However, the barques carried by the priests on the top register are going in the opposite direction and are consequently "leaving the temple."

PLATE 392 • NINTH PYLON, SEEN FROM THE SOUTHWEST

Fig. 128. Marriage text of Ramesses II

Length of the pylon: around 66 meters. Width: around 11.5 meters. Average slope of the lower courses of the north facade: 82° to 82°30′, taken by a protractor at that level (this needs to be carefully verified through triangulation).

If we insist on the necessity of taking extremely precise measurements, particularly for this pylon, it is to draw attention to the static problems posed by the hollow pylons, like the second and ninth pylons of Karnak. Their construction is of utmost interest: the exterior stone facings are formed from a single tier of blocks of varying thickness; on a height of several meters they are upheld by partition walls (second pylon). All the rest of the building is hollow, with the

exception of the stairway passage, which takes support in only a few places. The stairway generally goes from the east and climbs toward the west.

It is obvious that all the stones of the upper section are held up only by the enormous weight of the cap that serves in some way like the keystone of an arch: if a portion of it were missing, everything would collapse inward . . . and this is what has happened to the two hollow pylons of Karnak.[38]

According to the cadastral plan, the orientation of this pylon would be 18°30′ with respect to the east-west line. This fact is very interesting because the angles formed by the eighth and ninth pylons are complementary to 45° angles (to wit: 18°30′ + 26°30′ = 45°), and the importance of orientation in precisely this spot is underlined by the reuse in the foundation of the block of the "queen's chapel" that represents the ritual scene of stretching the cord. This implies a sighting taken on the circumpolar stars in order to define the temple's orientation.

PLATE 393 • NINTH PYLON, WEST WING; IN THE BACKGROUND IS THE TEMPLE OF KHONSU

PLATE 394 • NINTH PYLON: EAST WING
The bas-reliefs are of Ramesses IV.

PLATE 395 • INTERIOR STAIRCASE OF THE NINTH PYLON
This staircase climbs from the east entrance up to the level of the doorway's lintel. Starting here another staircase crosses the west wing and leads to the terrace.

---

[38]The western mole of this pylon threatened with destruction has been in the process of being dismantled since 1964, with an eye to its ultimate restoration. A large part of this pylon seems to have been hollow, because, before the construction, only the eight bottom courses, which rose to a height of 6.20 m, contained a "filling" of small blocks about 0.55 m × 0.24 m × 0.20 m. These blocks or *talatats* came from a building of Amenhotep IV and were arranged in alternating north-south and east-west beds. Starting with the eleventh bed, counting down from the top, three partition walls consisting of architraves assembled together by dovetails divided the interior of this wing of the pylon into four compartments filled with *talatats* arranged as previously described. (*Kemi* 19: 137–52)

These staircases constructed in empty space present an important architectural problem that never seems to have been studied.

PLATE 396 • NINTH PYLON: WEST WING, SOUTH FACADE

To the left of the large flagpole's location is an almost obliterated tableau that is framed by a sort of bas-relief false door. Flat inlaid stones mark out the site of the cornice, providing the sole protrusion beneath a frieze of uraei.

This tableau is the counterpart of the inscription that recounts the marriage of Ramesses II with the eldest daughter of the king of the Hittites represented on the southern facade of the east wing, which is a replica of the famous "marriage stela" of Abu Simbel.

Following the signing of the peace treaty between the two foes, the chief of the Kheta himself came to Egypt, in the middle of winter, accompanied by his eldest daughter and a large escort loaded down with rich presents, *after traveling through many mountains and difficult roads.*

The daughter of the Khetan high chief was found pleasing by Ramesses II, who married her and gave her these titles: *Great royal wife, mistress of the Two Lands, Maātneferure [she who sees the beauty of Ra],* name of the last hour of the night.

On the right is an offering scene that has been reworked several times. Horemheb's characteristic coiffure and style are recognizable here just as they are on the tenth pylon. The cartouches are in the name of Ramesses II.

PLATE 397 • THE KING IN THE TREE: RAMESSIDE BLOCK

PLATE 398 • NINTH PYLON: GRANITE PEDESTAL

This pedestal in Ramesses II's name, which is in front of the ninth pylon, retains no more than a piece of the foot of a colossus that can still be seen emerging from the excavations in the *Description de l'Egypte.* Consequently it could not have been broken until after 1800.

PLATE 399 • NINTH PYLON: OVERALL VIEW; IN THE BACKGROUND IS THE FIRST PYLON

In the foreground are the outside walls of the small monument of Amenhotep II (pls. 400–405) and the cloister wall that connects it to the tenth pylon.

PLATES 400–405 • MONUMENT OF AMENHOTEP II

After a painstaking study of all its anomalies, Borchardt showed that this small building of Amenhotep II was a *sed*-festival kiosk that had been destroyed by Akhenaten. It was restored in its original site by Seti I with the addition of several blocks of Akhenaten. (See Vandier, *Manuel d'Archéologie égyptienne,* vol. 2, p. 806) Its deployment directly upon the east-west axis of the court as well as the orientations of its walls seems to have been carefully studied in terms of the two pylons that enclose it. (See Lauffray, *Karnak d'Égypte,* p. 138) In the *A* section of diagram 19 there is a graffito depicting Amun's barque with an inscription from the high priest of Amun, Piankh, recounting an oracle that was sent to him by Amun-Ra in year 25 of the reign of Ramesses IX. In *B* there is a scene carved by the son of Pinedjem I, Masaherta, represented as seated before a table of offerings. (Barguet, *La Structure du Temple,* p. 251)

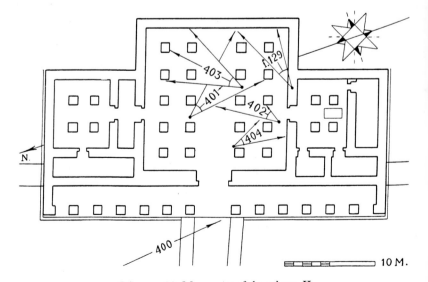

Diagram 20. Monument of Amenhotep II

PLATE 400 • MONUMENT OF AMENHOTEP II: OVERALL VIEW

This small edifice, constructed entirely upon a stylobate, consists of a large square room whose roof was supported by twenty pillars, and two smaller lateral sanctuaries that were fronted on the west by a portico of twelve square pillars to which one had access by a ramp.

In the background the east end of the tenth pylon can be seen, the corner of the court, and the east wall, on which bas-reliefs are carved that are said to be those of Tutankhamun.

PLATE 401 • MONUMENT OF AMENHOTEP II: SOUTHEAST CORNER

These square-sectioned pillars rest on a small pedestal and are topped by a capital in the form of a grooved cornice with a torus at the base and an abacus under the architrave. This type, though architec-

Fig. 129. Monument of Amenhotep II: pillar of the southeast corner, which is heightened by a stone that cuts through a line of inscriptions

turally rare, can however be found in the tomb paintings of the Eighteenth Dynasty.

The king, wearing different crowns in succession, is proceeding toward Amun in a west-to-east direction. The two horizontal lines of text under the tableaux specify that the king is celebrating his *sed* festival.

The tableaux that face the central bay are sculpted in light relief, as are those on the west facade of the first pillar to the left, on which the king is proceeding toward the south, whereas on the next pillar, the tableau is in sunk relief and the king, wearing the red crown, is proceeding north.

PLATE 402 • MONUMENT OF AMENHOTEP II: NORTHEAST CORNER

In the foreground is the dorsal facade of a pillar from the central bay, carved in relief. Behind it is the southern facade of a north pillar in the same bay, sculpted in sunk relief.

PLATE 403 • MONUMENT OF AMENHOTEP II: NORTHEAST CORNER

The tableaux on the inside facades of the central bay pillars and on those of the row in the background are carved alternately in relief and in sunk relief.

Note the flat stones in the foreground pillars, beneath the lines of inscriptions, that are inserted between the blocks of the pillars. These stones seem to have been added *after* the completion of the monument and covered with a roof, but for what purpose? When and how was this work executed? There are so many questions that remain to be answered.

PLATE 404 • MONUMENT OF AMENHOTEP II: PILLAR "RAISED HIGHER" WITH A REUSED BLOCK

The cornerstone that has been added beneath the line of inscriptions is of Amarnian style and is therefore of later date than the monument.

PLATE 405 • AMENHOTEP II PROTECTED BY THE SERPENT-GODDESS MERETSEGER: DETAIL

Black granite statue found at Karnak (see also fig. 123).

Very characteristic is the fact that the Hathorian horns are emerging from a blooming papyrus, which rounds off the symbolism of Hathor. The symbol of Neith is carved on the cobra's chest, behind the king's white crown.

PLATE 406 • TUTANKHAMUN

One of the two identical statues of purplish blue granite found in the cachette court of Karnak. Height: 1.57 meters.

Tutankhamun, "living image of Amun," was the first king after the death of Akhenaten and the quelling of the Amarnian schism that left Egypt in a dreadful state: its Asian empire entirely gone, the temple reliefs hammered out, the clergy of Amun disbanded, the country weakened and impoverished . . . at least so it appears.

Tutankhamun had a brief life, as did his successor Ay, but during their reigns the general Horemheb regained control over the Asian peoples and restored order to the country, then became king himself, at which time he concentrated all his efforts on restoring the religious institutions of Egypt, the temples, and the integrity of the worship, with the help of the clergy of Amun.

Not only does Tutankhamun's tomb contain an inestimable treasure characterized by the richness and beauty of its objects, but the painstaking detail in the expression of the symbolism makes it an inexhaustible source of information.

Horemheb was a great figure: *hereditary prince, count, wearer of the royal seal, private councillor to the palace . . . chief prophet of Horus.*

This is the first time the title "prophet of Horus" is encountered at Karnak.

Horemheb, "feasting Horus," was born in the capital of the eighteenth nome of Upper Egypt, *the castle of the king of Upper Egypt* whose symbol is the *flying falcon.* Reared by Amun himself, *Har-si-ese [Horus-son-of-Isis], his guardian was the protector of his limbs . . . the hue of a god* [neter] *was upon him. . . .*

When he came to the palace, *his every plan was in the footsteps of the Ibis [Thoth]. His decisions were in accord with the Lord of Hesret [Thoth] . . . pleased of heart therewith like Ptah.*

He administered the Two Lands for many years;

Fig. 130. Statue of Horemheb, cachette court
(photo Brugsch Pasha)

the *chiefs of the Nine Bows, South as well as North,* bowed down before him.

Then while he was *prince in all the world, Horus, lord of the royal palace of Upper Egypt,* desired to set him upon the throne and brought him to Amun, in Thebes, so that he could be confirmed in his office of king in the presence of the Great Ennead and of the *neters* of North and South. (Summary of Breasted passages from *Ancient Records*, vol. 3, §§ 24–32; see also Breasted, *Ancient Records*, vol. 23, §26)

PLATE 407 • PRESENTATION OF THE TRIBUTES FROM THE LAND OF PUNT

On the interior partition of the wall that connects the temple of Amenhotep II to the tenth pylon, the king is presenting Amun with the tributes brought by the high chiefs of Punt, the land of incense. He is wearing the characteristic wig with five rows of curls (pl. 408), and a trace of an Amarnian influence is noticeable in the depiction of the belly and the soft lines of the drawing.

Behind him are two rows of Puntish chieftains who, by their dress, countenance, and twisted goatees, are allied to the depictions of pharaonic nobles. They are carrying sacks of gold, skins, feathers, and cloth, but they are free, for they proclaim themselves as friends: *The great chiefs of the land of Punt say: "Glory to thee, king of Egypt, sun of the Nine Bows. As truly as thou art in life we have not known of the black land [Egypt] and our fathers have not trampled it down."*

PLATE 408 • PRESENTATION OF THE AEGEAN AND SYRIAN TRIBUTES

With his right hand the king is presenting the delicately wrought vessels, the horns, and the sacks of precious materials that are arranged before the naos of the seated Amun. The king is unarmed, but he is holding the *hek* scepter in his left hand along with the coiled ropes that bind the three rows of prisoners following behind him: *The miserable lords of Hannebu [Aegeans], the vile chiefs of Retenu [Syria] . . . terror is in their hearts.* (Wrezinski, *Atlas*, vol. 2, pls. 61 and 62)

The "vile chiefs of Retenu," recognizable by their fringed beards, their dress, and their capelines, are indeed enchained, which is to say again, subjugated by General Horemheb.

Despite the cartouches in the general's name, there are some who attribute this bas-relief to Tutankhamun.

PLATES 409–421 • TENTH PYLON

Horemheb built the tenth pylon, in which he reused numerous blocks from the temple of Akhenaten.

PLATE 409 • TENTH PYLON: GRANITE GATE

The gate measures 15.60 meters under the lintel. The double lintel adds 2.47 meters, which gives the gate a height of 18.07 meters not including the cornice.

This majestic granite gate consists of four registers of tableaux in the name of King Horemheb.

Going from bottom to top, these tableaux depict the offering of wine to Amun-Ra, water to Amun-Ra Kamutef, censing to Amun-Ra, and lastly, worshiping Mut, then Khonsu, four times.

The displacement of the stones in this gate has taken a quite surprising form: the upper six courses have pivoted in a solid mass, as if pushed by a violent deflagration.

The avenue of the ram-headed sphinxes that leads to the temple of Mut, mistress of Asheru, is in the background.

PLATE 410 • AMUN-RA: GRANITE BLOCK

Amun-Ra, master of the thrones of the Two Lands, master of Heaven, prince of Thebes.

Wearing a mortier crowned with two feathers that are each divided into fourteenths plus a fraction, this image of Amun again belongs to the pure hieratic style that Horemheb restored throughout Egypt when rebuilding and expanding the temples.

PLATE 411 • GATE, SEEN FROM THE NORTH, AND THE WEST COLOSSUS[39]

---

[39]On the north facade of the western wing Horemheb is "massacring the southern countries," while on the eastern wing Asian warriors, therefore the North, are represented in this ritual scene. This anomaly in regard to the general orientation is found again on the pedestal of the two white limestone statues (pls. 412 and 415). Although in the name of Ramesses II, these colossi seem to have been sculpted by Amenhotep III or perhaps Horemheb.

The inner side of the passage by the east door-post consists of only three tableaux: on the bottom the king is making offerings to a seated Amun (pls. 416 and 417); on the middle register the king is making the "great stride" with the vessels. He is wearing the white crown.

PLATE 412 • NORTHEAST COLOSSUS: PRISONERS FROM THE SOUTHERN COUNTRIES

The pedestal of the white limestone colossus is decorated on three sides with the "prisoners with the escutcheons," who symbolize the Nine Bows, that is to say, the vanquished, under the feet of the king.

The black peoples are on the left side of the king; therefore, as the statue is placed, they are on the west. Now, in Egypt *left* is said *iab.t,* that is, east (corresponding to the south). Their position is therefore correct with respect to the statue of the king but reversed in regard to the real orientation.

PLATE 413 • NORTHEAST COLOSSUS: QUEEN MUT-NEFERTARI

Queen Mut-Nefertari, the great royal wife, mistress of the Two Lands, is clad in a finely pleated linen robe held by a belt that is knotted under her chest. She is wearing a wig that is encased by the Mut vulture and capped by the double feather. The queen is resting her hand on the king's calf at the level of the ham.

The vanquished of the south are depicted on the western facade of the pedestal.[40]

PLATE 414 • THE TWO COLOSSI: WEST DOORPOST OF THE GATE

PLATE 415 • WESTERN COLOSSUS OF THE NORTH FACADE

The Asian warriors, bound with the plant of the North (fig. 131) are on the right side of the pedestal. As prisoners from the north they are in their correct position with respect to that of the king, since in

[40]"It was on the west side of the base of the eastern colossus that Legrain discovered, in 1913, four magnificent black granite statues, two in the name of Amenhotep Son of Hapu, two in the name of Paramessu." (Barguet, *La Structure du Temple,* p. 249, and *Annales du Service des Antiquités de l'Egypte* 14: 18)

Fig. 131. Asian captives attached to each other by the plant of the North

Egyptian *right* is called *imen.t,* west, and consequently corresponds with north. However, they are in the reverse position with regard to their actual orientation.

PLATES 416 AND 417 • GRANITE GATE, INTERIOR OF THE EAST DOORPOST: DETAIL

Amun's throne is surrounded by a border depicting the gold framing that is inlaid with a glass paste the color of lapis lazuli, turquoise, and carnelian. It is separated from its pedestal by a mat on which the feet of the *neter,* whose ankles are adorned with bracelets, are resting.

The king is wearing the triangular apron over which falls a front panel of pearls with a uraeus framed by ribbons. Rays are shooting forth from each corner, which are also each adorned with a small stylized head with big ears, making the trigonometric nature of this garb quite explicit.

Fig. 132. Tenth pylon, south facade: fragment of Akhenaten's obelisk

The lateral peroneal muscles on the outside of Amun's and the king's legs are accented by a curious stylization.

PLATE 418 • TENTH PYLON, SOUTHERN FACADE: EAST DOORPOST OF THE GRANITE GATE

As on the north facade, the doorposts include four registers. The bottom register is partially covered by a fore-gate[41] that separates Amun from the king, who is making him the offering of the white bread (pl. 419 and fig. 134).

A quite remarkable use of reused blocks should be noted here: the block on which the faces and crowns of Amun and the king are sculpted is a capital that has been sawed in two and laid on its side in such a way that Amun's head and feathers correspond to the abacus, and the crowned head of the king to the bud of the fasciculate capital. This is not a unique case.

PLATE 419 • TENTH PYLON, SOUTHERN FACADE, EAST DOORPOST OF THE GRANITE GATE: OFFERING OF THE WHITE BREAD

Horemheb is offering the white bread in the form of a long cone. This sculpture attains a classical purity in the silhouette, the face, and the symbols.

The king is girded by a diadem over his blue *ibes* wig topped by the horns of Khnum around which two uraei uncoil and fall to either side of the king's face, a detail that is specific to this side of the pylon. In fact, the same crown represented on the north, on the first register of the west doorpost, consists of only the two top uraei, the two feathers, and the disk; the face of the king is also sculpted on the planed side of a reused capital.

PLATE 420 • PEDESTAL OF THE COLOSSUS OF AMENHOTEP III

In the background are village houses and the Euergetes gate. In the center is the base of the gigantic colossus of Amenhotep III, of which only the feet remain.[42]

This statue was the "masterpiece" of Amenhotep, son of Hapu: *My lord made me chief of all works. I established the name of the king forever, I did not imitate that which had been done before. I fashioned for him a mountain of gritstone, for he is the heir of*

---

[41]According to Legrain, *A.S.A.* 14: 14-39, the fore-gate dates from Pedibastet and replaced an older, smaller porch.

[42]The round sculpted sandstone statue added to the left of the eastern colossus of Amenhotep III represents an unknown queen. The reclining sphinx in the foreground is in the name of Seti II.

Fig. 133. Pedestal of the colossus of Amenhotep III: nomes of Lower Egypt

Atum. . . . I conducted the work of his statue, immense in width, taller than his column, its beauty marred the pylon. Its length was 40 cubits in the august mountain of gritstone at the side of Re-Atum. (Trans. Breasted, *Ancient Records*, vol. 2, § 917)

Carved in a monolith of quartzitic sandstone (therefore from the North), this colossus represented the king Amenhotep III, standing and crowned, with one foot forward. Both feet rested on the pedestal made from another block of the same quartzite, which in turn rested on a second pedestal of red Aswan granite (therefore from the South).

The front foot measures 2.65 meters and the back foot 2.69 meters (it is a very full-fleshed figure). These measurements and the specification provided by Amenhotep that this colossus measured 40 (royal) cubits in the quarry, that is, 20.95 meters, allows one to calculate that it was actually 16.50 meters to the vertex and 20.95 meters with the crown.

Plate 421 • Tenth Pylon: East Facade

The slope of the east and west facades, measured by a protractor level with the lower courses, is around 80°. This exceptionally pronounced slope demanded further verification. The north and south facades fluctuate between 81°30′ and 82°, the maximum coefficient encountered up to the present time.

Plate 422 • Double Pedestal of Amenhotep III

Fig. 134. Tenth pylon, southern facade: eastern doorpost of the granite gate

A horizontal line of text on the facade of the quartzite pedestal, on both sides of the ankh of the axis, gives the cartouches of Nebmaātre (Amenhotep III) with the label *fraction of Ra* on the side with the setting sun and *heir of Ra* on the side with the rising sun.

Below that are two Iunmutefs (pillar of his mother), wearing the braid of the crown prince falling over their shoulders and holding a panther paw in their left hands. With the right hand they present their speech.

In the center, on both sides of the *Ra-master-of-heaven* disk, two falcons wearing the double crown are perched on the Horus name framed by the *ka*, which rests on an ensign holder provided with two arms, one of which holds up the long staff crowned with the emblem of the royal *ka*.

On the left (west), the name of the serpent deity of the North, Wadjet, is inscribed near the face of Iunmutef, who with his gesture is emphasizing this phrase from his discourse: *You will establish his annals in millions of years.* Meanwhile, the Iunmutef on the east is stressing the passage: *You have authentically established the series of his names in the capacity of Horus, mighty bull appearing in Maāt [truth].*

This pedestal rests on a granite pedestal whose facade consists of three pieces. In the median axis of the central one, the flowers of the North and South are linked around the *sma* sign and at the same time serve to bind the prisoners by the neck. On the east side these prisoners are the black peoples of the South, on the west side it is the Asians from the North. Here the orientation is correct with respect to the king and its actual location.

PLATE 423 • IUNMUTEF PRESENTING THE PROTOCOL OF AMENHOTEP III

The triple crown-prince braid here covers the temple and ends on the shoulder of the Iunmutef. The Egyptian name of this braid is *gmht,* used in the Ebers Papyrus (99.7), where it denotes the temple itself.

PLATE 424 • QUARTZITE PEDESTAL OF THE COLOSSUS OF AMENHOTEP III, WEST FACADE

On the west face of the quartzite pedestal, the first eight nomes of Lower Egypt, that is the North, are represented (fig. 133). (See also *Karnak*, vol. 5, p. 159 and figs. 1–11)

The androgynous figure is a "Nile" who is wearing the emblem of the Libyan nome upon his head. In one hand he is holding the vessel out of which comes the fertilizing waters and with the other the "foodstuffs" that are the fruit of the earth and the gift of the *neters*. A bull accompanies him.

PLATE 425 • AMENHOTEP SON OF HAPU

Black granite statue found at the entrance of the tenth pylon, north facade, in Karnak (see pl. 413). Height: 1.3 meters. Eighteenth Dynasty.

PLATE 426 • TENTH PYLON: SOUTH FACADE

The criosphinx avenue in Horemheb's name is more than 310 meters long and contains, from the time of Champollion, more than 120 sphinxes to which Seti II added his cartouches.

PLATE 427 • FIST FROM THE COLOSSUS OF AMENHOTEP III

PLATE 428 • FRAGMENT OF THE BLACK GRANITE PEDESTAL OF AMENHOTEP III

PLATE 429 • FRAGMENT OF THE BLACK GRANITE PEDESTAL OF AMENHOTEP III: DETAIL

To the east of the avenue of the sphinxes leading from the tenth pylon to the temple of Mut is a stylobate constructed with fourteen large granite blocks, of which six are of Amenhotep III.

These six blocks come from the pedestals of three black granite statues, two of which must have been symmetrical and of very great height. Recall that Ramesses III, then the high priest, constructed the temple of Khonsu with sandstone blocks taken from the funerary temple of Amenhotep III. It is this latter site that A. Varille suggests as the original site of these colossal statues.

Two of these blocks, which come from the lateral left side of two different colossi, depict curly-bearded prisoners bound by the plant of the North beneath the four lines of royal titulary.

Fig. 135. Debris of the Colossus of Amenhotep III

Three more blocks come from the lateral right side of the same colossus and depict Negro prisoners tied together with the plant of the South beneath the four lines of the protocol.

On the fragment that is represented here there is mention of Sokar, *neter* of the *amenti*, the land of the dead.

(See also *A.S.A.* 36: 202.)

PLATES 430–450 • TEMPLE OF MUT

The temple of Mut the Great, mistress of Asheru, built by Amenhotep III, is in almost total ruin. It is partially encircled by the lake of Asheru in the form of a crescent. The wall that encloses all of Mut's territory also surrounds two small temples, of which nothing remains but the lower courses.

PLATE 430 • MUSICIANS

A sistrum player, a harpist, and a tambourine player who are standing in the presence of Mut seated

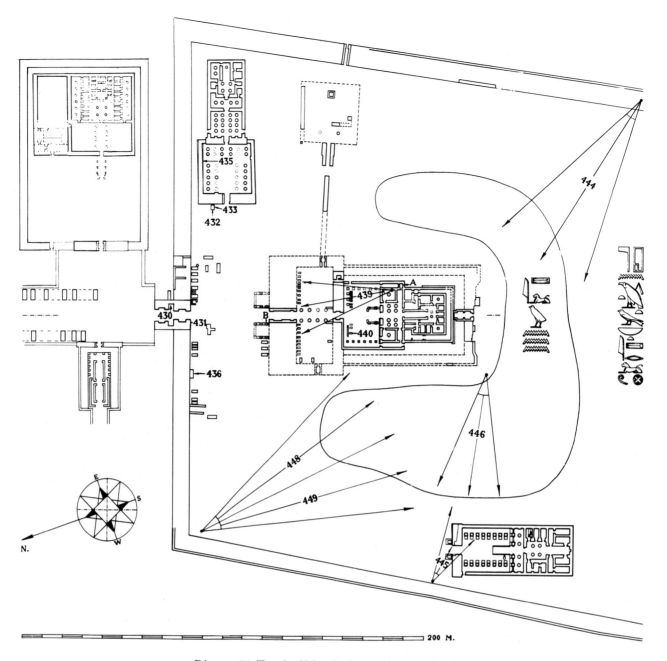

Diagram 21. Temple of Mut the Great, mistress of Asheru.

upon a throne are represented on the east doorpost of the passage of the Ptolemaic gate that crosses through the enclosure of the Mut temple.

Music, song, and dance have accompanied sacred ceremonies since the greatest antiquity. The harp is represented in tombs of the Fifth Dynasty; the sistrum players accompanied the leaving of the barques during the feast of Apet at Luxor (Eighteenth Dynasty); the tambourine appears later; until then the rhythm of the hymns and dances was stressed by hand clapping (see also pl. 336–337).

The long text inscribed beneath this tableau relates to the feasts of the temple of Mut.

PLATE 431 • PTOLEMAIC GATE OF THE
ENCLOSURE: WEST DOORPOST,
SOUTH FACADE

The frieze of the stylobate is composed of flowering papyrus and buds emerging from a base of wavy lines that signify water, in a style that is typically Ptolemaic.

PLATE 432 • OSIRIAN STATUE

PLATE 433 • OSIRIAN STATUE

This Osirian statue is attached to a stela whose edge bears the titulary of Ramesses II, but the vertical band that descends beneath the two crossed fists of the figure is a curious combination of the names of Ramesses II and Tuthmosis IV, which are superimposed together in the reverse direction (fig. 136): *King of Upper and Lower Egypt, master of the Two Lands, Usermaātre Setepenre, Son of Ra.*

The second cartouche of Ramesses II is not visible, yet the following is quite legible: *Neter-nefer, master of the Two Lands, Menkheperre, Son of Ra, of his breast, Tuthmosis IV, endowed with eternal life.*

This superimposition of the two royal names, in which the oldest appears the most clearly, is explainable, without doubt, by stucco work and carving. The union of these two names is reminiscent of the "poorly informed historian" who set down the story of the princess of Bakhtan, "naively" giving Ramesses II a part of the protocol of Tuthmosis IV (pl. 251). Recall that this princess was the younger sister of Maātneferure, the eldest daughter of the chief of the Kheta, who married Ramesses II. A portion of the tale of this marriage is carved on a magnificent alabaster plaque located in the temple of Mut (fig. 137).[43]

PLATE 434 • OSIRIAN STATUE

Currently in the Karnak storehouse, this Osirian statue bearing the Horus name of Ramesses II should be compared with that of plates 432 and 433. The outlines are similar, from the hieroglyphs down to the detail of the ear. The face seems to have been reworked to resemble Ramesses II (?).

PLATE 435 • CIRCUMCISION SCENE

The circumcision ceremony was mandatory among the Egyptians.

"They drink only from copper vessels, which they polish and clean every day with a great deal of care. . . . They wear clothes of linen that are always freshly washed and that they take pains never to stain. They have adopted circumcision in their search for cleanliness, and appear to think more highly of a perfect physical purity than any other adornment." (Herodotus, 2.37)

---

[43]For more on the Osirian statue of Tuthmosis III usurped by Ramesses II and Nectanebo see *A.S.A.* 25: 17 and 27: 152.

Fig. 136. Superimposition of Tuthmosis IV and Ramesses II

PLATE 436 • SPHINX

PLATE 437 • FEMALE BUST IN BLACK GRANITE

This decapitated bust is extremely curious: the block of black granite has been selected so that a clear vein encircles the breast, emphasized by the pliant shaft of the scepter ending in a flower of the South from which three "streams," similar to those of the *nekhakha*, are emerging. This scepter is always carried by a female figure, and it can be seen in the hand of the "black" queen Ahmose-Nefertari, mother of the Eighteenth Dynasty.

PLATE 438 • PTOLEMAIC BLOCKS FROM ONE OF THE SANCTUARIES

The splaying of a doorway is recognizable at the bottom, with its characteristic decor of baskets holding up the symbols for life and strength. Beneath the bar of the ankh are two arms holding *was* scepters, of which the upper hooks have been transformed, under the Ptolemies, into a head with big ears and an elongated muzzle.

The Wadjet serpent, the protective deity of the royalty of the North, is sculpted, with the body and the wings of a vulture, on the stone that is set on top, which probably once belonged to the inner facade of the lintel.

PLATE 439 • OVERALL VIEW OF THE RUINS OF THE TEMPLE OF MUT AND THE STATUES OF SEKHMET

Within the temple of Mut there are a great quantity of statues with the body of a woman and the head of a lion. Many of these are dedicated by Amenhotep III, others by Ramesses II or the high priest Pinedjem and Queen Henuttawy, and so forth. Each of them bears a different marker:

Sekhmet, beloved of Ptah; Sekhmet, mistress of the western desert; Sekhmet in the house of Bastet; Sekhmet the great; Sekhmet beloved of Sobek.

Each marker is connected to one or another of legends from the myth: the first is attributed to Sekhmet as the feminine principle of Ptah (pl. 313), the one after to the vengeful lioness or to Sekhmet, the bloodthirsty lioness who will become the peaceful cat Bastet.

The majority of these statues, which inhabit museums throughout the entire world, come from the temple of Mut.

PLATE 440 • STATUE OF SEKHMET

PLATE 441 • STATUE OF SEKHMET: DETAIL

Sekhmet, with the face of a wild beast haloed with a mane resembling the rays of the sun, is wearing a headdress whose rolls fall over her breasts, a crown with a uraeus with disks, and on her forehead, the two royal uraei. She is holding the key of life in her hand and the *wadj* (which opens). Sekhmet, associated with the myth of the Solar Eye, is one of the forms of Hathor, who was simultaneously Ra's daughter and the Eye of Ra.

PLATE 442 • BUST OF MENTUEMHET, FOURTH PROPHET OF AMUN

Black granite. Height: 0.5 meters. Twenty-fifth Dynasty. Found at Karnak in Mut's sanctuary. Currently in the Cairo Museum.

Mentuemhet, fourth prophet of Amun, prince of Thebes, and governor of the South, played an extremely important political role during the time of the Twenty-fifth Dynasty and the beginning of the Twenty-sixth Dynasty. This astonishingly realistic bust shows him as an older man. The eyes, accented by the bags beneath them, are small and keen. The fairly large nose indicates that Mentuemhet probably had Nubian blood in his veins; the mouth is full and very expressive. This is an admirable portrait made by a master sculptor. The striking hairstyle is not encountered on any other Egyptian statue (around 660 B.C.). (J. Vandier, *La Sculpture égyptienne*, notes, p. 90)

PLATE 443 • STATUE OF MENTUEMHET

Gray granite. Height: 1.35 meters. Found in two pieces, on March 3 and April 2, 1904, at Karnak.

Mentuemhet is standing in the hieratic position and holding the seals in his clenched fists. He is wearing the pleated loincloth and a ceremonial wig of tight curls.

The inscription on his belt reads: "Fourth Prophet of Amun, vizier of the city, Mentuemhet." Although the fourth prophet of Amun, Mentuemhet was the *high priest of the priests of all the neters of the South and North, and the prince of Thebes.*

During the reign of Taharka he was active in the restoration of the religious buildings of Thebes that had been sacked during Ashurbanipal's first campaign (666 B.C.), according to the inscription in his chapel within the temple of Mut (diagram 21, *A*): *I purified all the temples in the nomes of all Patoris, according as one should purify (violated) temples—after there had been (an invasion of unclean foreigners in) the Southland.* (Breasted, *Ancient Records*, vol. 4, § 905)

He then lists the numerous works that he executed in the temples of Thebes, constructing *the tem-*

ple of Mut, mistress of Heaven, in fine white sandstone, buildings, sacred lakes, barques, and statues for Mut, Khonsu, Mentu, Waset, Bastet, Ptah, Hathor Amun, Min, Thoth, and he says, *All these things which I have brought before you, there is no (lying) speech therein, no contradiction. . . . There is no lie in the place of my mouth.* No doubt can be cast on his words if one recalls the Ethiopian colonnades and all the evidence left at Karnak by the black kings.

PLATE 444 • THE SACRED LAKE AND THE TEMPLE OF MUT

In the foreground is the crescent-shaped lake of Asheru, which partially encircles the temple consecrated to Mut, the "mother," the lunar feminine principle par excellence.

Fig. 137. Alabaster block commemorating the marriage of Ramesses II and Maātneferure

In the background is the temple of Ramesses III, which was constructed in the image of the first court of the great temple of Amun, but of which nothing remains but the leveling courses.

PLATE 445 • THE TWO COLOSSI IN FRONT OF THE TEMPLE OF RAMESSES III CONSTRUCTED NEAR THE SACRED LAKE OF ASHERU

PLATE 446 • THE SACRED LAKE OF ASHERU AND THE TEMPLE OF RAMESSES III

On the outer south walls of this building Ramesses III had the record of his conquests carved, notably his victories over the Asians. He was the last truly Egyptian king and master of the Two Lands. Since the end of the Ramesside dynasty Thebes had known the pious domination of the high priests, then that of the Libyan kings of the North and the

Fig. 138. "Bes" sculpted in the round on a cylindrical surface (diagram 21, B)

high priests of the South. These latter were soon replaced by the "divine worshipers," while in the Delta the kings kept watch for enemy threats. The Persians, who had been trampled down several times under Ethiopian domination, invaded Thebes for the second time after the death of Taharka, and on this occasion the city was taken and sacked by Ashurbanipal's troops.

The memory of Thebes's capture and the treatment it received remained quite vivid, and a half century later, when the prophet Nahum wished to announce the fate awaiting Nineveh, he found no better example to illustrate his prophecy than that of Thebes. "Are you better than No-Amun [Thebes], that was seated in the middle of a river, surrounded by water, that had the sea for its rampart, that had the sea for its wall? Ethiopia and countless Egyptians were its strength, Kush and the Libyans were its auxiliaries. And yet it has been cast into exile, it has departed in captivity; its children were crushed on the corners of all its streets; a grim fate has fallen over its nobility, and all its high and mighty have been laden down with chains." (Nahum 3: 8–10) (Drioton and Vandier, *L'Egypte*, p. 530)

But shortly thereafter Egypt freed itself from the Assyrian yoke (Twenty-sixth Dynasty, 663–525 B.C.). The Saïte kings reigned in the North, and the divine worshipers in the South.

PLATE 447 • PLOVER IN THE LAKE OF ASHERU IN SPRING

This photograph was taken in the spring, at the time of average water levels (see also plate 452).

PLATE 448–449 • OVERALL VIEW OF THE LAKE OF ASHERU

The desert and the Libyan mountain chain. "The Three Brothers" are in the background.

PLATE 450 • SMALL HERD OF GOATS AT THE EDGE OF THE SACRED LAKE OF ASHERU

PLATE 451 • YOUNG GIRL FIFTEEN YEARS OLD

PLATE 452 • PLOVER IN THE LAKE OF ASHERU IN SUMMER

This photograph was taken in summer, at the time of low water levels, as is shown by the bubbles coming up through the mud.

"A time will come when it will appear that the Egyptians served their god with piety and zeal, in vain. . . . O Egypt, Egypt, nothing will remain of your beliefs but fables, which will seem incredible to future generations, and there will remain only the words on the stones to tell of your pious actions!"

(Pseudo-Apuleius, *Asclepius*, XXIV)

Fig. 139. Yussri

INDEX

Page numbers in italic refer to illustrations; suffix d *designates a diagram*